36 - PM
9    430

# PRISONERS OF THE EMPIRE

# PRISONERS
## of the EMPIRE

Inside

Japanese

POW

Camps

JEWISH

**Sarah Kovner**

 Harvard University Press

Cambridge, Massachusetts | London, England  2020

*For Lily*

Printed in the United States of America

First printing

Cataloging-in-Publication Data is available from the Library of Congress

ISBN: 978-0-674-73761-7 (alk. paper)

# Contents

UN BROKEN

Japanese Empire with discussed camps and capitals.

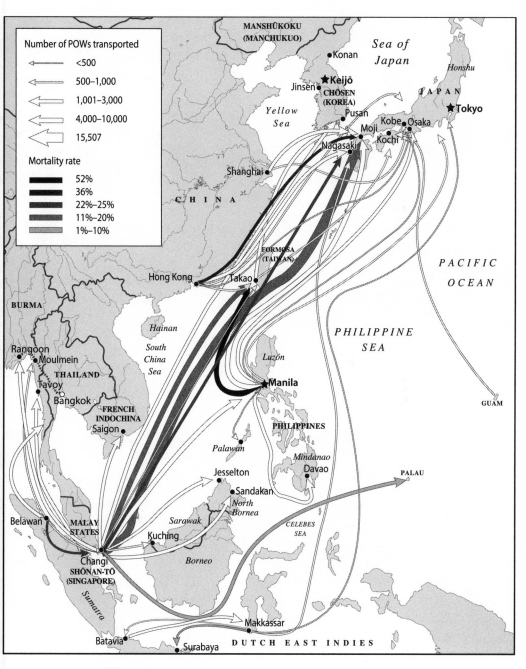

Legend:

**Number of POWs transported**

- <500
- 500–1,000
- 1,001–3,000
- 4,000–10,000
- 15,507

**Mortality rate**

- 52%
- 36%
- 22%–25%
- 11%–20%
- 1%–10%

Map labels:

MANSHŪKOKU (MANCHUKUO)
Sea of Japan
Honshu
Konan
Jinsen · Keijō
CHŌSEN (KOREA)
Pusan
Kobe · Osaka
Moji
Kochi
Nagasaki
★ Tokyo
JAPAN
Yellow Sea
Shanghai
CHINA
FORMOSA (TAIWAN)
Hong Kong · Takao
BURMA
Hainan
South China Sea
Luzón
PACIFIC OCEAN
PHILIPPINE SEA
Rangoon
Moulmein
THAILAND
Tavoy
Bangkok
FRENCH INDOCHINA
Saigon
★ Manila
PHILIPPINES
Palawan
Mindanao
Davao
GUAM
PALAU
Belawan
MALAY STATES
Jesselton
Sandakan
North Borneo
Sarawak
Kuching
Borneo
CELEBES SEA
Changi
SHŌNAN-TŌ (SINGAPORE)
Sumatra
Makkassar
Batavia
Surabaya
DUTCH EAST INDIES

Transporting POWs across vast expanses.

# INTRODUCTION

# A History Both Familiar and Strange

In two days in December 1941, the Imperial Japanese Navy and Army shocked the world with attacks on Pearl Harbor, Malaya, and Thailand. Japan invaded China in mid-1937, and careful observers had predicted Japanese military action. Yet most people in the United States and Britain were taken completely by surprise. In those days before email and free phone calls, before direct flights to Tokyo and Thailand, any threat from Japan seemed impossibly far away. But now Japanese forces rapidly advanced across thousands of miles of open ocean, from the Aleutians to the straits of Malacca, from the Marshall Islands to the Burma Road. In the first five months of the Pacific War, they took as prisoners more than 140,000 Allied servicemen[1] and 130,000 civilians from a dozen countries. Japanese commanders hastily set up hundreds of POW camps and civilian internment centers. Of the American POWs, one in three did not survive the war. And by the war's end, more Australians had died in captivity than in combat. Once far away, Japan and the Japanese became all too familiar to Western countries, above all as objects of hatred.

Ever since, memoirs, popular histories, and literary accounts have described how the Japanese systematically humiliated and abused their captives. Whether the tragic Lieutenant Colonel Nicholson in the 1957 film *The Bridge on the River Kwai*, or the heroic army airman Louis Zamperini in Laura Hillenbrand's best-selling book *Unbroken*, POWs are portrayed as martyrs to the unmitigated cruelty of their guards and camp commanders.[2] These accounts often present Japanese behavior as simply inexplicable. When they do offer an explanation for the harsh treatment of POWs, they often attribute it to Japanese military education and the bushidō code—a military ideology once applied to samurai, and revived and refigured over the course of the early twentieth century. The Japanese

1

d soldiers to feel extreme shame about being taken captive,
.uly inculcated contempt against any enemy soldier who willingly
..ered.

Considering that POWs in the Pacific accounted for only about 0.5 percent of Allied servicemen, popular understanding of this history has had an outsized impact on memories of the war. Sixty-five years after World War II ended, *Unbroken* became one of the longest-running best sellers of all time. The suffering of POWs in the Pacific is so familiar in popular culture that it can be invoked and immediately recognized without any context or explanation, whether as background to a character in a John Grisham thriller, or as the beginning—in media res—of *Call of Duty: World at War*, the blockbuster video game.[3]

Yet there have always been aspects of the captivity experience that resisted easy explanation. When Japan and Russia went to war in 1904, the international press and Western observers praised Japan's generous treatment of Russian POWs. Japan's scrupulous conduct forced Western powers to redefine international law as universal, rather than as the custom of Christian civilization. In World War II, many guards were not Japanese soldiers at all, but *gunzoku*—Korean and Taiwanese civilian employees. And even if Japanese notions of military honor could account for the treatment of Allied POWs, how could they explain the experience of civilian internees? This experience was different from what POWs endured, but was also difficult. Some men and women were even held in the same camps as POWs. This too has shaped how people remember the Pacific War, such as in the J. G. Ballard book (and Steven Spielberg film) *Empire of the Sun,* and the many other accounts of Europeans, Americans, and Australians rounded up in places like Shanghai, Hong Kong, Singapore, and Manila.[4] Finally, how do we explain why the suffering and death of Allied POWs became infamous in the United States and the British Commonwealth, while it hardly figures in Japanese popular memories of the Pacific War?

These questions call out for a comparative analysis. But English-language accounts usually lack an international perspective. Americans study Americans, and Australians study Australians. Very few even cite Japanese sources.[5] These accounts seldom mention Japanese and Japanese-American internees in the United States. Yet while the war was still being fought, the government in Tokyo focused on how the United States treated these civilian internees, and this treatment influenced how the Japanese handled Allied POWs. Finally, when assessing Japanese conduct, such as the execution of captured airmen, should we not compare it to Allied actions that Tokyo considered war crimes, such as the firebombing of Japanese cities?

English-language accounts also tend to underplay the large proportion of POW deaths that resulted from friendly fire, such as air and submarine attacks on Japanese convoys and bombing raids on Japanese cities, which Allied commanders carried out even when they knew they would likely kill POWs. It has been argued that more POWs died from friendly fire than from Japanese abuse and neglect.[6]

In this book I argue that there was nothing inherent to Japanese character or culture that led to the inhumane treatment of POWs. Rather than accepting as a given that Japanese society included a code of conduct that required inflicting cruelty on hundreds of thousands of captives, I will show that senior officials gave much less thought to their management than today's accounts assume. Far more people surrendered than commanders had anticipated. Pushed to their logistical limits, and fighting armies that were sometimes twice their size, Japanese commanders did not necessarily consider the care and feeding of captives a priority. It was Japanese inattention to the challenge of managing POWs, and lack of interest in caring for them, that led to many of the cruel and inhumane situations. But what stands out in the Japanese military's approach to POWs is its *unwitting* cruelty. Clearly, many POWs suffered and died because of abuse or negligence, including forced labor, malnutrition, and poor medical care. But accounts that ignore the Japanese side of the story cannot begin to explain why.

This study reveals that the Japanese government and military never made it policy to abuse POWs. There was never a mandate for officers or guards to mistreat, exploit, or shoot their prisoners. Official Japanese policy was to adhere to the Geneva Conventions, but even the officers who knew this—and many did not—often lacked the capacity to abide by it. Imperial planners never thought through what resources the empire would need in order to expand, and this created a series of dilemmas for a military unprepared to provide adequate logistics or labor. The Japanese government also failed to create a coherent system of administration or a clear chain of command, making it difficult to develop and enforce standards to prevent mistreatment or neglect. When Japanese officials and officers did consider the plight of POWs, they were deeply divided and ambivalent. It is not surprising, then, that conditions varied greatly between camps and that the experience of being a POW in Japan was dramatically different from camp to camp. Both crucial contextual factors and the variation in camp conditions make it impossible to reduce the POW experience to a simple morality tale.[7]

Tokyo could have summarily executed Allied captives from the start of the conflict, as they frequently did with Chinese servicemen (and as often occurred on the Eastern Front). Instead, they agreed they would be guided by the Geneva Conventions, allowed at least some prisoners to receive Red Cross packages, and submitted to the inspection of neutral observers outside war zones. Tokyo publicly insisted that POWs were well treated, to the point that some Japanese men and women grew resentful. The Japanese treatment of Allied POWs also takes on a different meaning when viewed in the context of how the Japanese government treated its own civilians and soldiers. The face slapping, forced marches, and rice gruel that seemed unusually cruel to Allied POWs were not unusual in the Imperial Japanese Army (IJA). Against this background, it is especially notable that the Japanese military court-martialed some guards found guilty of abusing prisoners. And over the course of the conflict, they greatly expanded their administrative capacity to provide information about POWs to Allied governments. Clearly, they cared how Westerners perceived their conduct, much more than they considered how other Asians—the ostensible beneficiaries of the "Greater East-Asian Co-Prosperity Sphere"—would react to comparable or worse treatment of Chinese, Indians, and Filipinos.

This book grapples with these seeming inconsistencies and paradoxes by exploring the captivity experience in the broadest possible context. That includes the long history of Japan's efforts to engage and compete with the West, whether through joining international organizations or imitating Western colonialism. Japan was the first non-Western nation to join the International Committee of the Red Cross (ICRC), and at times the Japanese chapter was the largest in the world. But long before 1941, the Japanese military began to consider some captives—Asian captives—unworthy of being treated as "prisoners of war." The inhabitants of Taiwan, and then later the Chinese on the mainland, were consistently dismissed as bandits, or "ben'itai." Not only were large numbers summarily executed, but the

4

*Table 1.*   Allied POWs in the Pacific War. Estimates of the numbers and mortality rates of Allied POWs vary greatly. These figures given here for the number of POWs, from the Tokyo War Crimes Tribunal, are considered to be very conservative. They do not include all of those who were captured but not accorded POW status, or Asian forced laborers.

| Country | Total POWs | POW deaths | Mortality rate |
| --- | --- | --- | --- |
| Britain | 50,016 | 12,433 | 25% |
| The Netherlands | 37,000 | 8,500 | 23% |
| Australia | 21,726 | 7,412 | 34% |
| United States | 21,580 | 7,107 | 33% |
| Canada | 1,691 | 273 | 16% |
| New Zealand | 121 | 31 | 26% |
| Total | 132,134 | 35,756 | 27% |

*Table 2.*   Differing estimates of American POWs. Focusing on POWs from one country shows how much estimates vary depending on the methodology.

| Source | Total POWs | POW deaths | Mortality rate |
| --- | --- | --- | --- |
| Tokyo War Crimes Tribunal | 21,580 | 7,107 | 33% |
| American Ex-Prisoners of War Association | 36,260 | 13,851 | 38% |
| Department of Veterans Affairs | 27,465 | 11,107 | 40% |

tens of thousands of Asian forced laborers who built the Thai-Burma Railway, and the Filipinos forced to march out of Bataan, died at even higher rates than Allied POWs.

Tokyo agreed to follow the Geneva Conventions, but only when they began to capture American, Australian, and European prisoners. They stipulated this would be done mutatis mutandis, meaning as Japanese laws and local circumstances permitted. Besides being constrained by massive logistical challenges, officers and men who experienced the comparatively lawless warfare in China were not accustomed to making fine distinctions. Understanding what that meant for POWs therefore requires analyzing the complex and sometimes chaotic conditions in different military theaters, and explaining how and why the hundreds of Japanese POW camps never coalesced into a coherent system. It means drawing on the perspectives of both guards and prisoners, and relating the internal life of these camps to the larger context of occupation policies, diplomacy, and international law.

We need to see both how policy was made and how it played out, comparing the fate of civilians swapped in exchanges, POWs transported to Japan on "hell ships," prisoners who were high-value propaganda assets, and those made to endure hard labor.

This account tells the story of individual prisoners and internees by focusing on specific camps and their commanders in the Philippines, Singapore, Japan, and Korea. It also highlights the decisions made by the most senior military and civilian leaders, both on the battlefield and back in Tokyo, Washington, DC, London, and Geneva. Notable here is General Douglas MacArthur, who first called for the internment of Japanese-Americans as retaliation for what he considered Japan's humiliation of Western captives. So too is Prime Minister Tōjō Hideki, who decided to use POWs to fill labor shortages, which subjected them to dangerous ocean voyages and harsh working conditions. We also need to understand more obscure figures, like Tamura Hiroshi, the last director of the Prisoner of War Information Bureau / Management Office, the Japanese government agencies charged with providing information on POWs and administering camps. Also playing important roles were the local delegate of the Swiss International Committee of the Red Cross, Dr. Fritz Paravicini, charged with visiting POWs in Japan, and the Swiss minister in Tokyo, Camille Gorgé. Their day-to-day struggle shows how high-level decisions made—or sometimes did not make—a demonstrable difference in who lived and who died, both during the war and in the war crimes tribunals.

Above all, we need to hear from POWs, internees, and guards themselves. Men like American counterintelligence officer Carl Engelhart, the rare Japanese-speaking POW, who understood far more quickly than most that IJA officers just did not know what to do with all their new prisoners; Alan Vernon Toze, a lance bombardier in the British Army, who was astonished to find starving Koreans desperate to break into a POW camp; and Dutch serviceman J. Oosterhuis, who became nostalgic for his favorite camp, only to become "a broken man" after a severe beating for stealing tangerines. We also meet internees held in the Philippines and Singapore, such as Mary Dorothy Cornelius, who resented the loss of status, and the fact that she had to wear a number, "like a convict," even more than the lack of food. The Japanese guards and officers also resist stereotype. Camp commander Noguchi Yuzuru gave stern speeches, but was really "a mild middle-aged man and anxious for a quiet life." Noguchi's own executive officer saved

6

lives when he refused to put emaciated POWs on yet another "hell ship." Park Byeong Suk, a Korean guard, was one of many to show small mercies, such as allowing a sick Dutch prisoner to avoid work.

Moving chronologically, the book reflects the journeys that captives themselves made, such as American POWs from the Philippines who were shipped to Japan, and then Korea; and British and Australian POWs who were shipped from Singapore to Korea and China, and thence to repatriation centers in the Philippines and home again. The chapters that follow therefore range across space, comparing camps in Singapore, the Philippines, Korea, and Fukuoka. Similarly, the book traces the divergent itineraries of guards, including men from Japan's colony in Korea, who along with Taiwanese colonials made up a disproportionately large number of camp personnel. The low-status jobs they filled were ones that in many armies are staffed by those considered unfit for combat. By following Swiss diplomats and representatives of the ICRC—who were some of the only neutral observers allowed into the theater—we can also see the impact of international law and nongovernmental organizations. Civilian internees, too, are part of the story, although their treatment was not governed by international law. They were often held at the same locations as POWs, could be keen observers of Japanese conduct, and frequently figured in negotiations and debates between the two sides. The book culminates with the war crimes tribunals, and the recasting of the Geneva Conventions in 1949.

Only an encyclopedia could cover all of the hundreds of camps and internment centers, and the coverage would be all too thin. I have focused instead on those camps that can answer key questions. That means highlighting the differences between the camps in the home islands, those in Korea—Japan's most important colony—and those in newly captured territories, farthest from the oversight of central authorities.

When we begin to see this history in all its epic scale, and to examine the Japanese treatment of POWs over time, the familiar account of Japanese conduct in the Pacific War takes on a different cast. It forces us to ask what changed in the years leading up to the Pacific War. This included the strategic use of a newly refigured bushidō. As we shall see, bushidō was an ideology that influenced both sides, with tragic consequences. It could indeed make some Japanese men condescend toward their captives, and military and civilian education and best-selling books made them fear the social consequences of surrendering. But so did the threat of capital punishment, and the expectation of being killed or tortured by Allied soldiers, who themselves came to suspect any attempted surrender to be a trap.[8]

To show that Japanese guards, camp commanders, and bureaucrats were human—all too human—even while they committed or abetted terrible crimes is one of my main objectives in this book. Some atrocities that occurred in POW camps were due to the cruelty of Japanese soldiers, but Japanese commanders and guards were not universally brutal. Some recognized the humanity of their Allied captives, and some even helped POWs escape abuse and death. And when Japanese bureaucrats made decisions that would prove disastrous for POWs, they were often responding to the overwhelming challenges of the war. The terrible consequences of their choices often were unintentional, arising as a by-product of decisions made for entirely different reasons. This does not excuse these choices, but it does cast Japanese soldiers and leaders in a different light, in contrast to narratives that portray the Japanese as intentionally and baselessly inhumane.

We also need to see POWs and internees as more than one-dimensional victims in a morality play. As much as conditions changed over time and varied between camps, there were important continuities in how POWs understood their condition. A deeper understanding requires that we explore the captivity experience through gender and race, but also class, which for military men usually mapped onto differences in rank. It can show how being a POW was not only physically difficult, but deeply disturbing, in ways that help explain why the plight of POWs continues to resonate in popular memories of the war.

By taking gender, race, and class into account, professionally trained historians have recently advanced our understanding of some of the most important aspects of twentieth-century history, whether the end of empires, the rise of popular democracies, or the spread of transnational social movements. These frames of analysis are among the most powerful tools of contemporary humanities scholarship and its commitment to understanding what it is to be human, including in the most extreme circumstances. But in recent decades, military history has had only a tenuous presence in academia. In fact, many military historians have perceived the academy to be either hostile or indifferent to their concerns, leading them, in turn, to deride or dismiss histories that focus on race and gender.[9]

At the same time, the POW camp is an unconventional subject for military history. As one prominent practitioner put it: "The essence of military history is combat; it is what makes our subject unique."[10] But is defeat and disarmament not also part of that experience? After all, until the second half of the twentieth century, modern wars typically ended with either one or the other side capitulating. Captivity is characterized by the *absence* of combat. Activities often identified with manliness and martial valor—such as physical conditioning and demonstrations of prowess, so central to most military history—have few, if any, outlets in a POW camp. Allied soldiers were supposed to attempt escape or commit sabotage. But typically neither course seemed practical in POW camps in Asia. Instead, POWs created weight tables to record their shrinking bodies, mended their gradually tattering clothes, and brooded about everyday humiliations at the hands of Japanese men.

Truly understanding the POW experience, an essential part of military history, demands the same analytical rigor that academic historians have used to examine much less consequential subjects. For instance, considering that Japanese notions of honor and manhood figure so prominently in popular explanations of the POW experience, analysis of how Allied POWs understood their own manhood and masculinity have been conspicuously absent. There were many masculinities even in the American army, depending on geography, class, education, and race. British services encouraged a masculinity of soberness and dispassionate reserve meant to represent an idealized national character.[11] Australians had to display expertise and also righteous virtue in their inevitable victories.[12] Rather than assuming that a uniquely Japanese notion of manhood dictated the conditions in POW camps, I will examine war as a site of competition over rival masculinities, both within and between different national communities.

While women are rarely mentioned in POW diaries or Japanese records, they were often present. Some camps held civilian white women and children as well as POWs. Japanese and other Asian women worked within camps as cooks and in other support roles. And when Allied men left the camps, they often worked alongside women toiling as farmers or other jobs usually held by men—men who were now off fighting the war. It is impossible to fully understand the POW experience without considering gender and acknowledging the impact that being held captive had on men's self-conceptions of their own manhood, even if that is only implicit in POW accounts of what made their experience so trying.

The same is true for understandings of race, which both reflected and refracted the experience of both POWs and internees. Many Americans, Australians, and British tended to consider the shorter, smaller Japanese men as literally beneath them. They were depicted as semi-civilized savages, primitives, children, or animals.[13] Newspapers described Japanese men as reptiles, or insects. Most commonly they were called apes, monkeys, baboons, or gorillas. Sometimes authors described them as mice and rats, cockroaches, vermin, with "beady little eyes." In groups they were referred to as "the Japanese herd."[14]

The American war correspondent Ernie Pyle compared perceptions of the Japanese to how GIs viewed the Nazi enemy. To servicemen, he wrote, the Germans were "still people." But the Japanese were "something subhuman and repulsive; the way some people feel about cockroaches or mice."[15] Others referred to Japanese "inscrutable minds." And in the race hierarchy of the United States, as John Dower and Gerald Horne have described it, fears of yellow, red, and black men were easily integrated.[16] This included American fears of an American black/Japanese alliance.[17]

Unfortunately, many books about POWs perpetuate views of Japanese people as inhuman and indistinguishable. One popular history insists that for them, "savagery was an almost sacred rite, a part of the code of Bushido." It continues, "The Japanese soldier obeyed no moral authority other than the emperor and the army. He listened to no inner voice of restraint. When he was ordered to scorch the earth or subdue the civilian population, he fixed his bayonet and took and did what he wanted."[18] To be fair, popular accounts, like Gavan Daws's *Prisoners of the Japanese,* do not claim to have any real interest in understanding the Japanese, or investigating their "warrior code, *bushidō.*" These books are about POWs, not their guards, and Daws makes no apology for simply reporting "in their words, in their tone of voice . . . what POWs say it was like." Crucially, for Daws, these POWs "were white men,* and yellow men had life-and-death power over them." By striving to preserve and sympathetically present the worldview of white POWs, no matter how racist, this approach ignores not just the "yellow men" who guarded them, but the tens of thousands of captives who were not white—who were, in fact, the majority of Allied troops who surrendered in the Pacific War. In this quotation, they are literally dismissed with an asterisk.[19]

This way of rendering the experience as a one-sided race war is unfair to POWs, and not just to the ones who are left out of the whites-only histories. Although many POWs and internees held racist views and were particularly humiliated to become prisoners of the Japanese, none could survive without gaining at least some understanding of their captors. They typically made distinctions between different Japanese guards and camp commanders, and many POWs showed empathy for the suffering of Korean and Japanese civilians outside the camps, who sometimes seemed even worse off than the POWs themselves. Most importantly, considering that "yellow men had life-and-death power" over POWs, any account that does not make a serious effort to understand the Japanese—in their own words, in the original—cannot ultimately explain why some POWs lived while others died.

It is true that some on both sides treated the war as a race war. But thousands of POWs switched sides, most notably those who joined the Indian National Army to fight for India's independence. Many other POWs worked in the Japanese war industry. This is famously—and controversially—depicted in *The Bridge on the River Kwai,* a story apparently inspired by Pierre Boulle's experiences in Japanese-occupied Indochina. These stories are not all wrong, and understanding how POWs could collaborate across racial lines, in the service of an enemy nation, is also part of their story.

For most Allied POWs, collaboration was a matter of survival, and thousands more captives, mostly Asians, were compelled to work in appalling conditions. But in many POW camps, men actually preferred to work, to relieve their boredom. Conversely, some Korean guards—themselves initially collaborators with the Japanese—conspired to free Allied prisoners and fight alongside them against their common enemy.

Collaboration of any kind was inimical to the Allies' military discipline, which required a strict separation from enemy soldiers. This discipline also mandated a distinction among officers and men of different ranks, a rule that was supposed to apply to POWs without exception. Allied officers tried to create societies in the camps on military models, viewing the camp as a continuation of the war. Each camp would have a commander and staff who would be responsible for their men.

Here again, the captivity experience disrupted hierarchies. Japanese commanders and guards typically refused to recognize the rank of officers, demanding that every POW salute their guards, no matter how lowly their rank. When they put their prisoners to work, they included the officers. Officers who tried to assert their privileges were often dealt with harshly. At Changi, in Singapore, the Japanese removed officers at will when it suited them. But at other times the Japanese did make distinctions as to rank, such as when they transported higher-ranking officers to separate camps in Korea and Manchuria. This unpredictability could be especially disconcerting for Allied POWs accustomed to the order and discipline of military life.

Popular accounts of captives in Japan tend to follow the simplified story line of Allied POWs ultimately triumphing over Japanese cruelty, a pat story that ignores the discrepancies among different POW experiences. This narrative did not materialize out of thin air. It too was a product of history. Memories of the war were shaped by Anglo-American announcements of atrocities, timed to justify the bombing of Japanese cities. The memories of POWs themselves were influenced by the structured interviews and questionnaires each was required to complete, which included questions about whether they had attempted sabotage or escape—very few could truthfully answer yes. And the accusations they made against the Japanese were collected not to provide an impartial account but for the specific purpose of prosecuting war crimes. The trials themselves treated history as a hanging judge, but were so often arbitrary and inconclusive as to leave no one satisfied. Questions of war guilt and reparations are still live issues in relations between Japan and several other nations.

In the immediate aftermath of the war, the perceived lessons of the POW experience changed international law, and led to new rules to protect both POWs and civilian internees. The Geneva Conventions of 1949 continue to be the main normative framework governing treatment of captives in wartime, which has frequently occasioned controversy over how the United States treats its own captives in the "global war on terror." But war crimes, tribunals, and possible prosecutions are not just a matter of case law and international treaties. They too are also the product of history and how societies choose to remember or forget.

# 1

# FROM AVATAR OF MODERNIZATION
# TO OUTLAW NATION

In 1873, a forty-five-year-old former samurai named Sano Tsunetami traveled to Vienna to lead Japan's first embassy to the Austro-Hungarian Empire. In the two decades since 1853, when Commodore Matthew Perry's ships arrived in Uraga Bay, Sano's world had undergone dramatic upheavals. He had witnessed the collapse of shogunal rule, civil war, and, in 1867, the "restoration" of the emperor Meiji to his throne. Sano and other Japanese of his generation had good reason to fear even more epochal change. Britain's defeat of China in the Opium Wars and Russian encroachment on Sakhalin and the Kuril Islands demonstrated the danger posed by European ambitions and rivalries. Clearly, Japan needed to rapidly learn and assimilate the rules of the international order, or risk going the way of a growing number of Europe's colonies and protectorates.

Over a period of seventy-five years, Japan sought to both engage and compete with the West by joining international organizations and imitating Western colonialism. This chapter explores how these two tendencies ran parallel until the force of Japanese imperialism and militarism completely overwhelmed internationalism. This trajectory is important context for the POW experience in Japan in World War II. In the nineteenth and early twentieth centuries, Japan's commitment to international organizations such as the Red Cross paralleled its own humanitarian reforms and encouraged it to adopt high standards for the treatment of war wounded and captive enemy soldiers. But Japanese imperial ambitions eventually drove them in the opposite direction, leading to the revival and refiguring of the bushidō code, an ideology that once applied only to the samurai class. This new bushidō involved fighting to the death and feeling shame, in some cases to the point of suicide, if taken captive. This chapter charts how the Japanese treated POWs—including Chinese and Russian soldiers—across several wars, revealing how this treatment changed over time as Japan shifted away from internationalism and toward imperialism.

Changes in warfare beginning in 1918 in the Siberian Intervention, and especially the harsh fighting on both sides in the second Sino-Japanese War starting in 1937, help explain why Japan moved away from international rules. So do changes in the Imperial Japanese Army (IJA) training that came to emphasize how Japan's only chance for victory in total war against superior Western forces was a bushidō-influenced emphasis on "spirit" and fighting to the finish. All this would have deadly consequences for allied POWs.

Sano Tsunetami was better positioned than most to find his way in this new order. Though born a low-ranking samurai, he was educated in Saga Domain, which was known as a center for technology and shipbuilding in an otherwise isolated archipelago, largely closed to the West for over 200 years. Men who grew up in such places became the elite of the new Japan. The story of how they traveled to Europe and the United States and, when they returned home, selectively adopted—and adapted—government institutions like a conscript army, civil service, and national universities, is well known. Less familiar is the twisted route by which Sano, and the nongovernmental organization he founded, also helped define Japan's twentieth century.[1]

That story starts even earlier, when another man, Geneva businessman Henri Dunant, visited a very different sort of place: the bloody battlefield of Solferino during the Second Italian War of Independence. It was 1859, an era when European nations and empires were already engaged in mortal combat. The violence and misery he saw inspired him to call for organizations of volunteers to be set up to help the wounded. He demanded "some international principles, conventional and sacred, which once ratified and agreed would form the basis for these national societies to help the wounded in different countries in Europe."[2]

Dunant's ideas were not entirely new. Since the seventeenth and early eighteenth century, armies in Europe made prisoners of the wounded rather than finishing them off, and in some eighteenth-century wars medics were considered noncombatants or granted neutral status.[3] But during the second half of the nineteenth century, widespread conscription meant citizens had a closer relationship with the men fighting, while technologies such as the telegraph and popular press, combined with rising literacy rates, raised awareness of what was happening on the battlefield in near real time.[4] Civilians' increasing awareness of the realities of war led to a new feature in international society, the rise of nongovernmental organizations. The

Red Cross movement was emblematic of this development. It was the work of private individuals, rather than religious or state institutions. The Red Cross, and the international agreements to which it gave rise, would set a new standard for the treatment of wounded enemy soldiers and POWs.

By October 1863, only a year after Dunant wrote *A Memory of Solferino*, delegates from sixteen countries had met and adopted ten articles to protect the sick and wounded as well as to provide the medical personnel to care for them. The Geneva-based "Red Cross" organization would link the national members and would serve as guardian of the rules.[5] Representatives from twelve European states met in Geneva and signed the Convention for the Amelioration of the Condition of the Wounded in Armies in the Field. The convention called for caring for the wounded without distinction as to nationality. It also asserted the inviolability of medical personnel, including the medical establishments and medical units of warring armies—all of which now would share the distinctive sign of a red cross on a white background.

This agreement was a watershed moment in the history of warfare, the first codified international treaty to protect sick and wounded soldiers. This First Geneva Convention, together with the 1899 Hague Conventions, formed the spine of a new international law of war. For the first time, international treaties governed military conduct, though in practice they functioned mostly as ideals—ideals that, when practiced, governed European behavior toward other Europeans.

Even with the rise of humanitarian organizations, improved communications, and emerging norms about inter-state war, the conduct of colonial armies did not change. The First Geneva Convention was thought to apply only in wars between civilized countries, not the brutal wars of conquest being waged to seize land and subjugate non-European peoples.

The fact that the Geneva Committee did not invite Japanese participation—supposedly because Tokyo was too far away—therefore had ominous implications.[6] Yet Japan was undergoing many of the same changes as European states, like Italy and Germany, including wars for national unification. Beginning in the 1830s, the shogun and some domains (fiefdoms) began to adapt European military technology, and by the 1850s, the central government introduced organizational reforms that would turn samurai into soldiers, if only on a small scale.[7] In 1873, the year Sano arrived in Vienna, the Japanese national government officially introduced conscription, and was rapidly adopting the telegraph and public education.

15

As chargé d'affaires in Vienna, Sano was responsible for Japan's participation in the Vienna Exhibition of 1873. Japan's pavilion would feature
the golden dolphins of Nagoya Castle, a model of the Great Buddha at
Kamakura, a Shinto shrine, a Japanese garden, Ukiyo-e works, and industrial art.[8] While mounting Japan's exhibition, Sano saw the displays of
Dunant's humanitarian organization that was starting to sweep Europe.

Sano was soon joined by the Iwakura embassy, Japan's first international
delegation, which stopped in Switzerland during its whistle-stop tour of
American and European capitals. On July 1, Itō Hirobumi, "father of the
Japanese constitution," and Iwakura Tomomi, leader of the eponymous del-
egation, visited Geneva. There they met with the chairman of the Geneva
Committee.

Aimé Humbert, author of *Japan and the Japanese* and signatory to the
1864 Treaty of Amity and Trade between Switzerland and Japan, attended
the meeting as a Japan expert. He observed that the International Committee was concerned with spreading the idea of the Red Cross, but could
not expect rapid advances in distant regions. "Generally men there are not
as well prepared as were the Europeans for a reform that requires a very
advanced level of civilization." Humbert reported that Iwakura and Itō
themselves recognized that it was premature for Japan to adhere to the
Geneva Conventions. But they promised to work toward these reforms after
their return to Japan, and authorized the Swiss to follow up with them.[9]

In fact, contrary to Humbert's estimation of its level of civilization, Japan
had a strong tradition of humanitarianism. The new Meiji government and
its allies suffered few casualties and took few captives during the Boshin
war of 1868–1869, but they treated defeated troops humanely or simply sent
them home.[10] Although no single organization provided medical care,
students of Dutch medicine staffed mobile medical units that treated all
combatants.[11] These practices were the precursor to Japan's international
reputation for the humane treatment of POWs, a reputation that lasted for
several decades.

At the same time as internationalists like Sano embarked on a campaign
to present Japan as a civilized nation, other Japanese sought to prove their
martial prowess. These two streams were part of a foreign policy aimed at
winning a place among the Great Powers. Meiji leaders adopted the slogan
"Rich country, strong army" (*fukoku kyōhei*). In 1868, after the defeat of
the Tokugawa, Japan had no central army, so Meiji leaders built one from
scratch. In 1869, former low-ranking samurai and now statesmen Yamagata

Aritomo and Saigō Tsugumichi traveled to Europe to study European models, especially in Prussia. These study trips were influential in forming Japanese institutions.

In 1873, Yamagata became war minister and led the creation of Japan's first centralized modern military. The victorious domains contributed to the creation of a new Imperial Guard. The new Meiji government considered a strong army essential to creating a Japan able to catch up with the West. After indigenous people in Taiwan killed Ryukyuan sailors in 1871, and Japanese subjects in 1873, the Meiji government launched the Taiwan expedition.[12] Its strategy of "indigenization" in Taiwan wreaked growing damage, essentially reorganizing Taiwanese society.[13] The Tokyo government also declared universal male conscription. Yet it left out several categories of people, and rich men could easily buy their way out. Conscription was so unpopular that in 1873–1874, riots erupted in rural areas.[14]

During the 1877 Satsuma Rebellion—the last gasp of disaffected samurai against the central government—the six-year-old army medical branch was still improvising and had few members. At the onset of the rebellion, a 2,000-man infantry regiment had just one chief doctor, assisted by seven others.[15] Sano and Ogyū Yuzuru, a former daimyō, or provincial military leader, founded the humanitarian society Hakuaisha (Philanthropic Society).[16] It processed donations of money and supplies. Sano himself provided handkerchiefs, and a few physicians served on the front lines. Many of the physicians were trained at the influential Juntendō School of Medical Studies, which specialized in teaching both Chinese medicine and Western surgery during the Shogunate.[17] Prince Higashifushimi Yorita, later known as Prince Komatsu Akihito, head of the cadet branch of the Japanese imperial family, agreed to be president.[18]

Sano's original inspiration for the Society is unknown, but he was likely influenced by his experience in Europe and knowledge of the Red Cross movement. For Sano, this Red Cross movement was a model of European civilization.[19] But the Hakuaisha was founded in an era when Japan's new elite were creating many more such humanitarian organizations.[20] Like the adoption of other aspects of modernity, the introduction of the Red Cross in Japan was a complex process in which European influences and late Tokugawa reform efforts came together. When it came to POWs and wounded combatants, the Red Cross was in some ways an extension of the earlier Japanese institutions and traditions that protected captive enemy soldiers.

Before a Japanese Red Cross Society could be accepted as a member of the International Committee of the Red Cross (ICRC), Japan's government needed to recognize it. And before Tokyo could sign the Geneva Conventions, the Geneva Committee had to judge it eligible. Japan, along with the Ottoman Empire, was deemed to have adequate morals, rule of law, medicine, and use of the appropriate emblem—a red cross or crescent.[21] In November 1886, they were the first two non-European countries to join the movement. The Hakuaisha became the Japan Red Cross Society (JRCS). The "Red Cross" was translated as "Red Ten" (Seki Jūji; Nihon Sekjūjisha) because the Japanese character for the number ten resembles a cross.[22]

After Geneva admitted the JRCS, organizers worked hard to recruit new members. Newspapers reported how Japanese medical officer Ishiguro Tadanori toured the nation, visiting schoolhouses to spread the message. The Meiji empress took a personal interest in the cause. In 1888, in its first humanitarian mission, the JRCS organized humanitarian relief after the volcanic eruption at Mount Bandai. Nearly 450 people were killed, and many more were injured. This mission led many Japanese men and women to identify the Red Cross as a medical and humanitarian organization rather than one associated with war. From 1890 to 1893, membership nearly doubled, from 23,569 to 45,317, likely due to advertising and road shows by Sano and Ishiguro.[23]

At the same time that support for the Red Cross grew, the Japanese government's efforts in building nationalism began to bear fruit. Meiji government leaders, most importantly Yamagata, had to figure out how to inculcate both military loyalty to the nation and a new military culture. They chose to adopt the values of the samurai class. Since Japan had seen little conflict for some 250 years, samurai, who comprised only a small percentage of the population, mostly worked as bureaucrats and clerks during that time. "Samurai ideals," therefore, needed to be created anew.

An important component was the 1882 Imperial Rescript to Soldiers and Sailors, presented by Yamagata to the emperor. According to the rescript, military service meant imperial loyalty.[24] In Japan it was read aloud in newly mandatory schools. Its influence was profound because it linked the military to the emperor. Together with changes in military education, military elites helped invent the tradition of "samurai values" in the military. These were used to create a culture in which soldiers were required to be loyal to the emperor until death.[25] The new military culture would eventually play a large role in Japanese treatment of POWs.

After the revision of the conscription law in 1889, the army experience increasingly delineated and even measured manhood, starting with the bodies of recruits.[26] Conscription inspections compared male subjects by height, weight, and other common characteristics.[27] Physical ranking by military authorities put men into categories that determined their military careers. After data was provided to families, these inspections and rankings began to define what manhood was.[28]

By the 1890s, Japan was beginning to industrialize and to build up its navy. An Army Staff College now trained officers and potential general officers.[29] There would be a long-standing rivalry between army staff college graduates and unit officers. Japan's now-professional military soon displayed both sound strategy and effective tactics. In 1894, with new martial confidence, Japan took on China in its first big war abroad, a contest over Korea. Tokyo deployed some 200,000 men with strong support at home.[30] They had the JRCS to serve as a medical auxiliary. Upon the declaration of war, the JRCS quickly held a conference to plan emergency funds for relief staff. They would eventually raise 75,401 yen and run ten base hospitals in Japan and four abroad.[31]

China had not joined the Red Cross. Even so, Tokyo committed to act in accordance with its tenets. The words of War Minister Ōyama Iwao provide a stark contrast with how European empires of the era conducted wars of conquest:

> The common principles of humanity dictate that succor and rescue should be extended. In obedience to these principles, civilized nations in times of peace enter into conventions to mutually assist disabled persons in times of war without distinction of friend or foe. This humane union is called the Geneva Convention or more commonly the Red Cross Association. Japan became a party to it in June 1886, and her soldiers have already been instructed that they are bound to treat with kindness and helpfulness such of their enemies as may be disabled by wounds or disease.[32]

Japan took prisoner some 1,500 Chinese in the course of the conflict. They allowed these prisoners to sit out the war and did not force them to work.[33] Ōyama told representatives of the Tientsin (Tianjin) Red Cross Society that Chinese wounded also were prisoners of war. He added, "We have great pleasure in assuring you that it is our strict rule to treat wounded and sick with the utmost kindness, to whatsoever nation they may belong." He added that the Chinese wounded were receiving treatment in Japanese field hospitals.[34] The JRCS treated almost 20,000 wounded, including Chinese and also Koreans, from Liushuchun to Pyongyang to Port Arthur.[35]

Yet Japan's record was not unblemished. In July 1894, when naval forces sank the British ship *Kowshing,* Japanese sailors rescued only the European crewmen and not the Chinese sailors aboard the ship. But it was a chaotic scene, in which these Chinese sailors continued to fire at them. Only half the Chinese sailors survived, escaping to either the islands or a French gunboat.[36] The Japanese were criticized abroad, but they were judged to have proceeded legally. On the other hand, the Chinese refused to join Japan in accepting basic principles of protection for the wounded. They were suspected of merciless treatment of the seventy Japanese captives they held.[37]

The Sino-Japanese War forced China to recognize Japan's influence in Korea, and Japan also gained control of Taiwan, the Pescadores, and the eastern portion of the Bay of Liaodong. The war attracted huge numbers to the JRCS, including the Meiji emperor himself. "I am more than honored by this distinguished assembly," he told delegates upon becoming honorary president.[38] In 1894, new members joining the organization totaled 71,705, and the next year another 65,392 signed up, for a total of 182,414. By 1897, membership had more than doubled again, to 455,638.[39] This was an almost twenty-fold increase since 1890. All of this greatly impressed foreign observers. The JRCS had become the largest branch of the Red Cross in the world.[40] For instance, although the United States had earlier been a pioneer in implementing practices to protect POWs, and already had a much larger population than Japan, the American Red Cross was far smaller, both in members and in financial resources.[41]

Four years after the war, at the 1899 Hague Peace Conference, Japanese delegates signed the Hague Conventions, which Japan ratified in 1900. These treaties formalized the laws of war and defined war crimes. Chapter II mandated that POWs should be treated humanely. It established the principle that "prisoners of war shall be treated as regards food, quarters, and clothing, on the same footing as the troops of the Government which has captured them." The Hague Conventions together with the Geneva Conventions are some of the earliest components of the international law of war and the concomitant idea of formal protections for a category of captured soldiers, prisoners of war.[42]

Chinese representatives also attended the conference. Unlike the Japanese—long masters of sartorial codes—they turned up in Qing dress. Internationalists within the Qing court saw ratification of the Hague Conventions as a route to international recognition, following the Japanese model. Yet within the Chinese court there was a split between internationalists and isolationists. The internationalists prevailed, but the ratification documents got lost during the chaos surrounding the Boxer Uprising.[43]

The huge popularity of the Red Cross in Japan made Sano world famous. When he died in 1901, several American newspapers ran obituaries.[44] The best tribute to him was the performance of the JRCS in the war with Russia that started three years later. The first "pagan nation" to sign the Geneva Conventions was also the first to defeat a white power in modern war.

During the Russo-Japanese War, military education instructed soldiers on the Red Cross treaties, coverage that later disappeared.[45] The Japanese government established the POW Information Bureau as the war began. Its purpose was to manage information on Russian POWs, a measure required to comply with the Hague Conventions.[46] The JRCS again provided care for wounded prisoners, many of whom were treated in Red Cross hospitals, most famously at Matsuyama in Ehime Prefecture. Medics and wounded prisoners who were considered unfit for military service were allowed to repatriate.

Some Russians complained about their treatment, alleging that the Japanese had neglected sick and wounded captured at Port Arthur. Red Cross files do not support these accusations.[47] Many of the almost 80,000 Russian prisoners were in poor health when captured. Nevertheless, almost 95 percent survived the war and returned to their families. Japanese captors treated Russian POWs far better than Russians treated the 2,088 Japanese POWs.[48] The Japanese even gave Russian officers private servants and took them on trips to hot springs.[49] The Japanese empress herself visited the Red Cross hospital.[50]

The ICRC, Europeans, and Americans were now well aware of Tokyo's humanitarianism, in part because of foreign volunteers who worked in Red Cross hospitals. For example, American physician Anita Newcomb McGee led a group of volunteer nurses to Japan and trained Japanese Red Cross nurses.[51] After the war the Japanese government sent a letter of appreciation to Dr. McGee.[52] Beyond foreign volunteers in Japan, many American and European observers judged that Japan was more civilized than Russia. In a 1905 book, Miss Ethel McCaul reported on her inspection trip. She was

GARDEN PARTY TO CELEBRATE RUSSIAN FESTIVAL IN THE SHIZUOKA QUARTER FOR RUSSIAN PRISONERS, JAPAN.
Пирушка русскихъ плѣнныхъ въ саду при помѣщеніи въ день русскаго
праздника въ г. Сизуока въ Японіи.

The Japanese government used the camps for Russian POWs at Matsuyama in order to impress Western observers. And observers noticed—Japanese treatment was shown in contemporary books, journalistic accounts, and postcards like this one. (Slavic-Eurasian Research Center Library, Hokkaido University.)

impressed by the medical officers' kind manners toward the wounded Russians. "The Japanese are a marvelously clever people," she wrote, "and their powers of organization extraordinary."[53]

Even then, there was an ominous contradiction in how the Japanese treated the Chinese and Koreans who worked for the Russians. Evidence suggests that they killed those who cut down telegraph lines, and also executed some Chinese who acted as interpreters for the Russians.[54] In fact, the precarious situation of Chinese in Manchuria during the war caused Chinese merchant-elites to found the Chinese Red Cross in 1904.[55]

In a peace agreement brokered by Theodore Roosevelt, Japan gained the Liaodong Peninsula and the strategic city of Dalian. This allowed them to set up the South Manchurian Railway and base troops in Manchuria, starting with the 10,000-strong Kwantung Army, formed to guard the railway and Japanese leased territory. The Treaty of Portsmouth also affirmed Japanese influence in Korea, setting the stage for annexation in 1910. Despite this victory, Japan gained neither territory on the Asian mainland nor reparations. A huge riot broke out in Hibiya in Tokyo in protest, and riots and meetings spread throughout Japan.[56] Yet victory in the Russo-Japanese War boosted Japanese self-confidence and increased its economic capacity to rival any Western power. The Japanese military was not just involved in Korea. In the 1910s, it sought to pacify Taiwan through fierce fighting.[57] The task of both the Army and Navy was then to prepare for the next war. For the Army, the likely enemy would be a revanchist Russia.[58] For the Navy, it was the United States.

Military leadership attributed Japan's 1905 victory in the Russo-Japanese War to the mental strength of Japanese soldiers. Subsequently, the IJA began to emphasize moral education. They tried to instill the modern conscripted army with the ideology of samurai warriors, and the idea that samurai did not mind death for victory. This mentality became a core value.[59] These ideas were extended into the family and into education.[60] Schools featured martial lessons, and war was increasingly a part of textbooks, children's literature, and songs.[61]

Despite treating Russian POWs well, even before the war the army discouraged its own soldiers from being taken captive, and captives were expected to apologize.[62] Approximately 2,000 veterans were investigated, and former captives could not go home until released. None were court-martialed, but some were subject to administrative punishment, and some officers lost their ranks. Yet this treatment was not universal, and depended on individual circumstances.[63] For instance, an Army interrogation committee exonerated one soldier: "We judge that this ex-prisoner's honor still remains and he should not be court-martialed nor punished, because he became a POW after he had wounded his head and fallen unconscious by enemy hands."[64]

Alongside the interrogation and occasional shaming of captured soldiers, the war led to a boom in writing about bushidō. The historian Oleg Benesch has argued that this writing prefigured 1930s ideas about captivity. A 1904 exchange in *Nihon*, a periodical, and *Taiyō*, Japan's first general-interest magazine, "The POW Exchange Student Debate," exemplifies this. Scholars debated whether Japanese soldiers should allow themselves to be taken captive, or should kill themselves instead.[65] The discussion revolved around a 1904 incident in which soldiers aboard the *Hitatchi Maru* refused to surrender to the Russians. Many officers killed themselves rather than be taken captive, and sensationalistic press coverage recounted their deaths. Although at that time, being taken a POW was not contrary to military doctrine, and Japan's captives were well treated, the incident provided material in later nationalist propaganda during the 1930s.[66]

At the same time that Japan celebrated its military success and the military spread its ideals of martial valor, Tokyo remained fully engaged in international diplomacy. This was the beginning of what is identified as Taishō democracy, when Japan was run by elected politicians who formed cabinets comprised of party members.[67]

Japan participated in negotiating the 1907 Hague Convention, later known as the Second Geneva Convention. It spelled out obligations in the realm of naval warfare. It also expanded the process for voluntary arbitration, and established conventions on the law of war and the rights and obligations of neutrals. In 1911, Japan signed and ratified it.

These laws of war, overseen by the ICRC, would be put to the test during World War I. During this war, about 8 million soldiers and 2 million civilians were held in captivity.[68] ICRC delegates inspected 529 camps, including camps in Japan. An International Agency for Aid and Information on POWs in Geneva facilitated the exchange of lists of prisoners and the dead.[69]Although this process was intended for POWs, some civilians came to be included.[70] The ICRC drifted into the role of mediator, as it recruited Swiss men to act as delegates and deliver care packages. It was thus in the unique position of observing and reporting on the conditions of captives on both sides.[71] In 1917, the ICRC won the ultimate accolade, the Nobel Peace Prize. After the war, Allied governments requested that the ICRC organize repatriation of prisoners to and from Germany, Russia, and the Austro-Hungarian Empire.

Japan entered the conflict mainly to gain control of German territories in Asia. In 1915, Tokyo delivered secret demands to the Chinese government, the "Twenty-One Demands" for special privileges. As Japan sought to increase its influence in China, it met resistance from the West, particularly the United States and President Woodrow Wilson. China refused Japan's most extreme demands, for placing Japanese advisors within the Chinese government. Yet Japan received much of what it sought, if only after the Paris Peace Conference. China was forced to transfer the German rights in Shandong to Japan, and to expand Japan's rights in Manchuria. This began the Japanese Army's predominant military influence in Japan's affairs with China. This influence would begin to overshadow both Japan's stated governmental position and its Foreign Ministry policy on matters such as China and the treatment of POWs.[72]

During the war Japan held some 4,500 German and Austro-Hungarian troops and colonists. They were taken at Qingdao after a short siege and brought to Japan.[73] Japanese authorities struggled to find places to put their new captives. At first most were kept in improvised camps in Japan Red Cross buildings, temples, or camps originally built for Russian captives.[74]

Some prisoners found the transportation and the lodging "crowded" and "unsuitable."[75] They complained about the "monotonous blandness" of the food. At Kurume camp, a former army barracks established in 1915, over 1,300 German POWs were crowded into sixteen buildings with holes in the walls. Accidents were sometimes punished by violence. The atmosphere elicited mild resistance, such as not appearing for evening roll call. Yet punishment was also mild, such as the withholding of mail or loss of excursions outside the camp.[76]

The ICRC asked a Swiss physician, Fritz Paravicini, to be its chief of delegation in Japan and visit the camps. Since 1905, Paravicini had practiced medicine and surgery in Yokohama, mostly for a foreign clientele. He was therefore well qualified to judge the well-being and health of the POWs. He also helped oversee the funds sent by the ICRC's central authority to the JRCS's Committee on POWs.[77] The JRCS in turn worked with the Japanese Imperial Office of POWs to ensure that the funds went to POWs. The POWs could buy what they needed at the camp store.[78]

Germany also had a "protecting power," the United States, responsible for looking after German interests in Japan during the war. On orders from Washington, two officials, including twenty-three-year-old Third Undersecretary Sumner Welles, visited eleven camps. Welles's report found that the "Imperial Japanese Government had shown a desire to safeguard every prisoner's health and welfare." Welles considered the food to be adequate, but he criticized the camps for overcrowding.[79]

Japan sought to follow international law, to demonstrate the extent to which they were a "civilized and cultured country."[80] Yet both captives and inspectors noted the problems at Osaka, and also at the former temple Matsuyama, where the camp commander's strict adherence to the rules meant swift punishment of infractions. During his next visit six months later, Welles visited Kurume. He found the former army barracks only slightly improved. Welles spoke some German, and so heard that the food offered to POWs may have been equivalent to what Japanese received, but the Germans found Japanese-style rations inadequate.[81] While POWs were compensated for work, the rate remained constant even as tremendous inflation racked Japan. Unfortunately for captives, Japan made it difficult for German prisoners to escape, though some tried. Most were found, but at least one made it all the way back to Germany.[82]

Despite overcrowding, poor food, and strict discipline, the majority of German POWs had a tolerable experience, and most Japanese showed good will. Entire school classes welcomed German POWs when they first arrived at Tokyo Station.[83] In one camp, prisoners found welcome remarks in German on the banners hung at the entrance of the village.[84] Bandō in particular became famous for its humane treatment of POWs.[85] In March 1918, a red-and-black poster in German and Japanese advertised a ten-day exhibition for the Ministry of Agriculture and dealers from Osaka, complete with packed lunches and Western-style food. It featured everything from metalwork to a puppet show to a butcher. The exhibition was so popular that it was extended for two additional days.[86]

During the war, local markets received an immediate economic benefit when camps bought ingredients for prisoners' meals.[87] An estimated $164 million in today's dollars was spent on Bandō and the other camps, including food for NCOs and privates, and excluding the cost of what officers purchased directly from local merchants.[88] Farmers began to raise cattle specifically to provide meat for POWs. The effect was so pronounced that Kumamoto citizens protested when the camp there closed. Some German POWs were so happy in Japan that they decided not to return home after the war was over. In both Japan and Germany the historical memory of this episode was positive.[89] The POW orchestra at Bandō became famous and was the first to perform Beethoven's Ninth Symphony in Japan. Now it is performed in Naruto every June. Cities like Naruto formed sister city relationships with German cities.[90]

By the beginning of World War I, Japan's economy was booming and could easily support a few thousand German and Austrian POWs. In 1941, circumstances could not have been more different. But in other ways what happened in World War I foreshadowed the Asian-Pacific War. One incident in particular left a lasting impression on the Japanese. Although no Japanese were prisoners of war in the conflict, about 600 Japanese civilians, mostly students, found themselves stranded in Germany after Japan declared war in August 1914. The Japanese embassy had successfully shepherded some 400 citizens out of the country, but the Germans interned the rest in humiliating and unsanitary conditions. Verbally abusive guards harassed the captives, forcing them to clean their own quarters.[91] By the end of 1914, most internees were released and left Germany, but their bitter experience was publicized in Japan.

In 1919 the Treaty of Versailles ended World War I. Even though Japan entered as an ally, it experienced a number of disappointments at the conference. It sought to confirm its control over Shandong and German Micronesia. Japan gained Shandong, but the League insisted that Japan control Micronesia as a League of Nations "Mandate." Japanese diplomats had also proposed an amendment calling for the acceptance of the principle of racial equality. It was quashed by Americans and British commonwealth delegations.[92] This enraged diplomats and others who argued it demonstrated the hypocrisy of Western idealism. Japanese diplomats also failed to achieve reparations for the wages and per diem expenses they had paid to German POWs.[93] According to the Hague Convention, these monies were supposed to be reimbursed by the German government after the war, but the Versailles Peace Treaty did not include this provision.[94]

Japan continued to seek international status with the Western Powers and joined the League of Nations as a founding member in 1920.[95] But Japan had reason to doubt it would benefit equally with Western countries from the creation of a law-based international system. Moreover, the war itself raised many doubts about the "established standards of civilization."[96] Its shocking carnage certainly influenced Japanese military commanders, who worried that Japan would be no match for European armies. The sheer number of combatants who surrendered and the protracted conflicts between occupying armies and hostile communities in places like Belgium showed the Japanese the necessity for strict military discipline both for their own troops and those who came under their control.[97]

In 1913, the Military Education Order already stated that making good soldiers was equivalent to making good people. During the war, the Army strengthened its intervention into national education. A 1918 textbook emphasized that boys' nature was strength and girls' nature was kindness. Masculinity was being strong and protecting the country.[98]

Experience with harsh fighting in the "Siberian Intervention" caused IJA leaders to increasingly view being taken prisoner as something dishonorable.[99] Tokyo had joined the other Entente powers in sending troops to support those fighting against the Bolsheviks during the Russian Civil War. Initially the ostensible purpose was to rescue former Austro-Hungarian POWs. For internationalists, it was a test of whether a modern Japan would live up to its treaty obligations or remain neutral. For others, it was an opportunity to stop the growth of Bolshevism in Northeast Asia and promote Japanese trade and investment.[100]

During the Intervention, Japan still sought to comply with international standards of POW treatment. Yet protracted guerrilla warfare in Siberia may have encouraged an indifference to human life in the IJA.[101] In May 1920, for instance, Russians massacred Japanese garrison troops and civilians at Nikolaevsk. This only prolonged the occupation, which lasted until 1922, two years after the other Allied powers had withdrawn. Perhaps in reaction to the harsh warfare, Japanese military ideology hardened and became less forgiving. Increasingly, officers viewed being taken prisoner as dishonorable.[102]

The Intervention was extremely unpopular in Japan, mostly because of the war's expense. In July and August 1918, Japan experienced riots against increasing rice prices, with attacks on the property of rice merchants in Tokyo.[103] One hundred thousand troops were deployed to put down the riots, and over 8,000 people were arrested.[104] Part of the reason for the price increases was the cost of the Siberian Intervention.[105]

Soldiers themselves became unpopular during this period, in part because of a growing socialist ideology among Japan's working classes, who focused on domestic issues rather than foreign policy. This isolated the officer class and created a preference for recruiting among rural farmers rather than urban workers.[106] Soldiers wore civilian clothes when off base, and families did not want their daughters to marry military men. One saying went, "Second lieutenants penniless, first lieutenants struggling, captains barely making it."[107] It is in this period that many of the military leaders in command during the war came of age.

Despite the difficult Siberian Intervention and the resulting economic hardships, Japan did enjoy vibrant party politics, a dynamic urban culture, and international prestige. Japanese diplomats continued to play a prominent role, such as at the world's first arms control negotiations, the 1921–1922 Washington Naval Conference. And although Japanese military ideology had turned against POWs during the Siberian Intervention, Japan was still committed to what we now call humanitarian projects. The nation played a leading role in widening the scope of the International Red Cross and in creating international civil society. In 1919, representatives from Japan joined counterparts from Britain, France, Italy, and the United States in Paris to found the League of Red Cross Societies, now called the International Federation of Red Cross and Red Crescent Societies.[108] It further expanded the focus of the Red Cross, from war relief and natural disasters to promoting health and preventing disease.[109] Even the Army improved its reputation by helping civilians after the devastating 1923 Kantō earthquake.

When it was first organized, the IJA was modeled on the French and German militaries. It used European-style uniforms, rank structures, weaponry, and modern tools of warfare. Military training sought to "perfect the self-discipline of the soldiers through military drill."[110] But this embrace of the West did not extend to social structure within the barracks. The Army sought to instill leadership, interdependence, and cohesion by building on existing Japanese societal values, especially that of family. Commissioned officers played the roles of fathers, petty officers were mothers, and conscripts were children. This family structure was instituted to educate soldiers in the military spirit and to mitigate resistance to military discipline. It also justified "private punishment" (i.e., corporal punishment) as *"benevolent behavior"* toward children.[111]

Officers used violence against soldiers who did not seem manly enough. In the Army, one soldier later testified that "informal punishments" were administered daily. Older soldiers punched young ones "to rile them up," and sometimes went so far as to break their eardrums. In the Navy, one sailor remembered that some hit one another with a "military-spirit injection cudgel" and made them faint.[112]

Despite—or because of—the unpopularity of the Siberian Intervention, the military worked on integrating itself into society. By this point, that included the schools. In the mid-1930s, games of war among children were common, preparing Japanese men for the real thing.[113] It was not just top-down military instruction that had created deep and intractable social transformation. New middle-class organizations would work to fan patriotism for the war, all in the name of modernity.[114]

The years 1924–1934 mark an important change, when Japan's Army, *Nihongun,* would become the imperial army, *kōgun.*[115] The charismatic and dictatorial Army Minister Ugaki Kazunari reduced the size of the army in order to spend more funds on new hardware and research.[116] This included an experimental tank unit, two regiments of anti-aircraft artillery, and two air regiments. These changes brought about resistance from elite officers, many of whom would later become military leaders. Ugaki's goals were not just to improve the national defense. He placed military officers in schools, aiming to unite the army and the people.[117] Ugaki's reforms were popular with politicians and the public, but they were expensive, and unpopular among military officers, who had to go teach in schools and found their promotion routes blocked.[118] They were also opposed by the General Staff, the traditional center of power, leaving the army factionalized and lacking a single strong leader.

During the mid-1920s, a faction of the IJA began to adopt an approach based on the idea that Japan's only chance to defeat superior Western forces would be an emphasis on "spirit" and fighting to the finish. Definitionally, this vision of a superior Japan did not leave room to follow international rules on POWs, and left no room for surrender. A chief exponent was Major General Araki Sadao, outspoken and erratic, who in May 1925 became chief of operations. He had support from—and supported—anti-Ugaki officers.[119]

In opposition to Ugaki's vision, Araki believed that *seishin*—superior morale, with spiritual training—could substitute for advanced weapons, and triumph over an army with material superiority.[120] In 1927, regulations further stressed spiritual training, while words like "surrender" were removed from the General Principles of Strategic Command.[121]

While Araki emphasized spiritual training, Japan was continuing to integrate itself in international society. In July 1929, former finance minister Hamaguchi Osachi assumed the office of prime minister, promising "fair and open politics" and contributions "to world peace and human welfare through cooperation with the League of Nations."[122] That same month, Japanese diplomats participated in a conference in Geneva to establish the rights of POWs in any future war and the responsibilities of belligerents. Each country involved agreed to create an information bureau for POWs and to transmit prisoner lists to the ICRC. The ICRC could talk to prisoners wherever they were found, "as a general rule, without witnesses." Additionally, prisoners were supposed to be given food and clothing equivalent to that provided to servicemen. Reprisals against prisoners were prohibited no matter what the provocation.[123] Many delegates, including those representing Japan, signed the new convention, and some began to plan for a convention that would extend protections to civilians.[124] After the meeting ended, the ICRC set up a commission of experts. It proposed two categories: enemy civilians on the territory of a belligerent, and civilians in the power of the enemy in occupied territories.[125]

By the end of the decade, Japan was experiencing severe economic challenges, which had started with the 1927 "Showa financial crisis," a financial panic that had led to the collapse of Prime Minister Wakatsuki Reijirō's government and eventually zaibatsu (business conglomerate) domination in the banking industry. Despite large-scale injections of public funds and a return to the gold standard, by 1930 Japan joined the worldwide Depression. It attempted a series of comprehensive macroeconomic policy measures with little success, leading many Japanese men and women to despair.

During these same years the army began to defy the civilian government. Araki asked the army to act against orders, and Kōmoto Daisaku successfully planned the assassination of the warlord Zhang Zuolin in Manchuria.[126] The "Young Officers' Movement," a loose grouping of unit officers (*taizuki shōkō*) too young to have been to the staff college, came out of the youth school–military academy system. Most were sons of military men. Primarily concerned with domestic revolution, they were also sympathetic to military goals in Manchuria.[127]

A particularly important moment in the history of the Japanese Army arose from army operatives' actions in Manchuria. In mid-1929, Lieutenant Colonel Itagaki Seishirō was posted as senior ranking staff officer at Kwantung headquarters. He joined his colleague from cadet days, Lieutenant Colonel Ishiwara Kanji, who ran operations in the Kwantung Army. The Kwantung Army was a key center for independent military activism and insubordination, part of a history in the IJA abroad that included attacks in Taiwan and Korea.[128]

In Manchuria, Itagaki and Ishiwara believed that civilian politicians— at the beck and call of special interests—could not confront the increasing threats to Japanese interests, especially communism in the Soviet Union and nationalism in China.[129] Ishiwara began reconnaissance to locate good targets in Manchuria. In September 1931, Itagaki joined him in a plot to plant explosives by a railway track near Mukden (present-day Shenyang), which they would blame on the Chinese. Even though it did almost no damage, the Manchurian incident offered a pretext for the Japanese to invade and take over Manchuria. The group acted independently, but the central government did little to rein them in, and the military followed up the group's action with a much larger action of its own: invading Manchuria.[130]

The Manchurian Incident had major effects: provoking Chinese hostility, increasing the Soviet presence in Northeast Asia, and awakening the United States to Japan's ambitions. Nevertheless, Itagaki and Ishiwara became heroes to many soldiers.[131] By 1933, the army in Manchuria increased to some 114,000 men.[132]

That same year saw the "October incident," a failed military coup by radicals within the IJA. It was just one of four attempted coups, four political assassinations, and twenty major domestic terror incidents in the period from 1930 to 1935.[133] What all of this shows is that certain renegade officers operated as independent actors. Increasingly, the Japanese government was unable to rein in the military, or rebellious officers within it. What happened in Manchuria is one example of how the Japanese military now functioned outside of civilian control.

Another incident—less famous, but no less telling—took place in April 1932. Kuga Noboru, commander of a battalion engaged in skirmishes in Shanghai, was captured by Chinese forces and released to the Japanese consul in Nanjing. Kuga viewed his capture as dishonorable, a sentiment made worse by colleagues who tormented him. Even a commander such as Kuga faced social pressure. Such pressure was all the stronger for lower-ranking IJA soldiers. Kuga's next act increased the stakes. He returned to the site of his capture and committed suicide with a revolver. Kuga became a hero to the Japanese. News coverage applauded this act, and praised his character. In 1932 alone several films and one play featured his death.[134] Leaders such as Kuga served as examples for IJA soldiers. Kuga's widely publicized suicide was a model of what to do after the dishonor of capture.

By this point, spirit and imperial loyalty were increasingly emphasized in military education over other aspects of warfare, such as developing superior technology. This was not an inevitable development: after all, Japan maintained leading technologies in fighter planes, battleships, and other military instruments during the latter half of the 1930s. But military education focused on the view that because Japanese soldiers had exceptional spirit, material factors were secondary. Texts like the 1930 Moral Training for Soldiers (bujin to tokusō), written for officers, provided examples of great soldiers and precepts of bushidō.[135] As military officers continued to work in schools, the military's prioritization of spiritual virtue and bushidō became increasingly apparent in civilian education as well. And influential writers such as Navy captain Hirose Yutaka and Tokyo Imperial University professor Hiraizumi Kiyoshi linked victories in the Sino-Japanese War and Russo-Japanese wars to superior morality. After the Manchurian Incident, many textbooks and texts for children on bushidō appeared, showing the extent to which military and civilian education overlapped and became mutually reinforcing.[136]

The actions of the renegade military actors in the Kwantung army occurred in the context of the weakening and eventual collapse of any semblance of representative democracy. In the wake of political assassinations and other violence, as well as economic crisis, military officers gained control of key positions in the government. After the May 1932 assassination of Prime Minister Inukai Tsuyoshi by naval officers, Admiral Saitō Makoto was appointed prime minister, ending party cabinets and civilian government in Japan. The admiral established an authoritarian regime with strong—though not complete—military control. For the next four years, political parties continued to wield some influence but were unsuccessful in forming cabinets.

On February 26, 1936, radical young IJA officers from the Kodoha (Imperial Way faction) attempted a coup d'état in the eponymous February 26 Incident. Their justification was what they identified as lack of respect for the emperor and an inadequately aggressive foreign policy.[137] The IJA officers led 1,400 officers in an attack on the prime minister's residence along with other sites in Tokyo, killing several senior political leaders, including Saitō.[138]

Meanwhile in the League of Nations, the Lytton Commission found that Japan's conduct in China had violated the 1922 Nine-Power Treaty, the League Covenant, and the 1928 Kellogg-Briand Pact declaring aggressive war illegal. Japan had been a founding member of the League of Nations. Tokyo argued that it was a local matter and none of the League's business.[139] Until conflict arose between Japan and the organization over the 1931 Manchurian Incident, the League was a centerpiece of Japan's policy to cooperate with the Western powers.

In February 1933, Matsuoka Yōsuke, the Japanese delegate to the League of Nations, voted no to the assembly's recommendation that Japan withdraw its troops from Manchuria and restore Chinese sovereignty there. After the vote he gave an angry speech and, while it was being translated, led the Japanese delegation out of the hall.[140] In 1933, Japan announced its withdrawal from the League of Nations, though they needed to wait two years until they could officially leave. Still, its politicians' hopes for equality with the West were dashed. Their departure resonated beyond Japan and was the nail in the coffin of an experiment in world government.

Yet Japanese politicians continued to attend international conferences and did not repudiate international agreements.[141] Business leaders and intellectuals also continued to participate in international organizations.

The 1930s saw companies such as Mitsui establishing foundations to work for advanced technology and fund medical research.[142] Just one year after Japan's withdrawal from the League of Nations, Kokusai Bunka Shinkōkai (later the Japan Foundation) was formed with a mission of "mutual understanding."

Many Japanese saw no contradiction between internationalism and imperialism. Some reconciled the two through the ideology of "Pan-Asianism." As Japan grew stronger, Japanese leaders evoked ideals like "Asian solidarity and identity" to assert a "common destiny" and a "Japanese mission" to lead.[143] Pan-Asian rhetoric like this was used to justify the creation of Manchukuo and the withdrawal from the League of Nations. But Pan-Asianism did not preclude Japanese participation in and even leadership of international organizations like the ICRC. And those Japanese who still favored a more liberal international order also sought to maintain Japan's position within these institutions, hoping in that way to stem militarism at home.

In 1934, the ICRC decided to go ahead with plans for an international conference in Tokyo to consider further expanding the Geneva Conventions to civilian internees. World War I had shown that civilians could be injured in war, and the idea was to protect them. For the Japanese, the conference would serve to counter the appearance of isolation. Prince Kan'in Kotohito, honorary president of the Japan Red Cross, would preside over the gathering, joined by several other members of the imperial family.[144] Hosting it meant Japan had to decide on whether to ratify two conventions its delegation signed at the previous meeting: the revised convention on Amelioration of the Sick and Wounded and the new convention providing expanded protections for POWs.[145] The Foreign Ministry recommended ratifying both, but invited opinions from other ministries.

In sharp contrast to the Japanese military's earlier history of leniency to POWs and acceptance of humanitarian interventions on their behalf, the Navy now raised strong objections to the POW convention. They gave several reasons to oppose it. "Because this Convention ensures more favorable treatment [to foreign POWs] than to imperial sailors, the Naval Discipline Ordinance, Naval Penalty Law, Naval Court Martial Law, Naval Prison Ordinance and so on would need to be amended. However, it is impossible to amend those laws because their purpose is to maintain the discipline of sailors."[146] They also objected to Article 86, which allowed third-party observers to meet with POWs without Japanese observers. This might threaten operational security. But other objections strained credulity. Because soldiers and sailors of the empire would never be taken prisoner, it was alleged, only the Japanese would be obliged to follow the treaty. It would also risk the expansion of bomber attacks, since enemy airmen would supposedly feel secure they would receive decent treatment as POWs even if they did not make it back to base. The Ministry opposed recommending ratification to the emperor.[147]

Army leaders also opposed ratification.[148] Tōjō too emphasized that Japanese military policy specified that capture was shameful, and death preferable. Ratifying the convention could be misunderstood as encouraging soldiers and sailors to become POWs.[149] At no point did either service address the moral and ethical concerns that originally inspired measures to protect POWs.

No formal decision in Japan had been made when more than 250 foreign delegates arrived in Tokyo. They stood on the sides of an open pavilion in the Constitutional Memorial Hall, overlooking a vast garden filled with 13,000 Red Cross delegates, one from every district in Japan. But in the pavilion one could also find Hayashi Senjūrō, who had been commander of the Chōsen Army during the Mukden Incident and the invasion of Manchuria, and was now minister of the army and later would become prime minister. There were also Navy Minister Ōsumi Mineo, who had supported withdrawal from the League of Nations and renegotiation of the Washington Naval Treaty. They were joined by Home Minister Gotō Fumio, who would become minister of state under Tōjō.

Yet the delegates in Tokyo might not have noticed the ominous presence of the Japanese military. Instead, it was Dowager Empress Nagako of Japan who welcomed the foreign representatives. The imperial family and high-ranking society entertained them at receptions and teas. They enjoyed a classic Noh performance, "Funa-Benkei," and Chikamatsu kabuki. Japanese women on the reception committee arranged shopping trips and escorted delegates to hospitals, schools, and tobacco factories.[150]

When not touring Japan, delegates discussed the "Tokyo Draft." The proposed convention addressed two distinct subjects: the status of enemy civilians, and enemy civilians on the territory of a belligerent or the territory it occupied. Representatives agreed on the principle of extending protections to civilians, but could not summon sufficient votes to formally approve the text.[151]

After the conference concluded, the cabinet finally took up the questions of whether Japan would ratify the conventions signed at the 1929 meeting.

It decided that Japan would join the convention on amelioration of the sick and wounded.[152] Yet the cabinet went along with the Army and Navy's opposition to expanding protections for POWs, viewing it as a benefit for future enemies.[153]

Japan was just one of nine countries, including Ireland, Finland, and Luxemburg, that signed, but did not ratify, the new Geneva Conventions. It was little noted at the time, perhaps because each had different reasons. For example, Ireland lacked an internment policy in part because of the presence of British forces in Ireland. Strict enforcement in the event of war would in theory mean that British and Commonwealth forces—some Irish themselves—would be held in Irish camps.[154] The Soviets did not favor an agreement that would permit the Red Cross or foreign powers to visit prisoners.[155]

In the end it is unclear how much this treaty mattered, because, by design, enforcement of the treaty depended on other nations. They decided what adherence to the Geneva Conventions meant and what would be the consequences of ignoring it. Even neutral states could still choose to respect and extend the Geneva Conventions. And protections for civilians were still not covered by treaty.

Other decisions provided more clear evidence to contemporaries that Japan was breaking free of the internationalist ideals and institutions it had helped establish. In 1935, Tokyo abrogated the Washington Naval Treaty that limited naval construction. The military continued to expand its hold on national political power still further. But for the most part, bureaucrats, party politicians, and a few aristocrats were not convinced of the necessity of full-scale military mobilization. Public criticism of the military could still be heard in the Diet.[156] In 1937, the Seiyūkai politician Hamada Kunimatsu openly attacked the military's intervention in politics in the Diet. An angry Army Minister Terauchi Juichi pressured the cabinet to dissolve the Lower House of the Diet in retaliation. Prime Minister Hirota Kōki's cabinet resigned.[157]

By mid-1937, the Army was the strongest force in Japan, but not strong enough to exercise unilateral power. It never controlled the Navy, or even the civilian cabinet. The Army could capitalize on the worsening international situation, domestic terrorism, and the weakness of political parties. Yet it was often forced to compromise with other elites. The military ultimately became successful at integrating its interests with bureaucrats and Japanese men and women through post-1935 public campaigns such as the Home Ministry's Election Purification Campaign of 1935–1936. The Konoe cabinet's 1937 National Spiritual Mobilization Movement, a federation of a wide range of nationalist and civic organizations, would work to ensure popular support of the war.[158]

Earlier that year, in July 1937, the Marco Polo Bridge Incident started an undeclared war with China, the second Sino-Japanese War. By this point, more than 100,000 Japanese troops were based in Northeast China, surrounding Beijing and Tianjin. On the night of July 7, Japanese troops crossed the border and exchanged fire with Chinese forces. Early the next day the Japanese attacked the Marco Polo Bridge near Beijing. Efforts by higherups in the government to deescalate failed. After months of fighting in August to December 1937, Chinese nationalist leaders and refugees were forced to retreat to Chongqing. This pitched fighting contributed to the evolving Japanese policy on POWs.

What started as a local incident in China had set off a chain of events that no one could control. The Japanese originally considered the conflict a limited engagement; they had little idea that they would be bogged down in China for years. They held off on declaring war because they did not want to recognize Chongqing as either a combatant or as a negotiating partner.[159] They also worried that officially declaring war might make the United States ban exports to Japan.

The Chinese nationalists also did not declare war. A formal state of war would have made it easier for Japan to blockade Chinese ports and cut off its supply lines. There was also a power struggle. Chinese nationalist leader Wang Jinwei, at the time rival to Chiang Kai-shek for leadership of the Kuomintang, consistently sought to steer away from war with Japan, believing the British and American allies no better than the Japanese.[160] By contrast, Chiang Kai-shek advocated an all-out declaration of war. This helped him consolidate his power, but even he would hold off on declaring war until after Pearl Harbor.[161]

This absence of a declaration of war had important implications for POWs. A formal state of war would have triggered legal obligations. Even though Japan had not ratified the 1929 Geneva Convention, it was party to multiple other international agreements that would have imposed legal limits on its conduct in China. Similarly, China might have signaled its expectations by invoking the POW Convention, which it signed in 1935.

Instead of declaring war, Japanese soldiers were instructed that the Chinese soldiers they faced were fighting for an illegitimate government that was preventing the Japanese from liberating the Chinese people. But military orders stipulated that Chinese captives were to be well treated.[162] Still, the military formed no organizational structure for managing POWs, and captives were under the jurisdiction and control of combat units. Seized Chinese soldiers were forced to work for the military puppet government or transported to Japan as forced labor. The lack of any overall plan led to many abuses, from petty misbehavior to torture and death. The worst episode of all occurred during the taking of Nanjing in 1937, when thousands of Chinese captives were summarily executed, some in grisly fashion. The Japanese claimed they were saving Chinese civilians from their own government.

The ICRC's work for the Chinese Red Cross that started in 1937 stopped in 1939, as they no longer had the means to distribute aid.[163] In Tokyo, ICRC delegates continued to negotiate with the Japanese and Chinese legations to restart Red Cross activities on the battlefield. The ICRC delegate in Shanghai pleaded with the two sides to honor the Geneva Conventions. Yet initially neither China nor Japan seemed very interested in ICRC offers to look after captured soldiers. Both sides were far more concerned with air attacks on civilians, but the ICRC only relayed their protests.[164]

While Japanese soldiers never experienced anything like the atrocities visited on Chinese captives at Nanjing, they had many reasons to be fearful if they fell into enemy hands. The Chinese claimed to abide by the terms of the Geneva Conventions and eventually welcomed efforts by international agencies to inspect camps. But conditions of captivity varied greatly, especially because there was no unified Chinese government. Forces led by Chinese Communists subjected captured Japanese to reeducation. Japanese POWs in Guomindang camps composed propaganda leaflets.

The ICRC sent delegate Ernest Senn to Chongqing, where Japanese POWs were held along with Chinese collaborators and German and Italian civilians accused of espionage. Over the course of Senn's repeated visits, the conditions of crowded camps gradually improved, despite famine and inflation caused by war. By 1943, Senn observed that the Chinese central government was keen to live up to Geneva Conventions, to "put themselves in line with civilized nations in the observance of humanitarian conventions"—and to get such treatment for their own POWs in Japan. Yet at least one journalist doubted their true commitment and claimed that the few camps the ICRC was allowed to inspect were "window-dressing."[165] Several provinces, such as Xinjiang, remained off-limits.[166]

One thing seemed clear to Japanese soldiers in China: If they were captured and managed to return home, they could be rejected or punished by their own state, or their own family. Those missing after a battle were listed as "battle deaths" and a commander could declare them dead even when no body was recovered. Thus, a soldier honored as "dead in battle" could bring dishonor on his family if he returned. Japanese soldiers who believed they could not return home roamed the Asian mainland.

At the same time that state-civilian organizations worked to support the war, the influence of the new bushidō was only continuing to grow. The 1937 *Fundamentals of Our National Polity* (*kokutai no hongi*) was written by academics and popularly read. Hundreds of thousands of copies were printed and over 2 million ultimately were distributed.[167] It provided reasoning for the war. "Loyalty means to revere the emperor as [our] pivot and to follow him implicitly. By implicit obedience is meant casting ourselves aside and serving the emperor intently."[168] Bushidō was stressed as a special Japanese characteristic, pairing Japanese spirit and loyalty to the emperor.[169]

This new bushidō reached its heights in the early 1940s, magnified by new media.[170] Sensationalized events featuring brave military deaths became fodder for articles and widely read books. Many interpretive texts followed. Among them was the popular 1939 *Bushidō Treasury,* featuring a preface by philosopher Inoue Tetsujirō, who expanded on his ideas from the Russo-Japanese War forty years earlier. It celebrated the heroism of Japanese servicemen, backed up with historical examples of pilots who carried no parachutes. And according to Inoue, no Japanese soldier had ever surrendered. This history was remembered differently by eyewitnesses.

Yet it is difficult to know to what extent we can blame bushidō for the acts of the IJA during the Pacific War. After all, the IJA needed capital penalties to make sure soldiers adhered to the policy not to surrender. Soldiers chose not to surrender because of the consequences they believed they would face from their fellow soldiers. According to a 1944 US military report, three-quarters of Japanese soldiers thought they would die or suffer severe consequences if they returned home.[171] Thus bushidō indoctrination in the civilian schools had worked, but only in the sense that soldiers feared being ostracized or worse if they were captured.

Japanese soldiers also believed captors would kill them. As John Dower famously argued, bushidō influenced American propaganda, and American actions: US forces considered Japanese attempts to surrender as traps, and attacked surrendering troops. They also desecrated dead soldiers.[172] According to another American military report, nearly 85 percent of Japanese soldiers thought they would die or suffer torture at American hands.[173] Bushidō as ideology, then, worked on both sides, influencing American behaviors and also IJA actions and ideologies. Being made to fear and feel ashamed of capture would naturally make at least some Japanese soldiers condescend toward or even feel contemptuous of foreign counterparts who seemed to accept surrender willingly.

Japan fought another undeclared war in the summer of 1939, this time against the USSR. Though Nomonhan (The Battle of Khalkhin Gol) is little remembered today, it was a major conflict in which 100,000 troops clashed. Some 30,000 to 50,000 men were killed or wounded. Ultimately, Japanese forces were out-generaled and forced into a humiliating retreat by the legendary Georgy Zhukov.

The conflict provided more stories of the kind celebrated by Inoue.[174] In one such episode, a soldier leaped aboard a Soviet tank, was cut down by enemy fire, and killed himself rather than risk being taken prisoner. In another, a major's wife in Harbin was tormented by a rumor that he had been captured. She shed tears of relief on news his body was found.[175] When men fell in battle, comrades often abandoned them on the field.

The Japanese army bureaucracy preferred to list all these missing men as "killed in action," rather than accept that some were POWs. But it estimated that 1,000–4,000 Japanese had been captured, most likely 3,000. The USSR had neither signed nor ratified the Geneva Convention of 1929. But one cease-fire agreement stipulated that all POWs were to be exchanged. The Soviets demanded exchanges on a one-to-one basis. In September 1939 the Japanese ended up returning 87 Soviet POWs for 88 Japanese (including two Manchurians). This was a bad bargain for the Japanese, who had little leverage. The Soviet POWs were overjoyed upon their return. The Japanese were downcast.[176]

Some released Japanese officers were prosecuted for espionage, and more were court-martialed for the crime of desertion under enemy fire. The unhurt were judged harshly, and the wounded got off more lightly. Officers had it the worst, because authorities maintained an unofficial but very real policy of pressuring officers to commit suicide before facing court-martial. For the Japanese military the policy presented a solution to the conflict between law and discipline. One released combat pilot was sentenced to two years and ten months and demoted one rank. But there were many more who chose permanent exile in Russia or Outer Mongolia. Veterans thought that more than 1,000 released Japanese POWs had remained in foreign countries.[177]

The most important consequence of this episode was to discourage any thought of again taking on the USSR, even when it was invaded by Germany in 1941. Yet it also taught Japanese commanders that they had little to gain from capturing enemy POWs, especially if their own forces surrendered in larger numbers. It also taught officers that being taken prisoner was potentially punishable by death.[178]

The Senjinkun (military code) announced on January 8, 1941, instructed soldiers "not to accept the shame of being a POW," making explicit what had been implicit.[179] It was better to die than to be captured as a POW. The code was reprinted in full in most newspapers. Elementary school students learned it at morning assembly, and junior high school students learned it as a song during music class.

Though it seems obvious in retrospect that at least some Japanese servicemen would still surrender, the no-surrender policy was an attempt to establish a norm and influence behavior. Unfortunately it had unintended consequences, such as leading officers and guards to feel contempt for the POWs they captured and detained.

By this point, political parties in Japan had vanished. In 1940, when politician Saitō Takao delivered a fierce antiwar speech questioning the war in China, he was thrown out of the Diet.[180] Aristocrats continued to have influence over choosing prime ministers. The Navy and bureaucracy prevented the Army from wielding complete control. Yet the Army had autonomy over its own affairs, even as it continued to suffer internal struggles.

In the end, the Army was able to win Navy support for an increasingly provocative strategy to bring China to its knees. Japan's military and civilian leaders considered themselves the natural overlords of Asia, and war was a chance to prove it. Japanese technocrats—whether "new military men," "new-new Zaibatsu," or "reform bureaucrats"—saw war as an opportunity to transform Japan's economy and apply their training in research, planning, and administration.[181] These ideas placed Japan at the center, then its colonies of Korea and Taiwan, followed by the "independent" (puppet) states of Nanjing-China and Manchukuo, and Thailand. Now, Japanese leaders were casting their eyes on Burma, the Philippines, and Java. A United States–United Kingdom–Netherlands oil embargo was particularly provocative, because Japan was critically dependent on oil imports. In September 1941, the prospect of running out of fuel set a hard deadline for negotiations to avert a wider war. They finally ran out of time in December 1941.

All of the political infighting in Tokyo and between Tokyo and military commanders meant that Japan—however formidable in a fight—was ill prepared for a protracted struggle. Its divided leadership had failed to devise a coherent strategy. By emphasizing morale over material factors, they ignored the immense logistical and labor requirements imposed by rapid and far-reaching territorial conquests. Even early successes—because of their sheer scale, and lack of planning for the aftermath—proved catastrophic, not least because the hundreds of thousands of the empire's new captives were treated as an afterthought. By the mid-twentieth century, Japan was far from being at the forefront of international humanitarian efforts, as it had been in previous decades. Now, as it dramatically expanded its empire, with domestic interests encouraging patriotism and support for the military, the plight of POWs was the last thing on the minds of its military leaders.

# 2

## SINGAPORE

# A World Gone Topsy-Turvy

There was no such thing as a typical captivity experience in the Pacific War. The lack of planning for either POWs or civilian internees, the protracted nature of the conflict, and the changing fortunes of Japanese forces created a vortex that sent captives in highly unpredictable and dramatically different directions. But the largest proportion of POWs entered this maelstrom at one particular place and time, the surrender of Singapore in February 1942, when the world's largest empire began to implode.

The fall of Singapore was a shattering blow from which British prestige never recovered. Humiliation came not just from the surrender of more than 100,000 British soldiers, many of whom had never fired a shot. It was what the defeat revealed about the decadence of colonial society and the incompetence of its leadership.

The Imperial Japanese Army (IJA) was not prepared for the rapid collapse of a brittle Western empire. Officers had no plan for managing 100,000 captives, and captivity conditions reflected this. Yet the Japanese did have both a plan and a policy for those of Chinese descent, who would be treated as a threat, to be ruled by fear. Conversely, Indian soldiers in the British Army would be seen as an opportunity and treated harshly only after they resisted or disappointed their new overlords, or when the need for manual laborers became paramount. As for the thousands of other captives, they were treated as little more than an afterthought until the Japanese realized their labor could also be mobilized to bolster the war effort. The experience of becoming laborers for another empire was utterly demoralizing.

To understand all this, we first need to understand what made Singapore special, but also what made it seem normal for those who ruled it from positions of privilege. Singapore was the keystone of Britain's empire in Asia because of its commanding position along the approaches to the straits of

Malacca, the main route for international shipping connecting East Asia with India, Africa, and the Middle East. The organization of the British Empire was complex, and "British Malaya" was no exception. It consisted of the federated Malay states, the unfederated Malay states, and the Straits settlements—Penang, Malacca, Dinding, and Singapore. The highest ranking British official in Singapore, the resident-general, also ruled over Malaya. Malaya itself was a protectorate, but the Straits settlements were a British Crown colony, answering to the Colonial Office in London.

Singapore was a transit point for some 40 percent of the international rubber trade. It was also a major storage and distribution center for petroleum from Sumatra and Burma.[1] In addition to rubber plantations, Malaya also possessed tin fields, and manganese, bauxite, and iron ore mines.

This economic hub drew in laborers and investors from across Asia and beyond. With its large numbers of Indians and Chinese, British Malaya was a multiethnic society, but it was also divided and subdivided by language, religion, and class. Singapore itself was polyglot and highly stratified. The 1941 population was 78 percent Chinese, 10 percent Malay, 8 percent Indian, 2 percent European, 1 percent Eurasian, and 1 percent "other."[2]

Some groups enjoyed distinct advantages. The Malays could work in the British imperial civil service, for instance, though often at a low level; the Chinese were excluded. While the state and federal executive and legislative councils had little power, Chinese leaders, usually businessmen, could participate unofficially.[3] Above it all were the British, enjoying the colonial experience at its brittle best. As a wartime ditty had it, they sat languidly at Raffles Hotel with "Its watery sun, its yellow sand, Its heavy humid sticky heat. . . . The frangapanni's cloying smell, And all the other smells as well."[4]

As important as Singapore was to the British Empire in Asia, it was no less critical for the Japanese. Alongside British and Chinese financiers, Japanese industrialists owned mines at Johore, Kelangtan, and Terenganu. Resource-poor Japan relied on Southeast Asia for much of its supply of critical minerals, metals, and petroleum.[5] The peninsula sent 2 million tons of iron ore to Japan each year. Tokyo therefore sought to extend its influence in Malaya through the Japanese resident community there. In the 1930s, Tokyo was publishing news bulletins and five newspapers—three in Japanese, one in English, and one in Chinese. At the same time, Japanese landowners, fishermen, and secret agents collected intelligence on British military outposts and strategic industries.[6]

In 1939, the British administration in Malaya began to prepare for a possible Japanese invasion. Authorities equipped hospitals to treat military casualties, and increased local agricultural production.[7] Yet the colony could not produce sufficient food, and relied on imports of necessities like sugar and, most importantly, rice. And starting in September 1939, London was distracted by the European war with Germany.

In early June 1940, the month France was defeated, the Japanese general staff pondered options for war, to include an attack in Southeast Asia. Aircraft from French Indochina and Thailand would first strike Singapore. Then the IJA would invade the Dutch East Indies. This would allow Japan to ready for war with the soon-to-be isolated United States. This thinking lay behind the July 3, 1941, decision for the southern movement. The Navy continued to plan for war with the United States, while the War Ministry emphasized bringing the fight in China to an end.[8]

British strategists actually predicted that the Japanese would attack by coming down from Malaya and assaulting Singapore's fortress and naval bases from the rear. In 1940 the British Chiefs of Staff considered the defense of Malaya "fraught with difficulty," since their forces would be vulnerable to air attack. But they hoped the Japanese would struggle with the "almost impenetrable" terrain and the difficulties it presented for communications.[9] The British maintained a sizable force. Yet, poorly trained and equipped, they failed to prepare adequate defensive positions. They were also poorly led, especially in comparison to their Japanese counterparts.

Lieutenant General Yamashita Tomoyuki led the invading force, beginning on December 8 with an amphibious landing on the northern coast of Malaya. His three divisions quickly marched—or bicycled—south through the jungle. Japanese troops advanced at maximum speed, taking calculated risks along the way. Lieutenant General A. E. Percival's 100,000 men were unable to counter effectively, even though they outmanned the Japanese almost two to one.

The final collapse came from a combination of factors: confusion and disorganization, leadership clashes, and conflicts both among the services and with civilians.[10] The root cause was that Britain sought to defend Asia on the cheap, with a strategy resting on "a promise never meant to be kept"—that is, reinforcements arriving from the rest of the empire, when the rest of the empire was already under siege. Neither did the US Pacific Fleet serve as much of a deterrent after Pearl Harbor. The soldiers themselves blamed their leadership, as recorded in one camp journal: "Singapore was lost in the rooms of the famous "Raffles hotel" / Where quartered the cream of the generals all scarlet trim and braid."[11] It was not "lack of numbers or a lack of planes," but a "lack of brains."[12]

In the midst of this ignominious defeat, with countless civilians dying due to Japanese shelling, and some—even hospital patients—massacred outright, British troops made sure to evacuate their own dependents. Others, both British and Australians, simply deserted. The British burned important facilities, adding to the hardship of those left behind.

With defeat, said one observer, later a POW himself, "everything changed; there was so much noise, noise of battle and the air was full of noise, everything was noise." And then, "all of a sudden it went just quiet, sudden dead quiet, from the noise to quiet suddenly. On the ceasefire, there was no more sound, no guns roaring, no artillery, no aircraft roaring overhead or anything. And it just stopped."[13]

After the February 15 surrender, the Japanese Twenty-Fifth Army took command and began to assert its authority over Sumatra, Malaya, and Singapore. In February 1942, the first issue of the new *Shōnan Times,* formerly the *Straits Times,* printed General Yamashita's vow "to sweep away the arrogant and unrighteous British elements" and join with the Malayan people to create the "New Order and the Co-Prosperity Sphere."[14] The country's official name became "Malai," and it moved to Tokyo time.[15] The working day became shorter, so everyone had time to grow crops and learn Japanese—"an obvious necessity with the inclusion of this country into the New Order of Asians for the Asian."[16] Much of the colonial administration remained, with Malays filling jobs of the bygone British, at less pay.[17]

Yamashita warned that the "Nippon army will drastically expel and punish those who still pursue bended delusions as heretofore, those who indulge themselves in private interests and wants, those who act against humanity or disturb the public order and peace and those who are against the orders and disturb the military action of Nippon army."[18] Yamashita sought to invite participation in the new regime while he also threatened to punish detractors.

Before the war even began, in November 1941, the Japanese high command issued orders for governing what they called Shōnan. They showed their awareness of the cleavages in colonial society and their determination to integrate Malaya into their own empire. Japanese authorities would treat Westerners and the ethnic Chinese in dramatically different ways. "Instruct the American, British, and Dutch citizens to cooperate with our military administration. If they do not, let them leave or take other appropriate measures on them."[19] Instructions regarding German and Italian citizens were similarly vague. "Respect the rights and interests of the citizens from the Axis, but firmly regulate their expansion."[20]

On the other hand, the Twenty-Fifth Army headquarters decided on a harsh policy toward ethnic Chinese. Under Japan's own Peace Preservation Law, revised in 1941, communists and other political opposition figures could be held even if they did not commit any crimes. The Twenty-Fifth Army's formal guidance was to "Instruct Chinese Singaporeans to defect from the Chinese communist party and cooperate with our policies." Yamashita had extensive experience in China, both in Manchuria, where he had been an advisor, and as chief of staff of the North China Area Army in 1938–1939. Harsh retaliatory measures—"genjū shobun" (harsh disposal)— were commonly used against any opposition. They were common in the Chinese-Japanese War after 1937. Others with military experience in China, such as Colonel Watanabe Wataru, deputy chief of the military government of Malaya and Singapore, argued that the Chinese in Singapore were anti-Japanese and should be treated accordingly.[21]

The Japanese belief that ethnic Chinese would oppose their rule resulted in widespread killing in Singapore and Malaya. Altogether, the Japanese killed somewhere between 5,000 and 50,000 in the "Sook Ching" (*kakyō shukusei; dai kensho*) massacre of Singapore overseas Chinese.[22] Yamashita himself gave the initial order to begin the purge of the Chinese, and he later praised the infantry brigade commander in charge of the Singapore garrison, Kawamura Saburo, telling him to continue his efforts.[23]

The actual execution of overseas Chinese was carried out by the sector commanders, who chose the time, place, and method of killing.[24] A few days after surrender, the Japanese military police in Singapore issued a notice that Chinese men between the ages of eighteen and fifty should visit registration centers. Their target was men who opposed the Japanese: communists, but also armed men, men who obstructed the Japanese, or men who disturbed peace and order. With a remit so wide, many others were caught in the net.[25]

All those who threatened "public peace" were taken to remote areas and shot. Each commander had his own method of massacre.[26] Nishimura ordered Chinese in the Ponggol Road area to congregate at Oehler's Lodge, and ordered the shooting of 300 at the beach. For the next three days, corpses could be found washed up on the beach or floating at sea. At Tenth

Mile Changik Road, another 200 or 300 were taken in Japanese trucks to Samba Ikat, and killed by machine gun and rifle fire. Chinese residents of Geylang District were rounded up and assembled at Tekuk Kursu English school.[27] After screening, some were removed and driven to 7½-Mile East Coast Road. Some 500 were then led off the road to trenches and killed by machine-gun fire.[28]

At Mata Ikan, Tanah Merah, and Changi Spit, civilians living in Jalan Besara were assembled at Victoria School grounds, and 700 or 800 were taken in batches and massacred. At the Singapore docks, Lieutenant Hisa-matsu Haruji and his unit arrived at Tanjong Pagar police station, and concentrated Chinese captives at assembly points. After interrogation, large groups were driven away to the Tajoing Pagar wharf and decapitated. "Headless bodies were subsequently seen on the Yacht Club beach at Tanjong Pagar."[29] At Fort Canning, Captain Goshi Kōsuke assembled Chinese men in his sector, and 200 to 400 men were selected, taken away in trucks, and shot on the Changi beaches. At Amber Road, about fifty Chinese men were executed.

The experience of surrendered British Commonwealth Forces was dramatically different. On February 16, the Australian Imperial Force was ordered to pile their arms in Tanglin Square. The next day, Australian POWs, commanded by Lieutenant General Percival, were marched to Changi, a huge military installation on the northeast peninsula—now home to Singapore's modern airport. They were joined by thousands of British, American, and Indian soldiers from the Singapore Garrison, plus the troops that had retreated down the Malay Peninsula. Altogether, 130,000 Allied troops were initially taken prisoner, including British Indians, Eurasians, and Portuguese from the volunteer forces of Malaya and Hong Kong.[30]

At Changi, POWs were housed in former British army barracks, including Selarang, Roberts, and Kitchner. Although Changi remained the biggest and most important POW camp in Singapore, captives were also held at several other installations. For instance, work camps that sprang up in April 1942, such as River Valley Road and Sime Road, became permanent areas for incarceration.[31] Change was the only constant in Japanese prisoner management.

The Japanese interned some 2,500 civilians—mostly British—in Changi prison, also on the peninsula. While most of the British civilians had been evacuated at surrender, some remained and were interned along with their wives. Most were associated with the colonial administration in Singapore and Malaya, or with the plantations and tin mines.

The Japanese also interned non-Malay/Chinese civilians who were either unable to escape or had decided to stay. Japanese administrators divided all the prisoners by nationality, an imperfect process at best, not least because they classified people by their appearance.[32] It appears that initially other European civilians were not interned.

Swiss neutral observers monitored the whereabouts of the captives, though they were forbidden to visit camps. More than 230 other Swiss went to Indochina. ICRC delegate C. A. Kengelbacher observed that Indochina remained the only place for them to find safety.[33]

Others willingly surrendered. Seventeen-year-old Sheila Bruhn-Allan, half Australian and half Malaysian, only went to Changi on March 8, 1942. She marched eight miles to the prison from Katong. Bruhn-Allan brought books and notebooks as well as personal items. She believed locals were angry in the main though she suspected that some thought the British "deserved it."[34]

British soldiers who found themselves disarmed and imprisoned, already shocked by the defeat, were further disoriented by the conditions of their confinement. They had certain expectations of POW camps, and Changi met none of them.[35] Captivity was supposed to be run according to the Geneva Conventions. They were still soldiers and expected to be treated as such. After all, that is what had happened in the main in POW camps during World War I and during the early years of World War II on the Western Front. But Changi was very different. First, it was a huge site, without sufficient Japanese manpower to supervise the POWs. And while the physical space was enormous, the buildings themselves were entirely insufficient to shelter everyone who was kept there. Changi prison was now bursting at the seams. Built in 1930 by American engineers, it was modeled on New York's infamous Sing-Sing.[36]

The POWs' standing Army orders were to attempt escape. Many interrogation reports describe how at least some POWs tried to do so, according to the answers they gave after they were finally released. Captain Mohammed Ahmadi, Ninth Indian Division, captured February 15, 1942, in Singapore, noted, "Prisoners escaped individually. Escapes were easy." "No outside help was required for escapes."[37] Mohan Singh said that "very few were caught and brought back. Many did not return."[38]

But captives in Changi faced a conundrum: even if they could escape easily, it was unclear where to go next. Lieutenant Kenneth Addy, for example, who was held at Changi from February 7 to May 6, said he made two attempts. He went to the beach, seeking a boat, but found only a canoe. He considered getting a boat and crossing the straits to Jahore, but rejected it as impractical. "Japanese supervision at this point was very poor but we were only at Changi for three months and did not plan anything definite."[39]

So the borders around Changi were initially rather porous, and escape seemed deceptively simple. The situation was both provocative and maddening for an army that may have begun to realize it surrendered too willingly, and now had to wait out the war crammed into their own barracks.

British civilians were also left uncertain and deeply unsettled. They were allowed to administer their own part of the camp. But upper-class Britons who were accustomed to local servants felt it "beneath their dignity" to clean.[40] All the married women at Changi were separated from their husbands and had little contact with them. And whereas other Europeans brought their children with them, many British women had left their children at home.

A poem from the men's internee camp newspaper summed up the prevailing sentiment in March 1942:

> The whole world has gone topsy-turvy
> The whole bally world has gone nuts
> You're threatened with typhus and scurvy
> And rely on just what I lack—guts.[41]

So whereas the Crown colony was a highly stratified and segmented society, Changi was a place where children were separated from their fathers, husbands from their wives, and even military rank was now met with derision. After all, many enlisted men felt that officers—whose incompetence led to their rapid defeat—had also lost their right to lead.[42] This meant that men felt a considerable degree of autonomy, which was recounted in wartime diaries and later in memoirs—some fictionalized—such as former captive James Clavell's *King Rat*. He described how some men seemed to thrive in the circumstances, like the title character. It brought out the worst in others, such as officers who stole from their men and men who fooled them into eating rat meat.[43] The closing scene of the 1965 film depicts caged rats killing and eating each other.

For other British prisoners, it was their captors who were subhuman, and this even though the Japanese had outfought and outsmarted them.[44] "The majority have a rather brutal appearance," British soldier A. A. Morris commented. "The shape of their heads is similar to that of a gorilla . . . their voices are guttural and some of their speech sounds like animal noises."[45] Yet the more the POWs scorned their Japanese, Korean, and Taiwanese guards—who scarcely bothered to guard them—the more they might have questioned their own self-worth and dignity.

For the men at Changi, perhaps the most unnerving aspect was how some British soldiers were choosing to switch sides to join the Japanese. Japanese official policy throughout Asia paid lip service to freeing Asians from the yoke of colonialism. But in Singapore, they actually did intend to free Indian POWs, to educate them, and use their labor.

The most dramatic example of this policy was Japanese support of the formation—and reformation—of an Indian National Army (INA), which sought to secure Indian independence from the Raj. Even here though, initial Japanese support of the INA dwindled when labor needs became paramount.

Nearly 60,000 Indian POWs were taken prisoner after the fall of Singapore, and they had already experienced difficult conditions. These Indian servicemen were among the least experienced men in the British Army, since most had been hastily recruited and trained in the early days of the war.[46] Many were unprepared for jungle warfare. The Ninth and Eleventh Divisions, fighting in Malaya, suffered massive losses during the retreat.

Veteran Indian officers had well-justified bitterness at their treatment in the British Army: they suffered inequities in pay and discrimination under the Raj. And those who were newly recruited were not career soldiers. What had the British done for them? It is not difficult to imagine how the collapse of Singapore's defenses and the flight of British officials did little to inspire loyalty. Additionally, the INA had charismatic leaders. Japan's own emperor had commanded that "all Indians be treated like brothers."[47]

The Japanese had first declared a new order for East Asia in November 1938, and in 1940 Foreign Minister Matsuoka Yōsuke announced the "Greater East Asia Co-Prosperity Sphere." Now that Tokyo was at war with what Matsuoka called "the white race bloc," encouraging—or forcing—other Asians to join them was a military necessity. Singapore resident Velauthar Ambiavagar observed:

Because the Japanese believed that the more people they had on their side, sympathizing with them, supporting them, the less trouble they would have in ruling the place, less danger there would be in any kind of organized activity that might result in sabotage of their war efforts. The less . . . the likelihood of trouble the smaller the number of troops they would have to station here to keep the people under control.[48]

In February 1942, the Japanese encouraged the formation of the INA in Singapore, just a few days after Indian POWs arrived at Nee Soon Camp.[49] The Sikh military officer Captain Mohan Singh of the 14th Punjab regiment led the first INA, formed to fight to free India from British rule. Senior Indian officers—VCOs (viceroy's commissioned officers) from the Hong Kong and Singapore Royal Artillery and the British Indian Army—were made to listen to Singh's fiery speeches. He attacked the British and asked for volunteers.[50] A few days later, Singh requested gunners, in particular, to man anti-aircraft guns and free up Japanese troops.[51] According to British Intelligence reports, many Muslims were not interested.[52] Yet for some Sikhs and Hindus, at least, the propaganda was persuasive. Minority Muslims may have calculated that they had more to gain by remaining loyal to the British and more to lose in independence.

Some 16,000 Indian POWs were formed into an INA division, a limit set by the Japanese.[53] Some were posted to direct traffic for passing Japanese units.[54] The IJA also made use of willing POWs as ancillary troops in Hong Kong and Hainan, where they became guards and police. Within the Allied POW camps, these INA guards became a source of tension, reportedly because of their aggressive behavior toward captives.

The Japanese used the INA troops, in particular Sikhs, as guards in the POW camp at Changi. This created conflicts between British and other POWS and the Sikhs who worked for the Japanese. That resentment led, in November 1942, to new Japanese guidelines. Thereafter, Indians were prohibited from entering POW spaces except when they were on duty, and they were no longer permitted to strike POWs for failing to salute. The order was meant to remove causes of trouble, but it left loopholes. Instead of slapping POWs, Indian guards put alleged offenders through drills or made them stand at attention.[55]

The policy of recruiting Indian POWs soon proved a disappointment, for the Indians as much as the Japanese. Contrary to the emperor's command,

Indians were *not* treated as brothers, not when they were given menial roles as Japanese auxiliaries. Mohan Singh had spoken of independence and a national army. Few Indian POWs were interested in taking over simple station duties to free up Japanese troops. When they were uncooperative, the Japanese turned hostile, treating them with contempt and sometimes brutality. This included slaps and other indignities.[56]

The underlying problem was that there was simply not enough manpower to staff Japan's rapidly expanding empire. When pressed to choose, Tokyo prioritized its immediate need for auxiliaries and manual laborers over the promise of Asian emancipation. On December 1, 1942, a Japanese decree made all volunteers into POWs—probably prompted by Japan's mounting need for fatigue labor in the islands of the South Pacific.[57] It was not just South Asians who were supposed to serve the Japanese. A new system of contract labor would also require other Allied POWs to work, whether at dockyards and railroad yards, or an airport in the northeast of the island.[58] The workday ran from 8:00 a.m. to 5:00 p.m., with one hour of rest. British officers initially supervised the men. The Twenty-Fifth Army Military Administration guidelines also called for making the British and British-affiliated civilians cooperate with Japanese policy. The idea was that those Singaporeans who followed Japanese guidance had freedom and could even be hired to staff the municipal government.[59]

As for the others, the Japanese priority was to get the British and Australians to give up information of military value. This was a major source of tension, since the British were under orders to resist, and General Percival asked if the Japanese were actually planning on following the Hague Conventions.[60] Interrogations of British POWs became constant.

Otherwise, the Japanese were largely indifferent to the fate of their captives. As often was the case in Japanese camps during this period, the British were captives but were not yet considered POWs. Colonel Sugita Ichiji and military intelligence officers under him controlled both the inhabitants of Changi and civilian internees. But Sugita had many other responsibilities, and a lowly lieutenant, Okazaki, was effectively the camp commandant, and was the only link between Sugita and the captives.[61]

POWs and internees were expected to be self-sufficient. For instance, the Japanese directed them to produce their own food. In May 1942, an Australian Imperial Force poultry farm was established, producing 40,000 eggs between 1942 and 1945.[62] But it was not nearly enough. Even when the Crown colony was under British control, it imported most of its food. The general Singapore population, not just the POWs, faced major food short-ages throughout the war.

From the POWs' point of view, another problem was adjusting to a reduced diet composed mainly of rice, the one foodstuff the Japanese did not expect them to produce on their own. For some with Asian experience, this did not at first seem so bad. As rice arrived, "memories of fine white rice cooked by expert Chinese and served in delicious curry tiffins flashed through many minds." But British army cooks did not seem to know how to cook it properly. And so they faced "a tight ball of grayish, gelatinous substance, nauseous in its lack of flavor and utterly repulsive."[63]

Badly prepared rice was cause for bitter complaint because food was critical, and not only as sustenance when there was so little to do. Meals broke the monotony, or were supposed to. Instead, there was little to discuss at meal times but how little food they had and how bad it tasted. Some even resorted to writing imaginary cookbooks.[64]

From early days, British and Australian officers also organized education and entertainment. "Changi University" offered instruction in agriculture, business, and general education.[65] Organized activities, which also included workshops and music, made captives feel they were all part of the same community, despite segregation between civilians and POWs and men and women.

Despite physical separation, women were often reminded of the men, whether using prisoner-made objects, wearing their metal tags, or in viewing a male performance. Mary Dorothy Cornelius recalled how men in the military camp made some "wonderful toys."[66] A July 1, 1942, poster advertised a concert featuring the music of Bach, Mozart, and Chopin.[67] One viewer remembered the concerts as "a great treat."

According to the Eighth Division's diarist, news bulletins came second only to food in the prisoners' lives. News material consisted of the propaganda organs *Nippon Times* and *Shōnan Shimbun*. Eventually even these stopped coming, and men became reliant on radios. In July 1942, POWs began to produce their own daily news bulletin, which lasted until April 1944.[68]

In *King Rat,* Clavell recounts how Changi POWs filled their time with gambling and trading on the black market. Yet this had its drawbacks as well as benefits. Those with valuables, ill-gotten or otherwise, could get food and medicine. Gambling raised prices for both and created a security risk.

This was especially true for stolen goods, because POWs might have to leave the camp to obtain contraband.[69]

Many a British soldier later reported attempts at sabotage, but it is difficult to know how successful they were. For example, British Private Robert James Ablett, imprisoned from February 15, 1942, reported that in disposing of ammunition at River Valley Camp, he supplied it to the Chinese instead of dumping it overboard.[70] Yet these reports may reflect the fact that POWs were specifically asked if they attempted sabotage on postwar questionnaire forms. In fact, the POWs did a lot of useful work for the Japanese. They leveled bomb shelters, filled shell craters, loaded and unloaded ships, located and disabled mines, and collected scrap iron for shipment to Japan. Even if they were aiding the Japanese war effort, and subject to beating and slaps, working was popular among POWs because leaving the camp alleviated boredom and allowed them to get more food. They could also loot dumps, and sometimes benefited from the generosity of Chinese traders and merchants.

All in all, many POWs did not consider their initial days at Changi particularly bad. The Australian Guy Round, who experienced camps throughout the empire, recalled the "carefree existence" of Changi.[71] "If it wasn't for the all-important question of food," Lieutenant Bailles concluded, "we would feel that as POW camps go we were quite well off."[72]

As for the internees, Mary Cornelius also focused on the food, which for her included coconuts, cracked open by a *parang*—a type of Malay knife—and vegetables grown at Sime Road. They always had tea, but, she noted, "We suffered greatly from anxiety." For Cornelius, the biggest source of anxiety may not have been the lack of food, but the loss of status. Most humiliating, to her, was the requirement that they wear a number, "like a convict."[73] But women like Cornelius and Sheila Bruhn-Allen were only able to record these feelings because of the laxity of the camp administrators—their diaries were contraband.

Unbeknownst to the POWs and internees at Changi, events elsewhere were about to change their lives drastically. In April 1942, US B-25s under the command of James Doolittle took off from the aircraft carrier *Hornet* and bombed Tokyo, killing approximately fifty people and injuring around 400 before they flew on to China. The Doolittle raid was a watershed moment in the war, after which Japanese military strategy and policies shifted. It was the kind of one-way mission Japan's military warned the enemy would stage if they could be confident captured flyers would be well treated. In metropolitan Japan, authorities began to develop policies and appoint new camp commanders who brought the initial period of relative laxity to a close. For POWs, this contributed to increasingly difficult conditions. The Army Ministry decided that Allied POWs should be used to address manpower shortages, both in Japan itself and in its growing empire. On May 30, Prime Minister Tōjō Hideki gave these instructions: "It is necessary to take care not to be obsessed with a mistaken idea of humanitarianism or swayed by personal feelings toward the prisoners of war which may grow in the long time of their imprisonment. The present situation of affairs in this country does not permit anyone to lie idle."[74]

In order to regulate prisoners as labor, authorities needed to amend the 1904 "Rules Governing the Treatment of POWs" (*furyo toriatsukai kiroku*). Tōjō faced some opposition to putting new regulations into place from Uemura Mikio, head of the Prisoner of War Information Bureau. Uemura pointed out that they were a violation of the Geneva Conventions.[75] Under the Conventions, Japan was proscribed from forcing POWs to work.[76] But Tōjō insisted that the decision was necessary because of domestic labor shortages.[77]

In June 1942, the devastating defeat of Japanese forces at Midway made it clear that the country was facing a long war. Tōjō explained his approach to POWs and its underlying logic in an address to the newly appointed chiefs of the POW camps that same month. While stressing that all relevant laws should be followed, he noted, "You must supervise them rigidly insofar as you do not become inhuman, and not let them remain idle even for a single day." He stressed that they should "make the local people realize the superiority of the Japanese people through the treatment of prisoners of war as well as make the local people conceive of it as the greatest honor that they are to be Japanese subjects [*shinmin*]." POW labor would be used to achieve the aims of the war.[78]

Some POWs had already been put to work, and others would be used for propaganda, as we shall see. But Tōjō's new policy and explicit instructions to camp commanders marked a turning point. The Japanese military and Japanese companies would henceforth use POWs to meet critical shortages: to load cargo, mine coal, and work in factories. Also of consequence was what Tōjō failed to address. Allied captives were in the wrong places: mainly Singapore and the Philippines. They were far from the mines, fields, and factories where they were needed most. For that reason, the Japanese began to move the POWs around their rapidly expanding empire.

The Japanese transported POWs across hundreds or thousands of miles from where they were captured to where their labor would be most useful. Moving POWs created a huge logistical problem, requiring ships and land infrastructure to move them. This transportation came at a time when many other tasks—offensive operations and the resupply of island garrisons—had an even higher priority. Overcrowding on dilapidated and defenseless ships, known as "hell ships" for their atrocious conditions, meant many captives died on the way, and some were so debilitated that on arrival they could not work.[79] Tens of thousands died because of these conditions, but also from Allied bombs and torpedoes.

A few hubs in Taiwan and southwestern Japan served as staging points as men were shipped to various other parts of Japan's empire. Servicemen above the rank of colonel and skilled technicians were moved to Taiwan, and other high-ranking prisoners to Korea.[80] Still other prisoners from Singapore were shipped to Malaya and Java. Indian prisoners were often sent to the South Seas.

Here the story of Allied POWs from Singapore intersects with one of the most infamous episodes of World War II, one that appears on the short list of Japanese war crimes and that was memorialized in the classic film *The Bridge over the River Kwai*. In 1943, the IJA ordered the construction of the Thai-Burma Railway by Allied POWs and forced Asian labor. The railway would be more than 250 miles long and was intended to supply IJA forces in the Burma campaign. In May 1942, the Army had already begun to transport POWs from Singapore to Malaya to work on the railway. At least 50,000 Allied POWs and over 200,000 Asian laborers were eventually sent to work on this infamous project, the site of some of the worst abuses of the war.[81]

The Thai-Burma Railway was the rare place where an IJA program put POWs at the center. But even here, it was mainly the lack of planning and inadequate logistics that created hellish conditions. The IJA sent POWs to unfinished camps, provided no preparation or equipment, and set a fixed date for completion of the railway—in the rainy season. Supervisors pushed laborers until they were "overdriven." But the severe conditions of the jungle did not spare Japanese and Korean guards, who likewise suffered from cholera, tropical fevers, malaria, diarrhea, and colitis.[82]

POWs could only imagine birthday cakes—or draw them, like this sketch from a soldier in the Second Battalion Loyal Lancashire Regiment. The surrender at Singapore was just the beginning of a long ordeal that would take them to Keijō, Korea, and then on to Kobe, Japan. (Lancashire Infantry Museum.)

In Singapore, policy changes began to be felt at Changi itself in August 1942 with the arrival of Lieutenant General Fukuei Shimpei and a team of bureaucrats and interpreters. Fukuei's arrival meant a tightening of security. When, in late August 1942, four POWs escaped from Selarang barracks in Changi, Lieutenant General Fukuei ordered all the allied POWs to sign the following statement: "I, the undersigned, hereby solemnly swear on my honor that I will not, under any circumstances, attempt escape."[83]

Compelling POWs to sign documents under oath to refrain from escape was a violation of the laws of war. So was the mistreatment Fukuei ordered when POWs refused to sign. He crowded 17,000 Allied POWs in the square around Selarang barracks. Under a blazing sun, and under the guard of Sikh soldiers armed with machine guns, they had to just stand and watch as the recaptured men were summarily executed.[84]

After five days, Lieutenant General Holmes finally relented and issued a written order that men should follow Imperial Japanese Order No. 17, prohibiting escape. Many of the Allied troops signed with fake names, including that of the infamous Australian outlaw Ned Kelly. But the episode is remembered as a low point. It was not just British POWs who were killed: on September 20, two Chinese who stole ammunition were caught and executed.[85]

Fukuei also prevented any outside relief. The month he arrived, the Japanese ship *Asama Maru* brought South African and Canadian Red Cross relief goods and packages to Singapore. The Japan Red Cross and the Prisoner of War Information Bureau stocked Red Cross parcels in warehouses instead of delivering them to POWs.[86] The Japanese later claimed that they were to be a reserve for the prisoners when conditions prevented incoming shipments from arriving. "Afraid of interfering," there was little the International Committee of the Red Cross delegate Fritz Paravicini could do.[87]

Before they surrendered or fled Singapore, British troops had destroyed the water pipes and other infrastructure as part of a scorched earth policy. Thus, in addition to food shortages, captives faced a growing threat of disease. Changi's water supply came from Johore, and the causeway carrying the pipes and the pipeline itself had been damaged. Antimalarial drains were choked with litter and wreckage, which contributed to a massive outbreak of cholera among civilians. Poor sanitation at the camp led to more disease: corpses, offal, rotting garbage, and unprotected latrines created ideal conditions for disease-causing flies that plagued the city.[88] Japanese action—including inoculation and the provision of B1 tablets—prevented such an outbreak among the POWs themselves.[89] They also provided timber to build fly-proof structures over the latrines.

Although the POWs perceived medical care they received as poor, at least some of it was simply different from what they were used to. For instance, Japanese doctors used moxibustion to treat dysentery, rampant in Singapore. Most Allied captives were unfamiliar with the practice. Japanese doctors were recruited from all specialties; the doctors at the camp were not always trained in or familiar with the diseases POWs contracted.[90] And within the Japanese military administration, military doctors had a low position, so that even when they requested medicine, they had low priority. The lack of supplies became a growing problem. Faced with raging disease, British, Australian, and Dutch medical officers did their best, but eventually lacked even bandages, sheets, or clothing.[91] Some were creative: Dutch physicians, for example, were adept at compounding extracts from leaves and grass to use as a medicine for endemic scrotum (swelling balls).[92]

Yet it was impossible to contain all contagious disease outbreaks, because of both the crowded conditions and what became near-constant prisoner movement into and out of Changi, as prisoners were shipped where they could be useful for the Japanese empire. IJA policy was for white POWs to work, "employed in the expansion of our production and on work conducted with military affairs." Other captives were to be released when possible, and made to work where they were.[93]

While disease was the greatest threat to the lives of POWs, and transportation by ship was increasingly dangerous, POWs were particularly enraged by the physical violence inflicted by guards. The IJA's history of interpersonal violence, used instead of formal sanctions, created endless problems between low-ranking Japanese guards and Euro-American POWs. Most captives did not realize this was a part of Japanese military training, and the particular ways it shaped soldiers' understanding of their honor and masculinity. Japanese conscripts, trained in a military that considered corporal punishment as standard, and surrender to be shameful, now were given total power over POWs. But these same notions of honor and manhood meant that Japanese guards thought it was better to punch or slap POWs once, rather than punish them officially. For them, informal punishments were less shameful.[94] They probably never imagined how humiliating it was for Allied POWs. Having already lost their status as colonial overlords, they now had to submit to Japanese men, who determined the kind of food that they ate, the medical care they received—indeed, their every bodily function.

As the war proceeded, the director of the Japanese Prisoner of War Information Bureau (POWIB; Furyo Jōhōkyoku), Hamada Hiroshi, showed that he, at least, was well aware that private sanctions were unacceptable to the Allies. At a POW camp directors' meeting on December 26, 1943, he argued that private sanctions were due to bad army practices and flawed thinking—that is, that private sanctions were preferable to shaming one's name and family by criminal punishment. He thought it often occurred because of minor misunderstandings due to cultural and language differences. Most infuriated Japanese conscripts had seldom encountered foreigners up to this point except through wartime propaganda. Later, the POWIB acknowledged that "Japanese people could be short-term." By this they meant that Japanese guards might not realize the lasting impact on prisoners when they reacted with violent anger toward trivial mistakes.[95] But, they insisted, "People who added sanctions as a very effective means to truly correct the delinquency of a prisoner without having a personal grudge are also good people."[96]

But Hamada knew that, as the war continued, the people who became guards were not the best people by the Army's own standards. As late as 1937, the majority of men conscripted into the Japanese army were class A or B.[97] As the war went on, the IJA kept lowering its standards to lower-level recruits. The draft age was lowered to 19 from 20 in 1943. Military obligations were increased, and student deferments ended. The army also stepped up recruitment of colonial subjects. In some camps, Japanese men still topped the hierarchy, but the bulk of the guards were colonial subjects. Hamada claimed that private sanctions occurred especially among non-commissioned officers or mercenary soldiers. Korean and Taiwanese guards inflicted a considerable number of these sanctions, but evidence indicates that guards learned the practice of private sanctions during their two-month training.[98] This training emphasized that Allied soldiers were taller and stronger. Colonial troops therefore were told to use physical violence to keep them in line. Being a camp commander or a guard was never a high-status job, and the guards knew it. As the war continued, it was colonial subjects and older, maimed, and recalled soldiers who guarded POWs and commanded the camps.

In Changi, the number and composition of the captive population was also changing. In November 1942, more British and Dutch troops were sent to Thailand. At the end of the month 2,200 POWs, including 563 Australians, were sent to Japan. Australians and others from the Dutch East Indies passed through Singapore on the way north.[99] Even within the former Crown colony, prisoners were continually shuffled from camp to camp, but some were deliberately kept separate. The Japanese continued to try to win over Indian POWs. They found it better to separate Indian and British troops to achieve this end. They did so with the help of Indian civilians.[100]

The biggest movements of all were of the Indian prisoners. Between December 1942 and September 1943 about 12,000 Indian POWs were shipped from Singapore to various islands in the Southwest Pacific, the Andaman Islands, and French Indochina. The largest convoy left Malaya in May, including not just men who had held out against collaboration but also men who had at one time been volunteers in Singapore and in building the Thai-Burma Railway. The POWs were proving useful as a labor pool not just in Singapore but at many points of Japan's far-flung empire.

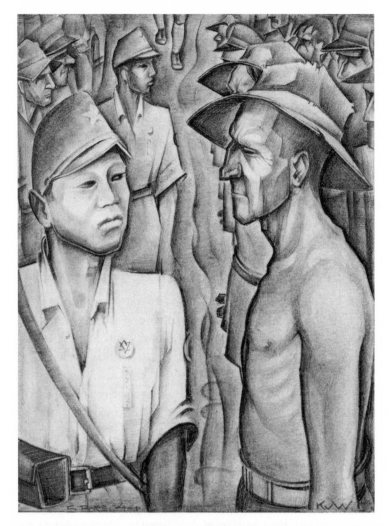

Korean guard looking at an Australian. In training Korean guards were told to use
physical force against larger and stronger POWs, and they felt there was good reason
to regard their captives warily. ("Roll Call," Kees van Willigen, Museon, The Hague.)

In November 1942, Major General Tsunemichi Arimura replaced Fukuei
and was placed in charge of the camps. Under his command, conditions
continued to deteriorate. In February 1943, the rice ration was reduced,
leading to a vitamin deficiency.[101] A Dutch POW who arrived at this point,
Lieutenant Pilot Observer Lambertus Kroes, recalled that "location not so
bad, but the food was absolutely insufficient, due to lack of vitamins my

lip split." In April he was moved to Japan, first to Moji, then to Yomotoko near Teira.[102]

In April 1943, there was a further reduction in POW numbers, as still more were shipped out. Australian strength dipped to fewer than 3,000, and fewer than 2,000 the next month. By June 1943, only 5,359 POWs remained.[103] This may have helped the food situation, but work became much harder. As the Japanese sought to complete the Changi aerodrome, they demanded the employment of unfit men, who worked long hours in the heat. Even their clothes began to wear out. POWs had to work, not just on projects prescribed by the Japanese, but to provide for the bare necessities for camp life. They had a broom workshop, and also made their own chalk, glue, and darning needles, but still faced constant shortages.

In July 1943, S. C. Bose's arrival in Singapore energized the remaining Indian POWs.[104] A "fiery orator," Bose was known for his speaking skill.[105] As one observer recalled, "When Subhas Chandra Bose spoke, women would throw their gold jewelry at his feet."[106] It is difficult to know what exactly motivated the men who followed him. M. Singh believed they were inspired by the idea of freeing India from British rule.[107] Most Indians were not believers in or loyal to the ideas of Pan-Asianism or its policy incarnation, the Greater East Asia Co-prosperity Sphere. According to Pitt Kuan Wah, "those who did it did it for self-gain."[108] But "The average Indian, yes, had a negative attitude toward the Japanese."[109]

As for the Japanese themselves, even if the liberation of Asia was not an original war objective, and could easily be cast off, Pan-Asianism functioned at different levels, often with deep effect. Many intellectuals shared this ideal, as did the Japanese soldiers in Southeast Asia who believed they were fighting for "the liberation of the Asian peoples." It also informed official policy. In April 1943, instructions on the "Handling of Indian Soldiers" stated that they should receive the "sincere protection of the Imperial Army." The document also contained briefs on Indian religions, and proscribed Japanese guards from hitting or making fun of a soldier in front of his colleagues.[110] The situation on the ground was often very different, but there can be little doubt that at least some Japanese policymakers were seeking to make the rhetoric of Pan-Asianism into more of a reality.

In November 1943, the representatives of six Asian governments—Japan, Manchukuo, China, Burma, Thailand, and the Philippines—met in Tokyo at the "Greater East Asian Conference" and discussed the future of Asia. Bose joined them. Pan-Asianism was explicitly defined against the West.

"The countries of Greater East Asia, with a view to contributing to the cause of world peace, undertake to cooperate toward prosecuting the War of Greater East Asia to a successful conclusion, liberating their region from the yoke of British-American domination, and assuring their self-existence and self-defense, and in constructing a Greater East Asia."[111] They issued a Joint Declaration, with the aim of fostering "common prosperity and well-being."[112]

Ultimately, INA troops were deployed all across the Pacific theater, and experienced some of the worst conditions of the entire war. Large numbers died from transport or illness, but some also from mistreatment at the hands of the Japanese.[113] It was even worse for the POWs. Many of the 12,000 who shipped out from Singapore to various islands in the Southwest Pacific were employed on labor gangs. They worked as coolies, for example, building huts. Japanese officers used corporal punishment to force them to work. The most notorious incident took place in May 1944 at Wewak in New Guinea. When American planes flew overhead, and an American patrol boat came to reconnoiter the coast near the camp, the Japanese guards took cover. Three Indian POWs tried to swim out to the boat but failed to make contact. When they returned to the shore, the Japanese immediately turned their machine guns on the POWs in an attempt to kill them all.[114]

As Indians shipped out of Changi, new contingents arrived. They even included some Italian submariners, who surrendered their boats when Italy capitulated in 1943. A few took oaths of allegiance to the Japanese and were assigned to the Imperial Navy.[115] But the others became POWs for the rest of the war. They joined the survivors of the USS *Houston,* sunk by Japanese torpedoes, as well as Colonel Thorpe's 131st Field Artillery Battalion, which had been captured in the Dutch East Indies. The actual numbers were highly variable, as contingents shipped out to Burma, Thailand, Borneo, Taiwan, Japan, or Korea. But all along, the plurality of Allied prisoners in Singapore were British Commonwealth soldiers, and their number rose again when men came back from the Sime Road Camp. Some returned all the way from Thailand to crowd into Changi.

As the number of POWs rose again, so too did their protests. For example, in September 1943, the ICRC wrote to Tokyo on behalf of the British government specifically regarding Changi.[116] Prisoners themselves also complained about their poor treatment to camp commanders. Here as elsewhere, it was the commander who was responsible for communicating with the prison authorities. The success of this tactic depended on the camp and the camp commander.[117] At Changi, for example, the British colonel E. B. Holmes wrote a letter of complaint in November 1943 to Arimura. In response, Captain Tazumi Motozō acknowledged that Japan was a signatory to the 1907 convention. But he pointed out that the convention also specified that prisoners must obey captors, and thus they had no right to protest.[118] In fairness, camp commanders like Arimura were given little support and were limited by Tokyo's scarce logistics. For example, Red Cross supplies depended on Army transport, and weapons and ammunition were always prioritized.

Overall, the changes in Japanese camp leadership and attitude made life considerably more difficult. Entertainment was restricted and the number of attendees at lectures was limited to twenty-five. Theatrical performances at the jail theater were limited to two per week. According to the Japanese administration, such limitations were justified because prisoners were getting more entertainment than their captors.[119] The Japanese may have had less tolerance for light entertainment because it had been years since their first victories and Japan itself was now under bombardment.

The effects of the Allied campaign made food ever more scarce. During the last months of internment POWs were living on little more than eight ounces of rice daily.[120] Later ICRC delegates would report that Dutch prisoners were more concerned about conditions their families were experiencing: "Great anxiety was expressed to us about conditions [in the] Dutch East Indies and internees camp."[121]

On November 4, 1944, forty Allied aircraft attacked Singapore, followed by another raid on New Year's Day 1945. Shortly after, the Japanese formed work parties totaling nearly 6,000 POWs to strengthen the defenses around Singapore and Johore Bahru. They dug tunnels and defense works. Men assigned to work were given better rations, but hard labor, long hours, and distance from the camp further taxed undernourished men.

By March 1945, POWs able to work received priority for food allocation. The Japanese Command issued only half rations for the sick, and three-fourths for the somewhat sick. They also forbade the pooling of rations. That same month, a Red Cross ship arrived with 1,200 tons of stores, and in April, the Japanese began small twice-weekly distributions. But the work was unrelenting, and the dollars POWs were paid lost much of their purchasing power. Firewood, always in short supply, was now largely unavailable. In June 1945, the end of work on the aerodrome meant fit men from the project became available for other working parties. Many were injured, and one was killed by dirt falling during tunneling. Other prisoners were also wounded during the increasingly severe Allied air raids.[122] By July 1945, air raids were a daily occurrence. In early August 1945, seven crew members of a downed B-24 were summarily executed.[123]

When Allied Forces finally reached Singapore in August 1945, ICRC inspectors reported that there were 30,500 POWs of all nationalities, mostly Indian, then half as many British, followed by Australians, Dutch, and Americans, as well as a few others.[124] About 4,600 internees also remained.[125] According to the ICRC's informants, the "health situation in Changi [is] probably better than in other POW camps though poor." Investigators discovered that some troops were paid and some received mail. There were three lots of Red Cross parcels, amounting to slightly more than one parcel per man. No clothing was issued, so many men were practically naked by the end of the war. But morale was high.[126]

The Indian POWs had had the worst of it.[127] Jack Winters of the US Marine Corps testified in an affidavit that the 4,200 men in River Valley Road lived in buildings with leaky roofs. Sanitation was poor, and there were many flies. All men in River Valley Road were required to work, loading supplies on transports.[128] At Tanjong Pagar, another camp, men received "beastly treatment."[129] Of 60,000 Indians captured at the outset of the war, 5,000 died of malnutrition, dysentery, and malaria.[130]

Almost 1,500 miles away, in the American quasi-colony of the Philippines, Americans and Filipinos faced a similar situation, in which Japanese lack of planning again resulted in needless suffering. The whole world had "gone topsy-turvy," as the Singapore internees' newspaper observed after just one month of captivity. Soon it would seem even more like "the whole bally world has gone nuts."

# 3

## THE PHILIPPINES

## Commonwealth of Hell

By far the largest contingent of American servicemen to become prisoners of the Japanese were those who surrendered in the Philippines. Like Singapore, the Philippines had been subjected to foreign rule long before Japanese forces arrived in 1941. Named after the Habsburg king Philip II of Spain, it was one of the oldest colonies in the Pacific before being taken by the United States in 1898. In 1935, the Philippines became a commonwealth, with the promise of independence after ten years. Yet the United States retained a "special relationship" with the Philippines that shaped the experience of the Japanese occupation and the treatment of American and Filipino POWs and internees.

Here again, a lack of planning and an indifference to POWs were the primary causes of neglect and abuse. In this case, it was a failure to anticipate the ferocity of resistance, and the challenge of keeping even their own forces healthy in the harsh and malarial environment of Bataan. The presence of large numbers of Japanese civilians—and MacArthur's decision to intern them—further poisoned the atmosphere. But the single greatest cause of high mortality among American POWs was the decision to transport them long distances to labor in Japanese war industries, combined with the determination of Allied forces to destroy these convoys, no matter what the cost.

Ironically, many Americans first came to the Philippines because they hoped to make their fortunes. They maintained a standard of living that was unattainable back home, and helped keep the Philippines a quasi-colony of the United States. Its economy remained dependent on the United States and a free-trade agreement between the two countries. Raw materials such as sugar, hemp, and coconut went duty-free to the United States, while manufactured goods such as textiles, steel, machinery, and processed food were imported from the United States.[1]

The Philippines held key strategic importance for the United States. Bases at Cavite and Subic Bay defended air and sea lanes from the Northern Pacific to Southeast Asia, and onward to the Indian Ocean, the Middle East, and Europe. The United States had made the island of Corregidor, in Manila Bay, into a fortress, and also maintained posts at Fort McKinley and Stotsenburg. Clark Field served as the primary base for long-range American bombers in Asia.

In 1937, Douglas MacArthur became military advisor to the Commonwealth government. He convinced Manuel L. Quezon, the president of the Philippine Commonwealth, that he needed to strengthen their defenses. But just as in Singapore, investment was inadequate. Quezon paid for advisors, basic training, and obsolete materiel. It was not until the formation of the US Army in the Far East (USAFE) in July 1941 that the Commonwealth received state-of-the-art American equipment.[2]

Tokyo also had a long-standing interest in the Philippines, starting with the large number of Japanese who had settled there. In 1903, Japanese first arrived to work as laborers.[3] Some became successful entrepreneurs, and their businesses made use of increasing capital from Japan during World War I. By 1918, seventy-one Japanese managed agribusinesses in Davao—on the southern island of Mindanao—and Davao's Japanese population reached more than 5,600. The vast majority of the Japanese in the Philippines lived in Mindanao, and almost 10,000 lived in the archipelago.[4] By the 1920s and 1930s many more Japanese had emigrated to the Philippines, part of a larger wave of emigration to Latin America and North America. In 1935, Japanese landowners controlled about two-thirds of the cultivated land in Davao.[5] The Japanese community included Okinawans and Japanese-Filipinos. According to the 1939 census, 894 Filipinos nationwide had Japanese husbands, with 740 children registered as Japanese citizens.[6] Most Japanese in Southeast Asia lived in the Philippines, and they sent the largest remittances home.[7]

Japan traditionally supported American rule in the Philippines. Since 1931, Japanese foreign policy had focused on China and Manchukuo. Some Pan-Asianists advocated a different policy, supporting Filipino nationalist Artemio Ricarte. When he was exiled to Japan, police surveilled him because the Japanese government still supported the US presence in the Philippines. He was an admirer of Japan since its victory over Russia and continued to live in exile there. But Tokyo sought mainly to look after Japanese emigrants and investments. The Philippines contained important resources, such as copper, chrome, manganese, iron, and coal.[8]

Starting in the 1930s, some diplomats and military men began to argue that Japan should turn to the South (*Nan'yō*, South Pacific).[9] Japan's Foreign Ministry began to openly argue for full independence for the Philippines, and for the idea that Pan-Asianism extended to the Philippines. By the late 1930s, the Japanese military was drawing up contingency plans for an invasion and occupation.[10] Both the Imperial Japanese Army (IJA) and the Imperial Japanese Navy (IJN) sent operatives there for reconnaissance.[11] They also employed a similar approach to Malaya: seeking to get resident Japanese merchants and businessmen to prepare, and also to provide information on the local political and economic situation.[12]

In June 1940, Japan began to send military personnel to French Indochina to block China from shipping military materiel by rail through Hanoi. The Vichy-controlled regime could offer little opposition. After August 1940 Japanese foreign policy explicitly turned to Southeast Asia. Two of the four powers that formerly dominated the region, France and the Netherlands, were under Axis occupation. Both the United Kingdom and the United States were focused on Germany. But it was not until June 1941, after the Nazi invasion of the Soviet Union removed the Soviet threat to Japanese Manchuria, that Japanese troops moved into French Indochina in force. This was in order to prepare for military action against the Dutch East Indies. In response, President Franklin Delano Roosevelt froze Japanese assets and embargoed exports as the threat to US possessions and interests became increasingly clear.

In July 1941, the same month Japan occupied all of Indochina, Roosevelt recalled MacArthur to active duty and made him commander of USAFE. It was composed of a US Army division and ten Philippine Army divisions in varying states of readiness. By the end of 1941, there were 23,000 US troops stationed in the archipelago. But this was a garrison force with little to no combat experience.[13]

The standing US strategy, known as War Plan Orange-3 (WPO-3), concentrated US forces in Central Luzon rather than dispersing to defend every beach and island. The core mission was to delay a Japanese invasion and prevent them from taking Manila Bay until American reinforcements arrived by sea. If they could not repel amphibious landings, they were to defeat Japanese forces in the field. If they failed again, they would seek to delay their advance while withdrawing to Bataan and Corregidor.

Together, the Bataan Peninsula and the island citadel could prevent the Japanese fleet from using the port of Manila even if the rest of the Philippines had fallen.[14]

MacArthur considered this plan defeatist, and had good reason to doubt that reinforcements would arrive in time. He insisted that if large numbers of Filipino troops were trained, equipped, and provided with air support, they could mount an aggressive coastal defense of the entire archipelago. He therefore assigned some divisions and supplies to the defense of the southern islands and Mindanao. But many US commanders were still uncertain as to whether the beaches were really to "be held at all costs."[15]

Even in 1941, a Japanese invasion seemed impossible to many. While some dependents were sent home, other American civilians were reluctant to leave. The State Department advised the American high commissioner, Francis Bowes Sayre, not to give "official notice" to leave. Sayre decided that because it was impossible to tell if, or when, an attack by the Japanese might occur, "it would be inadvisable to issue such a notice."[16] This evasiveness may have been an attempt to preserve the status quo: after all, if Americans left, Filipinos would begin to lose faith and question the US commitment to their defense.

When war came, MacArthur had a powerful asset under his command: thirty-five of the newest US heavy bombers, the B-17 "flying fortresses," which had the range to strike Japanese forces that were marshalling in Formosa (Taiwan). For that same reason, they were a prime target for the Japanese.

But MacArthur's focus was elsewhere. Instead of preparing his forces, he made it a priority to intern Japanese men, women, and children. He quickly interned about 40 percent of Japanese nationals in Manila and put some of them to work digging air raid trenches, in a direct violation of the Geneva Conventions. He also did nothing when Filipino policemen allegedly executed ten internees as a reprisal for the naval bombardment of Mindanao.[17] G-2 counterintelligence officer E. Carl Engelhart recounted how, even before servicemen heard the news of the attack on Pearl Harbor, MacArthur's G-2, Charles Willoughby, called and asked how long it would take him to pick up Japanese nationals for internment.[18] Soon after, another phone call came with the news from Pearl Harbor. Engelhart was ordered to direct the internment of Japanese citizens, starting with Japanese residents in Manila.[19] Nagashima Nobuko, who had been a fifth-grader at the Manila Japan School, described the experience:

On December 8, 1941, I was heading for school with my sister and brother as usual. On the way we ran into Mr. Nakamura coming back from the school. As soon as he saw us, he said, "I went to school, but Mr. Yoshimura told us to go back home as the war started." We were surprised and rushed home. We told our parents. Our father said, "It might be true. Get ready."

Nagashima continued:

The military policemen told us to get out and line up. Our father and his cousin Tatsuji brought the huge bags and our mother carried my three-year-old sister on her back, holding the case of medicine. My older sister and I brought kimonos in the bag. My little brother brought the water bottle, eggs, and rice balls. There were Japanese people with bags lining up along the street in front of our house. . . . Usually my Filipino friends would talk to me in a friendly way while we went, or we went together, but yesterday's friends are today's enemies. They turned a blind eye. . . . On the street, Filipino and Chinese people were standing and staring at us. Kiyo-chan started crying and I felt like crying.[20]

In Davao, where most Japanese lived, men, women, and children were also interned. During their confinement, their wealth and assets were confiscated by Filipinos. Later, those who had been confined returned to find that 95 percent of their homes were looted, and some burned to the ground.[21]

Meanwhile, for American servicemen, it was about noon on December 8 when "disaster really struck." While the B-17 crews were eating lunch, waiting for MacArthur to release them to attack the Japanese bomber base on Formosa, IJA bombers came in and attacked Iba Field, destroying most of the American fighter planes. Also hit was Apoarri in northern Luzon and Nichols Field on the outskirts of Manila. Soon Cavite Navy Yard was "practically removed from the map." The loss of air cover was a crippling blow to the defense of the Philippines.

In Manila, some residents realized they were in danger and began to make plans to escape. Ten days later, the SS *Corregidor* was delayed for hours by the "Clamor of Filipinos" seeking passage to get to Mindanao and other southern islands. It finally sailed with over 1,000 people on board, but veered into a defensive minefield and sank quickly, taking most of the passengers and crew.

The Japanese had already begun landing detachments at various points around the Philippines, both to prepare for the main assault on Luzon, and to interdict any reinforcements. On the island of Mindanao, Japanese troops quickly succeeded in taking Davao. American and Filipino forces retreated into the hills. In the days that followed, resident Japanese nationals worked to support the occupying force. Filipinos killed ten of them who were laboring in a kitchen, which the Japanese called a "massacre." Tokyo bitterly complained in diplomatic notes delivered by the Swiss.[22]

On December 22, the main Japanese Army invasion fleet arrived at Luzon.[23] Lieutenant General Honma Masaharu commanded an army of approximately 40,000 men. Among his forces was the famous Forty-Eighth Division, which had trained in amphibious warfare while based in Formosa. Japanese troops took a multipronged approach to Luzon Island. Troops approached from the north and entered through the Lingayen Gulf to the West. Japanese forces also approached from the southeast.[24] MacArthur had at least 65,000 to 70,000 troops in Luzon to oppose an invasion. But most of the Filipinos were poorly trained and poorly equipped. In some ways they resembled the Indian forces defending the British Empire in Malaysia.[25] Many more troops were dispersed among the islands. Honma, on the other hand, concentrated his forces for a quick advance.

MacArthur's army failed to hold the beaches. By nightfall the IJA was well positioned to emerge onto the central plain. On the afternoon of December 23, Field Commander General Jonathan Wainwright phoned headquarters at Manila to tell MacArthur that a further defense of the Lingayen beaches was not feasible. Returning to the original strategy, WPO-3, MacArthur ordered a withdrawal into the rugged Bataan Peninsula. On December 26 he declared Manila an "open city," leaving it undefended. Some troops headed to Corregidor, as did HQ personnel and nurses from Sternberg Hospital. Civilian employees—secretaries and typists—took home typewriters. Engelhart gave his secretary a case of baked beans.[26] The Japanese, for their part, bombed the docks and ships in port, which many, including MacArthur, considered an outrage. They were trying to prevent a rear echelon, headed by Brigadier General Richard Marshall, from destroying or carting away all useful supplies and equipment, which they continued doing until the last possible moment.

Engelhart arrived in Corregidor long after dark. Along the way, the troops could see the fires Marshall's men had set to destroy installations in Manila.[27] They fired antiaircraft guns at Japanese bombers, but they were out of range. Engelhart, at least, saw no planes shot down. Even so, Corregidor HQ claimed they had shot down a half dozen or so enemy planes.[28]

Luckily for MacArthur, Honma's directives were unclear, and he was uncertain as to whether he should focus on destroying MacArthur's remaining forces or first occupy Manila.[29] He finally decided to advance on the capital. On January 2, 1942, at 5:45 p.m., Japanese troops entered the city.[30] They released interned Japanese, among whom were nervous and fearful children.[31] Nakajima Yūko, a sixth-grader at the Manila Japan school, described the scene:

> "Banzai, Banzai!" A thousand people's shouts echoed in the dark sky in Manila. Since December 8, we had evacuated to the housing of Daidō Trade company. How strongly we had wished every day that soldiers would come, and peaceful days would come back. The soldiers we dreamed of now stand in front of us (9:00 a.m. on January 2). I am filled with happiness and appreciation toward soldiers who came here, I cannot help shouting "Banzai!" holding my national flag. . . . After that, the representative of the citizens made a speech to express our gratefulness and the captain gave a greeting speech. I could not stop crying during the speeches.[32]

Honma put the director of the military administrative section of the Fourteenth Army, Deputy Chief of Staff Lieutenant General Hayashi Yoshihide, in charge of the city. Ten months earlier, the First Department Research Section of the Army General Staff had decided administrative policies in occupied territories. In the Philippines, the priority was to destroy American military bases. Next, the Army Special Command was to win the trust of the Filipino government. Finally, the army was to focus on military measures, rather than political ones, except for assistance in creating a new economic system. There was no mention of what would be done with captured American and Filipino troops.[33]

Now that they actually occupied the Philippines, Japanese administrators confronted a colonial territory they had trouble understanding.[34] The archipelago was officially a commonwealth, and many elite Filipinos had been well served by years of American rule and had little appetite for Japanese Pan-Asianism.[35] Tōjō did not know how to win them over. On January 22, 1942, he announced that in the future the Philippines would be independent only if it understood and complied with the intentions of the empire.[36] The Quezon regime would not go along. Before escaping to Corregidor, Quezon had appointed Jose Abad Santos Sr., Chief Justice of the Philippine Supreme Court, as his deputy and acting president. Four months later, after Santos was captured, Lieutenant Colonel Kawakami, director general of military administration in the Cebu area, executed him by firing squad. Kawakami made the decision without getting permission from any superiors. Santos preferred to die rather than collaborate.[37]

When General Artemio Ricarte arrived from Japan, he sought to establish a Filipino dictatorship based on Andres Bonifacio's ideology—the spirit of unity, innocence, and fairness. But even before Ricarte arrived, the Fourteenth Army announced on the front page of the *Manila Tribune* a no-tolerance policy against resistance.[38] The Kempeitai (Japanese military police force) began to systematically enforce this directive. As in Singapore, Chinese were targeted. Though they made up only about 1 percent of the population, they would be active in the nascent resistance movement.[39]

Ricarte was handicapped by the fact that he had lived in exile in Japan for twenty-eight years and lacked contacts with current elites. He was not even invited to the meetings of the Japanese preparation committee. This may have been because Japanese civilian officials on the ground had a different plan than the military, or because Ricarte was viewed as a has-been, and therefore not treated as a real leader.[40] Instead, much of the Filipino ruling elite remained in place, mainly administrators trained under US colonial rule. Educated in the United States, they were Americanized, or at least Westernized.[41] It was they, led by Jose Vargas, who would determine the success or failure of the Japanese occupation.[42]

As the Japanese struggled to organize the new government in the capital, Filipino and American troops and supplies continued pouring into Bataan. The battle began in earnest on January 7, 1942. Unfortunately for Honma, he no longer had his best troops. The Forty-Eighth Division had been redeployed to Java. They were replaced by a brigade that was originally intended for garrison duty and lacked appropriate training and equipment.[43]

On January 30, MacArthur was told that there would be no further reinforcements.[44] Yet for almost three months, the two sides continued to engage in fierce fighting. In one battle, two entire Japanese battalions were surrounded and finally wiped out, and a third was badly mauled when it attempted to rescue them. During this period, 2,700 Japanese troops died and 4,050 were injured, while some 15,500 became sick from diseases like dysentery and malaria.[45]

But the Filipino and American defenders were also suffering high casualties and physical exhaustion, and started to run out of supplies and ammunition. On February 24, MacArthur evacuated his headquarters to Corregidor. Like the fighters in Bataan, the garrison there had to go on half rations. First to go were the cavalry horses, then mule meat. Reasonable quantities of rice were still available. But when Engelhart and others from G-2 visited friends in the jungle, they dined on roast monkey meat. Some "looked green around the gills."[46] The occasional submarine still visited and brought details of the "debacle at Pearl Harbor."[47]

On March 11, MacArthur escaped in PT boats with his senior staff, his family, and his child's nanny. When he arrived in Australia, he famously promised, "I shall return." MacArthur also allowed President Quezon and his family to evacuate by submarine, but not before Quezon agreed to transfer $500,000 to MacArthur's personal bank account.[48] Even without knowing about this payoff—which was worth about $6 million in today's money, and was almost certainly illegal—at least some of those who remained considered MacArthur's flight cowardly. This was especially true when he continued ordering them to fight to the last. One American brigadier called it "a foul trick of deception played on a large group of Americans by a commander in chief and his small staff who are now eating steak and eggs in Australia."[49]

To be fair, Roosevelt himself had ordered that the defense of the Philippines be "as prolonged as humanly possible." Quezon earlier suggested instead that both Japanese and US forces withdraw, so the Philippines would become neutral and independent. But in a message drafted by Dwight Eisenhower, FDR explained that it was "mandatory" to demonstrate to the rest of the world that "the American determination and indomitable will to win carries on down to the last unit."[50] Both MacArthur and the War Department understood this meant "no surrender." Roosevelt issued the same command to Wainwright on March 23.[51] Two weeks later, FDR relented and told MacArthur that he could let Wainwright decide. But MacArthur was now adamant that the men left in the Philippines should fight to their deaths, even after they ran out of food. "If food fails," he wrote, "you will prepare and execute an attack on the enemy."[52]

Thus, at this point in the war, it was not just the Japanese high command that insisted that troops must not surrender under any circumstances, and that anything less was dishonorable. MacArthur himself was insisting on a policy of "no surrender," even if it meant launching suicidal, "banzai" type attacks. But to many of those subject to these orders, it was "Dugout Doug" who had proven himself to be unmanly by withdrawing to the comparative safety of the tunnels on Corregidor, and then fleeing again rather than risk capture. These Filipino and American troops were exhausted after 120 days fighting. They were stricken by disease and surviving on scarce food and medicine. Their supplies and ammunition had all but run out. And they faced an overwhelmingly superior enemy.

After Honma received fresh reinforcements, he began his final assault on Bataan. Five days later, on April 9, Major General Edward King Jr. finally surrendered to Colonel Nakayama Motoo of the Fourteenth Army. King held out months longer than his counterparts in Malaya and Singapore, and General Wainwright on Corregidor continued to fight on. From the island fortress Engelhart could see Japanese troops moving south on one side of the road and American soldiers trudging north on the other side of the road. They were beginning "the terrible march into captivity, and the rest of us were now trapped on Corregidor."[53]

It is unclear how many captives were taken after the surrender of Bataan— perhaps 10,000 Americans and 62,000 Filipinos.[54] The Japanese would eventually have almost twice as many captives as their intelligence had originally estimated.[55] Civil servants and civilians were mixed in. Some Philippine Army units disbanded and the men were sent home.[56] But others escaped to Corregidor or the mountains of northern Luzon. The number of Allied POWs was therefore expected to increase. It was only then that the Japanese Foreign Ministry realized that they had to "think about the treatment of even bigger numbers of POWs from now on."[57] Either they had assumed the enemy would fight to the last man, a fundamental misreading of the US military, or they simply failed to plan and prepare for managing large numbers of prisoners.

From the Japanese military's point of view, the immediate priority was to move the prisoners in Bataan north to get them out of the way of the final assault on Corregidor. The campaign had already taken longer and cost more casualties than planned, and the lack of transport created an enormous logistical challenge.[58] Two hundred captured officers were transported in vehicles. But the remainder of Filipino and American captives would be marched some sixty-five miles to San Fernando. Then they faced a twenty-five-mile journey in overcrowded freight cars. Finally, they marched for nine more miles to Camp O'Donnell in north-central Luzon.

These prisoners were in no condition to make such a trip, especially when the Japanese would not spare water, food, or medicine.[59] This is today in the United States referred to as the Bataan Death March, and for Americans it is the most notorious POW experience of the entire Pacific War.[60] Corporal William Duncan later recalled how the march began a day after he was captured. As he marched near the Barrio of Balanga, Japanese soldiers standing along the side of the road beat him and the others with clubs and sticks as they passed.[61] Major William Dyess also reported brutal treatment. If POWs were found with Japanese money or Japanese-made goods such as shaving mirrors, they were hit with "crushing blows" or sometimes beheaded on suspicion of looting Japanese bodies.[62] After marching with little water and no food, some men were still not permitted to lie down, even at night. Some POWs, according to Dyess, were killed if they fell out of line. Three Americans and three Filipinos were buried alive. Another American colonel was horsewhipped after trying to help. In six days Dyess had one mess kit of rice.[63] Corporal William W. Duncan had the same recollection: "We were not given any food except on the last day, at which time the Japanese gave us a small portion of rice, about a handful of cooked rice."[64] Filipinos fit uncomfortably into this story. Many suffered alongside their American comrades, others watched sympathetically, or offered fried chicken or sugar cane. But still others sought to profit by selling food or water.[65]

On arrival at Camp O'Donnell, originally home to the 71st division of the Philippine Army, the camp commander, Tsuneyoshi Yoshio, told them that they were not POWs but captives.[66] By this point an estimated 700 Americans and 5,000 Filipinos had already died during the forced march. But Camp O'Donnell itself offered no relief. It was "in an appalling condition," Duncan recalled, with poor sanitation, inadequate supplies, and continued brutal treatment.[67] All the prisoners were suffering from malnutrition, and epidemics of malaria and dysentery were soon running rampant throughout the camp. There were no medical supplies other than a few aspirin tablets, a little tape, and a few bandages, though it was reported that quinine or sulfathiazole might be had for $5 a tablet.

Captain Mark W. Wohfield recalled that the "so-called hospital had patients lying in two rows on the floor which was saturated with feces, blood, and vomit—all of which was covered with flies." Captain Robert Edward

The Bataan Death March, remembered by many Americans as the most notorious POW experience of the Pacific War. Thousands died, most of them Filipinos. (US National Archives and Records Administration.) BRODSKY 2 BRODSKY BROS. DIED

Conn, also held at O'Donnell, later testified that the Japanese in charge deliberately withheld food and medicine from prisoners, and were directly responsible for the 1,547 American deaths in the camp.[68] It was difficult even to find a sufficient number of able-bodied men to bury the dead. According to one account, men who had collapsed from exhaustion were buried before they were actually dead.[69]

Altogether, Japanese treatment of POWs in the Philippines during the first months of their captivity may have been as bad as any in the entire Pacific War. It is estimated that one out of every six Americans who entered O'Donnell did not survive. The death rate among Filipino captives was even higher. Some of the reasons for this mistreatment were common to other theaters, while others were specific to the Philippines. First, as elsewhere, captives taken at Bataan were initially not regarded as POWs,[70] and they would not be accorded that status until formal POW camps were established in August 1942. This had several consequences, the most important being that their treatment was not a matter of official policy, but left to the discretion of the local commanders who took them into custody. It also meant that the names of the men taken were not reported to the ICRC. The records of those who died before they were in Japanese custody—enemy combatants killed in action—were also not transmitted. This is one reason why, even now, it is very hard to estimate the number who died in custody.

Japanese commanders considered themselves under no obligation to treat POWs better than they were able to treat their own soldiers. Members of the IJA often suffered from inadequate provisions and corporal punishment. Honma had repeatedly asked for more quinine and medical support, but received nothing until the end of April. The rate of infection therefore almost doubled as the Japanese entered the southernmost part of Bataan, which featured malaria-infested river valleys. Some 28,000 Japanese were hospitalized with malaria by the end of the month.[71] This helps explain why the level of brutality and privation was greater in the Philippines, where many of the Japanese were poorly trained and unprepared for the kind of fighting they endured before American and Filipino troops finally gave up.

One of those with no training was the camp commander himself. Tsuneyoshi was in his late forties, but still only a captain. Like many others who worked in camps, he had been discharged from the military only to be recalled to duty in 1937.[72] According to Tsuneyoshi, his prior experience in the Philippines included training NCOs and doing propaganda work. With little time to prepare and no previous experience operating a POW camp, on April 1 he was told that he would be responsible for a temporary camp with about 20,000 POWs.

As a branch commander, Tsuneyoshi had no power to obtain food or water beyond requisitioning it. He, and the small staff he was assigned, had little time to prepare the camp for the tens of thousands who would soon arrive. As it turns out, about twice as many showed up at Camp O'Donnell. Altogether, the surrendering troops outnumbered all the Japanese in the Philippines by almost two to one. While many of the POWs were weak from malaria and dysentery, so were their guards.

There were other factors unique to the Philippines. The internment of Japanese families, the destruction of their property, and the killing of

civilian workers in Mindanao may have spurred some to inflict reprisals. Most American and Filipino soldiers were likely unaware of these episodes. Instead, at least some of them hoped that the bravery and determination they showed while inflicting many deaths and injuries on Japanese
forces would win them respect.[73] They believed the manly way they fought
to the bitter end would ensure they would be treated as men. It likely had the
opposite effect. The Japanese were clearly frustrated about the heavy casualties they suffered when the outcome was never in doubt, as was evident
from the fact that the campaign effectively ended Honma's military career.[74]

While they marched Allied POWs out of Bataan, Honma's troops may
have been even more angry about the fact that their fight was still far from
over. General Wainwright refused to comply with demands that Corregidor
be surrendered at the same time Bataan capitulated. On Corregidor multiple batteries of 14-inch turret guns and 12-inch mortars continued to rain
thousand-pound shells on Japanese positions while American and Filipino
POWs were marched to the rear and out of range.

The Japanese now had to prepare to mount an amphibious landing on
the island citadel. Corregidor still had 12,000 defenders, including a reinforced Marines regiment, who were dug into tunnels. Even in Bataan, some
Americans and Filipinos had broken through Japanese lines and continued
to fight on, forming a guerrilla movement that became a growing threat to
the occupation. The message POWs got was that Corregidor's refusal to surrender was the reason they were treated not as prisoners, but as captives.

The Americans also believed that their treatment was meant to weaken
whatever loyalty to the United States remained among Filipinos. Filipinos
who fought by their side suffered the worst treatment. According to a later
report by the provost marshal general, "The Japanese commanders . . . made
every attempt possible to humiliate and degrade the Americans in the eyes
of the Filipinos."[75] Washington later alleged that among the humiliations
forced upon POWs was their use in propaganda. As the Japanese filmed
"Rip Down the Stars and Stripes," American POWs were forced to be photo-
graphed operating American military equipment.[76]

Wainwright finally surrendered Corregidor almost a month after the fall
of Bataan, but only after the US defenders inflicted heavy casualties on the
Japanese and destroyed most of their landing craft. Even then, Wainwright
initially insisted that he was only surrendering the islands in Manila Bay,
so US forces in the rest of the Philippines could fight on.[77] POWs taken from
Corregidor were made to march through Manila to Bilibid Prison. And

Japanese schoolchildren, soldiers, and civilians were admitted to internment camps and "encouraged to satisfy curiosity."[78]

Now that Corregidor had finally surrendered, and with it Japanese-speaking US intelligence officers, at least some of the Americans began to understand better the Japanese attitude toward their new captives. Initially they feared the worst. It was announced that "any foreigner who could speak Japanese is an enemy of the empire and should be hung or shot."[79] However, when Engelhart first came face-to-face with a group of officers and spoke Japanese to them, "the expression on the Lieutenant's face changed to one of relief."[80] Engelhart saluted the group. The officer returned it. Engelhart answered with his rank and name. He was questioned about where he had learned Japanese. He noticed that they were checking his statements against a dossier.[81]

Along with Engelhart, at least two other Americans he was aware of could speak Japanese. Where Engelhart could only speak what he described as "ordinary colloquial Japanese," "Pete" could speak polite Japanese, and the third only "pidgin Japanese." According to Engelhart, the "Japanese officers were very polite, almost respectful." He reciprocated by showing them where the mines were hidden.[82]

Americans who spoke fluent Japanese came to be regarded with suspicion by their comrades. One recalled them as tattletales.[83] It is difficult to judge in retrospect. What is clear is that they often had a more nuanced understanding of their captors than did other POWs. For instance, Engelhart realized that "the commander of the Japanese troops on Corregidor didn't know what the hell to do with us and he wasn't going to make any decision until he got some sort of indication from higher command. He's not going to risk any action for fear it might not comply with his commanding general's personal attitude."[84]

These Japanese-speaking POWs were among the first to understand that their treatment, rather than the result of some conscious policy, reflected the relative indifference and inattention of the high command during the first months of the war. Engelhart also realized that in the absence of new orders, Japanese officers and enlisted men would treat them as they had grown accustomed to treating captives in recent years. He feared that "Japanese military operations in China had shown no change from their ancient attitude that captives were subject to the whim of the captors."[85] While the Southern Expeditionary Army Group had formed the Fourteenth Army specifically to invade the Philippines, at least some of them, including Honma, had spent considerable time in China. The Six-teenth Division had been involved in some of the worst fighting, including the Rape of Nanking.

What was Honma's personal knowledge and responsibility for what was happening to Allied POWs? He was not oblivious to their fate. His officers told him that POWs "were dying at an alarming rate," as historian Yuma Totani notes.[86] On May 22, 1942—just one day—471 Filipinos and 77 Americans died at Camp O'Donnell.[87] Most Allied prisoners started to be moved out, but it took time.[88] By mid-June there was a new, more competent commander at Camp O'Donnell and death rates started to drop.[89] Japanese authorities moved senior officers like Wainright to Tarlac, and others to Cabanatuan or elsewhere. The sickest stayed on for a time, and in July a hospital was opened at O'Donnell to treat them.

It is hard to know what role Honma may have had. But in this period Honma was almost certainly focused, not on the fate of POWs, but on the challenge of redeploying his forces to end the last vestiges of organized re-sistance on the other islands. According to Major Dyess, high Japanese mil-itary and civil authorities made frequent visits and were aware of the con-ditions American POWs lived in. Honma also should have known what his troops were capable of. After all, he had been sent to Nanjing in 1938 to in-vestigate in the immediate aftermath of the atrocities there.[90]

Yet Honma's China experience had also impressed on him the difficulty of controlling the actions of subordinate officers and individual soldiers. After apologizing for an incident in Nanjing in which a Japanese soldier slapped an American diplomat, "he claimed it was exceedingly difficult to make sure that orders issued by the High Command were carried out at once by the private soldiers."[91] Others found such claims to be credible. In 1940, a Japanese Foreign Ministry official said that Honma was "powerless" to rein in "ruffianly younger officers."[92]

Honma's main task was to rapidly transform the Philippines into a trans-port hub for troops, labor, and materiel for Japan's still-expanding opera-tions in the Southwest Pacific. Having already disappointed high command with his conduct of the invasion, he now had to figure out how to use ex-isting political authorities to exert control. If Honma and his staff were con-cerned with Allied POWs, and wanted them to suffer abuse and humilia-tion, one would expect similarity in treatment for those captured at different times and places. But the Camp O'Donnell men found that was not the case after meeting captives from Corregidor upon arrival at Cabanatuan. To be sure, having endured the three-month Bataan campaign, the march that followed, and O'Donnell itself, they had started out in worse condition. The Japanese shelling of Corregidor had been horrendous, but the men there were adequately fed and relatively disease-free during the siege. Yet they were also treated differently after they surrendered. They were able to shower after arriving at Bilibid. And rather than marching, these 9,000 POWs were transported the rest of the way by rail, some ninety-five miles north of Manila.

Perhaps because they had not suffered as much death and disease, the Corregidor captives dwelled on lesser indignities. Colonel Paul D. Bunker, a West Point man who had commanded artillery batteries, was "highly incensed" that "every American, officer or enlisted alike, must salute every Japanese soldier, regardless of rank." Engelhart explained that everyone in the IJA saluted each other, "even Japanese buck privates." Moreover, "as far as the Japanese were concerned," Engelhart continued, "one of their buck privates outranked an American general. I then told him that failure to salute might bring a rebuke with a rifle butt."[93] Bunker said that he would "be goddamned if he would salute a Jap buck private."[94] But he admitted that "quite a few men and officers had already been slugged."[95]

Engelhart knew that many times guards beat prisoners not at random, or because of sadism, but because they did not understand why their captives did not follow their orders. After all, many Imperial Japanese conscripts came from rural areas and previously had little or no contact with persons who did not speak Japanese. Bunker asked Engelhart if the Japanese were not familiar with the Geneva Conventions and Rules of International Warfare. Engelhart said that he would bet that "not a single Japanese on Corregidor had ever heard of the Geneva Convention." To most of them, the phrase "Rules of International Warfare would be regarded as some sort of impractical silliness."[96]

When an indignant Bunker insisted that American troops were POWs entitled to civil treatment, Engelhart claimed that the Japanese did not even have a term for POWs. This was not quite true. Ordinary Japanese troops on Corregidor simply called them "toriko," or captives. An educated person would have known "furyo," meaning prisoner, from the characters. Yet soldiers who used these terms did not understand that POW was a legal category entailing specific rights and responsibilities.[97]

Engelhart argued to Bunker that they just had to wait patiently and hope for passable food, shelter, and clothing. Bunker passed the word that all Americans would henceforth salute all Japanese. Engelhart emphasized that "most of all, we had to avoid creating any confrontation or crisis, if we hoped to survive."

As Engelhart feared, attempts by some Americans to escape occasioned the worst episodes of punishment. As in the British Army, US military regulations expected troops to make an effort to escape if possible, but Japanese regulations strictly prohibited such attempts, and punished them severely. Three Americans were caught trying to escape from Cabanatuan. "They were beaten, turned over to a Judo expert who proceeded to break arms and bones wholesale. The next day they were left tied up at the main gate all day, marched out that evening to a hole prepared by an American detail and were shot, standing by their grave."[98]

In another such episode, six men were executed without trial for alleged black market activities.[99] A witness claimed they were completely innocent and were chosen to discourage further illegal behavior. For most POWs, it mattered little whether such incidents resulted from a lack of recognition of their legal status, a desire to humiliate them in front of Filipinos, or the whims of sadistic individuals. One of them, Captain William J. (Jim) Fossey, recalled a Japanese sergeant, named Hihara, in charge of the farm at Cabanatuan Prison Camp who beat many American prisoners. "I myself was beaten mildly but many were beaten more severely for no reason at all." In other instances, beatings occurred for the same reason Engelhart had tried to communicate to Colonel Bunker: "Many times when an interpreter was not available, prisoners were beaten merely because they didn't understand the orders."[100]

Yet the main threat to prisoners was death from disease, and the fact that so many—especially from Camp O'Donnell—were already so weak. The death rate at Cabanatuan rose after they arrived, as the number of POWs swelled to 7,300. The camp had inadequate medicine and food, and the rainy climate attracted mosquitoes and flies.

In August 1942, four months after defeat, *Asahi Shimbun,* one of Japan's oldest national newspapers, reported that the IJA accorded Cabanatuan official status as a POW camp. That same month, Changi was given the same status. As in Singapore, they put a relatively senior commander, Major General Morimoto Iichirō, in charge of the main camp at Manila.[101] Also in that same month, the most senior American POWs, like Wainwright, were transported to Formosa.

The new Japanese camp commanders began to assume more responsibility, at least to the extent that they evinced concern about leaving a record that might implicate them in the killing of prisoners. By year's end the death rate in the camps fell, and they declined at a much lower pace over the next two years—not necessarily because of improved treatment, but at least in part because the sickest had already died. One reason commanders had begun to take more interest in POWs is that, under Tōjō's new policy, they had begun to look at them as a resource. The new camp commanders were under orders to put them to work. And because of labor shortages, as more Japanese men were called up to serve, a growing number of POWs were transported to work in war industries. After relatively small movements like the one that sent Wainright and about 180 others to Formosa, much larger transfers started in October 1942, with several ships departing Manila with 1,000 to 2,000 POWs at a time. The ships moved POWs to central nodes in Formosa and Moji, then delivered them to Korea, China, and Manchuria, or wherever their labor was most needed.[102]

The *Tottori Maru*, for instance, carried 1,992 men, and made stops in the Formosan port city of Takao (Gaoxiong), then Pusan (Busan), Korea, before finally arriving in Osaka. In Pusan, the men were paraded through the streets. But they were also given winter clothes and at least occasionally fed a hot meal. Even so, they were packed in tightly, driven deep into the hold at the point of bayonets, and several died from dysentery during the voyage. Many more would have perished if the captain had not managed to evade a torpedo attack. He also granted the officers' request to bury their dead at sea with appropriate ceremony, and even provided an American flag to do the honors.[103]

Most of the men on the *Tottori Maru* disembarked at Pusan and went by train to Manchuria, where they worked in Mukden. The rest ended up working in factories in Kawasaki. "Industry needed our labor," remembered Robert Phillips, a flight engineer captured at Mindanao. "The army brought us up there and rented us out."[104] In early November, another 1,482 prisoners sailed on the *Nagato Maru* from Manila bound for Japan. They included Richard Gordon, who had been captured at Bataan and was destined to spend the rest of the war building a hydroelectric power dam near Hiraoka. He too recalled how his ship narrowly escaped being sunk by torpedo just outside Manila. At first they were fed fish and rice, and then just rice. Eight POWs died on board and thirty-four were hospitalized. Even healthy men were exhausted after spending weeks in a dark hold, and were unfit for work when they finally reached their destination. POW camps' medical staff were sent to Kita-Kyushu to try to speed their recovery.

A postwar report by the Prisoner of War Information Bureau observed that such voyages were debilitating, presumably because the men were already in a weakened condition.[105] The submarine attacks were also harbingers of a growing danger. This was the case even though the *Nagato Maru* appears to have been marked as a POW transport—even though it carried an even larger number of Japanese troops.[106] The pace of these transfers from the Philippines slowed, and large-scale POW movements did not resume until the summer of 1944.

All of the ships carrying POWs have been called "hell ships," but the experience of those who sailed in 1942 was very different compared to the horrific conditions that awaited POWs who shipped out of Manila later in the war. In earlier voyages, the men were crammed into dark holds with little space, but at least some, like Phillips, were able to remain on the deck. Even those below did not report the suffocating conditions of later voyages. Rations were extremely limited, but POWs were at least occasionally given hot meals. And the main cause of death was from illness already contracted before POWs came on board. Most importantly, the Japanese were still able to effectively protect their own shipping.

Unlike the POWs, most interned civilians remained in the Philippines to sit out the war. About 7,800 men, women, and children were held at locations such as the University of Santo Tomas in the capital city, Camp John Hay in Baguio, central Luzon, or Los Baños. Like in Singapore, these internee camps were self-run. The largest had its own newspaper, the Santo Tomas *Campus Gazette*. In its January 17, 1943, edition, it estimated the number of internees at more than 3,600 persons: 2,280 Americans, 577 British, 34 Poles, 28 Dutch, one Mexican, one Cuban, and one Nicaraguan. Some 1,350 of them were women and children. There was a school with fifty kindergarteners, as well as teams for softball, football, basketball, volleyball, soccer, and boxing.[107] Whereas the Japanese rejected an American request for an ICRC visit to Cabanatuan, the Red Cross had some success in getting information out of Santo Tomas. The news was sometimes grim. In 1943, for instance, the ICRC reported that a British internee suffered a nervous breakdown and her ten-year-old daughter contracted tuberculosis.[108]

The Japanese high command now gave some consideration to the POWs, if only because they might serve the war effort. There was less interest in the internees. Formally, they were the responsibility of the Foreign Relations Section of the Fourteenth Army's Military Administration Section.[109] But according to Honma, his subordinates had informed him that internees wanted to live as they chose—paid for by themselves. In 1944, the ICRC reported that delegated internees bought their own food and "preferred this system."[110]

But what was happening in the Philippines outside the camps would inevitably affect what happened within. The Japanese officials in Manila continued struggling to institute an effective administration. The military sought to work with Japanese residents, many of whom had contacts and connections within the elite Filipino community. Kanagae Seitarō, head of the Nippon Bazaar and the National Rubber Corporation, became adviser to the Japanese Military Administration. Takahashi Torao, a sales agent of Osaka Bōeki, was in charge of rationing beer. Balintak Beer Brewery supplied civilians, and San Miguel's higher-quality brew went to the military. Others became head of fuel and vegetable plantations.[111] Japanese companies had to cooperate. The Ohta Development Corporation managed a slaughterhouse which supplied Japanese soldiers with meat, took over rubber plantations in Cotabato, and ran vegetable plantations in Calamba. They sought to provide familiar foods for the Japanese, who could not import them from Japan. Farms attempted to grow Formosan rice. The Furukawa Company was one of ten companies ordered to manufacture miso.

Japanese-language newspapers such as the *Manira Shimbun* and the *Davao Shimbun* meanwhile stressed that resident Japanese were supposed to provide a "model of deportment" for Filipinos. This became especially important when some did not. On December 18, 1942, after seven Japanese were accused of greed and selfishness, new standards for morality were issued. "It is time that the Japanese residents of the Philippines instill in their daily lives the confidence that we are a race destined to lead the weak throughout our entire 2,600 year history as a race."[112]

Japanese men were also conscripted, and those who did not pass the requirements, but did have fluency, were made to work as interpreters. In Davao, Japanese were organized into civil defense brigades and assigned relevant duties. Monetary "donations" were required, as was "voluntary" labor.[113]

By the end of 1942, Japanese officials had gotten rid of political parties and began the process of institutionalizing the occupation. On December 4, Vargas passed executive order No. 109, which established the KALIBAPI as a ruling party to foster local support. Wachi Takeji, director-general of the Japanese Military Authority (JMA) and number two in command of the occupation, was in charge. The KALIBAPI was largely based on the Imperial Rule Assistance Association (IRAA), the statist party organized by Konoe Fumimaro in 1940.[114] Although the KALIBAPI was described as a "nonpolitical service organization," joining required swearing loyalty oaths to the JMA and the Philippine Executive Commission. It was illegal to form any other such group, and working for the government required membership. Japanese leaders used the KALIBAPI to attract Filipino support.[115] They established neighborhood associations, censored the media, and spread Japanese culture and ideas through education, including the teaching of Japanese (though Tagalog was also allowed).[116] But just like the IRAA in Japan, the KALIBAPI was a top-down organization. Many Filipino men and women distrusted it. Some displayed contempt. One popular song had the tagline, "I'm a slaphappy Jappy, since I joined the KALIBAPI."[117]

The Japanese, for their part, complained that Filipinos were "self-indulgent, idle, fickle, and frivolous. They adore the United States and make light of us."[118] Nevertheless, Tōjō continued to promise independence for the Philippines, formalizing this policy in a January 14, 1943, meeting between Imperial Japanese Headquarters and Philippine representatives. Tōjō's main reason was pragmatic: Japan could not do less than the United States, which had already committed to Philippines independence by July 4, 1946.[119] Left unsaid was that this was independence on Japan's terms. Economic policy served Japanese war aims—the "liberation" of Asia.

Yet from the beginning, the occupation authorities had to contend with a guerrilla movement that worked to undermine their initiatives. Japanese frustration created an atmosphere that was increasingly dangerous for both POWs and internees. The guerrillas were split into two organizations: the US Army forces in the Far East guerrillas, who were ultimately under MacArthur's command, and the Hukbong Bayan Laban sa Hapon (HUKBALAHAP, The Nation's Army against the Japanese), who worked independently in central Luzon. HUKBALAHAP built on agrarian and labor movements that aimed to reform landlord-tenant relations and combat economic dependency. From early 1943, MacArthur's command tried to integrate these organizations, with limited success. But even when uncoordinated, the opposition mounted by the guerrilla resistance movement did succeed in frustrating occupation policies.[120]

On May 6, 1943, Tōjō made a state visit to Manila to pledge independence for the Philippines. According to Satō Kenryō, who traveled with him, Tōjō thought such personal visits were effective in unifying Southeast Asian people. Tokyo sought to use propaganda to stress how important the Philippines was to the Greater East Asia Co-Prosperity Sphere, sending Japanese reporters and entertainers and others to Manila.[121]

In mid-June, Tōjō announced that the Philippines would receive the "honor of independence" within the year.[122] In an attempt to cement relations between Japan and the Philippines, in June 1943, ten officers were chosen for extra study in Japan. Leocadio de Asis was among them, which made him ideally placed to observe how Filipino dignitaries like José P. Laurel, Jorge B. Vargas, and Benigno S. Aquino were received in Tokyo. De Asis observed during the visit that "President Laurel literally gave us a discourse on his views about our coming independence, emphasizing the fact that freedom from any source, whether from America or from Japan, does not make any difference provided it is real freedom."[123]

At the same time, a new military commander took charge of the Fourteenth Army: Kuroda Shigenori. He took a more aggressive approach against the guerrillas. From July to September 1943, he instituted increasingly severe "pacification campaigns" in the hope that the threat would be removed before Japan bestowed independence on the archipelago.[124] After September, each unit had "discretion" to "conduct punitive expeditions."[125]

Another strategy was the formation of a Philippine Constabulary to fight the guerrillas and keep the peace.[126] Based on an old prewar unit, the plan was to increase its pay and its numbers to 40,000 and establish regional training schools. But the Japanese military did not want to arm the Constabulary for fear that its weapons would end up in the hands of guerrillas. In fact, the United States had placed its own agents within their ranks.[127]

On October 14, 1943, the Republic of the Philippines was established in Manila, ostensibly granting Filipinos independence while keeping Japanese-appointed political elites in power. The Philippines was to be a unit of the Greater East Asia Co-Prosperity sphere. Jose P. Laurel was its first president, and Aquino became the speaker.

Ricarte was left out. Before returning to Manila in 1942, Ricarte had toured rural areas. As he observed the abuses and violence of Japanese soldiers, who seized food and commodities, and tortured suspects, he became alienated from the Japanese military administration. Before the war even began, the Philippines was not self-sufficient in food, importing rice, grains, and canned foods. Now shortages were growing more severe, and Filipinos did not have even daily necessities, such as food or fuel.[128] Filipinos were ordered to perform compulsory labor, and join neighborhood associations under threat of death.[129] As for Japanese civilians, because they knew local society, customs, and language, they were mobilized to help collect information and stamp out the insurgency.[130]

By 1944, it was becoming clear that the policy of winning over Filipinos to help make the archipelago a bulwark in the defense of Japan's new conquests was failing. Japanese civilians—though long resident in the Philippines—were increasingly seen as part of a more and more oppressive occupation. Escaped POWs and internees were joining the growing ranks of guerrillas, and coordinating with the US command in the Southwest Pacific. The Japanese Army HQ responded with increasingly brutal methods.

According to American intelligence, in January and March 1944, the Fourteenth Army issued orders that guerrillas who were captured or surrendered should be executed. The orders bore the seals of the Fourteenth Army and the Kaki Force. "All surrendered persons and captured prisoners of war are to be murdered on the battlefield and their bodies counted with those who have met with death in battle."[131] It was to be done in isolated places so there was no police or civilian eyewitnesses.[132]

But the Fourteenth Army—already spread thin in 1942—had grown weaker as the best units were redeployed to shore up Japanese positions elsewhere. Carrier-based assaults on Japanese bases at Truk and Rabaul demonstrated the ever-increasing range of Allied air and naval power, while amphibious landings on Tarawa and the Marshall Islands pierced the outer ring of Japanese defenses. The IJN committed most of its remaining carriers to what was meant to be a decisive engagement in June 1944, only to suffer massive losses in the Battle of the Philippine Sea.

By 1944, the number of POWs in the Philippines had decreased, largely because so many had been shipped elsewhere. At the beginning of the year, there was an equivalent number of POWs and other captives.[133] It was in this context that the Japanese resumed shipping large numbers of POWs out of the Philippines to work in war industries. Already hazardous in 1942, sailing out of Manila Harbor in the summer and fall of 1944 now meant sailing into sea lanes that were directly threatened by Allied aircraft, submarines, and surface units. The Hague Conventions called for clear markings to protect hospital ships. There was no provision to protect vessels carrying POWs. But the ICRC recommended multiple times that these ships should carry clear markings, and that POWs should not sail on vessels that also carried military supplies.

What the Japanese did not realize was that the Allies had succeeded in decrypting their communications, and that the codebreakers were providing the US Pacific Fleet with Japanese convoy coordinates.[134] The Americans were aware that POWs were being transported on unmarked ships, but this did not stop them from attacking the convoys.[135] At this point in the war it was clear that Japan would be defeated, but Washington went ahead and sunk POW transports anyway.

Even without the threat of attack, conditions for POWs on these ships could be harrowing. Many prisoners were already in poor medical condition. Ships were typically cramped and supplies were short, and those departing Manila in July endured extreme heat. One of these ships, the *Canadian Inventor*, carrying about 1,100 POWs, took two months to reach the seaport of Moji. While the voyage was difficult, and many suffered dysentery, perhaps only one perished.[136] Another ship, the *Nissyo Maru*, left Manila with 1,600 American POWs, and took only a little more than two weeks to reach the same destination. But men aboard faced even more extreme crowding and endured worse dehydration. There was also sheer terror, when other ships in the convoy were struck by torpedoes, blowing up a tanker.[137]

Far and away the greatest danger to POWs came from friendly fire.[138] The *Nissyo Maru* escaped the submarine attack, but not so the *Arisan Maru*, which departed Manila for Takao on October 21 and carried 1,783 American POWs. On October 24, the ship was attacked by American submarines. The USS Shark fired torpedoes and the Japanese freighter broke in two. All but nine of the POWs perished at sea. The sinking of the *Arisan Maru* by a US submarine was the largest loss of American POWs in the entire war.[139]

Starting in August 1944, American aircraft began carrying out bombing raids on the Philippines. On September 21, they bombed Manila itself. The following month, MacArthur waded ashore with American forces in Leyte, joining up with guerrillas. By November 1944, guerrilla forces were severely hampering Japanese military operations.[140]

For the Japanese, it made sense to continue shipping POWs out of Manila bound for Japan because POW labor represented a resource for war industries, and the Philippines was becoming a lost cause. In late October 1944, the Japanese decided to move most of the remaining POWs at Cabanatuan Camp No. 1 to Bilibid, eighty miles away in Manila. They were mainly American officers, some enlisted Medical Corps Personnel, and about 100 civilians.[141] Among them was Lieutenant Colonel Dwight Gard, who had started the war at 185 pounds with a 38-inch waist. He dropped to 135 at Cabanatuan and now, at Bilibid, weighed only 122 pounds, with a 22-inch waist.[142] Though many were similarly weak or disabled, the Japanese judged these 1,200 to 1,600 prisoners "transportable cases." Only those even worse off, about 500, were left at Cabanatuan.[143]

On December 13, 1944, the captives from Cabanatuan joined others from Bilibid.[144] The total contingent of 1,619 were divided into three groups, and the groups then boarded the *Ōryoku, Maru*. On December 14, US intelligence revealed that POWs with intelligence value were on the ship, and would be questioned on arrival to Japan. Allied attacks had already reduced the number of Japanese warships, and so they sailed with limited escort. The *Ōryoku* cargo included hundreds of Japanese troops, ammunition, trucks and other supplies. The ship had no Red Cross markings, and anti-aircraft guns.[145] Aboard were also Japanese men, women, and children "loaded down with scarf-wrapped parcels and straw cases."[146] According to Dwight Gard, the voyage got off to a decent start, with "usual rice plus fish and sea weed which was enjoyed." But two days later, the ship was bombed in Subic Bay in eight separate attacks. Japanese guards threatened to shoot into the hold unless there was "absolute silence," presumably so as not to attract US submarines. Gard described the resulting scene.

> A REAL HELL ON EARTH. Men raving, crawling naked in the darkness, covered with slime—eels—making speeches—threatening to kill, shouting at the Nips—men shouting at their enemies (whether real or imaginary I don't know)—defecating in place—drinking urine—stealing canteens—slashing wrists . . . and drinking their own blood. Many men were murdered—some for their blood, but more had their heads battered in with canteens because they couldn't keep quiet. Major K and I formed a

team to handle insane men crawling from rear part of the shelf. Tried to keep them from piling up and shutting off the air. Wrestled with dozens and quieted insane men but only hit one man—Capt. Whittenberg. The Nips did shoot into the hold but don't know if they hit anyone because we were in absolute darkness. . . . I was among the first 100 to climb out. . . . Nips shooting at swimmers from bank. Looters on the ship. Shots on the ship. Bomb wrecking aft hold. Fire aft. Scene on beach—naked except for girl's skirt. Angry Nip guards. Grove of trees—not permitted to get water. Planes return to bomb ship, then bomb harbor positions around Olongapo.[147]

Fossey offered a similar account of the same voyage:

We were crammed into a small hold on the Ōryoku Maru on decks that would not permit standing and no room to lie down. We were given no water or food after the first evening. American planes bombed and strafed the ship. Prisoners were frantic, insane, and dying of thirst. Many drank urine, some tried to suck blood from the wounded and dead. Latrine buckets were overflowing and yet the Nips kept threatening to shoot down the hold and cut off our meager air supply if we didn't quiet the crazy. Many prisoners committed suicide, some were killed by Americans and thus quieted, to keep the Jap from shooting down the hold.[148]

Of the 1,619 prisoners, about 250 were dead.[149] The death and destruction was not just of POWs. "The deck cabins were a shambles of dead and wounded Japanese civilians, men, women, and children. Fifty caliber machine gun bullets had ripped through the cabin walls everywhere, tearing up humans, luggage, and American Red Cross parcels."[150] Japanese military personnel and guards also died. Lieutenant Toshino told Engelhart that the worst wounded would go back to Bilibid to the hospital, but according to Engelhart, they never made it there. En route, they were beheaded.[151]

About three weeks later, on January 9, 1945, 350 of these POWs were killed in a bombing raid at Takao, Formosa. About 500 more died during the voyage from Formosa to Moji. Thus, only approximately 500 men, out of the original 1,619, were alive when the ship reached Moji on January 30, 1945.[152]

At least twelve ships sailed out of Manila after July 1944. Japanese and American official and private records disagree about how many ships were lost, and how many POWs and civilians—Japanese as well as American—died during these voyages.[153] Credible estimates range from a few thousand to over 20,000. When all the ships that carried Allied prisoners in the Pacific theater are counted, at least twenty-four vessels were sunk. Together they account for a large proportion of all POW deaths during the war.[154]

There were good strategic reasons for the Allies to rid the seas of Japanese shipping. It was a decisive factor in the Allied victory. Japanese commanders also bear responsibility, because they did not mark the ships. So too do the naval personnel who chose not to rescue American servicemen, and those who mistreated them, or killed them outright. But the primary reason that their mortality rate was so high was the American decision to torpedo the ships regardless of the risk to POWs.

In February 1945, when US forces marched on Manila, a month of warfare led to some of the worst atrocities of the war. The IJA faced hostile guerrillas, who they thought were armed.[155] As the Japanese began to lose ground, they came to believe that some civilians were spies, as in Okinawa. This is one reason why the Army began to target civilians.[156] They first refused to let Filipino citizens evacuate.[157] The Army then committed organized massacres, executing pro-American Filipino citizens after identifying them as guerrillas. Many others—Chinese, Americans, Spanish, Swiss, and Germans—died as well.[158] Some, like Swiss citizens, were simply caught in the crossfire.[159] But Japanese soldiers also killed twelve Swiss men and women in "appalling circumstances." A father and son were killed with grenades.[160]

On February 13, 1945, the Kobashi Corps issued new orders: "The U.S. Army invading Manila holds about 1,000 people in the artillery. In addition, a few thousands of Filipino guerrilla including women and children. Anyone on the field, except Japanese soldiers, citizens, and construction units. Just kill them all."[161] In many areas soldiers were ordered to kill citizens passing by Army camps.[162] Ultimately, about 100,000 civilians were killed in the battle for Manila.

Altogether, more than a million Filipinos were wounded or killed during the Japanese occupation of the Philippines.[163] Among the Japanese, about 80 percent of their troops (498,000 of 625,800) never returned.[164] Long after shortages of food and medicine continued to afflict the archipelago, starvation was common, and even the water buffalo were slaughtered.[165] The suffering of the Allied POWs, as considerable as it was, was only a part of that bigger picture.

The Japanese employed a bifurcated policy toward POWs in the same way they did in Singapore. Authorities eventually showed some concern for western POWs, and actually treated them better than the ostensible beneficiaries of the Greater East Asia Co-Prosperity Sphere. Filipinos who resisted were killed outright—including their acting president, Jose Abad Santos, and large numbers of partisans. But much of the suffering of Allied POWs and internees resulted from Japanese logistical failures and inadequate planning for camps, not prior intent. For all its military successes, Japan was never fully in control in the Philippines. Its policies were reactive. We see that with the experience of the POWs, but it was true of many other aspects of the occupation that were a higher priority for Tokyo, such as effectively enlisting Filipino elites in the new order.

What was not well known to those suffering in Southeast Asia was that throughout the war, diplomats in Washington, DC, London, Canberra, Tokyo, and Geneva showed more concern for their fate. The well-being of captives was never a priority for policymakers at the highest level, but POWs and internees were extremely important for purposes of mobilizing public and international opinion, as both sides resorted to ever more extreme measures to defeat their enemy.

# 4

## A WAR OF WORDS

Very few neutral observers were allowed into POW and internee camps, and even fewer could visit captives on both sides of the Pacific War. Swiss citizens—both diplomats and International Committee of the Red Cross (ICRC) delegates—were in the unique position of being allowed to observe. They were able to see conditions in different camps, provide material and financial aid, and mediate an intensifying exchange of recrimination and threats. Washington and Tokyo made claims and counterclaims about the observance or nonobservance of the Geneva Conventions. Swiss observers were placed in an impossible position, as both sides threatened and carried out reprisals and made their observance of international law conditional on the conduct of the enemy. It was a war of words, but it had deadly consequences for captives on both sides of the conflict.

When countries break off diplomatic relations and enter a state of hostilities, it is the protecting power that must make inquiries and look in on POWs and internees. In the twenty-first century, Sweden performs some of the functions of a protecting power for the United States in North Korea. During World War II, the United States relied on the government of Switzerland, a technically neutral country, to play this role in Japan.

On December 18, 1941, after Japan had first begun its assault on Malaya and the Philippines, the US State Department requested that the Swiss government inform Tokyo that the United States would follow the Geneva Convention of 1929 and, furthermore, apply it to Japanese civilians on the basis of reciprocity. Washington hoped that the Japanese government would follow suit.[1]

The Americans set up a new POW Bureau and an Alien Information Bureau in the Office of the Provost Marshal General to assemble lists of captives.[2] A "special division" of the State Department had already been established in 1939 to look out for the interests of American nationals in war zones. This division was in frequent contact with the Swiss government.[3]

The Japanese government, for its part, established a Prisoner of War Information Bureau (POWIB) on December 27, 1941, to meet Japan's Hague

Convention duties. Under the Ministry of War, the Bureau was responsible for creating ID cards to identify POWs, gathering lists of POWs, and transmitting them to the ICRC, the Swiss, and the other protecting powers. It was also supposed to manage the wills and personal possessions of deceased enemy combatants.

It was not until the end of January 1942, after isolating American and Filipino troops in the Bataan Peninsula, and while advancing down Malaya's east coast to lay siege to Singapore, that Tokyo informed the Swiss government that they would observe the Geneva Conventions on POWs, though they would be applying them mutatis mutandis.[4] Washington took this to mean that Japan had committed to the Geneva Convention of 1929, "The Convention Relative to the Treatment of Prisoners of War." But Tokyo was indicating that it would have to be adapted to changing circumstances.[5] The Japanese had not yet indicated how they would treat civilian internees.

The Swiss legation in Tokyo, headed by Camille Gorgé, would play a central role in this unfolding drama, as would the leaders of the International Committee of the Red Cross. As an international body, the ICRC provided services to both Allied POWs in Asia and Japanese POWs in the United States. Responsibilities of the ICRC during World War II in Asia were laid out in the Geneva Conventions, and included negotiating for official visits with POWs, visiting POW camps, obtaining and providing information on POWs, and delivering and sending mail. The main ICRC delegate active in Asia during the war was Dr. Frederic Paravicini.

Both Paravicini and Gorgé had extensive experience in Japan. This was the same Paravicini who had inspected German POWs during World War I.[6] Gorgé was a seasoned diplomat who had served as legal advisor to the Japanese Ministry of Foreign Affairs fifteen years earlier. He prided himself on his good relations with his Japanese counterparts. He held regular meetings with them, and had great faith in what diplomacy could accomplish.

Technically, the functions of the Swiss government as a protecting power and the services of the ICRC were different: the Swiss government covered diplomacy, and the Swiss-led ICRC provided relief to prisoners of war. During the war, which involved hundreds of thousands of captives, the line between diplomacy and relief was not always clear, and the two organizations had significant overlap in terms of personnel. Gorgé and Paravicini understood their responsibilities differently, viewed the Japanese government differently, and displayed different temperaments. Yet the two would have to work together in their roles as intermediaries.

Senior Japanese officials were themselves divided over how to treat Allied POWs. Matsumoto Shun'ichi, head of the Treaty Bureau of the Foreign Ministry, foresaw enormous challenges. But, he argued, this did not mean they could not "apply the principles of the Geneva Convention wherever possible, unless in situations where there were insurmountable difficulties involved." Both Matsumoto and Foreign Minister Tōgō Shigenori said that in the absence of "any crucial obstacles," the Geneva Convention would take precedence over domestic laws and regulations that came into conflict with its provisions.[7]

For Army Minister Tōjō Hideki, on the other hand, mutatis mutandis meant "necessary revisions of the principles of international conventions could be made in accordance with the demands of the immediate situation and in accordance with Japan's domestic law." One such law, dating to 1915, called for the death penalty for prisoners who attempted to escape. Tōjō and Lieutenant General Uemura Mikio, the first head of the Prisoner of War Management Bureau, approached the challenge of managing Allied prisoners as an unfair burden, since they believed Japanese soldiers would not—or at least should not—surrender. The Japanese Red Cross, for its part, opposed Japan's proposal to apply the convention mutatis mutandis. Based on the experience of fighting in China, they thought it would be better to reject the American proposal than to risk condemnation for violating Conventions Japan had never ratified.[8]

At least some senior Japanese officials intended to follow the Geneva Conventions. But not nearly enough was done to act on that intention. In his postwar testimony, Odashima Tadashi, the chief secretary of the Prisoner of War Information Bureau, had no recollection of the War Ministry giving any specific instructions, and only a small proportion of War Ministry officials and theater commanders even knew that Japan had agreed to comply with the Geneva Conventions "mutatis mutandis."[9] On balance, the policy could be seen as a diplomatic dodge.

Japanese commanders were given broad latitude in the field. But the same was true on the American side, at least at the outset of hostilities. As we have seen, MacArthur put Japanese internees to work digging air raid trenches, in violation of the Geneva Conventions.[10] On February 1, 1942, after MacArthur heard reports that American civilians were subjected to "abuse and special humiliation" by imperial Japanese soldiers to "discredit the white races," he urged using interned Japanese as a "lever under the threat of reciprocal retaliatory measures to force decent treatment for interned [American] men and women." Secretary of War Henry L. Stimson agreed that the United States should "present the threat of reprisals." On February 2, the State Department demanded an investigation of Japanese conduct through Swiss intermediaries and warned that, depending on what they found, the United States might reconsider how, until then, it had treated Japanese nationals with "the most liberal treatment consistent with national safety."[11]

The Swiss were reluctant to take on Tokyo, as Arthur de Pury, chief of the Division of Foreign Interests, explained to the US chargé in Bern, J. Klahr Huddle. Japan had refused to provide any information from Manila, and divested their honorary consul there of his official status. Switzerland therefore had no way to make inquiries even about their own nationals. When Huddle pressed, suggesting that Bern could point out how neutral states were looking after Japanese in the United States, de Pury agreed that Tokyo was being unreasonable, but the Swiss had to protect their own interests: "Switzerland as [a] small neutral country should consider Japanese action as one of military necessity and make no representations against it."[12]

Swiss diplomats could still represent US interests in Japan proper, including Korea and Manchuria, and also Shanghai, Saigon, and Bangkok.[13] But for the remainder of the war, Gorgé struggled to get information on US nationals in other Japanese-occupied territories.

In mid-February, the Japanese Ministry of Foreign Affairs informed both the Swiss legation in Tokyo and the ICRC that it would apply the Geneva Conventions to civilian internees "on condition of reciprocity and as far as they are applicable."[14] It noted that Japan was actually treating those internees better than the Conventions required, because they could receive food and clothing from the outside and leave camps when conditions permitted.[15]

Reports about the situation of Allied internees varied greatly, but early on London voiced concern about captives in Hong Kong. The US State Department replied on March 14 that information from the Swiss government and the ICRC did not "give cause for alarm." In fact, it "indicates that the Japanese government is conforming to its undertaking" to apply the Geneva Conventions to both POWs and civilians on the basis of reciprocity. The State Department also reassured members of the public. One official noted that reports "do not indicate that American prisoners of war in Japanese hands are being mistreated." He further explained that "the treatment of Japanese prisoners of war and other Japanese nationals in the United States will naturally be influenced by the treatment accorded American prisoners of war and other American nationals under Japanese control," and that the Swiss had been asked to investigate.[16]

Reciprocity thus meant that Washington made the Swiss responsible for determining whether the United States should retaliate against Japanese and Japanese-American civilians. The War Department did not wait to find out. In February 1942, it was already moving ahead with mass roundups. On February 14, General John L. DeWitt, head of the Western Defense Command, recommended removal of "Japanese and other subversive persons," language indicating they were viewed as subversive *because* they were Japanese.[17] MacArthur's attitudes and events in the Philippines likely influenced DeWitt, since he had done three tours there. Five days later, President Roosevelt issued Executive Order 9066, which authorized the secretary of war and military commanders to designate areas "from which any or all persons may be excluded."[18] On March 22, Japanese-American residents of Los Angeles were sent to live in hastily constructed barracks in Manzanar, an arid, abandoned town over 200 miles to the north. This was just the first of many large-scale removals, which included both first-generation Japanese immigrants (*issei*) and their children (*nisei*).

Even so, five days later the State Department assured Spanish diplomats—who would have relayed this assurance to Tokyo—that the United States wished "to avoid mass internment."[19] But FDR was under enormous political pressure to act. In Los Angeles local officials were incensed upon hearing reports that Japanese who were longtime residents of the Philippines had landed with the invaders and lent them support in their conquest.[20] Secretary of War Stimson maintained that a Japanese invasion of the West Coast was a real possibility. Both he and Roosevelt were skeptical that people of Japanese descent could be true Americans.[21]

Whatever the motives, the internment of some 117,000 people of Japanese descent in the spring of 1942—often under harsh conditions, with little or no opportunity to sell their property—was bound to influence authorities in Tokyo. So were reports of vigilante violence, including attacks on Japanese homes and two deaths.[22] Material conditions for internees of Japanese descent in the United States were better than those experienced by most European and American internees in Asia. But some aspects of their situation—such as the fact that many were citizens—could make it no less wrenching.

Even without such provocations, it was difficult for Japan to accommodate Allied expatriates in the style to which many had grown accustomed. In 1941 Gorgé had already reported that Japan's Foreign Ministry had provided assurances of good treatment, but explained that "Japanese people are poor and contented with little from which facts arise difficulties concerning treatment of foreign internees."[23] Daily life for Japanese had grown increasingly difficult even before Tokyo went to war against the Western Allies. Winter fuel was scarce and expensive, and would-be shoppers faced long queues at bakeries, greengrocers, and butchers.[24]

The April 1942 Doolittle raid was intended to shake Japanese morale. It did scant damage to their military and industrial targets, but scattered bombs hit several schools and a military hospital. The Americans—including Doolittle himself—hoped that Japanese would understand the raid as a foretaste of the revenge that awaited them.[25] Tokyo decided to treat captured American flyers as war criminals. It would be some time before the Japanese attitude toward captured airmen was known in London, Canberra, and Washington. The Japanese showed far more concern about civilian internees. In May 1942, the Japanese Ministry of Foreign Affairs asked the US State Department whether internees in the United States could receive funds from family, draw on their bank accounts, or sell their property, as, they claimed, Allied internees in Japan were allowed to do. Tokyo even claimed to provide living expenses for those who had no means of subsistence, and expected reciprocal treatment.[26]

Initial reports on Allied internees from the ICRC appeared to confirm that, while conditions were sometimes Spartan, there was no systematic abuse. In July 1942, the State Department received an ICRC report detailing conditions in Kobe. At one camp, internees could play tennis and volleyball and had excursions twice weekly, but were still gaining weight because of their generous rations. Internees at another camp had three good meals a day prepared by Japanese cooks, and played billiards and ping-pong. At the third and fourth camps, conditions were tougher. Internees from Guam had tropical-weight clothing and shoes that were inappropriate for Kobe's colder climate. The funds provided by the Swiss were insufficient to buy warmer attire. Even so, the sick received adequate care and camp commandants were thought to be doing their best.[27]

Internees who were subsequently released described a variety of situations. Charles Copp, a teacher in a Japanese university near Matsuyama, reported that he had had "really excellent food."[28] The police officer in charge was "always friendly, kind and courteous. He gave us as much freedom as he dared." In fact, many foreign residents were not interned in camps at all, but were confined to their homes or even allowed to move about freely—more freely than Japanese and Japanese Americans on the West Coast. This included several hundred American, British, and Dutch residents in Shanghai.[29]

The earliest reports of treatment concerned civilian internees, but some of those released in exchanges came back with reassuring news about American POWs. Marian Olds, a nurse captured at Guam, was held at Zentsuji, in the center of a large training camp. She reported there was enough space to play catch, and meals consisted chiefly of rice and some fish. She pointed out that the diet was short in vitamins and fats, but offered no criticism of it. Observing GIs, Olds's impression was that they received treatment "on a par with that afforded Japanese soldiers in base camps."[30] Similarly, Paravicini reported to the ICRC that the Japanese seemed to do their best for the prisoners but "they themselves are content with little and this has to influence the living conditions in the camps."[31]

Japanese officials could read every word of the ICRC reports, which tended to discourage the inclusion of criticism. They also limited the ICRC to camps in Japan, Korea, Shanghai, and Hong Kong. The Swiss were not allowed to visit the camps in Malaya, the Philippines, or anywhere close to the fighting, despite repeated demands by Washington.[32] Because the Swiss could not go to where the worst abuses took place, their reports created a misleading impression. This helps explain why—after reassuring the American public and their British allies—Washington and then London reacted so strongly when they later learned about what was happening in places like Bataan and the Thai-Burma Railway.

The United States, for its part, claimed to allow representatives of the protecting power and the ICRC to visit all Japanese captives.[33] No one told the Swiss about a secret detention center near Stockton, California, where high-value POWs were interrogated.[34] Yet Tokyo was informed about some violent incidents through a report from civilian internment centers. Between May and July 1942, US guards on three separate occasions shot Japanese internees attempting to escape, killing three of them. And 117,000 Japanese were already ordered into custody, in or on their way to relocation centers, contrary to the assurance that the United States did not plan mass detentions.

In July 1942, the vice minister of war issued Japanese Army Secret Order 2190, which specified that flyers who did not violate the international law of war would be treated as POWs. Those who violated the international law of war were to be tried in a military tribunal.[35] The order became law in August, but was not announced until months later. This is also when the Japanese informed the Swiss minister that Japan would not recognize their representation of foreign interests in occupied territories.[36] In Shanghai, visits to camps required the permission of local commanders. In Saigon, the Swiss consul was told that—because of escape attempts—Japanese military authorities would not permit it.[37]

State Department officials at the Special Section, the officials responsible for dealing with captives, concluded that Tokyo was keeping a scorecard. When Japanese nationals suffered injustice in the United States, Japanese forces inflicted punishment on their American captives.[38] A September 23 telegram from Bern provided further proof. It reported that the Japanese government would intern more US citizens because the United States had provided no list of interned Japanese. According to the Swiss minister, if Washington provided more information, he would have a greater chance of helping interned Americans.[39]

In fact, it was really the Japanese military that decided such matters.[40] Gorgé repeatedly noted that the Foreign Ministry would have granted more concessions. For Japanese commanders, on the other hand, Allied prisoners and internees were a low priority, and they had little understanding of the ICRC and its activities.

The agencies set up to provide information to the ICRC and protecting powers, and more generally manage POW camps, were weak and internally divided. The head of the Prisoner of War Information Bureau (POWIB) and the Prisoner of War Management Office (POWMO)—the same person led both—had no command authority and relatively few personnel, and none of the three officers who held the position were particularly skilled as bureaucratic operators. The POWIB was parallel to the Military Affairs Bureau (MAB), itself a very powerful bureau, far more powerful than the small and temporarily created POWIB.[41] Many military commanders did not even submit information about POWs. With only twenty-five staff in 1941 and twenty-eight in June 1942, the POWIB did not have the manpower to manage even the reports it did receive.[42] To do anything, the POWIB

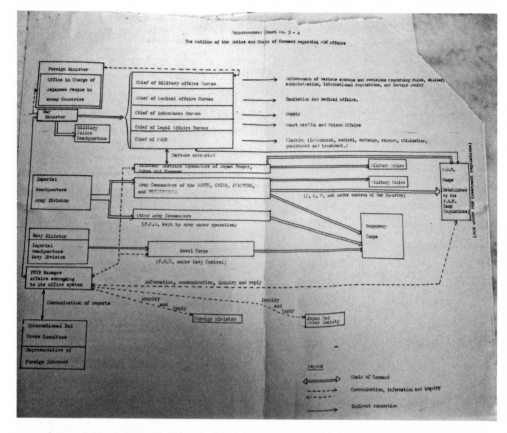

An organizational chart of the Prisoner of War Information Bureau. The interrelationships among departments and agencies responsible for POWs was so tangled and complex that Allied officials made many such charts to determine the chain of command. Even if senior officials wished to intervene and improve conditions in camps, it was unclear how to effect change. (US National Archives and Records Administration.)

needed the approval of the MAB. Any orders had to go through the Army Ministry, which issued the commands.[43]

The POWMO had an even bigger job, being in charge of planning logistics for handling POWs, but was even more inadequate to the task. Like the POWIB, it lacked strong political allies within the War Ministry. It is estimated that Japanese forces eventually set up some 378 camps, stretching from the Aleutian Islands to Burma to New Guinea. Yet the POWMO had direct responsibility for just sixteen main POW camps and 100 detached camps, all of them Army camps in Japan and its colonies.[44]

The head of the two agencies was never in the chain of command, and basically fulfilled a bureaucratic and managerial role: compiling, storing, and transmitting reports. He visited camps, structured ICRC visits, and issued guidance. Camp commanders, more focused on their direct reports, could decide whether to follow them. He could advise the War Ministry to issue binding orders, but if he had advised better treatment, he likely would have lost any influence, or lost his job.

Many sources attest to the fact that field commanders were surprised and unprepared for the large number of Allied prisoners who were suddenly in their care. Japanese forces were stretched thin over a wide geographic area, separated by thousands of miles of open ocean.[45] This made transport and communication difficult at the best of times, and especially when Allied aircraft and submarines were attacking the Japanese navy and merchant marine. After 1943, when the Japanese mainland suffered food shortages, authorities decided that diverting supplies to sustain POWs would "act to serve the interest of the enemy." Even the Japanese Red Cross needed to give priority to the needs of the military.[46]

Experienced and skilled governance was another problem. Camp commandants, many of whom were near or past retirement age, managed guard units that were dumping grounds for those found unfit for front-line duty—whether because of their low quality, illness, or injuries.[47] Many Korean and Taiwanese guards served as "civilian military employees"—that is, they were not proper soldiers of the Imperial Japanese Army. Some volunteered for service, in some cases driven by poverty, while the police strong-armed others.[48]

Even Korean men specifically recruited as guards received little training. Commanders told them that because they were physically smaller than most prisoners, they should use corporal punishment to keep them in line.[49] With little or no knowledge of prisoners' languages or customs, guards employed violence to maintain control.

Many prisoners were kept close to the front and on the move. As we have seen, the Japanese government did not classify them as POWs—and thus protected by the Geneva Conventions—until they were formally admitted to a camp under the administration of the Ministry of the Army. Until then, captives were the exclusive responsibility of the local commander who captured them. Neither did the POWMO have control of the conditions in which POWs were transported by sea. Many captives who died on ships never came under its purview.[50]

Those who represented the Japanese government were not themselves in control of or even aware of the conditions in which the captives lived. In the months that followed, Allied captives were shifted between many different kinds of camps depending on the vicissitudes of war and the need for prisoners' labor. Some who worked in the war industry even became the charges of private companies. And the management of civilian internees was no less complex. The POWMO managed civilian internees in Southeast Asia and the South Pacific, the Home Ministry handled those in Japan and Korea, and the Great East Asia Ministry (Daitō A shō) handled those in China. The Foreign Ministry was responsible for receiving requests from the protecting powers to visit individual camps and detention centers.

A simple request for the number and location of civilian internees was therefore not so simple, as Paravicini discovered in August 1942. Responsible for distributing some 7,000 relief packages from the American, Canadian, and South African Red Cross societies, he had to make rough estimates of what percentages should go to Japan and its many far-flung conquests, stretching from Shanghai to the East Indies. He reported being told that there were about 20,000 internees, and realized "it will take time, trouble and luck to get the right goods in the right proportions to the right places." In fact, there were more than 100,000 civilians interned just in the Dutch East Indies.[51]

Although Paravicini clearly needed help, it was a logistical challenge for the ICRC even to transport a new delegate to Asia. It required official recognition from the Japanese government and travel authorization on a ship bringing diplomats to Japan.[52] A newcomer had to know the country and its language, and be willing to challenge Japanese authorities. Moreover, it was thought that Paravicini would react badly if he thought he was being replaced.[53] And so the Swiss Foreign Affairs Department—on Gorgé's advice—agreed that Paravicini should take on one of the unemployed Swiss to work as an ICRC delegate in Japan.[54]

Paravicini required Japanese permission to deliver Red Cross boxes to the camps. With the August 1942 shipment to Singapore, for example, relief packages were loaded onto the *Asama Maru* and delivered into the hands of the Japanese Army. The Swiss there could play no part because they had no official status.[55] Instead, the Japanese Red Cross handled the goods under the direction of the Japanese military.[56] Once they reached the camps, matters were wholly beyond the control of relief workers. Some POWs received goods and mail, but many, if not most, did not. In 1943, the

ICRC resorted to smuggling vitamins to the Far East via Turkey and Romania.[57]

While the differences in the respective mandates of Switzerland as a protecting power and the ICRC seemed clear, dividing their responsibilities and coordinating their activities in the field proved impossible. In 1942, the Swiss and the ICRC agreed to cooperate in gathering lists of POWs and civilian internees and coordinating camp visits. The protecting power had exclusive responsibility for transmitting documents, such as death certificates, and in representing POWs or internees in any legal proceeding. But everything else was up for grabs. In principle the ICRC distributed material relief, such as packages and books, except when the interested parties asked the protecting power to do it. The protecting power seemed better positioned to provide financial relief, but the ICRC and national Red Cross sometimes took on this role too. Given the varied conditions delegates encountered, the ICRC explained that "no strict general rule can be established."[58] They were responsible for transmitting individual prisoners' demands, though the protecting power could also intervene. Repatriation of the sick or wounded could be undertaken by the ICRC, the protecting power, or both at the same time.

The overlap in mandates created confusion right from the start of the war in Europe. For instance, foreign governments were supposed to go through their national Red Cross committees to communicate with the ICRC, but they often approached the Swiss government instead.[59] Switzerland also gave the ICRC financial, material, and diplomatic support, and Swiss diplomats offered the services of the ICRC and monitored its activities. Because of the challenge of sending messages during wartime, Swiss diplomats often served as the ICRC's communications bureau. It was all too easy for foreigners to think the two were one and the same.[60]

Unlike the Swiss government, the ICRC accepted no limit to its mission. As an ICRC 1942 memorandum declared, it could "take any initiative it sees fit in the interest of prisoners or of internees."[61] Max Huber, president of the ICRC, offered the following opinion: "If Switzerland's role is to bilaterally manage the interests of the majority of the belligerent countries, then the ICRC's job is to watch over all the POWs and civil internees regardless of their nationality."[62]

Unfortunately for an organization with such an expansive vision, the ICRC was small and poorly run. Slow or interrupted communications and the frequent need for improvisation meant that personalities rather than formal procedure often dominated the decision-making process. Bureaucratic rivalries and the poor health of key individuals—beginning with Huber himself, and later Paravicini—had an outsized impact.[63] When the Allies were drawn into the Asia-Pacific War, the overlapping goals and mandates of Switzerland and the ICRC grew to be global in scope.

Neither the ICRC nor Swiss diplomats were able to obtain a complete list of POWs from the Japanese, despite repeated requests in 1942 and 1943. At this point it was unlikely that the POWIB itself possessed this information. Military commanders moved prisoners from camp to camp, and their number at any particular site could also fluctuate due to deaths or hospitalizations.[64] Even when Gorgé and Paravicini had the names and location of POWs, a request to see them followed a convoluted process. The request first went to the Ministry of Foreign Affairs, then the War Ministry, and then the Prisoner of War Management Office. Although the POWMO ostensibly decided on these visits, they were made according to Army policy and in consultation with the chief of the Military Affairs Bureau. It was the General Staff and front line commanders, citing military security, who vetoed visits outside Japan, Korea, and China. At a meeting of the bureau chiefs in 1942, War Minister Tōjō stated that the representative of the protecting powers could not visit places like the Philippines until the end of the war.[65]

Even if Japan had given the Swiss and the ICRC the right to inspect all camps across Japan's expanding empire, to process and deliver mail and packages, to ensure medical care, and manage property and legal affairs, the Swiss were completely inadequate to the task. Paravicini asked for patience from his superiors, explaining that everything he asked of a Japanese ministry, no matter how small, required multiple requests, many meetings, and "a lot of paperwork."[66] As early as February 1942 he asked to be relieved of any responsibility for civilian internees. The Swiss Foreign Ministry pleaded with the ICRC not to saddle Gorgé with all of the work.[67]

Gorgé's main job in Tokyo, after all, was to represent Switzerland and to protect Swiss national interests, not Allied POWs and internees. Gorgé struggled to track down Swiss citizens scattered across the Japanese empire and its newly conquered territories. The task was all the more difficult now that Switzerland had lost consulates in Manila, Hong Kong, Singapore, Medan, Jakarta, and Batavia. In June 1942, one Swiss diplomat was sent to Taiwan to wind up the affairs of the US and British consulates. He died in mysterious circumstances on his return voyage. The Japanese authorities declared it a suicide, but Gorgé and his colleagues believed there had been foul play, and the Japanese had reason to remove an "embarrassing witness."[68] In September, a Swiss citizen—the first of several—was arrested on suspicion of working for a foreign power.[69] The next month, the Japanese arrested eighteen Swiss in the Dutch East Indies, the same month that Japanese soldiers allegedly shot a Swiss Catholic missionary stationed in the Gilbert Islands.[70]

Despite such incidents, ICRC delegates had to remain strictly neutral. Paravicini believed they could not otherwise carry out their work. Gorgé, on the other hand, saw Switzerland's role as protecting power as requiring him to advocate for American interests. He became increasingly disgusted with the ICRC's inability or unwillingness to protest Japanese conduct, to the point that ICRC delegates could hardly bring themselves to mention the Geneva Conventions because of the angry reaction it typically provoked. This was why, according to Gorgé, Tokyo gave them favored access to camps and discriminated against him and other Swiss diplomats.[71] When the Red Cross finally obtained permission to send delegates to the Philippines, the Japanese could more easily refuse Swiss government requests to send their own inspectors.

Even in those camps they could visit, neither the ICRC nor the Swiss legation were ever able to interview prisoners without guards or the commandant being present. In May 1942, Paravicini admitted that his reports "usually emphasized the positive aspects," claiming that "it actually benefits the prisoners taken by the enemy and doesn't harm the prisoners here even if they don't like reading propaganda in the local press that we have described the camps like heavens on earth."[72] He believed, in other words, that emphasizing the positive encouraged good behavior. In fact, after having been told that their own government was scrupulously respecting international law toward POWs, the Japanese public would be all the more furious about alleged Allied war crimes.

After Japanese radio and newspapers publicized numerous stories that POWs were being treated too well, Lieutenant Colonel Akiyama Kunio of the Imperial General Headquarters Communications Department responded on the radio. He criticized members of the upper class for their sympathy to POWs, and said they were trying to avoid the war. He argued that it was impossible to be headed for victory, even if enemy ships were destroyed, while the United States remained in people's hearts. Lieutenant

Colonel Akiyama singled out a woman who said "okawai-sō ni" (what a pity) about Allied POWs. She became known as Ms. "Okawai-sō ni."[73]

The Japanese military leadership warned that "any member of the crew of enemy aircraft who is found to have committed cruel and inhuman acts shall be tried before a military court and suffer death or other severe penalty." The press alleged that the Doolittle raiders had machine-gunned children playing near a school. An article in the newspaper *Nichi-Nichi* recommended that captured airmen be beheaded without discrimination. According to Japanese radio broadcasts, authorities had already tried American airmen in military tribunals and sentenced them to death. Without hard information, Washington pressed the Swiss diplomats in October 1942 for answers: Had they been permitted to visit the prisoners? Were the flyers already dead?[74]

Washington lodged an emphatic protest, and asked the Swiss to repeat the demand that Japan adhere to the Geneva Conventions. According to Hull's December message, the "Japanese Government has not previously indicated to this Government that it would apply provisions of Geneva Prisoners of War Convention of 1929 only to [the] extent that its provisions do not change the effect of Japanese laws in force." In fact, back in February 1942, Tokyo had informed Gorgé that it would apply them mutatis mutandis, and Gorgé passed this information along to Washington. It is not clear whether the Americans were feigning surprise or were genuinely shocked at these events.[75]

The Japanese replied that prosecuting those who had admitted to cruel and inhuman attacks on innocents was a moral act intended to minimize the horrors of war. Even so, they commuted death sentences in certain cases. But the note did not say which ones, or answer the request for visits by the Swiss minister. Tokyo pledged to treat aviators who raided Japan as POWs, but only if they did not commit war crimes.[76]

When Washington finally replied in February 1943, almost two months later, it marked another escalation in this war of words:

> If . . . the Japanese Government has descended to such acts of barbarity and manifestations of depravity as to murder in cold blood uniformed members of the American armed forces made prisoners as an incident of warfare, the American government will hold personally and officially responsible for those deliberate crimes all of those officers of the Japanese Government who have

participated in their commitment and will in due course bring those officers to justice.[77]

The Americans, for their part, denied that they had "intentionally attacked non-combatants anywhere." It was true that the Army Air Force was still committed to the elusive goal of "precision bombing." Yet before the war began, Chief of Staff George C. Marshall himself warned that American bombers would "set the paper cities of Japan on fire."[78] This began in earnest once the deployment of the B-29 bomber brought them within range.

More and more, the exchanges between Washington and Tokyo via Swiss intermediaries became a dialogue of the deaf: The Americans continually accused Japan of war crimes and "cruel inhumane treatment," citing increasingly detailed reports by escapees, liberated POWs, and exchanged civilians.[79] The Japanese, for their part, pointed to the transport of Japanese nationals from Latin America for internment in remote regions of the United States, the separation of interned Japanese men from their families, and the shootings of POWs and interned civilians who tried to escape.

Upon reading reports of the violent suppression of riots at the Tule Lake detention center in November 1943, Tokyo cut off negotiations for any further internee exchanges. And after Japanese internees started a hunger strike and made a direct appeal for protection, Tokyo announced in March 1944 that it would intern US civilians in Shanghai in retaliation. This might have merely been a pretext.[80] But despite taking on the role of protecting power for Japanese interests in the mainland United States, Spanish diplomats did not report every alleged incident of mistreatment of Japanese internees, precisely so as to avoid provoking such reprisals, suggesting that they did have an impact.[81]

On both sides there were those who sought to deescalate this war of words. Washington delayed publicizing Japanese atrocities against POWs, in part because Roosevelt wanted to make sure the Red Cross could continue to do its work, and also out of concern that crossing this threshold might increase the likelihood of further executions. Yet beginning in 1944, the suffering and death of POWs would become a constant theme in Allied propaganda. The Office of War Information used their plight to accomplish specific political goals. It judged that it would "serve to nullify any voices that might be raised here if we should undertake bombing of Japanese cities," a view backed by joint staff planners.[82] Ironically, these bombings took a heavy toll on POWs themselves, as we shall see.

Similarly, the Special Division of the State Department had long warned that continuing to separate Japanese men from their families would provoke retaliation. They also struggled long and mightily to change the US Army's shoot-to-kill policy against attempted escapes. But they were largely incapable of changing the way the Army ran internment camps.[83] Neither could they control the behavior of American soldiers in the field, such as those who did not "treat with due respect the remains of fallen Japanese soldiers." The Marines even used the remains of Japanese men in a recruiting advertisement. The State Department could only assure Tokyo that it did not "countenance such depravity."[84]

The Japanese POWIB was similarly powerless. It asked the Japanese Army to provide casualty reports, sought information on court-martials, and tried to help the Swiss visit camps in Southeast Asia and the South Pacific. It also sought to have prisoners captured on the front lines quickly taken into official POW camps. The POWIB did not inform Gorgé of court-martials of the POWs in advance because they did not themselves have advance notice.[85] The War Ministry subsequently stopped the POWIB from giving the protecting powers information regarding the fate of convicted POWs. The chief of the POWIB advised the War Ministry and general staff that flyers should be treated as POWs even if they had committed crimes against humanity, but this opinion was rejected.[86]

Much of this information comes from postwar interviews with officials in the POWIB and the POWMO who were anxious to absolve themselves of any wrongdoing. Yet the ICRC itself judged that the Prisoner of War Information Bureau was in "bad odor with the military High Command because it sends in too many questions and requests which appear to have no vital connection with the prosecution of the war."[87] Moreover, much of the POWIB archive survived the war, and it provides ample evidence that the POWIB was relatively powerless to carry out the many requests of the Swiss legation and the ICRC.[88]

Personnel problems also continued to plague the ICRC. Paravicini, already in poor health, died in January 1944. His longest-serving assistant, Max Pestalozzi, seemed cowed by the Japanese. And Japanese authorities would have nothing to do with the ICRC delegate in Shanghai. The Red Cross representative in Hong Kong, Robert Zindel, had the opposite problem: his every move and every message were closely monitored, and he was never permitted to speak to prisoners.[89]

Gorgé argued that the ICRC had failed in Japan, claiming that it was only because he pressed the Ministry of Foreign Affairs that the ICRC was able to visit any camps at all.[90] The legation also kept far better records and statistics for POWs. When the ICRC needed information on a prisoner, they had to come to him.[91] Gorgé claimed that, unlike the ICRC, he never failed to point to injustices committed against the internees, even when it jeopardized his relationship with the Japanese Foreign Ministry.[92] Worst of all, the ICRC actually provided cover for Japan to continue disregarding the Geneva Conventions. He pointed out that the Japanese press made selective use of their reports to claim that prisoners were well treated.[93]

The Allied-Japanese war of words finally broke out into the open in January 1944, when British foreign secretary Anthony Eden spoke before the House of Commons on the "barbarous nature of our Japanese enemy." Despite knowing the obligations of a "civilised Power," as evidenced by the treatment of prisoners in the Russo-Japanese war, they now subjected their captives to "unspeakable savagery," and it was time to "make public the facts."[94] US secretary of state Cordell Hull also charged the Japanese with "cruelty," "inhumanity," and "fiendishness."[95] Canadian prime minister James Allison Glen stated before the House of Commons that "the evidence of Japanese brutality and organized sadism is so horrible and overwhelming as to be almost incredible."[96]

The press reacted swiftly. Washington "was full of a spirit of revenge," according to the *New York Times*. The chairman of the House Military Affairs Committee, Andrew J. May, suggested they should immediately dispatch the fleet and "blow Tokyo off the map." But Congress also demanded to know why abuses of prisoners had been kept secret.[97] In a February 2 editorial, the *Washington Post* agreed: "Why our military authorities, in the light of this knowledge, imagined if we hid the news of Japanese savagery there would be better treatment is a mystery. Why the diplomatists repeated the long course of fruitless note-writing which characterized our prewar dealings with Japan is equally curious. Hope, of course, springs eternal. But it is time we realize that it is primitive man we are dealing with."[98]

Of course, families of captives could not give up hope. After being given reassurances early in the war, to now hear that the Japanese were treating their loved ones with "unspeakable savagery" filled them with anguish. These families were all over the world, since colonial armies included

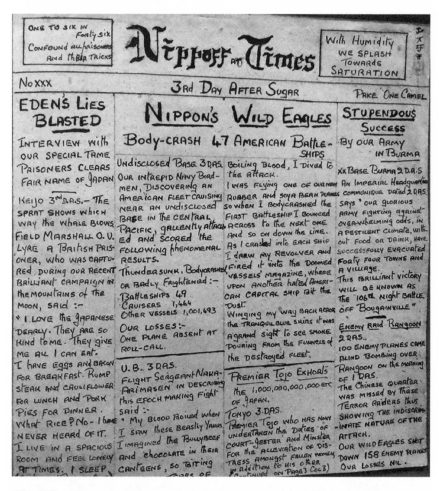

"Nippoff Times," a parody of a Japanese propaganda newspaper. Some POWs eventually became aware of the escalating debate about their fate between Allied and Japanese leaders. But at least initially it made little difference in their circumstances, other than as a source of amusement at the way it was reported. (Lancashire Infantry Museum.)

enlistees from dozens of different countries. As one Irishman, Ignatius Gregson, wrote to his government in Dublin: "As the father of a son in the Royal Air Force, now a prisoner of war in Japanese hands, we are naturally very worried after Mr. Eden's disclosures . . . why don't the three Catholic countries, Ireland, Spain, and Portugal do or say something?"[99]

With the release of long-held information to the public, the Roosevelt administration had intended to shame Tokyo into cooperating with prisoner exchanges and shipment of relief goods. The State Department sent an eighteen-page diplomatic note detailing atrocities that could be prosecuted after the war. But the Japanese answered by making their own charges, describing at even greater length abuses at the internment camps in the United States, such as internees who had been beaten and hospitalized.[100] The State Department replied that if Tokyo really cared about their internees, they would be doing more to improve conditions in Japan.[101]

The increasing outrage shown by US and British authorities is attributable in part to the fact that they were discovering more and more atrocities. But many of the worst incidents had occurred much earlier in the war.[102] In February 1944 Gorgé found that the Japanese Foreign Ministry already wanted to treat the question of war crimes as something that belonged to the past.[103] To the Americans this seemed like callous indifference. It may have been the opposite. At least in the Foreign Ministry, there may have been a realization that Japanese forces had committed atrocities, and that going forward they had to try to establish better control over conditions in camps.[104]

Even officials in the Ministry of War were sometimes surprised at what they found when they inspected POW and internment camps in occupied territories. In April 1944, a senior officer from the POWMO found that Dutch internees were being forced to serve as military comfort women for Japanese troops in Java. After he reported this to Tokyo, the brothels were abruptly shut down.[105]

By October of that year, a former Japanese ambassador, close to Shigemitsu, admitted to Gorgé, "We will not win this war."[106] He had already lost his own son, and felt that "this death, like hundreds of thousands of others, will have served exactly nothing. Our country will come out beaten and, moreover, ruined by the immense tragedy." If only, he continued, "they had listened a little more to the voices of his diplomats . . . But they did not exert any influence on the military camarilla."[107]

More than just bemoaning Japan's fate, Gorgé's interlocutor had a specific message, one he believed came directly from the Foreign Ministry. He commended Gorgé on his efforts on behalf of civilian internees and prisoners of war, and regretted how allegations of atrocities had "poisoned the fountains of peace." Gorgé felt vindicated: "It is regrettable that, among the military, they have not always understood that by insisting as I did on visiting prisoners of war and verifying whether they were humanely treated, I acted, ultimately, in the interests of Japan itself. He greatly hopes that

I will be allowed to do more to dispel fears abroad about the conditions in the camps."[108]

These were not just words. Beginning in mid-1944 there was rapid growth in the size and capability of the Japanese agencies responsible for managing POWs. A new director, Lieutenant General Tamura Hiroshi, took charge of the POWIB.[109] He had lived in California and Hawaii for ten years as a child, and entered the Army College in 1924. A veteran of the Kwantung Army, in 1944 he was ordered to Thailand but refused due to his poor health. Upon taking charge of the POWIB, he found it disorganized, with limited power to control policies.[110] Nevertheless, he made some attempts to improve conditions for prisoners.[111] Under his command, the POWIB grew to the point that it had 117 staff by August 1945, compared to just 52 in 1942.[112]

In June 1944, Tokyo also agreed to another exchange of internees and relief goods for POWs, though it would take four months to work out the conditions. Now that US submarines had made communications with overseas garrisons increasingly difficult, the Japanese used the opportunity for safe passage to transport VIPs and deliver war materiel. The Americans came to realize this, but decided to agree to these voyages nonetheless.[113]

Yet Japanese military authorities continued to refuse permission for inspection visits. A spokesperson pointed out that if American authorities held Japanese prisoners, the US government would "doubtless hesitate [to] authorize camp visits."[114] In fact, as US forces began to capture more Japanese, they used them as leverage. In August 1944, the Japanese requested a report on Japanese nationals in Saipan and New Caledonia. The Americans responded that the Japanese first had to fulfill their commitment to allow visits to camps in the Philippines and other occupied territories.[115] Four months later, Shigemitsu told Gorgé that Japan would recognize ICRC delegates and authorize their visits to the Philippines, Singapore, and Thailand, but only on condition that the Allies accord the ICRC permission to visit both POW and civilian internee camps in the territories that they occupied, namely New Caledonia, Saipan, Tinian, and Guam.[116] The ICRC responded that these visits must occur on a basis of reciprocity with an ICRC representative based in the Philippines. The Japanese proposed visits to Santo Tomás, the civilian internee camp in the Philippines, a POW camp in Singapore, and a POW hospital in Thailand.

The Japanese were offering extremely limited access, and only for the ICRC—not Swiss diplomats. Moreover, the US invasion of the Philippines soon resulted in the liberation of Santo Tomas, obviating this part of the offer. For this, Japan was calling for ICRC access to all US-controlled camps.[117] Nevertheless, the United States was clearly setting conditions for its own adherence to the Geneva Conventions. Even the British were taken aback. Anthony Eden protested that such a position would make it harder to hold Japan to a higher standard.[118]

Any prospect of an Allied-Japanese rapprochement over POWs literally blew up in March 1945, when a US submarine torpedoed a Japanese ship that had been guaranteed safe passage, reportedly mistaking it for a destroyer. The *Awa Maru* carried more than 2,000 Japanese, including many senior commanders and diplomats along with their families. The sinking—and Washington's initial refusal to take responsibility—enraged Tokyo, ended relief shipments for POWs, and provoked new threats of reprisals.[119]

Meanwhile, bitter fighting in Manila continued for a month after the capture of Santo Tomás, including Japanese attacks on the civilian population, among them Swiss and Spanish citizens. The Spanish resigned as Japan's protecting power in the continental United States, forcing Tokyo to turn to the Swiss. But the Swiss Federal Council had finally reached its breaking point.[120] Japanese soldiers in Manila had reportedly murdered eighteen Swiss men and women, including a young couple and their child who were burned in their home. Swiss citizens across Japan's rapidly contracting empire continued to face arbitrary arrest and could be held incommunicado for months. Of particular concern were the approximately 400 Swiss living in Malaya, the Dutch East Indies, and Borneo, including 120 women and 90 children, some of whom had not been heard from in two years.[121]

At an April 1945 meeting, the Swiss Federal Council considered expelling Japanese refugees who had fled across the border from Germany if Japan did not show contrition. That June, Bern demanded compensation of a million Swiss francs. The Swiss would take over Japan's interests in the United States only if Japan gave Swiss representatives access to occupied areas to work on behalf of the United States and Great Britain.[122]

In July 1945, Gorgé finally obtained permission to visit camps in the occupied territories. Gorgé congratulated himself.[123] But considering that by this point practically every Japanese garrison was isolated by air and naval blockade, Japan was surrendering something to Switzerland that it no longer possessed.

Tokyo's failure to work with Swiss intermediaries provides further evidence of its poor wartime decision making, especially when one considers how much it had to lose by mistreating its captives. What is less clear is whether the Swiss made any positive difference. One might well conclude that in the end they had achieved little, if their work was not actually counterproductive. Because they had visited only 11,300 out of an estimated 36,000 US POWs, their reports gave a misleading impression about the fate of American servicemen.[124] In the case of the ICRC, putting a positive spin on Japanese conduct gave Tokyo useful propaganda, and failing to demand adherence to the Geneva Conventions—including unsupervised visits— vitiated the significance of even these inspections.

Swiss diplomats, for their part, were less-than-innocent bystanders in all of this, especially when one considers US conduct. Above all, the Swiss played the role of "protecting power" for a country that used its reports to threaten reprisals against civilian internees, set conditions on its adherence to the Geneva Conventions, used Japanese POWs for leverage, and invoked Japanese conduct to justify firebombing civilian targets. Ironically, while the Swiss and the Americans both put great store in showing how Japanese POWs were well treated, the Japanese proved indifferent to their fate, at least until the later stages of the war.[125] They were far more concerned with the treatment of Japanese civilian internees.

But in the end, Japan's military leaders were prepared to sacrifice even the lives of their own citizens, as when they urged suicide on Japanese civilians in Saipan and Okinawa. And even at the beginning of the war they showed scant concern for Allied POWs and internees, initially failing to create agencies capable of providing basic information about their fate, much less ensuring decent treatment. While some in the Foreign Ministry and the Japanese Red Cross showed concern for the rights of Allied captives, there is no record of their ever successfully challenging the military on this score.

Yet wartime debates do show that both the Allies and the Japanese accepted that POWs and civilians had a right to expect decent treatment even when there was no formal treaty obligation. When Tokyo excluded Allied airmen, it invoked another humanitarian principle: the prohibition against bombing civilian targets. Moreover, both sides accepted that neutral states and nongovernmental organizations had a role to play in observing and reporting on their respective conduct. And Washington and Tokyo cared about how that conduct was communicated to the rest of the world.

The Swiss government and especially the ICRC clearly overestimated their capacity to carry out the roles accorded them, whether inspecting far-flung camps or delivering humanitarian aid to hundreds of thousands of captives. Yet it is hard to imagine that the situation would have been improved if the Swiss had simply gotten out of the way. Instead of assuming that the Japanese gave Swiss intermediaries permission to go to only those camps with better conditions, the causal arrow could have pointed the other way: these camps may have had better conditions because the Japanese knew that they had to account for what Swiss inspectors would find there.

Tokyo considered it useful to be able to claim that it was acting humanely, and was not indifferent when its conduct was criticized abroad. This will become even more clear when we examine what happened in the rare case in which senior Japanese officials took an interest in establishing POW camps, and issued clear instructions about the conditions in which captives would be held.

# 5

## KOREA

## Life and Death in a Model Camp

In April 1945, Lieutenant Colonel Jack Schwartz, a medical officer from Fort Worth, Texas, arrived as a prisoner of war in Jinsen, Korea, present-day Inchon. Schwartz had been captured in the Philippines during the Battle of Bataan three years earlier. He had treated survivors of the Bataan Death March and endured wretched conditions in several camps and prison hospitals. He was on the *Ōryoku Maru*, one of the ships that American naval aircraft had sunk. More of his fellow POWs died on the *Enoura Maru* en route to Formosa. Finally the *Brazil Maru* delivered him to Moji. After about three months in Fukuoka, Schwartz sailed for Pusan. After a comparatively comfortable two-day journey via ship and train, Schwartz and the other survivors finally arrived in Korea and were immediately impressed by the good conditions. "We were placed in a large, well-constructed frame barrack building and were there fed better than at any of our previous camps," Schwartz later wrote. "The Japanese camp officials, on the whole, were more friendly than any we had previously encountered."[1]

The relatively benign conditions of POW camps in Korea surprised Schwartz, and seem anomalous compared with common accounts of the POW experience. Almost unique among the hundreds of POW camps, the ones in Korea at Jinsen (Inchon) and Keijō (Seoul) were established and organized in 1942 on direct orders from Tokyo. They therefore indicate what happened when senior officials took an interest in the fate of Allied POWs in the first months of the war, and how the experience of captivity could have been different if they showed the same interest elsewhere.

It started in March 1942, the same month that the Prisoner of War Management Office was established. General Itagaki Seishirō, a former Army minister and chief of staff of the Chōsen Army in Korea, told the War Ministry that he and the governor-general wanted to bring 1,000 British and

1,000 American prisoners to Korea. They wanted to establish a "strong faith in victory" among Koreans and "stamp out the respect and admiration" among Korean people for Britain and America.[2] On March 23, Itagaki sent more concrete plans, laying out locations and policies. Camps would be located at Keijō, at the former Iwamura Silk Reeling Mill, and at Jinsen, in a former military barracks. POWs who were warrant officers or more senior ranks were not to work, and the rations were to be the same as those of the Japanese army. "Interning, supervision and guarding of prisoners should be carried out [so] as to leave nothing to be desired."[3]

The purpose of these camps was to make "Koreans realize positively the true might of our empire as well as to contribute to psychological propaganda work."[4] The camps were also intended to create positive impressions for an international audience. The International Committee of the Red Cross (ICRC) would inspect the camps regularly, and its findings would be communicated to governments and published in mass media around the world. Japanese journalists also reported on these conditions, taking photographs and filming newsreels for a domestic audience. These photographs were reproduced in the Western media. Allied POWs thus played roles not just in the internal Japanese struggle to maintain control of the colonies, but also in the larger international arena.[5] The photographs and newsreels were meant to show Washington and London as well as the International Committee of the Red Cross that Japan was treating Allied prisoners humanely.

Colonel Noguchi Yuzuru, a graduate of the Japanese Military Academy and lifelong Army man, was in command of the Korean camps. Like many commanders, Noguchi had retired from the army before his service as a commandant. Earlier Noguchi was responsible for training Koreans to be guards.[6] Ultimately, a total of 3,016 deployed, mostly to Singapore, Thailand, and Java. A much smaller number of Korean guards remained in the peninsula, perhaps because the Japanese perceived a political risk of having Koreans posted in their own country, a concern that proved prescient.[7]

The Japanese summoned the people of Pusan to come see the first Allied POWs when in August 1942 they arrived from Singapore aboard the ship *Fukkai Maru*. Most of these first POWs hailed from Britain and Australia, but a disproportionate number of the higher-ranking officers were British.[8] Only one of the Australians was a field officer. There were also senior Malayan and Netherlands East Indies government officials and technicians. The rest of the prisoners were mostly the surviving members of the Second Battalion Loyal Lancashire Regiment and the Yorkshire-based

Staged photo of a Korean guard. Many Koreans and other subjects of the Japanese empire believed they were signing up for an adventure, only to find that—as guards in a POW camp—the closest they came to real battle was in a posed photo in front of a painted backdrop. (Beeldbank WO2—NIOD.)

122nd Field Regiment, Royal Artillery. Japanese journalists watched and snapped photos of the crowded deck.

The sight of high-ranking Euro-American prisoners would have been impressive to Japanese and Korean onlookers. The men disembarked and then, as Japanese and Korean guards looked on, began a five-mile march through the Pusan streets. The arrival of 998 prisoners had such an effect that an estimated 120,000 Koreans and 57,000 Japanese lined the roads in Pusan, Keijō, and Jinsen. The Koreans sneered at British officers, according to a confidential report to the vice minister of the Army, Kimura Heitarō, by Lieutenant General Ihara Junjirō, chief of staff of the Korean Army. "[They] confessed their happiness at being subjects of the Empire and expressed their resolve to carry through the Greater East Asian War." One man reportedly said: "When I saw young Korean soldiers, members of the Imperial Army, guarding the prisoners, I shed tears of joy. I was so moved by the sight that I almost felt like shouting to those who weren't aware of the fact: Look! Peninsular youths are guarding the British soldiers!" Ihara concluded, "As a whole, it seems the idea was very successful."[9]

But even in Ihara's report, there were signs of trouble. Korean Christians were harder to convince, he said, since they were not able to "drive out completely their admiration for foreign ideas, due to the fact that their leaders were Europeans or Americans." But they were apparently "moved by the idea that they must establish a Japanese Christianity."[10]

The prisoners themselves knew that they were on display. Interviewed by the Japanese press after a miserable voyage, they slept in a school where hundreds of children gazed at them. As Australian prisoner Captain Guy Round put it, they felt like "lions in a zoo."[11] Like Schwartz, the aforementioned American officer, many POWs found the worst part of their captivity was not detention in camp but the deprivation suffered en route. After their six-week sea transit, a number of men collapsed during the march through Pusan.[12] After losing some of their number to hospitalization, the men quickly boarded a train and made their way northeast.

On their arrival at Keijō, the main camp, Noguchi delivered a stern speech to the prisoners.[13] "We will punish you, if you act against our regulations," he warned. "For instance, nonadherence to regulations, disobedience, resistance and escape (even an attempt to do so) are understood as manifestations of hostility." Neither would Noguchi tolerate complaints about housing, clothing, or work, noting that prisoners would inevitably experience changes in their lives.[14]

But prisoners gradually came to realize that Noguchi's bark was worse than his bite. Lieutenant Colonel Michael Elrington of the Second Loyal regiment—the senior commanding officer of the Keijō camp—knew Noguchi from the 1937 Shanghai Incident, when the Loyals patrolled the

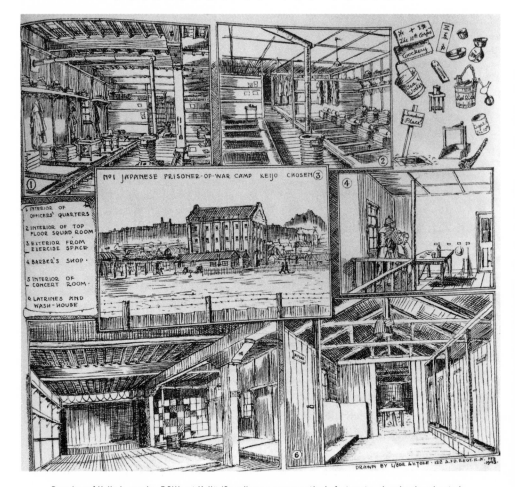

Drawing of Keijō barracks. POWs at Keijō (Seoul) were comparatively fortunate, sleeping in a heated brick building, with separate quarters for officers and men, and a hut with running water for bathing. Lance bombardier Alan Vernon Toze passed the time by creating a series of drawings of daily life. (Lancashire Infantry Museum.)

Shanghai Bund, and arranged a cease-fire between the Japanese and the Chinese. Noguchi reportedly used to invite Elrington over for the occasional chat over green tea. He had a habit of disappearing when there was trouble in camp.[15]

Noguchi could easily disappear because he was responsible for all of the camps in Korea. The one in Keijō initially held 433 British and Australian prisoners, who lived in the former Japanese Iwamura silk-reeling mill, a four-story brick building surrounded by a wooden fence. Up to sixty men slept in each room on tatami mats. They could wash in a separate hut with running water and a wooden trough, and bathe in a large Japanese bath where up to five men could fit.[16]

At Jinsen, the 482 prisoners lived in military barracks heated by Russian-style brick stoves.[17] One Lancashire Loyal recalled the prison dormitories as about eighty feet long by thirty-five feet, divided into sections, with a central passageway. Each prisoner was given a personal space of about six feet by two-and-a-half feet to keep his personal items, including eating utensils and bedding. They also slept on tatami.[18] Jinsen had running water, and like at Keijō, prisoners had two baths per week. Two smaller bathtubs were provided for prisoners with skin diseases. The camp had one toilet for every thirteen prisoners.[19]

Though obviously Spartan, these well-constructed camps, with heating and sanitary facilities, compared favorably to many others, especially O'Donnell in the Philippines and Changi in Singapore. The camps were not tightly sealed to the outside, and the prisoners soon realized this. Even so, only a few escape attempts were ever recorded. The most promising route was to Russia, some 200 miles away even from Kōnan. But few of the prisoners spoke Korean, and none could pass for a Korean national.[20] On the other hand, porous borders permitted interaction with Koreans, mostly women, children, and elderly men. Prisoners bought black-market food and newspapers from Koreans. On the way to work details or over the walls, men observed Koreans at work and at play. One drew Korean women doing laundry in a pond, and depicted the "cordial send-off" the villagers gave them on their way to work.[21]

While the facilities at Keijō and Jinsen were decent and even somewhat open to the surrounding community, the men lacked adequate clothes for Korea's severe winters. They had arrived from Singapore still wearing tropical-weight gear. As Captain Round, who had served with the Indian Army, observed, "In January and February at 30 below zero, you see the bullocks with icicles from their bodies."[22] But Koreans seemed even worse off: Private Harry Kingsley sketched Korean laborers sticking their arms into water to gather lily roots from frozen fields at an estimated 14 degrees below zero.[23]

POW diaries include many comments, both good and bad, on the weather, reflecting the tedium of captivity, as did the many references to food. According to the Geneva Conventions, prisoners were supposed to be fed the same as Japanese servicemen. Many POWs compared their diet to what Koreans ate. As Gerald Rosenberg, a private from the 85th Australian Light Aid Detachment, put it, "We cannot complain about the tucker as a whole even though at times it is very light. For we can see that the civilians outside are getting less than us." Dick Swarbrick, a private from the Loyals, observed, "This diet although very poor by Occidental standards was I must admit superior at least in quantity to what the average Korean got. And it was as good as what a Jap soldier got at least if my own observations were anything to go by."[24]

Rations from the Japanese army were supplemented by black-market activity, Red Cross boxes, as well as apples and other charity from the Koreans on the borders of the camp. Prisoners also produced food through farming and animal husbandry, though it is unclear how much of it they were able to keep for themselves. At Keijō they had a farm of 5,000 square meters, growing potatoes and vegetables.[25] By 1945 they had four hogs and 160 rabbits.

On the way to the farm, they would often see Koreans, sometimes in worse circumstances than their own. One of the ironies of the camps was that the prisoners often felt fortunate after witnessing what Koreans endured. Alan Vernon Toze, a lance bombardier in the British Army, described one episode:

> On arrival at [the] [f]arm a heartrending and shameful scene took place: lying in the road was a bundle of rags, which, when kicked by a native boss, proved to be a female of stunted structure and certain age, with blackened hands and a woebegone and tear streaked visage. She resisted all efforts by Jap soldiers etc. to eject her and escaping from them, shuffled to us and fell into our ranks looking pleadingly at us and wailing "America, America." She was then kicked and then as she passed me reached out a grimy paw and plucked my sleeve. I felt rotten but could do nothing about it.[26]

In one remarkable incident he found that Koreans were so desperate to escape their poverty that they attempted to break into the camp. In June 1943, "100 [K]oreans threw a riot outside the camp gates, tried to get in: the guard was turned out with fixed bayonets, took 1/2 hour to disperse them. One presumes poor devils are starving."[27] But this was the only such incident. Much more common are reports of receiving food from Koreans. In 1942 Australian corporal Alex Johnstone reported, "I scored an apple from a kid today."[28] A few days later, "Cec[il] brought me back half an apple and my little Jap guard friend (or should I say Korean) gave me a packet of cigs."[29]

The POWs' diet was irregularly supplemented from time to time by Red Cross packages. Japanese records indicate that by February 1943 Jinsen had received 250 comfort boxes with canned beef, sugar, cocoa, and salt.[30] Of course, we do not know what prisoners actually received.[31] Japanese camp management used the packages to supplement the salary of commissioned officers, themselves inadequately fed.[32] Under the guise of "sampling," camp staff also ate and trafficked in relief goods. Although prohibited by international law, this practice was not forbidden until November 1944.[33]

Even so, occasional and incomplete package deliveries were better than the total embargo that prevailed elsewhere. And there were other contributions besides food that bolstered morale. The Neutral Committee of the World Alliance of the YMCA provided books and musical instruments.[34] The Swiss legation provided a guitar, mandolin, and a violin.[35] Jinsen's library grew from 130 volumes in 1943 to 482 in 1945, though 125 of the books were Bibles.[36] The other books were mainly novels, but the library also contained a hymnal, a how-to guide to pottery, a biography of Brahms and, crucially, a compendium of card games.[37] Prisoners could also read the propaganda organ *Nippon Times*. Corporal Johnstone of the 2/15th Field Regiment, originally attached to the Command Pay Staff of the AIF in Malaya, created elaborate recipe books.

Card games like poker, pontoon, and bridge occupied the prisoners for long hours even though guards sometimes confiscated the playing cards. Gambling was strictly forbidden but it went on nonetheless.[38] POWs also played sports. At Jinsen they organized a baseball league, where the Red Sox faced teams named after the hard realities of camp life—Banjo (*benjo;* toilet) Squatters, Yasmui (*yasumi;* break) Giants, and the Tatami Pressers. Camp bookies set the odds.[39] Perhaps because prisoners had other activities to choose from, by 1945 few attended weekly church services any longer at Keijō, and Jinsen had no chaplain.[40]

What we usually hear in accounts of POW camps, such as the Thai-Burma Railway or the mines at Kinkaseki in Taiwan, is backbreaking work. But in Korea, camp commanders struggled to find labor for the Allied soldiers. They were paid for their work, but could only spend their savings at the cafeteria, where often there was not much to buy.[41] Near Keijō there were few large-scale civil engineering projects to absorb prisoner labor. Eventually POWs in Korea farmed, cared for livestock, built roads, and repaired harbors and airfields.[42] Others worked as miners or stevedores. For commissioned officers, work would be voluntary and unpaid.[43] They chose to do it nonetheless. But it appears there was less pressure put on the men to work than in other POW camps elsewhere in Japan's empire.[44]

At Keijō, prisoners worked at an Army warehouse forwarding supplies to the Chōsen Army (Chōsen Gunsō Rikugun Sōko), or loading and packing raw materials. Some prisoners worked within the camp making army uniforms, or at the carpentry workshop.[45] Imperial Japanese Army (IJA) management also hired out prisoners for loading and unloading railway trucks at Ryusan, small civil engineering jobs, and "one very pleasant job"—"building a racecourse for a wealthy Japanese civilian who provided us with good food and was very gentle and manly towards us."[46]

A third camp in the colony, Kōnan, was originally opened in September 1943 to supply workers for a carbide factory owned by Nippon Chisso.[47] Some prisoners were grateful to be transferred, even though it was 190 miles from the Manchurian border, and thus featured a harsher climate. The food appears to have been better, with daily rice, vegetables, and fish— at least in the fall and winter. But some had to work at scorching furnaces making dangerous chemicals.[48] And as one private, Lionel John Apps, later wrote, "Sanitation was a disgrace to a so called civilised nation."[49]

Allied military prisoners were a source of great interest for Koreans as they worked. And POWs appear to have looked right back. Because many Korean men had dispersed through the empire, to attend schools, to fight in the IJA, or to provide labor, there were a disproportionately large number of women and children. Johnstone reported that dozens of spectators watched prisoners doing excavating work for a new track at Jinsen railway. "Kids by the hundred stood on the railway embankment and threw cigarettes, apples and turnips down, but the guards stopped them." It was not just prisoners who worked, though: "On one side of the railway embankment were working Korean women and on the other us."[50]

While the work was not unduly onerous, the fact that POWs—a society of men—were now working alongside women seemed both remarkable and unseemly. Sometimes prisoners needed the help: "loaded skip was too heavy to lift," Toze recalled, "so a young Korean woman dropped her bundle and lifted the handle on to my shoulder for me!"[51] Rosenberg observed, "The native power is for the main part women and girls—poorly clad and badly shod. Some women work with a child on the back, one working behind and one in the pouch—very humane conditions I don't think." It was far more "manly" for men to work with—and for—other men.[52]

While prisoners sympathized with Koreans and felt uncomfortable to be working alongside women, they often resented one another. The constant shuffling between camps and worksites undermined unit cohesion and rank hierarchy. There was already significant tension from the outset between officers and enlisted men. Initially a large proportion of prisoners who had arrived from Singapore were senior officers. In these camps the Japanese permitted them to wear insignia designating rank. According to Dick Swarbrick, a British POW in 1942–1943, the officers had lost their men's trust following the surrender at Singapore. Officers were able to regain respect by standing up to the Japanese and using their own money to buy supplies for the others.[53] But POW representatives—officers—complained continually to the ICRC that morale was suffering because, living in close quarters with enlisted men, officers were not receiving the deference they deserved.[54]

POWs might have complained even more, but this risked physical punishment. As we have seen, Japanese officers and men were trained in a system in which face-slapping was common. But the testimony later given at the war crimes trial—a trial in which prisoners were encouraged to testify against guards—indicates that abuse was not systematic, but instead the sometimes random acts of particular guards. As one British sapper held in Kōnan, Richard Biggs, later recalled: "not knowing the language we did know we were going to get slapped until [they] stopped one they would just walk up and draw one off."[55]

Korean guards became notorious for their mistreatment of POWs. Leonard George Mills, a gunner also held in Kōnan, recalled that, "Korean guards were very brutal, even more than Japs."[56] But Toze had a different experience: "Korean guards away from their own country seem to have earned dreadful rep[utation], ours may have been superior."[57] Round also found that they were not easily stereotyped. He recalled the compassion of "The Christian," who obtained medicine and other items for prisoners with little concern for himself. Others, such as "The Pig," were quite different. He "delighted in striking us on the flimsiest of pretexts."[58]

While many cases evidenced a particular guard's predilection for violence, others meted out punishment only for particular infractions. These included trafficking in or possessing prohibited items, arguing with guards, and black market exchanges—attempts to either buy goods or trade ciga-rettes. In September 1943, for instance, British private Matthew Thompson was accused of stealing an apple. Thompson was made to stand at atten-tion and punched until almost unconscious. Upon returning to the camp, Captain Terada Takeo, adjutant at Keijō, hit him with a heavy roll of paper. Tatsumi Ushihara, a civilian interpreter and UCLA graduate, slapped him in the face.[59] Noguchi lectured Thomson and sentenced him to eight days of solitary confinement.[60] The most serious infraction was an escape at-tempt. After an officer and a noncommissioned officer attempted to es-cape Jinsen while on work patrol, they were quickly recaptured and sen-tenced to eight years and six months of jail at Seidaimon Civil Prison.[61] This was the longest sentence given at the prison, where terms ranged from two to eight years.[62]

There is some evidence that Japanese misconduct was kept from No-guchi. What Noguchi liked least was anything that presented the camps negatively to the outside world or to the ICRC. Men who preserved evidence of Japanese misconduct risked severe punishment, like British private David P. Lomasney. He brought an empty Red Cross can of beef into camp as evidence that the Japanese were eating Red Cross supplies. He was taken to military HQ, questioned, beaten, and told to sign a confession.[63] In the summer of 1943, after being unjustly accused of stealing toothbrushes, Aus-tralian private Arthur Clark was struck with fists and beaten by Captain Takeo. Ushihara, the interpreter, beat him with a cane after Clark wrote a letter to his wife telling her that he could survive without the Red Cross parcels.[64]

Suspected sedition brought even harsher treatment. In July 1943, Lieu-tenant R. B. Pigott, a British POW, was confined for alleged circulation of anti-Japanese propaganda. Piggott passed a letter to an elderly Korean whom he knew that contained figures of American aircraft production, shipping, tanks, and manpower, along with an estimate of Japanese forces. It was signed "Freedom."[65] While Round described this as a "trivial matter," it is not difficult to see how the Japanese authorities, already concerned about the loyalty of Koreans, might have viewed this as more serious.[66] Guards took Piggott to Ryusan MP camp, where "third degree methods" were used to get a statement that implicated others in the camp. Prisoners coped with the abuse through humor, creating nicknames for their tormen-tors, such as "The Kicker," or more ironic ones like "Smiler" or "Peaches and Cream."

But even taking these incidents into account, POWs in Korea were treated less harshly than their counterparts in places like Burma, Changi, and Camp O'Donnell. One way we know this is by evaluating the experience of prisoners who arrived from those other theaters, such as Schwarz's group from the Philippines. On February 1, 1945, Noguchi's executive officer, Lieutenant Isobe, inspected the contingent after it arrived in Moji, the main port of Kyushu, on their way to Korea. He described the Americans as filthy and emaciated. Out of the 1,619 who sailed from Manila, only 556 made it to Moji, and 300 of those subsequently died.[67]

Isobe judged that immediate transport to Korea was impossible, and instead put the men in the charge of the Western Army. Fifty-three of the 193 died in the next three months due to improper medical facilities and a poor diet.[68] On April 26, Schwartz's party finally arrived in Korea, and joined a group of twenty enlisted men—all that remained after the rest of the Commonwealth contingent shipped out. They were then sent to Jinsen, where they were surprised by their good treatment.[69]

At this point Jinsen was no longer a propaganda camp, which reflected a larger policy shift to stop highlighting good treatment of POWs. As the War Ministry stressed in December 1943, news on prisoners would be censored so that domestic reports would avoid anything that gave the impression that prisoners were "too well or too cruelly treated." But one American officer, Lieutenant Colonel Arthur Shreve, identified another possible reason for their good treatment. He wrote in his diary in April 1945: "The trip [from Pusan], for one exception, has been so comfortable and the food has been so good that I am sure that the Japanese have come to the realization that they are losing the war."[70]

Even so, the Americans were struck by the "sadism" of one man, the camp doctor, Mizuguchi Yasutoshi. Schwartz, a doctor himself, later recalled: "Two officers died while we were in this camp, both of amoebic dysentery, and I made many requests before their death for amebicides, but was always refused."[71] Even though American Red Cross supplies were available in the camp, Mizuguchi would not distribute them. The guards' defense counsel, Waldo P. Johnson, argued in his 1947 defense of Mizuguchi that Lieutenant William King had suffered greatly in the Philippines and on the voyage to Japan and Korea. He was seriously ill upon arrival, and his inevitable death "could hardly be said to have been contributed to or accelerated by Mizuguchi."[72] But it seemed clear that American Red Cross supplies were in the camp and were not used to aid King. Mizuguchi disappeared from the camp in July 1945. Shortly after, the Japanese turned over to prisoners a considerable amount of dressings, drugs, quinine, vitamins, and plasma.

In August it became apparent to the POWs at Kōnan that their long ordeal was almost over. On August 9, Gerald Rosenberg heard that Russia had entered the war and was on the march through Manchuria. Air alarms doubled and tripled in number, and they tried to pack camp stores and shift rations to safe positions.[73]

On August 12, a Korean guard told Rosenberg that a commander by the name of Otaki had ordered that if the Russians took the camp before a general armistice, the POWs would be shot.[74] The Korean guards wanted the prisoners to break out after "exterminating all Japanese." But Rosenberg concluded that "this was impossible owing to the fact that there were shifts at the factory and a hospital full of sick."

Several accounts in Korea, Thailand, the Philippines, and elsewhere, relate similar rumors—that prisoners would be put to death if Japan faced defeat.[75] In Java this appears to have intersected with the colonial situation, where Korean guards resented their imperial occupiers—they planned to arm POWs and eventually to take over.[76] Guards fearing for their own lives may have spread these rumors.

We have seen evidence from Singapore and the Philippines that massacres were sometimes ordered by commissioned officers, including high-ranking ones. At the Tokyo Tribunal, prosecutors also used soldiers' diaries, which contained evidence of orders to massacre, as well as battle reports of massacres, which included records of the ammunition used and deaths. It is clear that commanders and guards had grown increasingly desperate in the later stages of the war. But was there a plan or policy to kill all the POWs?

An extract from the journal of the Taiwan camp headquarters in Taihoku is often cited as evidence: "In any case it is the aim not to allow the escape of a single one, to annihilate them all, and not to leave any traces."[77] Yet it was not a high-level decision from the Taiwan Army, much less from the War Ministry. The document is *from* the Taiwan POW camp HQ *to* the 11th Unit, to be reported to the commanding general of the Military Police and the commander of the Taiwan Army.[78] If there were a central order for a massacre, there would have been no need for a camp HQ to inform higher-ups. Instead, it would have been the Taiwan Army command handing the order down to its subordinate units, the camp HQ and the

11th Unit. Moreover, there is no documentary evidence of any such order from the War Ministry.[79] By the end of August 1945, the POWIB had learned that at least one senior officer was aware that the order had been issued, but not who had planned it or drafted it.[80]

So rather than proving that there was a common policy or plan to kill all POWs, the Taiwan document suggests quite the opposite. Moreover, this document was describing what should be done in an emergency situation when a large uprising could not be suppressed without firearms, or when Allied POWs might turn into a hostile force. If enemy forces landed in Taiwan, POW camp headquarters would first concentrate and confine POWs. Only in emergency circumstances would they be killed. This was a last-ditch strategy by a camp commander if the security situation got out of control.

There is also a March 11, 1945, order by Vice Minister of War Shibayama Kaneshirō: "The handling of prisoners of war in these times when the state of things is becoming more and more pressing and the evils of war extend to the Imperial Domain, Manchuria and other places, is in the enclosed summary. We hope you follow it, making no mistake."[81] The summary ordered that guards should prevent POWs from falling into enemy hands, and that if necessary they should be moved.[82] But it did not order their deaths. Instead, it provides more evidence for the increasing desperation of Japanese forces by 1945.[83]

Rather than ordering POWs to be killed, Tokyo prohibited any such action. In June 1945, Riku-a-Mitsu 2245 ordered that POWs should be released if it was unavoidable, and "violence such as killing or injuring POWs should be prohibited." This was based on the previous year's Mitsu 1633, which ordered that if liberation became inevitable, POWs should be freed and "efforts made so as not to give an excuse for arousing the hostile feelings of the enemy, for propaganda material, or for taking reprisals."[84]

But officials also sought to protect themselves. On August 20, a radio message went out instructing POW camp chiefs to destroy incriminating documents and to transfer or conceal guards and other personnel who had mistreated POWs and internees.[85] Just two days later, on August 22, the chief of the War Controls division sent a telegram instructing command to "afford fair treatment to all prisoners since the future disposition of our nation will depend on the methods we employ to effect this transfer."[86]

Finally, and most importantly, few mass killings of POWs actually took place when defeat came. This included in Korea, where captives at Keijō discovered in mid-August that the war was coming to an end and that the US Army and the US Navy were ceasing military operations. They had a system where newspapers were smuggled into the camp by work parties from a Korean schoolboy who charged a pack of cigarettes for the trade. The "Camp Japan expert," Lieutenant Peter Baker, figured out what was happening.[87]

In Jinsen, when the blackout ended and riots occurred outside the camp, prisoners started to get excited. The next day the commandant told the Anglo-American prisoner representative that a cease-fire had been declared. On August 19 the POWs were paid in full the savings from their labor, on August 21 they were allowed to read the *Keijō Nippō,* and on August 24 they were allowed to listen to the radio.

Compared to POWs at camps in Kawasaki and Hakodate, where almost a quarter of captives lost their lives, those imprisoned at Keijō and Jinsen had been lucky. Just 2.7 percent of Commonwealth POWs in Korea did not survive the war.[88] Moreover, the majority of these deaths took place shortly after POWs arrived because of the harsh conditions of transport. Much of the same is true of the Americans.

So how do we assess and understand these camps in Korea? While many historians highlight unit cohesion as a key factor in determining who survived captivity, pluck and esprit de corps do not seem to have been a major factor, at least in this case. The population of prisoners in Korea was transient, with significant tension between officers and enlisted men. It was common practice for officers to enjoy special status in POW camps, whether in terms of work, correspondence, or access to black market goods. But the unique circumstances at Jinsen bred resentment. After all, when officers made up a large proportion of the camp population, otherwise customary demands for special treatment—or at least immunity from physical punishment—may have come across as special pleading. Rather than leading and representing the POWs as a group, the large number of officers formed a class apart. They may have appeared to represent themselves above all.

Whether they were officers or enlisted, upon arrival in Korea prisoners had adequate facilities and relatively good sanitation. They received army rations supplemented by occasional packages and food they managed to grow or raise, along with gifts from Korean civilians. The work was not, for most, particularly grueling. Even men working at the nitrogen factory at Kōnan ate fish, vegetables, and rice. And as much as they suffered from the cold, POWs from temperate climates fared even worse when exposed to tropical disease. Many of the prisoners in Korea enjoyed periods of leisure and at least sporadic correspondence with loved ones. Moreover, with important exceptions, the guards whom the prisoners encountered do not appear to have been particularly brutal.

Even the official US military history of the postwar military presence in Korea concluded that "the Japanese need not be blamed too severely for such minor abuses as face-slapping." Quoting Lieutenant Colonel Elrington, it agreed that "'the fault lies with the system rather than the individual. Soldiers in the Japanese Army normally fared little better at the hands of their superiors. Japan can easily feed twelve soldiers on the daily food cost of one American Private.'"[89] Six years after the war had ended, Major W. J. Holohan commented: "It is only those unfortunate people who have suffered the rigor and the utter helplessness and hopelessness of life in a POW camp [who] can realize the situation and our camp was a model."

Perhaps none of this should surprise us, since the Japanese Army designed Jinsen and Keijō as show camps. But they lost that purpose by 1943. If, as Elrington and Holohan found, the camps were still unusually well run, it was in part due to its management. And yet, even in what was intended to be a model camp, one in which the commanders officially proscribed violence, prisoners could be subject to abuse. A sadist such as Mizuguchi appeared to have free rein. Along with the confiscation of care packages, the Mizuguchi case shows how, even when supplies were ample, prisoners might still suffer. This suggests that Japan's straitened circumstances—however important—is not, by itself, a sufficient explanation for the deprivation of prisoners. After all, Korean civilians who may have endured even harsher wartime conditions often went out of their way to aid POWs.

Viewed in a larger context, what is most unusual about the camps in Korea is how, if only for a time, senior military and political leaders seriously considered the proper treatment of Allied prisoners. Ironically, it was not merely or even mainly to conform to international laws of war, but to provide a model for Japan's colonial subjects. And although conditions deteriorated in some respects, they never reached the level where other camps, like O'Donnell in the Philippines, first began. Instead, the initial design appears to have created a set of practices and precedents that continued to shape relations between guards and prisoners long after Jinsen and Keijō ceased being propaganda camps and most of the original prisoners had moved on.

Of course, physical punishment was also part of the culture in POW camps in Korea, whether or not commanders prohibited the practice, and a character like Mizuguchi could push matters quite far. But the surprising degree of autonomy officers enjoyed also meant that others could act to protect prisoners' welfare, such as when Isobe rejected the idea of immediately subjecting Schwartz and the other survivors from the Philippines to another ocean passage.

The history of the POW camps in Korea indicates that when senior Japanese military leaders concerned themselves with Allied POWs, they wanted them to be decently housed, not overworked, and given provisions equivalent to those provided to Japan's own soldiers. This raises the question of whether POW camps might have been different—and better—in the rest of Japan's wartime empire if senior officials had created policies and practices with more general applicability.

Yet POW camps did not exist in a vacuum. Even those camps in Japan itself, directly under the purview of the Prisoner of War Management Office and the Prisoner of War Information Bureau, could become chaotic and cruel when the main islands were isolated by blockade, cities were bombed from the air, and men, women, and children suffered deprivation.

# 6

## CAPTIVITY ON THE HOME FRONT

The Fukuokan camp was without question, excepting the hell ships, the worst experience of all." So declared Captain John Albert Goodpasture Jr., who was asked in 1946 to recount his experiences in multiple Japanese POW camps.[1] Like Jack Schwartz, he had survived the attacks on the *Ōryoku Maru*, the *Enoura Maru*, and the *Brazil Maru* en route to Fukuoka from the Philippines. He "narrowly escaped being torpedoed on the third ship and [was] without food or water sufficient to sustain life for many days." Most of his comrades did not survive the journey. But captivity at Fukuoka killed many more. Goodpasture blamed the camp commander, Sakamoto Yuhichi, "for not having taken action to save the lives of these men." At the same time, he condemned Japanese doctors for gross negligence.

The experience of POWs in Fukuoka remains infamous for Japanese brutality, including forced labor, execution of flyers, and even medical experimentation on POWs at Kyushu University. These experiences led former Allied POWs, as well as Chinese and Korean forced laborers who worked at Asō Mining Company and Mitsubishi Mining Company, to organize and seek compensation.[2]

How then can we explain the postwar assessment of a Dutch POW who said that his camp in Fukuoka was the most comfortable of all the places he had been held during the war, "with its heated dining hall, beautiful bathroom, good camp direction, my many friends and its good food"?[3] After examining hundreds of accounts, Major General Archer L. Lerch of the US Provost Marshal General judged that "in most established prisoner of war base camps in Japan proper, Manchuria and Korea, the food ration authorized and the housing, medical service, and other facilities and services provided prisoners of war were not far below the same type facilities and services authorized and officially provided personnel in the Japanese army."[4]

This chapter analyzes why accounts of the POW experience in Fukuoka are so sharply divergent, and what factors explain how they varied between camps and changed over the course of the conflict. Possible explanations include Ministry of War policies, the decisions of commanders like Sakamoto about whether and how to implement them, and the conduct of junior officers and guards. At least some of the captives might also have resented and resisted any situation in which people they once considered their inferiors were now their lords and masters.

But whereas accounts of POW camps often depict the camps in isolation, even frozen in time, this chapter emphasizes how Japan as a whole experienced cataclysmic change over the course of the conflict, leading to widespread deprivation that fundamentally altered the context of allied captivity. And the POWs themselves—from many different places, and from different classes and ranks—were also changed by these years of captivity, such that similar conditions might have been experienced differently at different points in the conflict.

The chapter follows groups of Allied POWs who spent time at one particular branch camp, Fukuoka 1. These captives came from Wake Island, Java, the Philippines, the Dutch East Indies, Malaya, Singapore, and other parts of Kyushu. Fukuoka 1 itself moved three times, and underwent various command regimes, like many other camps in Japan. But it was always under the purview of the Prisoner of War Management Office (POWMO) and the Prisoner of War Information Bureau (POWIB) in Tokyo. So what happened there can be compared with what Japanese policymakers prescribed.

The main reason POWs were brought to Japan, and to particular places in Japan, was to put them to work supporting the war economy. As more and more men went to fight, businesses and factories experienced labor shortages. The national government had already made efforts to improve the situation with the 1938 National Labor Mobilization Law, which authorized the emperor and government ministers to conscript labor. But as more men were drafted, companies continued to face shortages. The government first sought to fill them with colonial labor. In 1939, approximately 85,000 Koreans were forcibly brought to Japan.[5] In 1941, authorities turned to women: the Patriotic National Labor Cooperation Ordinance required that women between fourteen and twenty-five years of age join the Patriotic Labor Corps.[6] Yet the war economy required more and more workers.

In early 1942 Zentsūji was the sole POW camp in the homeland. It was set up far from Tokyo, in the northeast corner of Shikoku, the smallest and least populous of Japan's four main islands. The Ministry of War soon established POW camps in other regions: in September, in Osaka and Tokyo,

Japan's two largest cities. In November, a camp was established in Fu-kuoka, on the northern shore of Kyushu, the third largest of Japan's main islands, in the southern part of Japan. In December a camp was established in Hakodate, in the south of Hokkaido, the second largest and northern-most of Japan's main islands. Thus, by the end of 1942, camps were distrib-uted throughout Japan.[7]

The Western District Army (Seibu hōmengun) ran the camps in Kyushu. It controlled how POW labor was used, whether for military aims or mining. The Imperial Japanese Army (IJA) camps were divided into main, branch, and dispatch camps. The IJA set up these branch camps and smaller dispatch camps, and supplied them with food and clothing, except in the early period. Initially the Seibu army did not have the capacity to pay or manage a large number of POWs.[8] It therefore delegated to factories the responsibility for guarding and paying POWs. Dispatch camps were set up in 1944 to address a lack of manpower. In these dispatch camps, private companies provisioned the guards and POWs, and organized their labor.[9] Some branch camps also provided companies with labor: in Kyushu, many prisoners worked in mines or for industrial groups.

Japanese companies were willing to go along with this, a decision that remains controversial to this day. Although the government did not order companies to requisition POW labor, shortages made it hard not to. Com-panies could simply fill out the necessary forms, stating the period they would need POWs and how many hours they would work, and address them to the Ministry of War and the local commander. The companies would provide lodging, pay, medical treatment, and a canteen.[10] Sometimes the head of the POWMO would follow up to make sure that "the factory actually needed POW labor or whether they needed more and as to how the factory was treating the POWs." Then they would make a plan as to whether the camp should have more or fewer POWs.[11]

The camps in Fukuoka, as elsewhere, were established for the most part in industrial areas and near mines. The IJA opened branch camp Fu-kuoka 1 in the fall of 1942 at Kumamoto, a former castle town in Kyushu. It lay about 45 miles south of Fukuoka City, not far from the coast of the Bay of Nagasaki.[12] The compound was 1½ acres, with wooden barracks sur-rounded by a wooden fence. But like many other camps, POWs there would have considerable contact with the outside.

In November 1942 approximately 260 British servicemen arrived in Fu-kuoka from West Java, on board the *Dai-nichi Maru*. Once POWs arrived in the Japanese archipelago and were assigned to camps, they were under the command of the chief of the Army General Staff, who in turn placed them under local army control. In Japan, prisoners were formally registered as POWs, and the camp director was supposed to prepare a POW identification card. One copy was kept at the camp, and one was sent to the POWIB. Although international treaties specified that these cards should be sent to the International Committee of the Red Cross (ICRC), adherence to this policy was haphazard. The POWMO had a tiny staff and, until 1944, when Major Takata Masaru created a filing system, no formal process for gathering and transmitting this information.[13]

The first POWs in Fukuoka were mainly from the Royal Air Force 21st Light Anti-Aircraft Regiment, and had been captured during the Battle of Java and temporarily held at Changi. Among them were twenty-three officers, the most senior being Lieutenant Colonel Martin D. S. Saunders. The British prisoners were under the charge of Captain Sakamoto Yuhichi. He was average height for a Japanese man during this time (five feet, six inches), but struck the prisoners as short and solid. He commanded twenty-two guards, who led their captives to wooden huts. Some POWs found the huts inadequately constructed and leaky. But hygiene and sanitation were "fairly reasonable," according to one former wood machinist.[14] These first prisoners also received two sets of clothing. For food they were given a large cupful of steamed rice and about half a pint of vegetable soup three times per day.[15]

Bombardier Robert Metcalf, a former grocery man, found the food to be of "poor quality."[16] He and the other POWs were supposed to receive supplementary food from the Red Cross.[17] Accounts differ on how these Red Cross supplies were divided and how they were used. One captive recalled one issue of Red Cross supplies while he was a prisoner at Kumamoto, where he received "half a tin of condensed milk and a quarter of an apple pudding." Additionally, three tins of corned beef per man were added to cookhouse supplies at Fukuoka 1. Every two weeks, captives received half a cup of sugar and cocoa.[18] One captive recalled that men received boots from the Red Cross. But they were not allowed to wear them to work. Instead, they were only to be worn in camp at night and on rest days. It is not clear why, but it may be that Captain Sakamoto did not want people to see that POWs had new boots when so many Japanese civilians were suffering deprivation.

But these Red Cross supplies only came later. In the meantime, many of the POWs were already in bad shape when they arrived in Fukuoka. During the first five months at the camp, the hospital was practically always full, with as many as seventy men suffering from diarrhea. The hospital building was small and very poorly heated, so there were equally as many seriously ill in the barracks. Thirty-seven died in the hospital the first month. Prisoners found medical supplies inadequate. They consisted of what was left when the men were captured, and later a small quantity of Japanese medicine. For beriberi, Japanese medication—"Wakomoto tablets"—were supplied, but at the price of 2 yen for a small bottle of 200 tablets.[19]

Some of the medicine on hand would likely have been no better than placebos, at least according to an account by an American prisoner, Colonel William North, who arrived in January 1945. He noted that "the medicines and supplies issued at this camp as well as the other camps where I was interned were medicines which had been sent as relief supplies by the United States to Japan after an earthquake or typhoon I believe in 1923." He later testified to seeing "several crates of these supplies with their original packing and shipping instructions. Some of these supplies were crated in 1918 and had been given to the Japs after the First World War. For the most part the medicines were stale and unusable."[20]

It is hard to assess who was responsible for this situation. North reported that "when the Japanese medical officer would prescribe medicine, the Japanese medical orderly [medical officer] Hata would delay filling the prescription and issuing the medicine."[21] Lieutenant Colonel Saunders, on the other hand, judged that Hata was initially "fairly decent" and only later became "very hostile."[22] It does not appear that the Japanese were uniformly indifferent to the fate of the POWs. For instance, the most seriously ill servicemen were sent to the military hospital in Fukuoka to receive more intensive care.

Moreover, POWs in Fukuoka 1 were not initially forced to work when they were ill, as occurred later. The Mancunian Metcalf worked in the cookhouse for the first six months, before being hospitalized. Subsequently he joined the other captives in building an aerodrome, located about half a mile from the camp. Lieutenant Colonel Saunders dug trenches alongside the others. The Geneva Conventions strictly regulated the use of POW labor. But this depended on several interpretations: Did working with scrap iron contribute to manufacturing tanks? Exactly what was undesirable or "degrading"?[23] In Japan as in the United States, captives' labor helped outfit troops.[24] But Saunders judged, "We were not unreasonably hard worked."[25]

All in all, concluded Saunders, "general conditions were fairly reasonable as judged by Japanese standards." Still, he had only harsh words for the commandant. He focused his ire on practices that he found personally humiliating. Saunders judged Sakamoto "an uneducated man of a brutal and callous temperament." But it was the translator, Katsura Takeo, who was the "undisputed power behind the throne." Saunders accused the two of being "entirely responsible" for the "beatings and indignities to which men in their camps were subjected."[26]

Saunders was bitter about "the well-known Japanese dictum that to be taken a P.O.W. was a disgraceful act" and considered this ideology to be the major influence on prisoner treatment at Fukuoka 1. He recalled that Sakamoto had "on several occasions made that very plain to me." Saunders added that "at one camp, after evening roll-call on the anniversary of our arrival in Japan, the Senior Japanese N.C.O. made us all a speech in which he emphasized that he considered us cowards, and that any treatment was good enough for us."[27]

Many of the POWs, in Fukuoka as elsewhere, describe being slapped or beaten, though usually after disciplinary infractions—often quite minor. These beatings usually came at the hands of Katsura or the guard Horsumi, according to Saunders.[28] Galixtro Garcia was beaten for almost 3½ hours for possessing a penknife.[29] Albert Cleave was beaten for not returning his ration of corned beef. David Adams was severely beaten by Sakamoto and given five days in a cell just for taking a corncob while working on the aerodrome. POWs were made to count off in Japanese; those who could not do so were sometimes slapped in the face.[30]

What Saunders found particularly intolerable was how officers and enlisted men were treated equally. Worse, "not only were we treated exactly like the men but all of us were treated like the lowest Japanese privates." He could not stand how "he and other officers were required to salute [the] lowest Japanese soldier down to [the] latest joined recruit."[31] As an officer, he had expected better.

When Saunders compared his treatment to that of the "lowest Japanese private," he implicitly acknowledged how common face-slapping was in the Japanese Army. As we have seen, men in the Japanese Army may have considered it preferable to the alternative. Lieutenant General Hamada Hiroshi, future chief of the Prisoner of the War Bureau, touched on the issue in a POW camp directors meeting in 1943. He described these ad hoc punishments as a "traditional bad army practice" and attributed it to flaws of Japanese culture. Hamada may have considered it a "bad army practice," but evidence suggests Japanese soldiers on the ground disagreed. Unofficial punishment like face-slapping was better than criminal punishment, which disgraced one's name and family. Hamada implicitly confirmed that military personnel took a different attitude when he attributed this kind of practice not to official policy but to the behavior of low-ranking army men and hired guards (koyōnin).[32]

On March 9, 1943, the Ministry of Home Affairs updated and tightened Russo-Japanese War era regulations for the punishment of POWs to deal with the dramatic increase in POW labor.[33] Japan's formal stance was that torture and private sanctions did not occur, except for isolated cases in domestic POW camps.

Manpower shortages in the army meant wounded veterans were recruited to staff temporary camps run by the companies. They got a pay bump, but may have borne grudges against men whose compatriots had injured them.[34] These Japanese NCOs and hired guards would likely have had little, if any, prior contact with Europeans and Americans, increasing the risk that cultural misunderstandings and language barriers would lead to this kind of punishment (shiteki seisai).[35] On the other hand, the British Army and Americans previously stationed in the Philippines had generally only encountered Asians in a colonial context, and almost never in positions of authority. Some of them considered face-slapping or beatings by Japanese to be the worst form of humiliation. Many did not come to the camps with high regard for the Japanese in general and found it difficult to understand—literally—what was expected of them.

We can get a sense of the POWs' attitudes toward guards from the fact that in Fukuoka 1 Allied men called a guard named Honda "Bucktooth" and another "Freckles."[36] Still another guard was jokingly referred to as the "One-Armed Bandit." The humor would not have been appreciated by wounded and disabled veterans, who made up a growing proportion of guards assigned to temporary camps after August 1943.[37]

Commanders came from the reserves or second reserves. The IJA also faced shortages of lower-rank personnel. Dispatch camps in particular still lacked a sufficient number of petty officers and soldiers. Most concerning was the shortage of interpreters.[38] Some of the companies operating dispatch camps provided their own guards, who received little to no training in how to treat prisoners. Some likely suffered from undiagnosed and untreated post-traumatic stress disorder, and their resentment of POWs may have led to some of these abuses, as Utsumi Aiko argues. Others were re-cruited from Korea and Taiwan and may have learned to follow the example of veteran guards during their two-month training sessions.[39]

While POWs were usually objects of pity, both then and now, at least some of them may have given inexperienced or disabled guards reasons to worry. As a Dutch detainee later recalled, about some of the construction workers captured on Wake Island, "every single one of them had a rather colourful past of manslaughter, rape and so on."[40] Moreover, while the ratio of guards to prisoners varied over time, it could range as high to sixty to one.[41]

In a session of the Diet in February 1943, the same month Japan was forced to withdraw the last of its troops from Guadalcanal, the vice min-ister of the Army, Kimura Heitarō, argued for changing the 1905 War Pris-oners Punishment Act.[42] Kimura sought to update the regulations from the time of the Russo-Japanese War and to toughen punishments for POWs who committed infractions. Kimura claimed that the 1905 War Prisoners Punishment Act was inadequate, and further that the Japanese government had "regretted it," given that "some Russian POWs showed disobedience by resisting the guards or behaving violently or beating the members of the POW camp." Kimura, speaking for the government, noted that Japan had thousands of POWs, "and their nationalities and qualities are very different and complicated." This was likely even more worrisome to Kimura now that more and more of them were coming to Japan. But his answer was to add rules to the War Prisoners Punishments Act.[43] In March 1943, the Ministry of Home Affairs updated the regulations governing POWs, adding penal-ties for resistance, including capital punishment and life imprisonment, as well as shorter sentences.[44]

In 1943, as the danger of Allied bombing of Japanese cities increased, Japanese military authorities debated whether captured US airmen were war criminals or POWs.[45] This was already an issue after the Doolittle raid in April 1942.[46] A year earlier, the chief of the POWIB had argued to the Ministry of the Army and to the general staff that airmen should have the protected status of POWs. But he lost this argument.[47] Because the alleged crime had already occurred, the government could not simply issue new laws. Tōjō instead issued new military regulations, itself a six-step pro-cess.[48] Legal Affairs drafted the regulations under the premise that these air raids were indiscriminate and violated the 1923 Hague Draft Conven-tion on Air Combat. The question of whether or not an attack had violated international laws determined whether a captured combatant was to be treated as a protected POW or subject to punishment—even death as a war criminal.

On the other hand, in February 1944 the vice minister of the Army prohibited guards from inflicting punishment on POWs without authorization. The POWIB had tracked many such incidents and named the culprits for punishment. For example, in 1943 in Hakodate, Takeshita Toshio beat a POW with a bamboo sword for shirking work. Kanamaru Matsuzo beat a prisoner for stealing medicine. Tanaka Jun'chiro beat a prisoner who stole cucumbers from the Omimato munitions dump. And Imai Kiyomi slapped a POW who "did not show an obedient attitude." Some guards were taken before Japanese military justice. Court-martials (*gunpō kaigi*) punished soldiers for transgressing the rules and harming civilians or others.

But this policy was never consistently applied, most likely because of power politics in the military. At some companies employing POWs, such as Asano Cement, guards who inflicted private sanctions were punished. Yet only a total of eighty-three were punished for this practice, accounting for only a tiny fraction of all such incidents. Moreover, the vice minister's memorandum did not provide for any specific steps likely to reduce the prevalence of this practice, such as new training. Instead, wounded veterans and imperial youth from the colonies continued to mete out ad hoc punishments.[49]

One of the challenges the guards faced at camps like Fukuoka 1 was that they had to move and move again, at the same time as new POWs— accustomed to different camps—came and went. In the fall of 1943, authorities moved Fukuoka 1 to Tatara-cho (Kashii) in suburban Fukuoka, where the 230 men from Kumamoto were joined by another 74 American, British, and Dutch captives.[50] In April 1944, additional Dutch, British, and American civilians from Wake Island joined the camp.[51] The new captives included physically weakened men and hospital cases.

Saunders, the commander of the British contingent that was first held captive in Fukuoka 1, later claimed that, "despite all their greatest efforts, the Japanese failed to quench the general spirit of optimism which always prevailed amongst us." But to the extent that unit cohesion and morale mattered for individual survival, these comings and goings could only hurt. Saunders himself argued that it was the presence of these new captives that explained "the heavy death-roll in the two months that followed." For him, "responsibility for these deaths must lie with the higher authorities which ordered the move." But Saunders argued that Sakamoto's "callous and indifferent attitude" also "materially contributed to these deaths."[52]

The numbers of Americans and Dutch at Fukuoka 1 began to grow in 1944, both before and after Fukuoka 1 moved once again in April of that year. Now it was located within a city, Ōaza-Mushiroda, alongside an airport. Some prisoners called it Hirao, after its address (Higashi Hirao 3-chome). The camp was located at the foot of the hills surrounding the airfield, but outside the airfield's boundaries. It was supposed to be a summer camp for light work. Some of the POWs worked as mechanics on planes, or on trucks used to haul building supplies. Others constructed airfield bomb shelters. Still others mined coal and later worked at a lumberyard near the camp.

In the same month Fukuoka 1 moved to Ōaza Mushiroda, a number of American civilian contractors captured on Wake Island were transferred to the camp. Under international law, civilians should not have been kept in a POW camps, but in fact this practice was not uncommon.[53] In May and June 1944, Dutch and Malayan POWs arrived. The British identified them as "mostly natives."[54] At Fukuoka 6, Dutch POWs mined coal for Takamatsu mining company, later Nippon Mining Company. At Fukuoka 17 (Ōmuta), prisoners mined coal at the Miike mine for Mitsui. Prisoners at both camps were stabbed for attempting escape.[55]

Dutch serviceman J. Oosterhuis originally served with the Fourth Infantry Battalion based at Tjimahi (Cimahi) near Bandung, in the Dutch East Indies. In the summer and fall of 1944, Oosterhuis was held at Fukuoka 6B in Mizumaki, a notorious camp where the labor consisted of mining coal. Many died there, and an Australian was allegedly murdered there after attempting to escape. Oosterhuis recorded that he was imprisoned for 2½ days in an "eiso," a 2.5-x-2.5-meter cell without windows or furniture. Initially he was actually happy to be fed, and away from the Japanese. "Then it felt like torture because it was so cold, boring and uncomfortable."[56]

Perhaps unsurprisingly, a constant topic of conversation among POWs was which camp was the best. The most common answer was none. Oosterhuis wrote that some "have been defeated by the terrible cold," and were inclined to forget all of the horrors inflicted upon them in previous camps. But Oosterhuis observed that there were big differences between a camp like 6B and some of the others, which he actually recalled with real nostalgia on his arrival at Moji: "I wish I was still in our comfortable 9th camp. . . . [Now] we're living in a large stone Y.M.C.A.-building here, not as cold as the wooden barracks, but no heating either. There is a beautiful dining room though, and an even more beautiful heater, which seems to be only for show."

The ICRC could also observe and report variations between different camps, but only when local commanders gave permission. We do not have any inspection reports for Fukuoka Branch Camp No. 1, but the inspection reports for other camps do indicate what conditions POWs there had experienced and also what other camp commanders believed was appropriate in the treatment of POWs. On July 25, Dick Mouravieff informed Geneva via cable that Colonel Sugasawa Ijū, initially commander of the main camp in Fukuoka, would allow visits to camps under his command, such as Fukuoka 6B.[57] He said that POW health was taken into account when assigning work, both hymn books and wafers were distributed, and that "POWs treatment regarding army same as Japanese army."[58]

The Swedish were the protecting power for Dutch civilians in Japan. So it was the Swedish minister in Tokyo, Widar Bagge, who visited camp No. 11. This was the first visit to Yamano City Camp by a protecting power representative. Bagge also met with the spokesman for the Dutch POWs, though all the time he was accompanied by Colonel Sugasawa as the camp commander.[59]

Fukuoka No. 11, located near a coal mine, held 389 POWs, of whom 147, or just under 40 percent, were Dutch. Bagge found that the POWs were continuously losing weight and strength, though the camp had a vegetable garden and domestic animals, eight goats and ten chickens (the goat milk was just for the hospital). According to Japanese authorities, a doctor from the Mitsui Mining Company visited the captives daily in the mines. They needed medicine, such as the early sulfa-class antibiotics sulfapyridine and sulfathiazole, and worried about the cold and the lack of protein. Sulfapyridine and sulfathiazole were used in Britain at the time, but had many side effects, especially for people who proved to be allergic to them. Four POWs had died already: one from pneumonia, and three from intestinal disease.[60]

Bagge found that although morale "on the whole could be considered good, it was nevertheless true that a few of the men seem unable to stand the strain and let themselves go in spite of their stronger comrades' attempts to help them." He believed that this was due to unaccustomed hard work. But the prisoners were also concerned about their families in the Dutch East Indies. Neither were they allowed newspapers, as "these might have a

Prisoners of war in the Mitsui Tagawa mines, Fukuoka. POWs throughout the Japanese empire worked in a variety of capacities, and often for private companies. (Beeldbank WO2—NIOD.)

disturbing influence on the prisoners' minds." They could not even read books, because all of the books in camp were in English. On a later inspection, Bagge found the look of the prisoners "rather gloomy and not very satisfactory."

When Oosterhuis, together with forty-four other men, was moved to another Fukuoka camp in December 1944, he was struck by the cold—zero degrees Celsius. But otherwise his first impressions on arrival were good. For instance, the only work was "an hour of messing around" a day.[61] But Oosterhuis observed that as many as 25 percent of the captives were sick: as noted above, the facility had been built as a summer camp. Captives waited to move to a winter camp six kilometers (3.7 miles) away, which they themselves built.

That same month, 104 Canadian Red Cross packages arrived. These were to be saved until Christmas. After the butter and cheese had been sent to the hospital and the meat and fish to the kitchen, what remained was sent to the barracks: one can of powdered milk, one box of raisins, one bar of milk chocolate, one small bag of salt and pepper, one jar of jam, one small bag of sugar (about 250 grams), one box of cream crackers, and one box of tea bags. The day after that, 670 American Red Cross packages arrived.[62]

Oosterhuis meticulously recorded these details. He commented that the food was "slightly better and more copious," but altogether not very different from that at the previous camp. On the other hand, it was much more difficult to get information on events outside of the camp. Oosterhuis had recently heard that sixty-three Dutch messages of twenty-five words each had arrived at Red Cross headquarters. Additionally, two of the camp members were each allowed to send a ten-word telegram, and thirteen of them (including Oosterhuis) were allowed to fill out a 150-word "broadcast form." In the same month, Red Cross representatives met with prisoners' representatives, who requested clothes, shoes, medicine, and letters from home.[63]

On the first day of Christmas, camp officials handed out goods from the Red Cross, after a can of corned beef, fish, a half can of powdered milk, and a bar of soap had been removed from each package.[64] That left the prisoners with one box of raisins (or prunes), one box of cheese, three cans of "so-called cheesebutter," a half can of powdered milk, 100 sugar cubes, two bars of vitamin chocolate, one can of coffee, one jar of jam, one can of liver pâté, two cans of pork pie and 5½ packs of cigarettes.

Oosterhuis recorded the contents of these packages because otherwise there was so little news and so many hours of boredom. The opportunity for work was therefore not necessarily unwelcome. He worked alongside other men in the camp.[65] He noted that officers in Hirao—unlike other camps—were doing all the work before the other prisoners came. They had no say in what was going on in the camp, and were allowed to talk to neither the prisoners nor the camp commander.[66]

One day he was sent to the station to unload wagons filled with gravel. This was considered a good job, because it presented the opportunity to obtain extra food. In the camp there was little to no food available for purchase. But when men went to the station, they could usually get their hands on some vegetables or other food. One time one of the guards made soup for the entire "station party." Another time Oosterhuis got caught trying to smuggle some tangerines into the camp, and was beaten by the guards. After that, he wrote, he began to understand the expression "a broken man" a little better.[67]

To read his account, it seemed Oosterhuis spent much of his time not working, but simply being cold, eating, and sleeping.[68] But on January 18, 1945, the new Fukuoka 1 camp at Hakozaki was finally finished. Prisoners

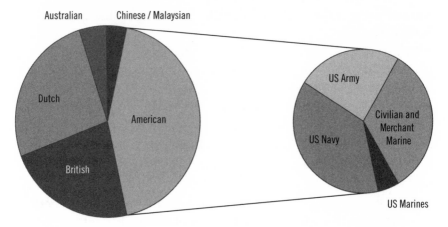

Breakdown of POWs and Internees Held in Fukuoka 1. By combining information from multiple sources it is possible to identify the nationality of 615 people who were held captive at Fukuoka 1 over the course of the war. The branch of service is known for only 120 of the 265 Americans, and the exact makeup of the camp at any given moment is even more difficult to determine. But even rough estimates based on incomplete data—such as the number of Norwegians, Canadians, South Africans, Indonesians, and New Zealanders—indicate the extreme heterogeneity of the camp population. (Data sources: US National Archives and Records Administration; Dutch National Archives; Mansell; Find My Past.)

moved to the camp, carrying their luggage, walking ninety minutes through a blizzard. It was situated along the bank of the Ubi River, and immediately below the Kagoshima railway. Subsequently, the camp moved yet again within Fukuoka City. For some prisoners who had started out in Fukuoka 1, this was their third move. But the new camp looked much more comfortable. It was built under trees and the barracks had wooden walls. It was within a grove of pine trees—perhaps for protection from bombing raids.

A large new contingent of Americans, including Captain Goodpasture, Carl Engelhart, and Jack Schwartz, arrived at Hakozaki in the dead of winter 1945. They included 193 men who had been captured in the Philippines almost three years earlier. At this point there were hundreds of prisoners at Hakozaki—Americans, British, Dutch, Australian, Norwegian, Canadian, South African, New Zealanders, as well as Indonesian, Malay, Arab, and Chinese captives.[69] Engelhart reported that British men of the "other ranks" greeted them. To the British, the Americans seemed like "walking skeletons."[70] They arrived by truck after a four-hour train trip from Moji. British escorts helped them out of trucks and into the barracks.[71]

On arrival, the Americans ate tea with sugar and *lugao* (in Filipino, rice mush with salmon). They were each given a pile of seven blankets, according to one source. Each barrack had a stove that gave at least "the illusion of warmth." They could have a bath each day. And the men learned they would also receive long underwear and an overcoat.[72] The next morning, guards processed the prisoners, compiling a roster and weighing the men. By this point Engelhart, the Japanese-speaking G-2 officer captured at Corregidor, weighed only 85 pounds. He had an interview with a Japanese officer, who gave him cigarettes and more for his commanding officer, Colonel Curtis T. Beecher, of California.[73]

According to Engelhart, prisoners ate regular meals and received additional Red Cross parcels of food once a month. These parcels also included cigarettes. But Captain William Fossey, from Oklahoma, remembered the Red Cross parcels differently: "It is well known that Japanese would not give us Red Cross parcels sent to us from the States. They would rob packages of cigarettes, food, etc." Supplies were low: "They denied us the bare necessities of food, medicine, clothing and warmth."[74]

So how do we understand different accounts from soldiers belonging to the same unit, on a specific question like the distribution of Red Cross parcels? In this case, it appears that the situation may have changed over time, and the difference was party attributable to the actions of a particular Japanese doctor, First Lieutenant Danno Kazuo. An American sergeant in the medical department, Dr. James Robert McIntosh, originally identified Lieutenant Danno as the camp doctor from February 1945 until May 1945.[75] Until Danno's arrival, McIntosh claimed, food supplies were inventoried and held for sick POWs. But Danno allowed Japanese personnel to eat them, as he himself did. He stopped distributing daily food and medicine for POWs and instead distributed supplies once every ten to fourteen days.

McIntosh "personally saw Danno eating food which came from parcels, while holding sick call for POWs." "Almost every day, when I cleaned out Danno's office," McIntosh reported, "I would find wrappers and empty cans which had once contained Red Cross food supplies. To my knowledge, this did not occur prior to the arrival of Danno." Moreover, "Danno would not excuse a POW from work unless he had an extremely high temperature or had a visible external injury."

It is hard to assess how many American POWs would have survived at this point with better food and medical care. As we have seen, many were sick when they arrived at Fukuoka 1, and they already looked like "skeletons."

As Captain Goodpasture himself explained, Fukuoka was the worst experience of all, except for the hell ships. But this was "probably partly due to the fact that we arrived in a very distressful physical and mental condition... There is no question but what many who died here died from mental distress in a defeated attitude, as we had about reached our rope's end." Engelhart agreed: "It was too late for some of our comrades and once more I began jotting down the names of friends who died, this time in POW camp no. 1, Fukuoka."[76] Altogether, fifty-three Americans died in the three months following their arrival.

Witnessing the deaths of friends who had helped one another survive years of mistreatment made the stealing and cruelty at Fukuoka 1 all the more intolerable. Gerry Nolthenius was captured in the Dutch East Indies in March 1942, then was sent to several POW camps, the last being Fukuoka 1. The grim death statistics and "the oversupply of vermin" were striking to him, but so too was "the terrible corruption in the camp."[77]

Certainly by this point, in the last few months of the war, punishment was no longer restricted to face-slapping or beatings because of rule breaking. Many of the guards themselves were breaking the rules by stealing from prisoners and beating POWs who reported them. Some of the guards were still soldiers, like those from the Seventy-Second, Seventy-Third, Seventy-Fourth, and Seventy-Fifth Coastal Artillery. But military guards were often in the camp for only about a month, rotating in and out. Civilian guards, on the other hand, were a constant presence for POWs, day and night. One officer said, "Most often beatings by these guards took place after the Japanese officers left the camp."[78] During roll call, the civilian guards ransacked the POW quarters and stole articles. Prisoners who reported them were beaten. Some guards, like Matsunaga Shigenori, did not participate.[79] But "Bucktooth" (Honda) always did.[80] Henry Forsberg accused "Bucktooth" of killing a man and noted "he was continually beating the men."[81]

In Fukuoka 1, like in many other camps, it was the translator, in this case Katsura, who was the most prominent and visible face of the enemy. Even the camp commander was never seen by many POWs. Katsura, on the other hand, personally oversaw the formal punishment of POWs for alleged infractions. American colonel William D. North himself had been slapped by Katsura. "Katsura slapped me without provocation, and quite severely."[82] He had also reported hearing from Captain Kostecki that "Katsura beat an

American to death in the camp."[83] Captain Kostecki was the representative or liaison officer between the Americans and the Japanese medical officers. He was in closer contact with Katsura than any other American at the camp, and personally had to sign the death certificates—often under duress.[84] William J. Fossey remembered Katsura as being particularly cruel. "This sergeant had spent much time in the United States before the war, spoke good English, but was mean by nature."[85]

Punishments included standing at attention for long periods of time in the bitter weather and being shut in a "dog box." The box was made from slats with wide cracks between and so constructed that it was impossible to stand inside. The prisoner consigned to the "dog box" was allowed one blanket in the bitter cold and no shoes. Major Roby was given this punishment for a minor infraction of a camp rule. He was first severely beaten by Katsura and had to remain in the "dog box" for several days, suffering frostbite of both feet and severe exposure. Previously an American prisoner had been assigned to the same punishment for tearing a Japanese blanket. He died from exposure.[86]

Camp Commander Sakamoto Yuhichi sought to enforce regulations, including corporal punishment of POWs for "stealing food and clothing from the warehouse."[87] Sakamoto argued that he had only carried out his duty based on "the regulations of the army and commands of my superiors."[88] But Sakamoto was actually said to have gone above and beyond to provide food and medical supplies from Fukuoka City, attempting to purchase it himself, and insisting to subordinates that they should not commit corporal punishment. POWs' deaths were due to factors beyond his control: their fifty-day sea transport or the fighting they had experienced before their transport.

No doubt, no matter who was in charge of the camp, everyone close to a city in Japan in 1945 was now in danger. Following a particularly devastating attack on Tokyo in March 1945, in which approximately 100,000 Japanese died, the US Army Air Corps began systematically firebombing smaller cities all across the country. Essential workers were barred from leaving the cities, even though they lacked shelter. Only farmers now had adequate food as the government experimented with new sources of nutrition, such as dolphins and silkworms. A seven-day workweek was now standard, tuberculosis was on the rise, and even boys and girls as young as twelve were put to work in the fields or as janitors. Throughout Japan there was a serious shortage of shoes, clothing, and coal.[89]

All of this further poisoned the atmosphere in POW camps. While Japan remained responsible for its captives, and it is impossible to condone the way many were beaten and otherwise abused, the deteriorating conditions outside created basic structural constraints that made it increasingly difficult to protect POWs. Already, at the end of 1944, the home minister had warned the war minister that citizens were complaining that POWs were getting better treatment than they were.[90]

This resentment and a desire for revenge were preconditions for the attacks and summary executions of captured American airmen. In Ishigaki-jima, on April 15, 1945, an American bomber was shot down and three crew members were captured after their parachute descent. After interrogation, two were beheaded, and one was stabbed with a bayonet. Their bodies were cremated and the ashes discarded in the sea.[91]

In May 1945, ten B-29s bombed Tachiarai airport, near the border of Kumamoto and Ōita Prefectures. One lost control, eleven men parachuted out, and then they fled on foot. In Seiwa village, hundreds of villagers ran after one soldier, Robert C. Johnson, who eventually committed suicide. In Azamihara village, Leo C. Oenic was surrounded by hundreds of armed villagers, who shot and stabbed him even though he did not resist. The bodies of Johnson and Oenic were brought to the police station and left for a day outside. Villagers attacked the corpses.[92]

The police caught the remaining nine men and brought them to Seibu Army headquarters. Because Tokyo prisons were full, only the aircraft commander was sent there. All others were to be "appropriately" dealt with locally, meaning they would be executed. Army doctor Komori consulted with Prof. Ishiyama Fukujirō and instead decided to do medical experiments on the men.[93]

With these "experiments," the treatment of POWs descended to a new level of inhumanity. On May 17, 1945, sometime after 2:00 p.m., these eight airmen were brought into an experimentation room at the university. According to the testimony of Higashino Toshio, a student at the time, Prof. Ishiyama Fukujirō and around ten colleagues were in attendance, along with soldiers. They ran a number of experiments to test organ function, including the liver and the heart. Because the IJA was short of saline solution, they were determined to find an alternative before the United States invaded.[94] One experiment therefore entailed injecting diluted sea water into blood vessels to determine if sea water could be an alternative to saline. It was performed four times on the eight airmen, and killed them.[95]

On June 19, 1945, the city of Fukuoka itself was firebombed. The next day, captured flyers were taken to Fukuoka Municipal Girls' High School and beheaded in a mass execution.[96] Some Japanese actually considered it to be humanitarian to quickly kill prisoners who would otherwise suffer torture under interrogation.[97] Others thought that crewmembers who were seriously injured after their aircraft was shot down would die soon enough, so it would relieve their pain.[98] When superior officers made those choices, it was the subordinates whose hands got dirty.[99]

By this point most of the Americans at Fukuoka 1, including Schwartz, Engelhart, and Goodpasture, had shipped off to a comparatively comfortable camp in Korea. In June 1945 the POWIB reported that there were 399 POWs left in Fukuoka 1.[100] According to some accounts, the camp had little work for the prisoners, so guards spent a lot of time "bullying" them. For example, they required malnourished and exhausted POWs to stand in line time after time.

But as much as POWs hated the beatings and other punishments Katsura and the guards inflicted on them, by 1945 those were not the greatest threat of death or injury. Instead, it was bombing by US Army Air Corps B-29s. The practice of establishing camps near mines and industry also meant they were at greater risk in these raids. "Almost every day they would come over and bomb us," Ellis recalled. "We weren't permitted to get in any foxholes or anything. We had to just stand there and watch our men get killed by bombs."[101] "Our whole camp was bombed and burned," as Moss later reported. All the men sick in the barracks at the time were lost.[102]

The fact that Fukuoka 1 was located directly alongside an airfield made the danger from bombing particularly great. Airfields in Kyushu were high-priority targets before and during the battle of Okinawa. The POWs were not exempt, because in most cases the Japanese did not mark their barracks as POW camps. Perhaps the most unfortunate POWs of all were those at Fukuoka 2, in the port of Nagasaki, and camp no. 14 (Fukushima), located one mile from ground zero of the atomic bombing. Ten sick POWs who remained in the building died when the atomic bomb was dropped on August 9. Altogether, thirty-five air raids hit POW camps in 1945. An estimated 318 POWs died, and 591 were injured.[103]

Had the Japanese Army purposely exposed POWs to air raids? A 1945 policy proscribed moving POWs out of range. After all, from the perspective of the Southern Army, it made no sense to risk the loss of their labor. POWs were "highly regarded as excellent technicians and laborers," according to policy, so "shifting them to other places greatly affected production." Another concern was that if POWs were moved, Japanese laborers would run away.[104] In the end, Army policy ordered POWs away from air raids, but only if it did not interfere with labor needs.[105]

POWIB chief Tamura enacted this policy, but claimed he attempted to evacuate POWs from camps near bombing targets. His limited success demonstrates the POWIB's lack of power.[106] But when Tamura became chief, Japan was losing the war and faced US invasion. He told the War Ministry that POWs who were employed in possible areas of attack should be evacuated away from the Pacific coast. If Japan had not surrendered, Kyushu would have been the initial target of the American invasion. In the end, most, but not all, POWs were moved to safer places.[107]

The cruelty and chaos in Japan's POW camps reflected what was going on all across the country. Especially in the last months of the war, POWs were denied adequate food, but so were Japanese civilians; Japanese children of this generation were literally stunted by malnutrition.[108] POWs were made to work, sometimes under tough conditions, but so were Japanese of all ages. Guards abused their authority and brutally punished any sign of disobedience, but so did local Japanese officials, who attacked civilians who dared to resist orders. POWs were often on the move, in temporary or inadequate housing. But now so were many Japanese civilians, as their homes were systematically destroyed by bombing or to create firebreaks.

The worst episodes in the Fukuoka camps were therefore not emblematic of the entire POW experience. Instead they reflected the suffering and chaos that was occurring outside the gates, and the bitter feelings among many Japanese as their homeland was systematically destroyed. Despite there being no overall policy to make POWS suffer, they did suffer considerably. Even for those who were not directly exposed to bombing, the situation was incredibly fluid, changeable, and capricious. That was one reason more it was so demoralizing.

# 7

## ENDINGS AND BEGINNINGS

On August 15, 1945, Emperor Hirohito announced that Japan would accept surrender, "enduring the [unavoidable] and suffering what is unsufferable."[1] Few understood Hirohito's formal way of speaking. But Japan had already endured carpet bombing, firestorms, and two atomic bombs. Sixty-six cities were devastated. It was estimated that 9 million people were homeless. Around 4.5 million were critically injured or ill. Close to 3 million Japanese were dead, including 1.7 million servicemen.[2] Somewhere between a quarter and a third of Japan's wealth had gone up in smoke.

While the emperor's address was broadcast over the radio in Japan and Korea, the recognition of defeat came at different times in different places.[3] From Seoul to Singapore, from Fukuoka to Manila, some guards had already deserted, while other soldiers would never surrender. Most waited obediently for instructions, and some were even made to fight with the Allies against anticolonial movements in the Dutch East Indies, French Indochina, and Korea. Allied officials faced the question of what to do with them all—not just the 6.5 million Japanese civilians and 3.5 million soldiers stranded all across Asia, but all the non-Allied civilians, dual nationals, stateless persons, and "natives" who were displaced by war, or suddenly unwelcome in places they had long called home.[4]

The soldiers had become "Japanese Surrendered Persons," a term proposed by Japanese officials to avoid shaming those who were ostensibly prohibited from being taken captive by their official *Instructions for the Battlefield*. These officials thought it was just another name for POWs.[5] But it meant that they lacked the protection of the Geneva Conventions.[6] The British decided they would "apply parts of the Convention but not quote it as authority"—a position not unlike the Japanese policy of accepting the Geneva Conventions mutatis mutandis.[7]

These decisions were made according to prewar logic. Imperial powers had already divided the world, and now they decided where to put various people. The Allies wanted to prioritize freeing fellow countrymen. But they could not move with equal speed everywhere. Logistics were tricky, Americans alone had ample transport, and everywhere they were confronted by the challenge of having to move millions of other people—some of whom were wanted for war crimes. But the first and most urgent question was simply to locate the POWs and civilian internees. Where were they, and what help could be provided to them quickly?[8]

During the war, Allied officials had only limited information about POW camps: their approximate number, some locations, and estimates of the number of captives each held. Information came from the International Committee of the Red Cross (ICRC), escaped POWs, and Japanese POWs themselves. In mid-August, Admiral Chester Nimitz, Commander in Chief for the Pacific (CINPAC), had a plan for freeing POWs called Operation "Blacklist."[9] This July 1945 assessment estimated about 36,000 personnel of various categories located in approximately 140 camps.[10] These estimates were not far off, but the exact locations of most camps were unknown, and the timetable soon accelerated after the destruction of Hiroshima and Nagasaki. On August 12, staff officers in Manila began teaching an eight-week course to prepare teams for evacuating captives. Topics included filing methods and determining which civilians were eligible for repatriation.[11] Japan's surrender three days later abruptly ended this training period after just four days. For the Americans, freeing POWs was a priority mission, "second only to military operations and to the maintenance of the forces of occupation."[12] On August 16, American planes began dropping supplies throughout Japan and Korea, even though they were not yet sure where exactly the POWs might be to receive them.

From late 1944, Allied powers planned that theater commanders would lead recovery and repatriation, with each responsible for a different zone.[13] CINPAC had primary responsibility for the four main islands of Japan, about 100 adjacent islands including Tsushima, and Korea below the 38th parallel.[14] The initial plan was to go in phases. In the first phase, the Eighth Army backed by the naval forces of the Third Fleet was assigned to the islands to the north and east of Honshu, west of Yokohama and Tokyo. The Sixth Army—which had been preparing to invade Kyushu—would take the south, assisted by the Fifth Fleet. Korea and the China coast were initially the responsibility of the Tenth Army, but were reassigned on August 12 to the XXIV Corps together with the Seventh Fleet.[15]

William H. Halsey, commander of the Third Fleet, put Commodore R. W. Simpson in charge of liberating, evacuating, and providing med-

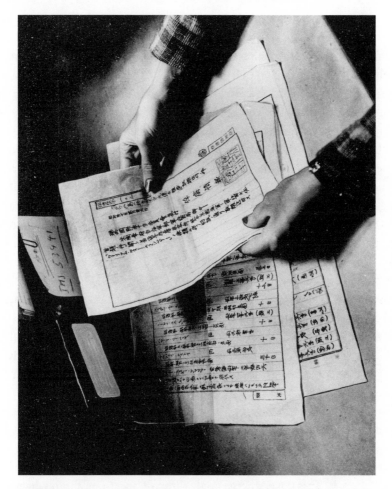

One of the first lists of American prisoners of war. Allied commanders initially had only a vague understanding of the numbers and location of POWs awaiting repatriation. Lists provided by the Japanese government, like this one, were incomplete and inaccurate. Authorities in Tokyo themselves struggled to keep track of their movements. (US National Archives and Records Administration.)

ical care to Allied POWs in his area of operations.[16] From August 15 to 29, Simpson organized and trained special medical units, communications units, and minor landing forces. The plan was to make amphibious landings with medical personnel, go to camps to provide immediate care, begin evacuation of the most seriously ill to hospital ships, then move ambulatory POWs.[17] The Third Fleet would provide air protection and reconnaissance, and the port of Yokohama would serve as the main base of operations for those requiring medical care and evacuation to the United States.[18]

On August 27, the Japanese gave the Allies a "yellow list" of camps. It might have been correct at one point. But in the last few months of the war, Japanese commanders moved Allied prisoners away from the heavily bombed Pacific coast.[19] The list was clearly incomplete and inaccurate, naming just seventy-three camps. Two days later, US commanders dispatched aircraft of the 314th Bombardment Wing to verify the location of these and other camps on the Japanese archipelago. On August 31, aircraft of the same wing were sent to Hainan Island, then the areas around Peking (Beijing), Hong Kong, Shanghai, and the Mukden area of Manchuria. This reconnaissance verified the existence and location of fifty-seven additional camps, a number that was expected to increase.[20] New detailed information was provided by aircraft carriers, photographic coverage, and other intelligence.[21]

Before any of the American forces were on the ground, Swiss physician Marcel Junod was already seeking out POW camps. He had arrived in Tokyo on August 9, after a considerable delay, to head the ICRC delegation. The Americans would also work with Dr. Fritz Bilfinger, another ICRC delegate, the Swiss government representative, Dr. Weidmann, and Swedish representative Mr. Walden.[22]

The suffering and devastation all around them struck the delegates and presented an enormous logistical challenge to any POW evacuation plan. In an August 30 telegram Junod reported that 80 percent of hospitals were destroyed or seriously damaged. Conditions in two hospitals were "beyond description."[23] This posed increasingly difficult questions about what could be asked of the Japanese. "I have come to the conclusion," he wrote, "that it is utterly impossible to ask the Hiroshima Chapter of the Japanese Red Cross society to assist us in the POW evacuation. After seeing all there and with the Japanese Red Cross not even in a position to meet the most urgent demands for the most primitive necessities, I have told them . . . we would try to manage without them."[24]

The next day, Bilfinger reported that he had visited two camps and had eight more to go. But he too was most struck by what he saw in Hiroshima: "I shall never forget it all my life . . . it is not at all exaggerated, and I strongly recommend you [Junod] to come yourself at earliest opportunity to see for yourself these conditions."[25] In Fuchū in Hiroshima, it took four days just for a telegram to reach Tokyo.[26] Allied High Command ordered, "No one can pass through Hiroshima."[27] The city had been a major transport hub, so its loss created a cascade of logistical problems, such as diverting trains through Kyoto, one of the only Japanese cities to be spared bombing. The ICRC also relied on supplies from Hiroshima. But the Japanese assisted them in carrying out their work. The Prisoner of War Information Bureau (POWIB) searched for a locomotive so Bilfinger could visit internees in Miyoshi. A Japanese captain struggled to procure a car so he could visit Hiroshima.[28] Bilfinger made it to Miyoshi and reported "working literally day and night."[29]

Bilfinger faced many unforeseen challenges. He ran into the crew of a B-29 at a camp that the ICRC had not even known about.[30] In Miyoshi he met the crew from the Netherlands hospital ship *Optennoort,* captured on December 19, 1942. "The joy of these internees to see us was indescribable and I shall never forget the handshakes of these happy Dutchmen." On September 2, he wrote to Junod that "the crew, medical officers, and nurses must be considered as protected personnel and should have been freed immediately upon seizure of the ship."[31] But what about the ship itself? Bilfinger wondered whether policy on evacuating POWs and civilian internees would differ. Specific cases only raised more questions.

On September 9, Bilfinger wrote from Onomichi, where he had encountered former camp representatives for POWs. "We have found a source of beer which is very much appreciated." A 12:00 p.m. daily broadcast for POWS instructed ex-POWs and internees to stay in place.[32] "This is sound advice, will make things go faster. Doesn't appear evacuation of Hiroshima is imminent, presumably 6th Army commander will start with Osaka. We join the POWs in wishing for evacuation . . . for ourselves."[33]

Unsurprisingly, ex-POWs did not always want to stay in place. Some streamed to Kyoto for sightseeing and others to Osaka in hopes of contacting the Allied vanguard.[34] "Some prisoners even went into business, one Australian opening a hotel in Kyoto."[35] To Bilfinger this was chaos: The Sixth Army had not yet arrived, but ex-prisoners, led by Australian Major Campbell, organized their own evacuation center.[36] Bilfinger reached Campbell, and also got in touch with Major Mitchell, the first Eighth Army officer in charge of evacuation that he had encountered. Mitchell was eager to get going with evacuation, but did not seem to understand or appreciate the work already done by the ICRC. "Our people were pretty well sidetracked," Bilfinger wrote. It was only when Mitchell realized he lacked necessary information on camps in Hiroshima that he accepted help.[37]

The evacuation of POWs from Japan accelerated once American processing teams finally began to reach the camps.[38] Each team had nine officers and twenty enlisted men, including one officer and one enlisted man each from Great Britain, Australia, Canada, and the Netherlands. There were seventy of these teams altogether, reflecting a 1:500 ratio with the expected number of POWs. This included the Sixth and Eighth Army, and the Sixth Corps (this included the XXIV Corps in Korea).[39] Eighth Army medical officers provided medical care. Those who required hospitalization were moved to hospital ships, including the *Marigold,* the first US ship to enter Yokohama, and the USS *Rescue.*[40] As soon as practicable, captives were to be liberated, evacuated to Tokyo, and processed.

The American center of operations for all these activities was Tokyo, "A fantastic monument of ruin to American aerial power," as *Los Angeles Times* reporter James Mcglincy observed: "burned out trolley cars stood on their tracks and tall smokestacks were tombstones for factories pounded into dust and rubble." Japanese he saw in the streets "appeared to be still suffering from shock."[41] Freed captives and freed civilians would be treated in the Forty-Second General Hospital.[42] By September 3, they had established facilities in the Yokohama dock area. By September 4, hospital personnel began processing the first group.

Officers and nurses made up a welcoming committee that gave former captives candy and cigarettes on arrival. A band played popular American songs. When the former captives reached the hospital area, after traveling some fourteen to sixteen hours, they disrobed, and what was salvageable was sent to the quartermaster depot. After putting on fresh clothes, they were served a hot meal.[43] Afterward, personnel sprayed captives and their clothes with DDT. A nurse took personal data, followed by a physical. If a captive was not sick, he was given new clothing and then went to General Headquarters processing. Eventually the processing center could deal with three people per minute.[44]

Military officials compiled records showing the nationality, branch of service, date and place of recovery, and physical condition of evacuees. They sent one copy to ICRC representatives.[45] Interrogators classified former captives for evacuation according to status. All who were ambulatory left Japan within twenty-four hours of arrival in Yokohama.[46] Men were served a meal, disrobed, bathed, given a physical examination, given new clothes, and admitted directly to a hospital ship.[47]

Alfred A. Weinstein, a surgeon taken captive in the Philippines and later shipped to Japan, described the scene:

> We clambered aboard the U. S. S. *Rescue* and were promptly told to strip and throw our lice-covered rags overboard. Into a steam-filled shower room we crowded. Oh, the first heavenly thrill of plenty of soap and piping-hot water squirting through the needle valves of the shower! We scrubbed and scrubbed our bodies, peeling off one layer of filth after another. We squirmed with pleasure under the jets. As we left the showers, medics with flit guns sprayed our heads and bodies with DDT while we pirouetted slowly, arms raised. In freshly washed pajamas sweet with cleanliness we walked through a line of docs who checked us over quickly. On the softest mattress, between the whitest sheets I have ever seen, I slipped into bed in the hundred-bed ward.[48]

It took the men some time to get used to the food—Weinstein describes throwing up from poached eggs—but also the onslaught of sensations, feeling safe and finally in control of their lives again.[49]

The Sixth Army, which had been preparing to invade Kyushu, assumed responsibility for POWs west of Osaka with the assistance of the Fifth Fleet. On Osaka Bay, across from Kobe and Shikoku, Wakayama was the base for evacuation teams for POWs and civilian internees in Western Honshu and Shikoku. It was selected because of its central location and rail links. Rear Admiral R. S. Riggs ran the center starting on September 4. Riggs and his team made their home at Mampa Ro, a small hotel on the beach on Wakanoura Bay. They originally estimated 10,000 POWs. It turned out that a more realistic number was 2,600. Biggs planned for "mentally defective" people and women and children to be sent immediately to hospital ships.

On September 14, the first POWs arrived from Shikoku. By September 15 at 3:00 p.m., all the American sailors and marines, as well as POWs from the Netherlands, Australia, and Britain, had been processed. Contrary to their expectations, they found only a handful of civilians, and no women or children.[50]

In Kyushu, Rear Admiral Frank G. Fahrion commanded the naval forces supporting the Sixth Army's evacuation mission. On September 11, his forces landed at Nagasaki. The Fifth Fleet under Admiral D. C. Ramsey had

Some of the most famous images of Allied POWs show how they became emaciated from malnutrition and disease during their captivity. But large numbers of Japanese servicemen were also starving by the end of the war, such as these sailors in the Marshall Islands, who were subject to blockade and bombardment. (U.S. Navy, 80-G-347131.)

first cleared the port of mines. Nagasaki was an excellent natural port, but just over one month earlier had been hit by the world's second atomic bomb. During their time at Nagasaki, medical officers saw how the atomic bomb had devastated the city. Fahrion established a medical and processing station on the waterfront and brought in a hospital ship.[51]

On September 12, Recovery Team No. 9 aboard the *Chenango* (CVE-28) docked in Nagasaki.[52] On landing, Private First Class J. W. Gianes wrote in his log about the extensive damage from firebombing. "One ruined shipyard still holds the hulls of what looks like two unfinished tankers." Japanese soldiers also looked worse for wear: "Boy, what scrawny little specimens."

The next day he visited camps 17 and 25. "It was a moving experience. God what they've been thru." Gianes was surprised by the reception he and his team received from the Japanese:

> The people are practically bending over backwards being nice to us, and are so damn polite it seems funny as heck. I was sur-

prised, but the POWs harbour no resentment towards the Japanese civilians. According to them the civilians are more inclined to be friendly than not but were too afraid to do other than follow the dictates of the military who are the core of inception of all the hateful actions and atrocities that were perpetrated.[53]

Gianes encountered Dutch, British, Australian, and American prisoners, though many had left before he arrived. Ex-POWs, led by a senior officer, sometimes held former guards prisoner. Some did all they could to be kind, and gave the former guards food and clothing. He observed how organized the camps were with Allied camp commanders, "their military discipline and courtesy puts our own [men's] to shame." He noticed a number of Chinese, but because they were outside his mission, he ignored them.[54]

The camps were incredibly diverse and not just in terms of the many nationalities represented. For instance, there were 381 men left at Fukuoka 1, including Gerry Nolthenius, Henry Forsberg, and James McIntosh. More than a hundred were not actually POWs. About a third of the captives were American (153), a third British (140), and the remainder Dutch and Australian, as well as one Norwegian and one Canadian.[55] In the entire camp, there were just four officers.

Gianes noted that for a month, army planes had been dropping supplies into the camps.[56] Teams were accompanied by some medical personnel, but others remained at the station. At Nagasaki, recovered personnel were given medical exams. They then filled out questionnaires which covered a range of topics: a summary of military / naval experience, date of capture, type and degree of sickness, mistreatment or punishment in camp, quality and quantity of food, and occupation as prisoner. In the end, they obtained more than 9,000 statements.

Most of the POWs completed processing in thirty-six hours or less. The teams at Nagasaki evacuated 9,061 captives in all. By September 22, this evacuation was complete and POWs from Western Japan, along with recovery teams, were en route to the Philippines.[57] There they joined POWs and former internees from all across East Asia, including British, Australian, and Canadian male personnel, and later the Dutch. At Nichols Field, a medical processing group was set up to separate former prisoners into two groups: those needing hospitalization and those able to proceed directly to the depots.[58] The Fifth Replacement Depot managed male personnel, and the Women's Replacement and Disposition Center processed women and children. The command maintained a 1,500-bed general hospital, and at the two reception centers near Manila, two infirmaries and a number of dispensaries operated.[59]

Meanwhile, in Tokyo, the 42nd Hospital had completed processing by September 21. What work there was, was assumed by the 608th Medical Clearing Company and the 30th Portable Surgical Hospital at Atsugi Airfield.[60] In all, the Eighth Army freed and evacuated 23,985 persons.[61] Americans and Canadians were flown to Guam, Saipan, or Manila.[62] Most other nationals were flown to Okinawa and then to Manila. C-54s flew as many as 1,600 men per day from Atsugi to Okinawa and then to Manila.[63] Similar numbers were transported to Guam.

"I'm glad for POWs that evacuation is progressing so rapidly," the ICRC delegate Bilfinger observed. "We seem to be completely forgotten except if it were not from the presents from Heaven, which are being dropped in a somewhat reckless fashion." Gradually Bilfinger warmed to the Americans, establishing "perfect understanding and collaboration," and crediting the Americans with "the same understanding and speed and efficiency which the Japanese almost made us forget."

Evacuating prisoners from Manchuria, Korea, China, and the Pacific Islands was an even greater logistical challenge. Because Tokyo had surrendered before Allied troops arrived, the Americans felt they had to land as many troops as possible in Japan before the formal surrender on September 2. They lacked sufficient ships to move troops everywhere simultaneously. Therefore, CINPAC prioritized Japan and Korea over China.[64]

At Jinsen, in Korea, the Japanese announced the end of the war on the day after the surrender.[65] The next day, men began to leave the camp to get chicken and buy sake.[66] But on August 20, a B-29 flew over the camp and dropped leaflets ordering the POWs to stay where they were.[67] Japanese guards still patrolled the camp with bayonets.

As elsewhere, the US military planned "liaison teams and recovery teams" to deliver food, clothing, medical supplies, and other necessary equipment.[68] But because Captain George Stengel, the commanding officer of the POW liaison team, did not reach Seoul until September 6, American B-29s made three parachute drops of clothing and food.[69] In a cruel irony, the heavy pallets caused multiple deaths and injuries. At Keijō, a Korean woman was hit and died. At Jinsen, the damage was still worse. A prisoner's leg was broken, one Korean was killed, and eight Japanese were injured.[70]

U.S. planes dropping supplies. Parachuting supplies was the fastest way to help POWs in the days immediately following Japan's surrender. But the heavy pallets also posed a real hazard, in some cases causing injuries and even fatalities when they crash-landed. (US National Archives and Records Administration.)

Guy Round recalled going with the Japanese staff by truck on August 29 to pick up canned foods and cigarettes dropped by the B-29s. He also recalled Korean independence leaders, some of whom were political prisoners. During the war they had been held in prison with POWs in the civil jail. Now they sent cars to pick up the POWs and bring them out to dance halls. Guy Round later recalled one such evening at a dance hall where a former political prisoner gave a speech and then sang the patriotic song "Aegukka."

In Seoul, on August 6, Lieutenant Colonel M. Elrington, who had been the senior Allied officer at Keijō, visited the Chōsen Hotel to dine with newly arrived American officers. The next day Captain Stengel and Captain V. H. P. Boeck, the medical officer of Headquarters Company, XXIV Corps, went to Keijō and spoke with Elrington and Noguchi.[71] The prisoners there were primarily British. Elrington and his staff helped process the prisoners quickly, and the 158 POWs were told about the plans for their evacuation to Manila. After several hours of answering questions "ranging from the atomic bomb to what the people in the United States and England thought about the surrender in Singapore," an inspection of the camp was made. Stengel noted they "were given to feel that their problems and future welfare are matters of concern to their Military establishment and their country and all that could be done to get them home as quickly as possible."[72]

That same day, Stengel and Captain V. H. P. Boeck, the medical officer of Headquarters Company, XXIV Corps, first visited Keijō, then Jinsen.[73] Together with the British POWs at Keijō was Carl Engelhart, the Japanese-speaking G-2 officer. By now the prisoners in Jinsen were primarily American. Among them were Lieutenant Colonel Curtis T. Beecher and the senior medical officer, Lieutenant Colonel Jack W. Schwartz.[74]

On September 8, advance elements of the Seventh Infantry Division arrived at Jinsen.[75] On September 9, Lieutenant General John R. Hodge, commander of the XXIV Corps of the US Tenth Army—and future military governor of South Korea—landed with his troops to receive the Japanese surrender. Koreans initially welcomed American troops, but the jubilation dimmed when Hodge announced that Governor-General Abe Nobuyuki would be kept in office. Hodge planned to use Japanese troops to maintain order.[76] Some prisoners found themselves in the capital celebrating Korea's independence. The correspondent for the London *Times* noted that as a crowd of about 500 Koreans waved flags, Japanese troops fired on them, killing two and wounding ten others.

Repatriation soon began for Allied POWs from Korea—now United Nations Prisoners of War—and for civilian internees. The hospital ship *Relief* moved to Jinsen and recovered 168 Allied POWs, 138 of them from the Philippines, and 30 British from Singapore.[77] US forces also liberated 158 British and Australians from Keijō, most of whom had been taken prisoner in Singapore, but also two Americans.[78]

As in Yokohama, military officials provided former POWs with food, clothing, and medical supplies. After they filled out questionnaires, they went to the Philippines to complete processing. Matters were more complicated for everyone else—for example, stateless persons, such as White Russians and German Jews, Italians, Vichy French, Turks, and Germans, and the Koreans who would soon be subject to US or Soviet military occupation.[79]

Meanwhile at Kōnan, now in Soviet-occupied territory, Korean men and women were kept outside the gates even after the Japanese surrender.[80] Stengel arranged to fly to Pyongyang to manage the situation. On September 15, he and some members of Recovery Team No. 7 flew there. At about the same time, another plane flew directly to Hamhung. Its passengers included Lieutenant Venner, two American enlisted men, an Australian enlisted man, and Mr. Barsdell, an Australian war correspondent. At Pyongyang, the Russians received Captain Stengel with courtesy. But the deputy chief of staff of the Twenty-Fifth Army refused to let him go on to Hamhung to evacuate the prisoners, citing the foul weather. So Captain Stengel returned to Seoul.[81]

A B-29 flew over the camp at Kōnan with the intention of dropping supplies, but some of the packages hit a building occupied by Red Army troops, narrowly missing a colonel. This brought an order that any planes flying over the camp would be made to land.[82] On September 20, Soviet planes intercepted the next B-29, but the pilot judged the designated field too small for a safe landing. The Soviets followed the American plane and fired, forcing the B-29 to crash. But the incident ended peacefully. Korean fishermen picked up the Americans and a repair crew arrived from Guam. On September 21, the American POWs finally left for Kanko. Russian officers accompanied them and kept the Koreans and Japanese away. On September 22, 302 British and 52 Australians were also liberated from the camp.[83]

In Manchuria as well, many POWs were liberated by Soviet troops. On August 23, evacuation of four camps near Mukden (Shenyang) began. There were 1,673 prisoners: 1,323 Americans, as well as British, Dutch, Australians, Canadians, and French. They included high-ranking officers such as General Jonathan W. Wainwright and General A. M. Jones, and British senior officials like Lieutenant General Arthur Percival, Sir Shenton Thomas, and Sir Mark Young. The Dutch POWs included A. W. L. Tjarda van Starkenborgh, former governor-general of the Netherlands East Indies, and Lieutenant General Hein ter Poorten, former commander of the Royal Netherlands East Indies Army. Some of them were sickly and emaciated. But the Russians reported that "treatment had not been unduly harsh except in the case of POWs who tried to escape." The Mukden-Dairen Railway line opened on September 6, and arrangements were made with Russia for the evacuation of remaining POWs through Dairen.[84]

In China, arriving US troops found themselves in a complex situation. China had been fighting a civil war since 1937, with some 14 million to 20 million dead.[85] Hundreds of thousands of Japanese and Chinese puppet troops were still armed and at large. The Japanese withdrew from the south and concentrated the North China Area Army, commanded by General Tada Hayame, along the Yangtze River Valley and the east coast around Shanghai and to the north. But when the forces withdrew, the Communists demanded that they surrender. Okamura, who commanded the China Expeditionary Army group—in charge of the Northern, Central, and China puppet armies—refused. He said he would surrender to Chiang Kai-shek. Chinese puppet forces numbered about 505,000. US policy was to assist the Chinese central government, but not to the extent of supporting it in civil war.[86]

US commanders estimated it would take about thirty days to evacuate American POWs from this chaotic situation, based on the Twentieth Air Force's ability to carry out supply drops. The US Army had little idea how many camps existed in China. According to the POW Information Bureau, there were six in Mukden (Manchuria), two in Shanghai, nine in Taiwan, and eleven in Hong Kong.[87] The Allies did not know where all of them were located. Just supplying thirty days of food and medical requirements for an estimated 69,000 persons required all available cargo parachutes from the Philippines to the Marianas.[88] Eight B-29s were lost flying these missions, due to either accidents or friendly fire. Finally, prisoners were freed from Tientsin, Yangchow, and Canton during the first week in September. On September 5, forces landed in Taiwan, and evacuation began that week.[89] But at Hainan, transports from Hong Kong did not even arrive until the middle of September.

In the rest of Southeast Asia, the evacuation moved even more slowly, in part due to even more limited resources. At the Potsdam Conference, British Command had agreed that "after some months" Southeast Asia Command could expand to include Siam and territories formerly with United States South West Pacific Area command.[90] In August 1945 MacArthur sped up the timetable and delegated these territories to Britain so that he could move troops to Japan.

Lord Mountbatten, commander of South East Asia Command, had just fought successful if exhausting campaigns in Burma and India. The former Dutch colonies (Java and Sumatra) and French colonies (south of the 16th parallel) comprised 100 million people and 700,000 square miles of territory.[91] The territory under his control had therefore increased some 50 percent overnight. In no way was Mountbatten ready for this challenge.

Nor was Britain, which by some estimates had lost one-fourth of its national wealth during the war.[92] Mountbatten was short on troops, supplies, and shipping, and therefore had to rely on the Americans. He also lacked up-to-date intelligence, especially for the former Dutch and French colonies.[93]

British HQ, now responsible for Java and Sumatra, had few Dutch staff, and little information about or understanding of the former Dutch colony.[94] On August 24, a formal Anglo-Dutch agreement gave a British commander working through Netherlands Indies Civil Administration responsibility for Java and Sumatra. The Australians had responsibility for the outer islands.

Mountbatten's mission was to ensure Japanese surrender and disarm former troops, to evacuate Allied POWs, and to repatriate Japanese soldiers and civilians. In the East Indies and Indochina, he was to prepare the territory to hand it over to the Dutch and French. He established a RAPWI (Recovery of Allied Prisoners of War and Internees) organization to lead relief in six regions: Java, Malacca, Singapore, French Indochina, Thailand, and Hong Kong. As of August 17 there were only forty teams for 150 camps. POWs at Changi took to calling the RAPWI organization "Retain All Prisoners of War Indefinitely."[95]

The process of ensuring peace on the cheap did not go smoothly. While evacuating Allied POWs, Commonwealth forces also had to repatriate some tens of thousands of Japanese civilians and 716,000 Japanese military personnel. Punitive policies in the last few months of the war meant growing hatred of the Japanese. Residents faced famine, disease, and violence. All this happened in a context of burgeoning anticolonial movements.

The British Special Operations Executive (SOE) first had to figure out where the captives were and then assess their condition.[96] On August 28, before evacuation started in Singapore, French Indochina, and the Dutch East Indies, the SOE ran two operations to evacuate captives.[97] In Operation Birdcage, SOE agents dropped leaflets, instructing POWs to remain in the camps.[98] Then, in Operation Mastiff, airborne parties flew in medical officers, who triaged captives, while the SOE supplied food.

After surrender, approximately 20,000 POWs remained inside the camps. According to an August 30, 1945, telegram from an operative in Mergui camp in Thailand, of 600 POWs, 200 had so far died. Another 200 were not expected to survive. SOE operations involvement may therefore have saved many from death. News of the Japanese defeat traveled slowly, in part due to remote locations and difficult terrain. At Kanchanaburi, POWs had heard the news before those further out in the inhospitable jungle. The SOE considered it safer for an official body to organize evacuation.[99] They used a leaflet drop to inform POWs to stay where they were. By the end of September most British POWs had been evacuated.[100]

But the main show would be in Singapore. Mountbatten would personally conduct the surrender ceremony. He ordered Allied troops to set sail from Sri Lanka and Burma. On August 28, they arrived in Malaya. On August 30, nine Royal Australian Air Force Catalina seaplanes landed in Singapore. The main British force arrived on September 4. Three days later, a headline in the *Straits Times* proclaimed, "Singapore Is British Again."[101]

Some 77,000 Japanese troops surrendered to the British.[102] British troops relieved the Japanese of their swords—and of their possessions. Japanese captives were forced to work "at the double" on Padang Cricket Ground for Mountbatten's appearance.[103] Others were forced to labor long hours in sometimes humiliating conditions in warehouses and cleaning sewers. Any perceived disobedience was repaid with rifle-beating and kicking.[104]

The *Straits Times* reported on the September 12 surrender ceremony at the municipal building, today Singapore's city hall. As in Japan, pageantry was on full display, with the hoisting of the Union Jack for the first time in 1,374 days. The British national anthem played and British bugles sounded. Mosquito bombers flew over. Ex-prisoners and internees looked on as Mountbatten approached and went to the Signature Room. Seven Japanese officers followed him to "boos and hisses." They proceeded to present the instruments of surrender signed by General Itagaki Seishirō and stamped with his name.[105]

The next day, the Second Australian POW Reception Group arrived.[106] Their commander, Brigadier J. E. Lloyd, had arrived five days earlier, and found few operational public utilities and conditions "bordering on chaotic." The Australians requisitioned "unreliable and unsuitable" local civilian vehicles.[107]

Lloyd directed that Australians in Singapore remain in Changi during the repatriation process. Captives in British-run territory had a very different experience than those in Japan and Korea. The Americans evacuated POWs quickly. But the British—short of supplies and ships—kept thousands of Allied captives in camps.[108] Ex-prisoners in Singapore had expected to be "liberated" and not kept in "the place of their wartime imprisonment."[109]

But British and Australian authorities also thought that, considering the condition of the POWs, there might be good reason to delay their return.

On September 1, 1945, Australian officers reported 5,560 former Australian POWs in Singapore, including 4,611 at Changi, 741 at Krangi, and 208 at Adam Park and Tanjong Pagar. According to a rapid classification, none was judged "fit to travel by troopship on ordinary rations." Some required sea ambulance transport, some hospital ship, and some were unfit to travel at all. The Dutch reported about 400 Dutch POWs, including 325 officers, and reported 99 deaths. As elsewhere, "the general opinion, however, was that the enemy behaved reasonably well."[110]

Lieutenant Colonel G. Gibson and Lieutenant Colonel Glyn White, a former POW himself, reported on the situation after the Royal Australian Medical Corps took over the Singapore General Hospital. Most POWs suffered from malnutrition and vitamin deficiency, and many had malaria or dysentery.[111] The Japanese had treated malaria with Atrebrin. There was no cholera or typhoid in Singapore, and less tuberculosis then doctors anticipated. All in all, the "hygiene of camps is extremely good," and Lieutenant Colonel Glyn White had kept good records. For his part, Lieutenant White praised the Australian Army Medical Corps in Malaya: "The greatest of credit must go to them for the years of arduous conscientious work carried out in spite of every frustration and obstruction. Medical officers have worked without thought of their own health or personal welfare."[112]

The health challenges POWs faced were actually fewer than Australian officers expected. But even for those who were relatively well, returning home would be a difficult trip. Doctors judged it a tough transition from an "oriental type of diet." "[In] their present condition many troops are so wasted . . . that minor complications, undue fatigue or exposure or even sea sickness may indirectly lead to fatal collapse." White concluded that men should be treated before repatriation. Lieutenant Colonel W. A. Bye, the senior Australian Imperial Force physician from Changi, home to 85 percent of POWs, agreed, even as White admitted that others might consider it "too gloomy a view."[113]

Medical officers therefore judged that even though relatives would find delays "irksome," transport would be safer if former POWs first were treated. It was not just the food. Military officers argued that repatriation would confront former POWs—who had lived under "conditions difficult for us even to imagine"—with social, emotional, and physical challenges. POWs, after all, had been "regimented beyond all normal conditions of the serving soldier." "Their reactions of suspicion and their responses may be almost automatic." "It's as logical to expect their bodies to recover completely" as it is to "expect minds which have lived and striven to maintain judgment and pride while in the custody of a barbarous enemy to become adjusted again simply by the fact of their return to Australia." The extremes of return "has been likened to that of a diver who has been working at a great depth in the ocean, and so subjected to great pressure."[114]

Mountbatten himself was mainly concerned with reestablishing British prestige and authority. After the formal surrender ceremony at Singapore City Hall, a new colonial occupation took shape headquartered at the Cathay Building, formerly Japanese headquarters and the site of Bose's Free India speech. The British employed some 7,000 people and requisitioned 2,227 houses and 51 institutions and clubs. To uphold British authority, Mountbatten used some 2,000 Japanese surrendered persons to break strikes. But not all the Japanese accepted such ignominy. More than 300 committed suicide, and others joined the Malayan communists.[115]

From Tokyo, MacArthur decided that theater commanders could use Japanese Surrendered Persons (JSPs) as they saw fit, as long as Allied forces could guarantee security and repatriation was not delayed. At MacArthur's headquarters, the British Staff Section clarified that "Japanese may NOT be enslaved," and should be paid.[116] But Mountbatten used JSPs to administer POW camps, to control food supplies, and to continue fighting. The JSPs must have been useful, since Britain delayed their repatriation until 1947.[117] Some only went back in January 1948.[118]

Meanwhile, the Dutch also needed someone to fight their battles in the East Indies. While in 1942 Queen Wilhelmina had pledged eventual independence and participation in a commonwealth, this was too little too late for many nationalists. By August 17, their charismatic leader, Sukarno, previously detained under Dutch rule, proclaimed the Republic of Indonesia. Many Dutch had spent the war in camps that in some ways replicated the racism of the prewar Dutch East Indies. They were sure the Indonesians would welcome them back. But reports that the Japanese had given arms to Javanese suggested problems to come.[119]

On August 28, leaflets went out to POWs and detainees in Dutch and English. "The JAPANESE Government has surrendered. You will be evacuated by ALLIED NATIONS forces as soon as possible." POWs were ordered to stay where they were, and notified that air drops would augment their supplies.[120] On September 6, the Imperial Japanese Army proclaimed they were still in charge, and ordered POWs and internees in Java to remain in place. They warned that "any precipitate action on your part could make things more difficult for your wives and children. Be patient. We are doing all we can to bring you safely together again as soon as possible."[121] Dutch command seconded these instructions.[122]

On September 8, the first British officers landed in Java and Sumatra, with the challenge of finding and freeing 100,000 captives.[123] The British again told POWs to stay put, but many people ignored the order. On September 15, British forces also landed in Jakarta. Two weeks later it was clear that the Japanese could no longer maintain order, and on September 28, Mountbatten established positions in Java. On September 29, British Indian troops landed in Batavia. They limited themselves to Batavia and Surabaya on Java, Medan, and Pedang on Sumatra.

The Dutch who landed in Java were astonished. On October 1, Lieutenant Governor Dr. Hubertus J. van Mook returned to find signs proclaiming his death. The red-and-white Indonesian flag was the only flag visible in Batavia. "Merdek" graffiti proclaimed independence.[124] According to a wartime Office of Strategic Services (OSS) agent, J. F. Mailuku, "the great mass of people are violently anti-Dutch."[125] This number included former Korean guards.[126]

Lieutenant Colonel London, a representative of the Commander in Chief, Australian Military Forces, warned Lieutenant Colonel Tarooda, commander of Kokas Forces, not to purchase food from the Indonesians or Chinese. Instead, men should go into the jungle and collect sago palms to eat and to catch fish to eat. Troops were also ordered to leave Allied nationals alone.[127]

Even though the Dutch thought the Japanese troops were a "potential danger," they lacked sufficient troops or shipping of their own to regain control of their colonies. From October 1945 onward, the JSPs tipped the security balance for the colonial powers.[128] By late 1945, both French and Dutch colonial administrators saw the usefulness of Japanese troops. According to a Strategic Services Unit report, many British officers described the Japanese troops as "good blokes." The Dutch opined that only Japanese "brutality" could work with the "natives."[129] As elsewhere in Southeast Asia, in the fall of 1945 Japanese POWs were sent to work loading and unloading supplies, farming, and doing forestry work and camp construction. In Sumatra they guarded oil installations. In southern Vietnam, JSP forces assisted the British—probably decisively—in helping regain control from the Vietminh, who were intent on winning independence from the French.[130]

All along, the occupying powers also faced conflicts among themselves: the Dutch resented the British, and the precedence supposedly given to French Indochina.[131] Mid-October saw conflict between British, Dutch, and Japanese troops and Indonesians. But by November, all camps were cleared, and 223,250 internees had been processed by the end of 1945.[132] But at the same time, "murder, kidnapping, arson, and robbery" became the order of the day in Java.[133]

As critical as the Allies had been during the war about the outrage of POWs being put to work or even being mobilized as troops in the Indian National Army, they did much the same thing as soon as they had the need and the opportunity. The JSPs worked as coolies in Singapore, where the British made use of these "docile and disciplined" troops to replace Indian laborers "sweeping latrines" and collecting trash.[134] The Japanese participated in British-run military operations against independence movements in the colonies of two foreign powers.[135] Japanese POWs were also used to reconstruct Singapore and maintain law and order in Burma.[136] In the Soviet Union, meanwhile, captives taken after the war's end toiled in Siberia. Even the high-minded Americans used Japanese troops and police in Korea.

The forced labor and corporal punishment of Japanese POWs might be seen as punitive, or even poetic justice. But in fact, hundreds of thousands were pressed into service, not just former guards or Japanese suspected of war crimes. Moreover the use (and abuse) of JSPs was not some plan worked out in advance. It was not unlike the use (and abuse) of Allied POWs during the war: a function of military necessity, with little or no thought given to their protected status as POWs. And whereas the INA were volunteers, the Japanese POWs used to break strikes, or put down colonial uprisings, had no say in the matter. And all this happened while guards and camp commanders were being pursued and prosecuted for their mistreatment of Allied POWs.

It was an ironic end to the story of captivity in the Pacific War. One and all—whether Japanese or Korean, American or Australian, French, Dutch, or Indian—were prisoners of empire. In some ways, though, and for some people, a new chapter was beginning. Investigation and prosecution of their guards and camp commanders began in Tokyo, and then throughout the former empire. Many of the sites of abuse in Allied POW camps became the sites of war crime trials.

# 8

## UNDUE PROCESS

By the end of 1945, all Allied POWs had been evacuated and shipped home. But the investigation and prosecution of their guards and camp commanders was only then swinging into high gear. It had started with the POW repatriation process itself, which typically included filling out forms and answering questions to document POWs' experiences. Investigators needed these statements from POWs to both identify and convict war criminals. In most cases, they were taken three to four weeks after POWs were freed.

These questionnaires and medical exams revealed "many instances of brutality," as noted in the Commander in Chief for the Pacific (CINPAC) report on the surrender. But the same report noted that this was not the whole story: "Close questioning often brought out that the prisoner had been guilty of breaking some petty but strict prison rule. A considerable number of the older men stated that the camp treatment, though extremely severe, was on the whole not too bad. They expected quick punishment when caught for an infraction of the rules, and they were not disappointed."[1] On the other hand, the physical deprivation could be extreme: "All complained of the food, clothing, housing, and lack of heating facilities. Malnutrition was common. Many serious cases of beriberi and tuberculosis required hospitalization." And yet the same was true of many Japanese at the time—millions were homeless, malnourished, and in need of medical care.

The follow-up interviews of POWs are usually treated as reliable accounts of what happened in the camps. But they were rife with inaccuracies. For example, one American sergeant captured in Corregidor later found that his exit interview got his name wrong. It also contained a written account of an incident that never occurred.[2]

Collecting evidence to make cases would have been difficult under the best of circumstances, considering how many witnesses and suspects were on the move. The Japanese made it more difficult when, the day before the surrender, August 14, the War Ministry sent a telegram directing the destruction of confidential documents. Lieutenant General Tamura of the Prisoner of War Information Bureau (POWIB) in turn directed subordinate officers to burn documents, and many camp commanders did the same.[3] This seemed highly incriminating in retrospect, but this was not unusual behavior when a military command faced defeat. American forces did the same at Corregidor in May 1942.[4] Moreover, the POWIB did not destroy all of its own papers, and they were a key source of evidence in the war crimes trials.

In addition to logistical difficulties, prosecutors faced tremendous challenges created by new legal concepts. Who was responsible, and how should they decide? Prosecutors sought to assign overall bureaucratic responsibility to the POWIB / POWMO (Prisoner of War Management Office) and its only living leader, Lieutenant General Tamura Hiroshi, and also to the military leaders who supposedly held command authority, like Yamashita Tomoyuki. Also prosecuted were camp commanders, including Fukuei (Fukuye) Shimpei, commandant in 1942 of Changi, Tsuneyoshi Yoshio from Camp O'Donnell, Sakamoto Yuhichi of Fukuoka 1, and Colonel Noguchi of Keijō. So too were guards, doctors, and interpreters.

Some of the men who committed abuses, like Tsuneyoshi and Fukuei, were tried and sentenced in some way that resembled justice. But others, like Tamura and Yamashita, were prosecuted for being in the wrong place in a bureaucratic hierarchy. Like the treatment of POWs, the treatment of accused war criminals was haphazard, and highly variable. Whether the accused person was executed, imprisoned, or eventually pardoned depended on much more than guilt or innocence.

To respond to accusations of crimes against POWs, War Minister Shimomura established the Investigation Committee on POWs (Furyo kankei chōsa iinkai) on September 20, 1945.[5] Its chair was then Vice War Minister Wakamatsu Tadakazu. Tamura was made one of the three vice chairs, with the director-general of the Army Service Bureau, Nasu Yoshio, and the director-general of the Judicial Bureau, Fujii Kiichi. In addition to investigating serious incidents regarding POWs, and any other incidents reported by Allied forces, they were to look after the return of Japanese POWs.[6]

It may seem surprising that the International Prosecution Section (IPS) of the Supreme Command for the Allied Powers (SCAP) would accept the appointment of Tamura to serve on the Investigative Committee on POWs.[7] After all, he would be responsible for collecting documents, compiling statistics, and observing war crimes trials—trials that would eventually

First commander of Camp O'Donnell receives his sentence. Tsuneyoshi Yoshio swore that he did not have food, water, or medicine adequate to care for tens of thousands of sick and malnourished POWs. He was sentenced to life imprisonment at hard labor, but was released early in a general amnesty.
(US National Archives and Records Administration.)

include Tamura himself. Yet only Tamura could do the job. The first POWIB / POWMO director, Hamada Hiroshi, had committed suicide in Bangkok in September 1945. His successor, Uemura Mikio, was now a Soviet POW, and would commit suicide in Khabarovsk in March 1946. Neither left personal papers. The POWIB records were often the only documentary evidence of how POW camps were administered. In effect, Tamura and the remaining POWIB staff were made to investigate themselves. The POWIB did not finish investigating and sorting the data on allied POWs until August 1952. Five years later, the Bureau was abolished.[8]

The most high-profile "class A" suspected war criminals were Japanese political leaders, like Tōjō. They were arrested in the days just following the formal surrender. In Japan, the Judge Advocate Corps led the investigation. After the first wave of high-profile arrests, they started rounding up B / C suspects, such as camp commanders.

In mid-October, eight Imperial Japanese Army (IJA) veterans were arrested in Korea, including Colonel Noguchi, Lieutenant Colonel Okazaki (the commander of Jinsen), and Captain Gotō, his counterpart at Keijō, Captain Terada, Goto's adjutant at Keijō, Lieutenant Moritomi, paymaster, Corporal Ushihara—a "notorious" interpreter—and the prison doctor Mizuguchi. Three days later, seven more of "lower notoriety" were arrested, for a total of fifteen. The men were held in a stockade in the vicinity of Inchon.[9] On October 25, 1945, in Japan, Sakamoto Yuhichi, commandant of Fukuoka 1, was arrested.[10] Also arrested from Fukuoka 1 were Hada Masato, the medical orderly, and Katsura Takeo, the camp interpreter.

Japanese arrested for war crimes trials were generally held near the place of their capture, whether in Changi in Singapore or in jails in Hong Kong, Burma, Malaya, Indochina, and the Dutch East Indies. Many sites of abuse of Westerners in POW camps became sites of war crimes trials for those accused after the war of crimes against POWs.[11] Those taken to Tokyo were brought to Sugamo Prison, "an enormous block of two storied, modern, reinforced concrete buildings." Surrounded by a tall concrete wall, it lay in a nearly destroyed part of north Tokyo. The Japanese designed it to accommodate 3,200 inmates, but American standards were for 1,800. Japanese war crimes suspects were segregated from foreigners. Oil-burning stoves heated cells equipped with camp beds, tables, chairs, blankets, and electric light. "It is like turning over the pages of history," an International Committee of the Red Cross (ICRC) representative observed, "to walk down the cell block which houses men who dreamed of 'greater Asia.'"[12]

As prosecutors prepared for trial, the POWIB was not as forthcoming as it might have been. But at whose behest remains unclear. Staff felt no responsibility for what happened in the POW camps. According to a 1955 report by the POWIB, unnamed Japanese authorities instructed personnel in the POWIB not to provide "unrequired info to Allied forces prosecutors." Documents were to be classified into two categories: active release, and release only if required.[13]

The POWIB was also not entirely helpful to prosecutors for more mundane reasons, especially a lack of personnel competent in English, common to almost every part of the Japanese government during the early period of the Occupation. Major Takata Masaru, wartime secretary in charge of compiling and investigating information, reported he needed another forty people. Few wanted to work for the POWIB, since many Japanese had close relatives or friends who were arrested or under suspicion. The POWIB also could not pay competitive wages. A "girl clerk" earned a mere 45 to 60 yen per month, scarcely enough for basic sustenance.[14]

Investigators were not solely dependent on the POWIB. They could also interview guards and camp officers already in custody.[15] Even those POWs who were repatriated and living in the United States were reinterviewed. For instance, in 1946, the Long Island daily newspaper *Newsday* reported on the Army's search for POWs willing to give testimony. Thousands of repatriated former POWs were asked to help. Four lived in the region. The War Department coordinated with the Veterans' Administration, the Attorney General's office, and the War Crimes Branch of the Civil Affairs Division. Eight officers from MacArthur's legal section returned stateside to supervise.[16]

Investigators had to positively identify Japanese who had committed crimes, a tricky process, given that many soldiers shared surnames with war crimes suspects, others gave false names, and military units had burned their papers.[17] In December 1945, new warrants were still being issued.[18] By the end, Allied investigators compiled an enormous amount of evidence, collecting tens of thousands of affidavits from American and British Commonwealth POWs in Tokyo, Manila, and San Francisco. According to a 1949 US report, more than 100,000 Japanese personnel were also questioned.

Prosecutors tended to focus on what they judged to be more serious cases. For instance, in 1946, British authorities chose to make cases only against those who would receive sentences of more than seven years.[19] About 9,000 suspects were released without trial and shipped back to Japan.[20] They had to make these decisions quickly. Of 708,000 Japanese Surrendered Persons in British control at the end of the war, after six months only 203,000 were left.

The International Military Tribunal for the Far East (IMTFE), also known as the Tokyo Tribunal, prosecuted the class-A war criminals—the Japanese leaders who had planned the war. In addition to the Tokyo Tribunal, national trials were held throughout Asia to try lower-level personnel.[21] The trials had already begun in Guam in September 1945, and eventually were held in more than fifty places.

The Americans managed trials at Tokyo, Yokohama, and the Philippines. The British and Australians tried alleged war criminals at Singapore and in Burma.[22] The Australians conducted trials in Morotai as well as Darwin. The Dutch organized their own trials in the Dutch East Indies, including

Batavia. The Soviets, Chinese, and Taiwanese all ran their trials in their own fashion. Scholars estimate approximately 2,362 trials with 5,707 defendants.[23] Camp commandants and guards were sometimes tried in groups. All this meant as many different versions of justice as countries where crimes had taken place, and trials depended on the local political situation and different legal systems.

The first major trial, held in the Philippines, was among the most famous. General Yamashita was held in custody from the moment he capitulated. Before accepting his surrender, MacArthur first made certain that General Arthur Percival, who had surrendered to Yamashita at Singapore, and General Jonathan Wainwright were present to witness his humiliation.

The prosecution of Yamashita showed how much conditions varied in different trials, and also how dramatically the trials themselves could transform the concept of war crimes. Though the international tribunal was already being planned, MacArthur decided that Yamashita's trial—and that of Honma—could not wait. Always a publicity hound, he wanted them to be prosecuted quickly to gain maximum press.

On September 24, he set out the orders for how the trial would be conducted. The charge was made by Colonel Alva C. Carpenter, a member of the "Bataan Gang" who had evacuated with MacArthur in 1942. Now chief of the Legal Section, Carpenter charged that Yamashita had "unlawfully disregarded and failed to discharge his duty as commander to control the operations of the members of his command," permitting them to commit "brutal atrocities and other high crimes" against Americans and their allies, in violation of the laws of war.

As we have seen, Allied POWs were treated terribly in the Philippines, especially during the Bataan Death March and the first months of captivity. Transportation in hell ships was horrendous. Filipino men and women also suffered tremendously during the war, caught up in some of the worst fighting in Southeast Asia. The guerrilla struggle—and Japan's reprisals—affected the entire population of the archipelago. In the end, more than a million died, more than 100,000 civilians just in the month-long battle for Manila. Japanese troops were accused of multiple atrocities, including the murder of Catholic priests, mass sexual assault, and bayoneting of whole families.[24]

In Manila, as in other theaters, a War Crimes Investigation Detachment was given the role of investigating war crimes and making recommendations for trial.[25] American judge advocate generals established lists of POW camps and sought war criminals.[26] These crimes occurred in a former US colony, and though the Americans expected Manila to take over the trials, the United States ended up meeting a large part of the cost and dominated the highest-profile prosecutions, such as that of Lieutenant General Honma Masaharu, convicted of war crimes and shot to death by firing squad, and General Yamashita Tomoyuki.[27]

Investigators had great difficulty establishing whether Yamashita himself personally ordered mistreatment of POWs or massacres of Filipinos. Indeed, it was unclear whether he was even aware of what was happening in POW and internment camps. There was no evidence he had been to Santo Tomas, or cared about the conditions there.[28] As an army field commander, he was not directly responsible for POWs unless lower-ranking officers sought his involvement, or he chose to be involved.

None of this gainsays the fact that Japan's conduct during the battle of Manila was atrocious. But the worst crimes took place when Yamashita was isolated in Baguio after retreating into the mountains. As an Army man, he had only limited authority over Navy troops who committed these acts. He appears to have mentioned his concern about food shortages in the POW and internment camps to Major General Kira Goichi, his quartermaster, and issued a forced requisition. But it did not help Yamashita's case that one of the witnesses, General Kou Shioku, claimed that POWs were treated better than Japanese soldiers in terms of food and clothing, and suffered no corporal punishment. This defied all evidence presented by other witnesses, who detailed starvation and beatings. But again, the challenge was establishing Yamashita's direct responsibility. The "hell ships," for instance, were not even under Yamashita's command.[29] Prosecutors also failed to prove that he intended to massacre POWs.

US captain Norman Sparnon, head of translations in the Allied Translator and Interpreter Service of the Southwest Pacific theater, testified that there was neither an order from Tokyo nor one from Yamashita for the killing of POWs. If there had been, the number of copies in a unit the size of the Fourteenth Army would have been considerable, so it was unlikely that they missed it.[30]

Yamashita was charged with the crimes of his subordinates simply because he was in command. Up until this point, no court had ever made a commander liable for the crimes of his subordinates without showing any involvement, or even knowledge, of such crimes.[31] Five generals, none with legal training, finally convicted Yamashita for a "willful disregard and failure to discharge his duty."[32] On December 7, 1945, he was sentenced to death.

Yamashita impressed his lawyers, who sought to reverse his conviction. His lawyer, Harry E. Clarke, appealed to MacArthur, who upheld the sentence, as did the Supreme Court of the Philippines. In 1946, Yamashita cited his habeas corpus rights in an appeal to the US Supreme Court. The majority refused the appeal, but two Supreme Court justices issued fierce dissents. Justice Frank Murphy faulted the military commission for convicting the accused for "a crime unheard of in American legal history." Some 80,000 Japanese citizens signed a petition to allow Yamashita to commit *seppuku* (suicide). Instead he was hanged in February 1946.

The Yamashita case is important because it became the basis for "command accountability," the legal doctrine of hierarchical accountability for war crimes. Set in Yamashita's trial—the first major trial by the Allies—it is now known as the Yamashita standard and has become part of international law.[33] Yet the United States did not use "the Yamashita standard" at the Tokyo Tribunal. Military commanders could be held responsible only if they knew crimes were being committed and failed to take steps to stop them. And fault required evidence of "negligence or supineness."[34]

Even if Yamashita had been acquitted at Manila, he still would likely have been put on trial for what happened under his command in Singapore at the outset of the war. In October 1945 the British war crimes chief investigator, Cyril Wild, conducted a lengthy interrogation. Himself a former POW and fluent in Japanese, Wild demanded to know how Yamashita could have been unaware of the killing of Australian POWs and the massacre of thousands of Chinese. He came to believe Yamashita when he claimed subordinate commanders and the Kempeitai (Japanese military police force) carried out such crimes on their own. Even so, no one escaped with their honor intact. "Senior officers are generally willing to give away their subordinates," Wild concluded, and "junior officers and other ranks are [also] ready to incriminate their seniors."[35]

After Yamashita, hundreds more were put on trial in the Philippines.[36] US cases in Manila covered crimes against POWs and civilians: 35,000 POWs and 90,000 civilian victims.[37] By 1946, about 57 percent were civilians, the rest were POWs. As in the Dutch East Indies, the majority of trials covered crimes against civilians. Most trials were of mid-ranking officers, but there were also camp guards, like a civilian guard at Cabanatuan accused of shooting and killing a POW. The trials dealing with POWs also focused on Davao, Bilibid Hospital, and Nichols Field.[38]

Manila sentences differed from those elsewhere because many more of the accused were sentenced to death. In 1946, of 136 accused, 65—or 47 percent—received a death sentence, more than six times as many as in Yokohama.[39] Another 20 percent received life sentences. On January 1, 1947, the Philippines government took over the class-B/C trials in Manila. They judged 151 civilians in 73 cases, and 137 were found guilty.[40]

The British also mounted a major effort to identify and apprehend those directly responsible for war crimes against Commonwealth forces. Beginning in January 1946, they conducted 305 war crimes trials throughout Southeast Asia.[41] There were seventeen British war investigation teams who collected evidence, which was then examined by teams of legal officers. As the seat of Southeast Asia Command, Singapore was the site of 131 British trials, covering not just events that occurred on the island, but on the Thai-Burma Railway as well.[42] Thirty cases dealt with crimes in Singapore alone, including treatment of POWs and civilian internees, most famously those kept in Changi.

The commandant at Changi in 1942, Major General Fukuei (Fukuye) Shimpei, was tried in late February 1946 for the Selarang Barracks incident. He faced two charges: forcing the 17,000 men to sign the statement promising they would not escape, and executing four POWs.[43] Found guilty, two months later he was shot by British firing squad on the same spot where the four had died.[44] Major General Arimura Tsunemichi, commandant in Malaya from December 1, 1942, to March 1944, was attached to the Western Army in March 1944. In September 1945 he was taken prisoner by the Soviet Union, and he died years later in a Soviet POW camp. Major General Saito Masatoshi became commander from March 1, 1944.[45] He was arrested on September 11, 1945, convicted of war crimes, and hanged.

More junior officers and enlisted men were also put on trial. Who could be punished, and why, could seem arbitrary. This included those Japanese guards accused of committing crimes against POWs in Korea. In May 1946, they were shipped to Japan for trial.[46] From June to September 1947, twelve Japanese men—"Yuzuru Noguchi et al."—were tried in a single Yokohama trial.[47] Noguchi and Okazaki were charged with their failure to "perform specific command functions," while subordinates including Terada, Ushihara, Mizuguchi, Uchida and the others were charged for specific acts against POWs.

Men being debriefed in Manila. Liberated POWs were given questionnaires to complete in order to document their experience for potential use in war crimes tribunals. The questions themselves, such as whether they had attempted escape or sabotage, could influence the way they described the conditions of their confinement and how the Japanese meted out punishment even for lesser offenses. (US National Archives and Records Administration.)

The defense counsel criticized the rules of the trial, such as the acceptance of *ex parte* affidavits decided by a judge without the defense lawyers being present, hearsay evidence, "evidence other than the best," and medical conclusions by lay witnesses.[48] There was also a question of jurisdiction, when a US-run court judged Japanese soldiers alleged to have harmed British or Australian prisoners. Only two of the five initial members of the judges' panel remained throughout the whole trial.

Noguchi's counsel pointed out that the conditions at the Keijō and Jinsen camps were superior to all others: acts of mistreatment were fewer, the percentage of illnesses lower, and deaths comparatively more rare. The prosecution did not contradict this evidence.[49] Noguchi and Okazaki were tried based on the principle of command responsibility: that they were criminally liable for acts perpetrated by their subordinates "if they knew or had reason to know that their subordinates were committing such crimes, and did not take all necessary or reasonable measures in their power to prevent their commission."[50] Based on this logic, Noguchi was sentenced to twenty-two years in prison, Okazaki received twenty years, and the doctor, Mizuguchi, was condemned to death by hanging.[51]

The treatment of the commander at Fukuoka 1, Sakamoto Yuhichi, was similarly tough. According to his clemency report, he was "a serious-minded and upright soldier and did his duty faithfully." He sought to "maintain a stern attitude toward those who went against regulations."[52] Corporal punishment was a sanction of POWs as punishment for "stealing food and clothing from the warehouse, stealing other people's personal effects or for neglecting their work."[53] Sakamoto argued that he had only carried out his duty based on "the regulations of the army and commands of my superiors."[54] Sakamoto was also accused of failing to distribute Red Cross supplies. But the clemency report pointed out that these were not his to distribute. They had been taken to Fukuoka to prevent their destruction from air raids, and Sakamoto needed authorization to distribute them.

Sakamoto was actually said to have gone above and beyond to provide food and medical supplies from Fukuoka City, attempting to purchase them himself. His clemency report argued that it was not Sakamoto who provided medical care, but the American lieutenant Coslucky and one Dutch officer. Further, the report argued he was not to blame for the death of the ten POWs. Instead their death was due to factors beyond his control: their fifty-day sea odyssey or the fighting they had experienced before the journey. Finally, though he was accused of not controlling his staff, he told "his subordinates never to beat or strike the prisoners of war and never failed to control them."[55] The report argued that Sakamoto had no criminal responsibility.

Nevertheless Sakamoto was sentenced to life imprisonment at hard labor. The evidence was based on an interpretation of command responsibility that was not uniformly applied even in the US Army. Instead, "the record shows that the accused made an effort and did improve the camps to which he was assigned during the period covered by charge and specifications, that the death rate was not uniformly high and was influenced by the assignments of two groups of POWs in extremely bad physical condition."[56] This was referring to the Americans from the Philippines who arrived in 1945 after a horrendous odyssey. While conceding that Sakamoto was "a strict disciplinarian," he "punished Japanese subordinates who disobeyed his instructions regarding the treatment of Allied POWs."[57]

Hada Masato, the medical orderly at Fukuoka, was convicted of mistreating and abusing POWs, refusing to provide them with medical supplies, and misappropriating and withholding Red Cross supplies. He was sentenced to life imprisonment.[58] Katsura, the interpreter, was sentenced to forty years of hard labor, and ordered to serve twenty-five years at Sugamo.[59]

Who then ultimately was responsible for all these camps, and all these crimes? And what punishment was appropriate, considering the tough sentences meted out to lesser figures, whether individual camp commanders, translators, doctors, or guards? The 1948–1949 prosecution of General Tamura, the head of the POWIB / POWMO, was how prosecutors put the whole POW camp system on trial.

In the course of the trial, it became clear that Tamura had visited camps on several occasions and was likely aware of mistreatment. Prosecutors alleged he showed "willful and unlawful disregard and failure to discharge his duties."[60] Still, it is hard to determine his personal responsibility. Major Andrew Russell, who had been held at Omuta Miike branch camp (Fukuoka 17), a Mitsui Mining Company camp, sent a letter to the head of IPS stating that the head of the POWIB had visited the camp and "shown sincere interest in the health and welfare in the men of the camp." He had even returned to the camp and, after the second visit, told the commandant "to inform all prisoners that there was to be no more abuse at the hands of the civilian mine workers." According to Russell, "this was the first concrete evidence . . . that the abuse, brutality, and mistreatment was not a policy by higher headquarters but was a result of local prison policy."[61]

Some evidence indicates Tamura attempted to eradicate the use of personal punishment by prison officers, such as the investigation and punishment for beating POWs after infractions such as shirking work or stealing food and medicine. But other evidence showed that guards made use of disciplinary guidelines instituted under Tamura, and during the entire war only eighty-three guards were punished for such acts.[62]

As in Singapore, lower-ranking officers—themselves at risk of prosecution—were ready to testify against their generals. Colonel Fukumoto, head at Fukuoka, alleged that Tamura had decided punishment cells should be made smaller, and may have instructed that POWs in Fukuoka be given less food. Captain Hirate Kaichi, in charge of Hakodate, accused him of saying that POWs were being treated too well. According to Hirate, on an inspection in February 1945, Tamura instructed him to not feed prisoners while they were imprisoned there, and to make them work harder.[63]

It is clear that Tamura knew about abuses in POW camps, both abroad and in Japan. He knew about "private punishment," even if he tried to reduce its use. He had the authority to demand information from commanders and did little to act on prisoners' protests. He or his subordinates may have been involved in decisions to omit sections of ICRC reports and/or leave them blank. He was clearly guilty of not holding up his end of the ICRC conventions, even if he was unable to do so, either from a policy perspective, or from a lack of personnel. In at least one case, Tamura deliberately covered up incriminating information, and asked others to do the same. When he requested that camp commanders provide materials on the Thai-Burma Railway, he specifically instructed them to downplay "matters that are considered negligence on our part which must be concealed or ignored as much as possible." The memo requested that materials be arranged "to state concrete facts as much as possible so as not to create an impression that we are distorting or concealing the facts and to make effective our counter-protests to protests of the enemy countries."[64] It was only at the end of the war, in August 1945, that instructions were sent calling for better POW treatment, if only because the Allies were soon to arrive.[65]

The attorney appointed to argue Tamura's case, E. N. Warren, had been a defense lawyer at the Tokyo Tribunal. Warren cross-examined witnesses who argued that Tamura did in fact have authority. But he presented no witnesses or exhibits, and his defense was limited to putting Tamura on the stand. Warren did not question Tamura, and asked only a few follow-up questions.

But the trial still showed how little actual authority Tamura had. Although he knew camp commanders and officers from his time at the academy, and he and his two predecessors were all generals, none was powerful politically, much less within the dominant faction of the Army. Tamura additionally was recovering from illness. He could only send camp commanders instructions, not orders, and these had to go through military or garrison commanders. To enforce policies, Tamura was reliant on the prime minister or the minister of war.[66]

The root problem was the limited authority of both the POWIB and the POWMO. The POWIB had been set up as a provisional government agency affiliated with the Ministry of War, mainly to provide information for each POW. The POWMO was nominally in charge of planning logistics for handling POWs.[67] But it was parallel to the far more powerful Military Affairs Bureau, and required its approval. Any orders had to go through the Army Ministry, which issued the commands.[68]

The Ministry of War laid out the responsibility of the POWMO in a November 22, 1942, memo: it was limited to "matters of minor importance," accommodation, handling, allowance, transfer and labor of POWs, correspondence, relief, and foreigners entering camps.[69] Considering them "matters of minor importance" was itself a telling phrase.

Numerous charts introduced as evidence showed Tamura was not in the chain of command.[70] Even prosecution witnesses emphasized that point. As Sanada Jōichiro, Military Administration section chief put it, "as far as the chain of command, the prisoner of war administration chief has no responsibility."[71] It would be more accurate to describe his responsibilities as bureaucratic and managerial: compiling, storing, and transmitting reports. Yet Tamura's administrative functions laid him open to responsibility.

While Tamura made few active decisions that resulted in harm, he did not do much to prevent prisoner mistreatment either. But if the goal was to identify who was ultimately responsible for POW abuse, it is clear that high-level officers at the Ministry of War and officials in the powerful Military Affairs Bureau were the ones who set major policies on POWs.[72]

Tamura himself did not blame Tōjō or camp commanders, but instead pointed a finger at senior officers in the Ministry of War. In a September 1947 letter to the prosecutor, Tamura alleged that at the Tokyo Tribunal, General Mutō Akira and Lieutenant General Satō Kenryō "sought to evade the responsibilities concerning the POW affairs, by attempting to minimize and limit the meanings of the various laws and regulations, especially the War Ministry Organization Law and other regulations which defined the duties of the POW Information Bureau and the POW Administration Division."[73] Tamura continued:

> The Military Affairs Bureau had been the pivot of the whole army administration . . . the Army Ministers and Vice Ministers were often ROBOTS just acting at the will and manipulation of the Chiefs of Military Affairs Bureau. This was an apparent and acknowledged fact among the Army circle, and the staff of that Bureau were deemed brilliant and imposing as well as often looked upon with hatred and animosity.[74]

It was Tōjō who was ultimately responsible for the fateful order in 1942 to mobilize POWs for labor, "Disposal of POWs" (*Furyo shori yōkō*).[75] The order set in motion many of the horrors that followed. Other Ministry of War policies resulted in mistreatment of POWs: Tōjō's decision to prosecute aviators in military trials by court-martial, punishable by firing squad, and the March 1945 "Outline of Disposal of POWs according to the Situation" resulted in POWs being exposed to air raids.[76] The chief of staff of the General Staff and the War Minister approved all major policies and projects such as the Thai-Burma Railway. The Army Ministry also gave generals in the field broad discretion in how they treated captives. The lines of command were very complex, and each commandant of each POW prison camp came under either the military commander or the garrison commander.[77] As was revealed in the Tamura trial, these commanders' priorities were very different from those of camp commandants; above all, they prioritized winning the war as expeditiously as possible.

Commanding generals had broad authority because of the exigencies of battle and the distance and difficulty of communications. Many of the most infamous events of the war happened outside Japan.[78] Within Japan, policies were also set by the military district commanders and the camp commanders. As one officer said in the trial against Tamura, "the Army Commander and his staff had no time to devote to POW matters in 1945."[79] The main concern of the IJA of Hokkaido was preparing for operations against the invading US Army forces. So camp commanders acted on their own.

In the context of Occupied Japan in 1948, where political considerations were paramount and guilt was assumed, it is almost impossible that Tamura would not be found guilty. But the specific question was command accountability, and whether he had *willfully* disregarded his duties. Because he did not have chain-of-command powers, it was obvious Tamura had no such authority.

Prosecutors failed to ultimately assign command responsibility to the POWIB / POWMO and Tamura himself. Under MacArthur's rules that governed Yamashita's trial in Manila, Tamura might have been hanged. But the different rules in the Tokyo Tribunal—and the bureaucratic mess of the Japanese Army—saved Tamura's neck.

After final arguments, the verdict was announced and Tamura was sentenced. In the end, the tribunal found Tamura guilty of a single charge. He was sentenced to just eight years of hard labor. It was a relatively light sentence. It seems that the trial ended in this fashion because of a plea deal between the tribunal and the defense.[80] In 1962, Kanase Kunji, one of his two defense lawyers, reported that a member of a tribunal had approached Warren asking for an early conclusion so that he could take advantage of a job opportunity with SCAP. The defense agreed, provided the verdict would be equivalent to the seven-year prison sentence of the former wartime foreign minister Shigemitsu Mamoru. According to Kanase, Tamura and his family supported it.[81]

Tamura's trial was therefore a synecdoche for the story of Allied captives in the Pacific War. He was a high-level bureaucrat, but headed a powerless agency. Prosecutors assembled twenty-two witnesses and 459 exhibits to try to portray Japan's POW camps as a complex system, but the ultimate truth was still elusive. Clearly abuses, suffering, and tragedy happened under Tamura's watch, but was he actually responsible? Even those formally charged with finding out gave up, seeking a better opportunity. Unable to fix responsibility on any one person, or explain the specific policies that led to so much suffering, it was easier to imagine that everyone involved—down to the lowliest guard—was a war criminal.

In the fall of 1947, authorities freed about half the prisoners held for the International Military Tribunal for the Far East.[82] The last British trial occurred in December 1948. The last American trial, targeting Admiral Toyoda Soemu, who directed Japanese battles at the Philippines, Saipan, and Leyte, ended in 1949.[83] Toyoda was the only one acquitted after the war. Trials soon wound up in Taiwan, the Dutch East Indies—with Indonesian independence—and French Indochina. Australia was the last of the Western Allies to hold a war crimes trial, in April 1951.[84]

Trials continued in the People's Republic of China as late as June–July 1956, with four cases, and 1,062 defendants (1,017 found not guilty).[85] The Soviet Union held half a million Japanese captive in the USSR from 1945 onward. It tried alleged war criminals in the December 1949 Khabarovsk trial. Twelve former Kwantung officers and "doctors" were put on trial to expose an American "cover-up" on Japanese biological warfare. It is unclear whether this was meant as a show trial, as propaganda, or as a means of projecting Soviet influence.[86] But the last of the Japanese POWs did not go home until 1956.

Long before this, the United States and the United Kingdom had adopted a policy of clemency: an administrative act that allowed the reduction or removal of a sentence.[87] SCAP worked together with the Japanese, and by 1950 SCAP had already established both a remission system and a parole system. As memories of the war receded and the postwar occupations ended, it became harder to convince governments to keep Japanese POWs locked up. Maintaining prisoners was expensive and administratively burdensome, and therefore most prisoners did not serve their full sentences. At Sugamo there was even a shortage of hard-labor tasks. Only 599 of 1,000 at Sugamo were so employed.[88]

By the turn of the 1950s, Japanese men and women pressed for the end of the trials, for clemency, and the repatriation of those convicted.[89] They agitated through letters to newspapers, petitions, rallies, and most astoundingly, tour buses to Sugamo Prison. War criminals, who published books and memoirs, became an issue in Japanese politics.[90] Japanese war criminals imprisoned abroad were gradually returned to Japan and put in Sugamo Prison.[91]

In 1952, the Allied Occupation ended with the San Francisco Peace Treaty. The US-Japan Security Treaty came into force, and Sugamo Prison came under the jurisdiction of the Japanese Ministry of Justice. It was overwhelmingly clear that the war criminal issue was complicating the resumption of ties with the United States.[92] In 1953, the sentences of Japanese on death row in Muntinlupa Prison in the Philippines were commuted, and the prisoners were transferred to Sugamo. Others were simply pardoned. All were repatriated to Japan.[93] When China and the Soviet Union returned most war criminals between December 1953 and March 1954, the Western Allies faced additional political pressure to release the men held at Sugamo.

Sakamoto, the Fukuoka 1 camp commander, was not an atypical case. In May 1953, the National Offenders Prevention and Rehabilitation Commission of the Japanese government recommended clemency, finding that the original sentence was a misunderstanding.[94] Suda Toshio, governor of Sugamo, had taken the same position.[95] His recommendation was based on Sakamoto's "excellent record," and the four persons in his home needing support.

Sakamoto's parole documents narrate his labor history, farming, and woodworking. His carpentry was also praised. Sakamoto received a prison rating of "excellent." He "performed his duties in an exemplary manner. At all times he has worked with a minimum of supervision and has been completely trustworthy." Ironically, while serving time for his inability to meet his responsibilities running a POW camp, Sakamoto was a model prisoner. Two years later, in 1955, Sakamoto again applied for parole. The governor of Sugamo, Toshio Suga, approved it, and so did the Ministry of Foreign Affairs.[96] Sakamoto was originally sentenced to life in prison with hard labor. But he ended up serving less than twelve years.[97]

Pressure to release prisoners came from all sides, and not just the Japanese public. For the Allies, continued imprisonment was an impediment to the new realities of the Cold War. America now considered Japan an important ally, and had created a security policy where US troops were permanently stationed on military bases there. Others also sought to establish a new relationship with Japan. The USSR and even China saw little advantage in holding Japanese war criminals, and releasing them was a relatively easy way to improve relations with Tokyo. On Christmas Day 1958, Sugamo released the last of its nineteen inmates, and in 1964 China freed its last prisoner.[98]

By this point the Japanese government had begun to describe the suffering of POWs—and the punishment of their guards—as being the result of a simple misunderstanding. According to a 1955 POWIB report, the West and Japan had different understandings of what being a POW meant.[99] The Allies did not consider it shameful. Even if individual freedom of movement was constrained, individual rights and honor should be retained. For Japanese officers, just being a POW was equivalent to being a coward, and captives would therefore be treated as criminals. It was therefore difficult for them to understand the perspective of being a POW.[100] The report reiterated the now familiar point that, from the guards' perspective, using so-called private punishment like hitting was better than official punishment. The report went on to describe such violence as a negative tradition of the Japanese military and even as a "Japanese tendency."[101] This too had the effect of absolving individuals of any direct responsibility.

But rather than any fundamental rethinking about Japanese treatment of Allied POWs during World War II, it was the shift in the political climate that led more and more of those accused of war crimes to be granted early release. Japan's imperial order had disintegrated and the Cold War security regime had begun. Japan had become an American ally, and its constitution now forbade it to conduct war. By treaty, American troops remained stationed throughout the archipelago. Former war criminals were set free. But the misunderstanding of what happened in Japanese POW camps and civilian internment centers had hardly come to an end. It was only just beginning.

# 9

## PRISONERS OF HISTORY

# Renegotiating the Geneva Conventions in the Wake of War

In May 1949, as negotiators gathered for the Diplomatic Conference on the Geneva Conventions, one member of the Japanese delegation already felt alienated from the whole exercise. "Why engage in war at all?" asked Ayusawa Iwao, a Quaker and labor activist. "Humanity would much prefer a world where there is no protection offered to prisoners of war, wounded, sick, shipwrecked in war etc. but where there was no need of much [protection] because nations agreed to settle differences by negotiation and not resorting to the work of bombs and bombers."[1]

Ayusawa and the rest of the Japanese were attending only as observers. They were not included among the fifty-nine states with formal delegations.[2] For four years the Japanese had stood on the sidelines as the International Committee of the Red Cross (ICRC) organized a series of preparatory meetings, culminating in this three-and-a-half-month conference in Geneva. After its terrible defeat in World War II, Japan was still under military occupation. From 1946 to 1949, the victors of that war had also negotiated the Universal Declaration of Human Rights and the Convention on the Prevention and Punishment of the Crime of Genocide. Japan, meanwhile, was made to witness a whole series of war crimes prosecutions, both for senior military and political leaders and for hundreds of guards and POW camp commanders.[3]

Japanese representatives therefore had virtually no role and no apparent influence when, on August 12, the final act was concluded, and the four conventions were opened for signature to all states.[4] Japan would not even be permitted to join the signatories until it formally concluded a peace treaty in San Francisco in 1952 and thereby regained its sovereign rights to enter into international agreements.

Yet, when we consider the longer historical perspective, Japan could actually be seen to have had a big impact on both international law and societal understanding of how captives should and should not be treated in wartime. It was in no small part the experience of fighting the Japanese that gave negotiators so much difficulty in working out new treaties. Some of the same diplomats wrestled with many of the same questions that all sides had debated in the course of the Pacific War.[5] What if neither side formally declares war at the outset of hostilities, as in the Sino-Japanese War?[6] How could belligerents ensure adequate food for POWs when even their own troops starved, as did men in the Imperial Japanese Army (IJA)? What of prisoners accused of war crimes, such as the American fliers downed after the firebombing of Japanese cities—did they still have the protection of the Geneva Conventions?

The 1949 Geneva Conventions still stand as the main normative framework governing the treatment of civilians and POWs in international conflict. Typically scholars have analyzed them in the context of international law and its application to subsequent conflicts. Historians concerned with the history of international organizations have studied them from that perspective—namely, that of the ICRC and its internal history.[7] Much less attention has been devoted to the specific historical circumstances that influenced negotiators—not only the war itself, but also the years leading up to it and its complex aftermath.[8]

To be sure, Nazi atrocities also had a big influence on the negotiations in Geneva. Yet the thinking behind many of the new provisions, including those on the treatment of civilians, actually were based on ideas first put forth in Tokyo, at the Fifteenth International Conference of the Red Cross in 1934. And notwithstanding the silence of Japanese observers in Geneva, few countries had so much at stake—not only in terms of what representatives said about wartime Tokyo's conduct, but also in whether and how the new Conventions would be applied. After all, in 1949 tens of thousands of Japanese captives still remained in labor camps in the Soviet Union. They would continue to be put on trial for war crimes, as were those held by Australia and the People's Republic of China (China did not free its last prisoner until 1964).[9]

The victors of World War II, above all the United States, the United Kingdom, France, and the USSR, would have a preponderant role in creating the 1949 Geneva Conventions. But Japan was present even when it was absent. Bringing it into the picture helps us see the shortcomings of the process itself. In essence, it focused on the wording of provisions meant to prevent new war crimes, but without considering the context that really explained why such crimes took place—both in the Pacific War, and in the decades that followed. The negotiators also never accounted for the complex dynamic when both sides committed atrocities, as occurred in the Pacific War. Together with what neutral observers judged to be "victors' justice" at the Tokyo trials, these shortcomings help explain why the Geneva Conventions would continue to be ignored in a whole series of Cold War and colonial conflicts, including the wars that "Japanese surrendered persons" were ordered to fight in order to restore imperial rule.

In February 1945, the International Committee first went public with its plans to revise the Geneva Conventions.[10] The ICRC was already vulnerable to attack for its unwillingness or inability to stand up against the worst crimes perpetrated by the Nazis. But senior ICRC staff in the Pacific were also failing utterly in protecting Allied POWs, civilians, and even their own staff.[11] Max Huber, the former ICRC president, wrote to the big five: the United States, the United Kingdom, France, China, and the Soviet Union.[12] He assumed from the outset that the war's victors would rewrite the rules. The ICRC, which would be responsible for providing technical assistance through the drafting of the conventions, sought to present things in the best possible light. One ICRC report suggested "the ill-treatment of many prisoners of war was due, not to the convention itself, but to its non-application."[13] They pointed out that the ICRC had advocated for millions of POWs, making over 11,000 visits.[14] This was impressive on its face. But the scale and ferocity of the fighting far outstripped the ICRC's capacity. Most Allied captives in Asia, for instance, rarely saw even a Red Cross package, much less an inspection visit.

The drafts that would eventually be voted on required a whole series of international meetings, the first of which was convened by the Swiss Federal Council in Geneva, headquarters of the ICRC.[15] In October 1945, the neutral members of the "Mixed Medical Commission" met. During wartime it examined sick or wounded prisoners and decided on their eligibility for repatriation. In the summer of 1946, the international committee convened a "Committee of Experts," with 145 delegates from National Red Cross societies from fifty countries. After studying the Committee's proposals and preliminary drafts, they unanimously recommended the revision of the Convention Relative to the Treatment of Prisoners of War.[16]

These groups provided the ICRC with information based on what had been learned from wartime experiences. But even though representatives of many countries participated in these preparatory meetings, when they finally got down to modifying or adding specific provisions, leadership in the preceding conflict is what ensured a place at the table. An April 1947 "Conference of Government Experts for the Study of the Conventions for the Protection of War Victims" included representatives from just fifteen countries that had detained or lost large numbers of prisoners of war and civilian internees.[17]

The experts assessed a range of issues that reflected the experience of the recent war, especially how the POW convention should be arranged, how to reinforce the Conventions' application, and how to make the requirements of the Conventions better known when it counted most. Could the Conventions be applied when a belligerent captured very large numbers of POWs, as occurred both at the beginning and the end of the Pacific War? What about POWs who lacked a protecting power—a neutral government acting on their behalf when the two belligerents did not have diplomatic relations? What penalties should be applied when the Convention was violated?[18]

The experts amended the existing Geneva Conventions and established a preliminary Draft Convention for the Protection of Civilians in Time of War, once again taking up the project that had been abandoned after the 1934 meeting in Tokyo. This process provided the working draft for the Seventeenth International Red Cross Conference, which met in Stockholm in August 1948.[19] The ICRC based this earlier draft on the experiences of World War I, when observers realized that it was essential to legally protect civilians as well as servicemen. The draft had sections on the status of enemy civilians, enemy civilians on the territory of a belligerent, enemy civilians on the territory occupied by a belligerent, and implementation of the convention. Delegates planned to discuss it at the 1940 Diplomatic Conference, but the war prevented this meeting.[20]

Representatives of fifty governments and fifty-two national Red Cross societies attended the 1948 Stockholm conference. Sweden, neutral during the war years, had acted as a protecting power for Japanese in Hawaii, and the Swedish Red Cross had engaged in much international relief activity. The wartime heroism and rescue missions of Swedish Red Cross president Count Folke Bernadotte won worldwide fame.[21] At the Stockholm Conference, as at other conferences, the ICRC and the League constantly jostled for influence. The League, for instance, preferred that civil wars should not be covered under the Geneva Conventions. Their view finally prevailed.[22]

The priorities of the most important League members also reflected their wartime experience. The American delegation, for instance, focused on clarifying language on food, prohibiting POW labor clearing mines, and improving prisoner transport.[23] The State Department gave the US representative, FDR's former law partner Basil O'Connor, detailed directions. As president of the American Red Cross and chairman of the Board of Governors of the League of Red Cross Societies, he would be in a strong position to press for these measures.[24]

Whitehall considered revision of the Conventions essential, and had extensive experience from the war that showed the problems all too clearly. Yet even as the British supported the ICRC, they did not agree that the Conventions should be expanded to cover internal conflicts as well as external ones. They may have been thinking of the series of anti-insurgency campaigns they were waging in Malaya and Palestine. Unlike the United States, Whitehall kept its plans from the British Red Cross.[25]

In September 1945 the Soviet Union declined to join the initial discussions or even communicate with the ICRC.[26] Moscow disapproved of ICRC policies during World War II and viewed it as soft on fascism even before it began. This included Red Cross actions dating back to the postrevolutionary Russian civil war and the ICRC's attempt to practice humanitarianism during the Spanish Civil War. During the negotiations, the Soviets and their clients argued that the ICRC should have excommunicated fascist countries in which leadership used national Red Cross societies for their own aims. The Soviets also blamed the ICRC for not doing more to protect Soviet prisoners in German hands, nearly 60 percent of whom had died. When the war ended, the Soviets accused the ICRC of a spurious concern for the plight of war victims, which encouraged POWs and internees not to return.

The Soviets would not attend ICRC gatherings to plan for the 1949 meeting, nor even reply to ICRC communications. But they sometimes allowed their Red Cross representative to attend international gatherings. Thus, other countries had to guess at Soviet intentions, inferring Moscow's position from the position taken by other socialist countries, especially Yugoslavia.[27]

In the end, the Soviets would attend the conference, and sign the Geneva Conventions, but they registered their reservations. Most significant was their opposition to article 85—that an individual's status as a POW would be unaffected during proceedings on war crimes trials and they would continue to have the rights of POWs. The Soviets were later joined in this opposition by all other communist countries.[28]

In the summer of 1949, China was still undergoing civil war. Representatives of Chiang Kai-shek's nationalist government emphasized how the Chinese had suffered during the Asia-Pacific War.[29] Captured Chinese soldiers had for the most part not been treated as Allied POWs. Nan-Ju Wu, the head of the delegation, pointed out that during eight years of conflict "the state of war had not been recognized by one of the belligerents." It was essential to specify the rights of belligerents and neutral parties in this situation.[30]

As a wartime occupied country, France was in a peculiar position, particularly because of what happened in French Indochina.[31] The colonial government in Hanoi remained loyal to Vichy, and French forces had collaborated with Tokyo. This had allowed Japan to set up support bases in Indochina. In March 1945, the Japanese took complete control and took French soldiers prisoner. In postwar Saigon, France had prosecuted 230 Japanese war criminals—most for crimes against French nationals—notably the four officers responsible for a March 1945 massacre at Lang Son.[32] But French forces in Indochina were primarily composed of colonial troops, many of which remained in Indochina after 1945. POWs from the Pacific War played less of a role in France's approach to the negotiation than for the United States or the United Kingdom. For Paris, the important POWs were the ones who had been captured by the Germans, and their experience is what shaped French preferences. French postwar activities also influenced their position. In 1949, the French still used German POWs for labor and were not following ICRC recommendations to repatriate them.[33]

As for the three observers from the Japanese Red Cross, they were not even able to present their views. Prince Shimazu Tadatsugu, president of the Japan Red Cross Society (JRCS), would have been able to speak directly to the concerns of the other powers.[34] He worked for the JRCS during the war and was personally responsible for the distribution of Red Cross aid to Allied servicemen. Because of their war experience, he and his colleagues knew how much—or how little—the shortcomings of the Geneva Conventions explained the suffering of POWs. As Ayusawa's letters suggested, the problem was not the Geneva Conventions themselves, but instead leaders who subordinated all considerations to military expediency. During the war, Camille Gorgé of the Swiss Legation in Tokyo repeatedly noted in his communications to Bern that the Foreign Ministry would have adhered more closely to the Geneva Conventions, but it was really the Japanese military that decided such matters. For Japanese commanders, many struggling to supply their own troops, Allied prisoners and internees were a low priority, and they had little understanding of or appreciation for the ICRC and its activities.

Instead of learning about the logistical and political context that actually explained why so many Allied POWs in the Pacific suffered deprivation, the delegates at Stockholm and Geneva focused on the language of specific provisions. To be sure, some of them also had direct experience, only it was that of the POW. They included the Australian POW Wing Commander Reginald Henry Davis. Men like Davis and R. H. Wilson, the Australian Red Cross representative who had been held captive in a POW camp in Korea, knew that reciprocity did not guarantee adequate rations: food that barely fed IJA soldiers doing guard duty could mean malnutrition for Allied troops doing hard labor. In the same way, former captives knew the importance of regular communication home and what happened when guards sat in on ICRC interviews with POWs.

So these were the kinds of issues negotiators focused on—essentially re-fighting the last war. The Japanese government, on the other hand, did not press its own views on these or any other issues, and insisted on its neutrality. Foreign Ministry officials were well aware of the extent to which the Asia-Pacific War shaped the Conventions: "It appears that the treatments accorded to prisoners of war and civilian internees by Japan during the Second World War were taken into consideration in revising some articles of these conventions," it blandly noted in a letter to the ICRC after the meeting. "As Japan has renounced war in her constitution, it is unimaginable that these conventions be applied to Japan as an active belligerent." But they were nevertheless concerned about how they would eventually be applied to Japan as a neutral country.[35]

Officially Japan had "no opinion" on POWs or civilians. But the Foreign Ministry had good reason to worry that, as a neutral country with no military, Japan might not gain protection from the new Conventions. In a future conflict, in which Japan itself might again become a battlefield, they would be unable to hoist a flag distinct from that of military authorities, since Japan would have no military. Similar objections applied to protections for

Fifty-nine nations sent formal delegations to Geneva to negotiate expanded protections for POWs and civilians in wartime. The Japanese could only look on as observers. (© M. Wasserman, 8/12/1949, ICRC Archives V-P-CER-N-0000B-08.)

religious and hospital staff, which referred to "the military authority." Should it not be changed to the "competent authorities"?[36]

These concerns were given no attention when in 1949 delegates met in Geneva to finalize and approve the draft ironed out at Stockholm. The former home of the records of the Central Prisoner of War Information Bureau, the Palais de la Conférence, was remodeled to serve as headquarters.[37] Official languages were French and English, although the Soviet representative chose to speak in Russian. Geneva provided entertainment to the delegates when they were not negotiating: a boat trip on Lac Léman and an official reception. Other delegations sponsored small dinners. The US delegation, first among equals, received twenty-seven invitations.[38]

Because Japan remained under occupation, two representatives from the Supreme Command for the Allied Powers (SCAP) were included in the delegation from Tokyo: Alva C. Carpenter, chief legal adviser to General

Douglas MacArthur, and George T. Hagen, his assistant. Future ambassador to the United States Asakai Kōichirō, director-general of the Central Liaison and Coordination Office, joined Ayusawa. The Office coordinated between the Japanese government and Allied Occupation authorities. A 1949 letter from Saitō So'ichi, general secretary of the YMCA, put the best face on things: "We are very grateful to hear that two Japanese, as observers, are allowed to participate in the international conference to be held in Geneva." The letter continued to thank the ICRC for their "kind understanding and generosity towards Japan."[39]

The four played peculiar roles, as representatives of both occupiers and occupied, with the two Americans serving as mere observers at a diplomatic conference where the other Americans were some of the most important participants.[40] The Japanese / American Occupation representatives could only sit back as the actual delegates debated how to prevent future belligerents from treating POWs the way Japan had done during the war years. For instance, article 11 of the 1929 convention had specified that food rations of prisoners should be equivalent to those of troops at base camps. The US Department of State commented that this was "a standard recalling the familiar 'fishhead and rice' diet of American prisoners of war in the Pacific."[41] Delegates therefore sought to require that food for POWs should be adequate to keep them in good health—specifying quantity, quality, and variety.[42] In rewriting the conventions, the delegates considered basing them on daily caloric intake, comparison with civilians, periodic weight checks, and additionally taking account of the habitual diet of POWs.[43] They did not address what would happen in theaters where food was lacking, such as Singapore, Korea, and Japan during World War II. Even in the United States, where food had been plentiful, evidence suggests that the United States used restricted pay and rations as a disciplinary measure on German POWs.[44]

The Pacific experience influenced other changes in the Conventions as well. What kind of work could captives be asked or required to perform and in what condition? Article 31 of the 1929 POW Convention provided that prisoners' labor should have no "direct relation" to war operations and prohibited "unhealthful or dangerous work." But in an age of total war, it was not always easy to identify what was, or was not, related to war operations and what kind of work would be deemed unacceptable. "In Japan, for instance, prisoners of war had been employed under conditions which were perfectly normal for Japanese workers but intolerable for prisoners from

Western countries," Roberto Moll, from the Venezuelan Ministry of External Relations, pointed out. "Further, working conditions in tropical
countries could be very hard for prisoners coming from temperate zones."[45]
In 1949, US representatives argued that a new and simplified formula should
regulate the employment of prisoners of war. Articles 50 and 52 of the new
Conventions limited compulsory work of prisoners of war to specific categories and prohibited compelling prisoners to clear and dispose of mines.[46]

The Australians, more of which had died in POW camps than in combat,
were particularly intent on learning from the last war. The Stockholm text
went too far in "permitting delegates to talk to prisoners of war without
witnesses," argued the former captive Wing Commander Davis, "Practical
experience had shown the drawbacks which that entailed."[47] He further
suggested that those responsible should be "commissioned [officers],"
because during World War II, Japanese authorities had placed NCOs in
charge of prison camps.[48]

Perhaps most important to the Australian delegation was guaranteeing
communication between POWs and their families. Tens of thousands of
British and Australian captives "could not send any messages to their
next-of-kin, or to their other relatives, and for years could receive no
message in return." This was a central part of the ICRC mission, but this
was not instituted in Japan until 1944. Wing Commander Davis pointed
out, "As you may know, neither the Protecting Power nor the International Committee of the Red Cross could do anything to organize a
system of communication to and from these camps." The ICRC Central
Committee had sent over 55,000 telegrams to the Prisoner of War Information Bureau and almost 2,500 to the JRCS. Yet in December 1945, one
Japanese official was unable to state the "total number of telegrams received and dispatched as no records had been kept." The process almost
guaranteed lost messages: When a telegram was received, officials underlined the camp address that the ICRC had included, and forwarded it by
mail. But the POWIB never bothered to check that the POW to whom it
was addressed was in the underlined camp, despite the constant transfer
of captives.[49]

When the war ended, the Australians discovered that there were more
than sixty camps of which they had not been informed.[50] Wing Commander Davis himself, an advisor to the Australian delegation, was taken
prisoner in Sumatra and held in captivity for more than two and a half
years. During his captivity "he, and the majority of his comrades in the

various camps to which they were moved from time to time, never received one message nor were they able to communicate one message, and it was not until the end of hostilities that their relatives found that in the meantime tens of thousands of prisoners had died." He continued, "Therefore, my Government wants to see that a similar state of affairs never occurs again."

US representatives also emphasized that captives should have "all the judicial guarantees which are recognized as indispensable by civilized peoples." During the war, a Japanese civilian court tried and convicted American fliers downed over Japan. And in Manila, three British internees who had escaped Santo Tomas were sentenced to death by a military court.[51] American representatives sought to clarify which laws should apply to whom. Stipulating regular courts-martial and codes of military justice would also avoid cases like that of Yamashita Tomoyuki, the Japanese commander in the Philippines.[52] While the majority of the US Supreme Court denied Yamashita's defense application for petition for writs of habeas corpus, their decision was controversial even at the time it was decided, and raised questions of "victor's justice."

The British emphasized a different issue. Their key concern was how captives should be treated when belligerents had not formally declared war, as in the case of the Sino-Japanese War. Joyce Gutteridge, delegate from the UK mission, argued, "The United Kingdom Delegation feels that it is of particular importance that all such questions should be decided upon according to the general 'rules of international law,'" when Japanese occupiers acted as if international law was not applicable.[53] She claimed that British citizens in China in particular had suffered. It is hardly clear that British internees suffered more than others—especially compared to the Chinese. Yet the issue had a wider significance. If belligerents did not declare war, the conventions would be meaningless.

In the end, the Americans and British were largely successful in achieving their aims. Instead of the old standard that food rations should be equivalent to those of garrison troops, now "the basic daily food rations shall be sufficient in quantity, quality and variety to keep prisoners of war in good health and to prevent loss of weight or the development of nutritional deficiencies. Account shall also be taken of the habitual diet of the prisoners."[54]

They also achieved provisions regarding work conditions for prisoners, ensuring communication, and the applicability of the Conventions when war was not formally declared.[55] In a 1955 report of the US Committee on Foreign Relations, the State Department affirmed that "the United States can well be proud of its efforts at the Diplomatic Conference to elevate the standards of treatment applicable to war victims."[56] In fact, because the Geneva Conventions so closely reflected the American position, the United States was the first major power to sign.[57]

The ICRC was also satisfied: "It is no exaggeration to say that POWs in present or future conflicts are covered by a veritable humanitarian administrative statute, which not only protects them from the dangers of war, but also ensures that the conditions in which they are held are as satisfactory as possible.[58] After 1949, the set of common treaties that governed war began to be called "the Geneva Conventions," as a "tribute to the city of Geneva, headquarters of the ICRC and also to Switzerland as a whole."[59]

In light of the treatment of POWs in the wars that followed, these words now seem overly optimistic, if not hollow. But even at the time, they hardly protected POWs held even by signatories to the Conventions, as the Japanese knew all too well. After the Soviet Union entered the Pacific War, they took more than 600,000 Japanese prisoner. Even as the Soviets participated in renegotiating the Geneva Conventions, they subjected their Japanese captives to forced labor under brutal conditions.[60]

ICRC Tokyo delegate Margherita Strahler pressed Geneva for news of their fate, "which has been awaited with eagerness for so long."[61] Yet the ICRC did virtually nothing to help them. Three months after the signing of the Geneva Conventions, General Douglas MacArthur, head of the Allied Occupation, pressed the US State Department to draft a letter to the Soviets to designate an international body to negotiate on behalf of the Japanese. Yet even in mid-1949, the State Department was more concerned to avoid "embarrassing the Swiss [government] or Int[ernational] Red Cross by giving Sov[iets] opportunity to attack their integrity."[62] Kessler of the ICRC had phoned the deputy head of the delegation and State Department legal assistant Raymond T. Yingling to say that it would be "very difficult" for them to offer assistance. Yingling said he would not embarrass the Swiss.[63]

What explains this idea that showing concern for Japanese captives in Siberia would have been too "embarrassing"? Part of the problem may arise with their definition: the Soviets called them *internirovanie*, the Japanese *yokuryūsha*, both words that mean "internee." The United States referred to them as "POWs" in internal documents, but in public statements called them Japanese Surrendered Personnel (JSP) or Surrendered Enemy Personnel. But these men were certainly POWs, and perhaps some of the most unfortunate POWs of all: servicemen who had been captured in the last days of the war by an army that they had not even been fighting, and kept in Siberia to perform hard labor for as long as eleven years after the war ended—far longer than the war itself. The ICRC may have found it easier to ignore them during the tense negotiations of the Geneva Conventions. It was not until December 1956 that the last of these Japanese prisoners was allowed to go home.[64]

The prisoners were prevented from suing the Soviets for compensation by a 1956 Soviet-Japanese Joint Declaration. Nor did they receive compensation from the Japanese courts. Plaintiffs based their case on the 1949 Third Geneva Convention. But Japanese courts denied their claim because Japan had not signed the Convention until 1953.[65] The fact that Japanese at the 1949 conference were mere observers now meant that the Japanese POWs had no protection.

It was the Japanese Quaker, Ayusawa, who was the most prescient, and from the first days of the Geneva Conference: "It began in a spirit of cooperation, a most convivial atmosphere," he reported. "But already a few . . . have begun to reveal their selfish stands with selfish but unconvincing arguments."[66] The delegates could not even agree on a preamble, much less the soaring language found in the opening of the Universal Declaration of Human Rights.

In the end, as Ayusawa concluded,

> The best or the only thing that actually solves these questions will be for each nation to adopt as Japan had done under the new constitution, a policy not to resort to arms for the settlement of international problems and to renounce the right of a nation to engage in war and to adapt and enforce a treaty to that effect that would have been far better and more worthwhile than to establish elaborate rules—which every nation in war tries to evade about the treatment of war prisoners and interned civilians.[67]

# CONCLUSION

# Never Again, and Again

Compared to their counterparts in 1941, Americans today are more familiar with Japan, and the Pacific nation no longer seems even remotely threatening. For most Americans, the Japanese have ceased to be objects of hatred. And the US government looks to Japan as a loyal ally, both now and in future conflicts in East Asia. American presidents and Japanese prime ministers still invoke the lessons of the Pacific War, even as they contemplate these potential new wars. But what were these lessons, and what have we actually learned from them? When we look beyond the usual narratives, what can the POW experience in Japan tell us about Japan, the Allies, and World War II, in all their human complexity?

Popular memories of what Allied captives endured in the Pacific War tend to invoke the very worst episodes as representing the essence of the experience. But for those unfortunate people who found themselves prisoners of the Japanese empire, whether and how they survived was more like a terrible game of chance. It was usually better to be a civilian internee than a soldier, better to be captured in Singapore than in the Philippines, better to surrender at Corregidor than Bataan, and better to be transported to Japan in 1942 than in 1944, when convoys were routinely attacked and sunk. But someone who survived the Bataan Death March, the most hellish of the hell ships, and a stint at Fukuoka 1, might end up at a camp in Korea originally built to showcase Japan's honorable treatment of POWs. Conversely, some civilian internees endured appalling treatment, or much the same treatment as POWs, since they were often kept in the same camps.

The experience of their captors was also incredibly varied, and is impossible to reduce to stereotype. War criminals responsible for the worst atrocities could escape trial and punishment, and many of those who were convicted were released early. A low-level Korean guard like Park Byeong Suk, by contrast, could be sentenced to years in prison and a lifetime of shame for slapping the face of an Allied officer.[1] Still others, mere bystanders, might be killed at the very end of the war, when a pallet of supplies for POWs crash-landed on top of them.

Given the variations in the captivity experience, we cannot begin to understand it without analyzing it comparatively and viewing it within a broader context. To start with, even a well-provisioned army with a coherent chain of command can struggle to cope with huge numbers of enemy soldiers who have suddenly surrendered. At the end of the war in Europe, for instance, the US Army held over a million German POWs in the Rhine Meadow camps. They were not accorded POW status, or allowed ICRC visits. They were kept in open enclosures, with no shelter, and limited to a diet of 1,200 to 1,500 calories a day—less than half as much as was given American GIs. Some 32,000 died in just three months.[2]

The Imperial Japanese Army (IJA) had much more tenuous logistics in 1941–1942, far fewer men available for guard duty, and much less time to prepare to care for hundreds of thousands of POWs and internees. The treatment of captives was just one of many examples of poor planning and strategic incoherence, but it turned out to be unusually important. After all, the goal of the early campaigns was to quickly surprise and overwhelm Allied positions, so they should not have been so surprised when so many surrendered. Considering that Tokyo's overall strategy depended on persuading the Allies to agree to a negotiated peace, they should have realized that the neglect or abuse of prisoners would make this more difficult. When reports of this mistreatment emerged, it helped rally support for the firebombing of Japanese cities and the demand for unconditional surrender. Japan's mishandling of its early military victories thus contributed to the totality of its strategic defeat.

But there was no overarching policy or plan to make POWs suffer, or starve them, or work them to death. There was little policy of any kind. POWs were simply not a priority. Even if there had been a clear policy on POWs, there was no institutional capacity to implement it. Regulation of the camps was ostensibly left to the Prisoner of War Management Office, a bureaucratic entity with no control over the camps. The camps were run by individual officers, and sometimes NCOs, in far-flung locales, who reported through a convoluted chain of command. They were given broad latitude in how they maintained order and met demands for POW labor.

This latitude meant that conditions differed dramatically across the vast Asia-Pacific theater.

Overall rates of death among Allied POWs in the Japanese empire were appallingly high. But some camps, such as Jinsen and Keijō in Korea, had very low casualty rates. Moreover, a large proportion of prisoners—the exact proportion is impossible to determine—died because their ships were sunk through friendly fire guided by Allied intelligence, in a ruthless campaign to destroy all Japanese shipping notwithstanding the price paid by POWs. The sinking of the *Arisan Maru* by a US submarine killed more than two and a half times as many American GIs as died during the entire Bataan Death March.

Even the more fortunate captives, such as the American officers who were driven out of Bataan rather than being made to march, or the British officers in Korea, lived through tough conditions and witnessed unimaginable suffering. But the reasons were specific and local, not a goal of high-level decision makers in Tokyo. This is an important distinction, and it becomes even more clear in an international and comparative framework. In 1941–1942, the same period the Japanese scrambled to improvise a policy to cope with Allied POWs, Germany implemented a program that clearly aimed at exterminating large numbers of Soviet prisoners right from the start.[3] It was high-level policy to kill all communist Commissars. Hitler refused to change this order even when he was told it was discouraging Soviet troops from surrendering. Those Soviet POWs who were not summarily shot as suspected communists were provided no shelter and no medical care during the Russian winter. As a result, by the end of the war as many as 57.5 percent of Soviet POWs in German hands died, about double the rate of mortality among Allied POWs in the Pacific.

The great exception to this lack of any high-level policy aiming to inflict suffering on POWs was the treatment of the Chinese. Here there is significant evidence that Japanese commanders planned to deal with them harshly from the outset, in China and throughout Asia, including both civilians and servicemen. Sometimes captured Chinese soldiers were considered "bandits" and immediately killed. In other cases the Japanese military corralled Chinese civilians, used them as laborers (*kajin rōmusha*), and used others as forced labor (*kyōsei rōdō*).[4] Thousands more Chinese suffered from medical experiments with biological weapons. This stands in contrast to Chinese authorities, who toward the end of the war captured Japanese soldiers and held them.

Tokyo called the war in China an incident (*Shina jihen*), and therefore the Geneva Conventions did not apply.[5] In the vast majority of cases the Chinese servicemen were not treated as POWs. Many other Asians died at Japanese hands, of course—most infamously, laborers on the Thai-Burma Railway, who were worked to death. But here again, these men were not considered POWs covered by the Geneva Conventions.

As for Allied POWs, they experienced wildly different conditions, depending on when and where they were captured, the physical conditions and climate, proximity of the camp to Tokyo, and, perhaps most importantly, the camp commander. But also important was the immediate context. After all, starvation and bombing in the surrounding community inevitably affected what happened inside the camps. Some Japanese resented POWs, and Koreans in one case rushed the gates because they believed that the POWs had better lives than they did. As Japanese men and women suffered, so too did POWs.

Some situations led to clear abuse, as when the IJA forcibly marched POWs at Bataan in the Philippines or Sandakan in Borneo, or transported them on the hell ships. The quixotic Thai-Burma Railway, where Japanese officers made hundreds of thousands toil, and close to a hundred thousand died, was another notorious case. As atrocious as the conditions were for Allied POWs and Asian laborers, Japanese servicemen also suffered at the hands of their commanders. IJA troops in the Philippines, Thailand, and Burma suffered high rates of diseases like cholera and malaria. They also tended to receive inadequate medical care. They too subsisted on a meager diet, albeit one that was more familiar to them. When Allied POWs died from attacks on transport ships, or aerial bombardment of cities, so did Japanese servicemen and civilians.[6]

Some of the worst atrocities were inflicted on captured airmen. Those caught during missions to bomb Japanese cities might suffer beheading, death by martial arts or even by biological experiments, while others were summarily executed. But it is worth considering what might have happened if the roles had been reversed. How would residents of Los Angeles, Chicago, and New York have treated captured Japanese airmen who were firebombing their cities? After Americans buried their dead, including large numbers of their children, would Japanese prisoners have been accorded all the protections of the Geneva Conventions, assured foreign diplomats' visits and Red Cross care packages?

As we have seen, many other Allied POWs described the physical conditions of captivity as "not so bad." Official postwar reports found that POWs in camps in Japan and Korea were treated much like Japan's own soldiers. But that could mean conditions were quite harsh, even for the guards. These camps could be relatively open to the outside world, and some POWs actually welcomed work as an opportunity to obtain food or simply as relief from boredom. Even in places like Changi, POWs were sometimes given a surprising degree of autonomy in running their own affairs. This was even more true of camps for internees, which were largely self-run and meant to be self-sufficient.

But even when the physical conditions of camps were tolerable, many POWs and internees found life in captivity difficult to endure. In reading prisoners' diaries, government reports, and contemporary news coverage, it is impossible to ignore the influence of both implicit and explicit racial hierarchies in how the POW experience was felt and portrayed, whether in Changi or Korea. For example, in his memoir, the Australian Guy Round recounted a poem that accompanied a Christmas Card in his diary. "The Nip in nineteen forty-three / Was Ichi ban to you and me / But soon in nineteen forty-four / Your Ricksha boy he'll be once more." In his diary he wrote, "These cartoons were entirely free from anything which could give offense to our captors—or so we thought. But the deeply ingrained inferiority complex of this simian race caused them to plead the most fantastic interpretation on these very innocent cartoons."[7] One article in the *Nor Bars,* the Loyals magazine, described a Japanese guard searching for contraband: "something unusually grave considering their rice-distended features are actually creased into a display of emotion! Oriental impassivity is shattered, hands and tongues begin to move briskly. Deplorable lack of zen." After the confession and seizure of a contraband item, "the Japanese officer's eyes grow yet slittier and mien more menacing." When the contraband is discovered to be merely a penny whistle, "oriental equanimity [was] restored."[8] Another poem, "Things I Wouldn't Like to Be," reads like A. A. Milne.[9] "I wouldn't like to be a Jap / And wear a silly little cap / And look an awful sap / I wouldn't like to be a Jap." It continues, "I wouldn't like to be a Jap / And kneel and crouch to have a crap: / I'd sooner sit like normal chap / I wouldn't like to be a Jap."[10]

First-person accounts emphasize the humiliation of bowing to their captors, having to speak in their language, and acting according to their norms, such as sleeping on Japanese-style mats and using Japanese toilets. They also objected to wearing number tags, and calling out their numbers in Japanese—a language with which very few were familiar. For many, this is what was most objectionable. Colonial officials and colonial soldiers who previously policed imperial domains found themselves under the control of men whom they clearly viewed as members of an inferior race, if not another species. Recall how, for Captain Round, being paraded in Pusan felt like he was a "lion in a zoo."

As we have seen, Japanese leaders in Tokyo, and occupation officials in the Philippines, did see the spectacle of Allied POWs as serving their goal of dramatizing the rise of Japan and the fall of the old Euro-American imperial order. In some places, like Korea, they literally put POWs on parade. Allied POWs were not wrong to think that, in some cases, their humiliation resulted from political calculations. Ironically, their colonial troops paid an even higher price, as the Japanese would be even tougher on Indians and Filipinos who refused to change loyalties.

But what Allied POWs most often complained of as being particularly humiliating, such as being made to salute lowly Japanese privates and slapped if they refused, only reflected IJA practices. Japanese military culture itself was strict, and POWs were expected to assume the lowest positions in the hierarchy. Moreover, Japanese enlisted men from rural areas would seldom have encountered non-Japanese speaking foreigners. In some cases they simply did not realize that POWs did not understand their orders. Guards who had come up through this system, or were trained by those who did, were encouraged to use corporal punishment to keep POWs in line, especially because Euro-American troops were physically larger. They saw nothing wrong with physical punishment for disobedience. They considered this "private punishment" a good way to deal with misbehavior, and they themselves preferred it to the risk of disgrace through more formal sanctions. But few POWs understood the practice. They themselves had seldom encountered Japanese. It was all too easy to portray their behavior as animalistic.

Recall too the hypermasculine military culture that American, Australian, and British soldiers brought to the camps. They considered the shorter, smaller Japanese men literally beneath them. POWs were held by what they regarded as subhumans, as apes. And yet the Japanese lectured them about their lack of honor for allowing themselves to be captured. At the same time, POWs were limited in their own expression of their masculinity, deprived as they were of bodily markers such as military uniforms, and diminished in their bodily autonomy.

A situation in which bitter enemies suddenly stopped fighting was bound to seem strange. At the least, POWs lost out on their chance to fight a heroic war. Few medals were awarded for being a POW. And it was difficult to follow injunctions to attempt escape or sabotage when chances of success seemed scant and punishment could mean death. The condition of captivity was meant to be stable, and many elements of military culture remained in effect. But the actual captivity experience was often chaotic, with men of different ranks, services, and nationalities mixed in together. It disrupted the hierarchy of ranks that structured military life. It was also literally unsettling, since POWs were so often on the move, taken from place to place with no notice and no explanation. And it was isolating as well, since POWs—as well as internees—had little or no contact with the outside world, or even with immediate family members who might also be in captivity.

But many of these observations also applied to guards. It was a low-status position, and typically reserved for colonial conscripts, or those who were too unfit, injured, or traumatized to fight at the front. They too had little or no opportunity to display bravery or otherwise distinguish themselves. The camps were meant to be largely self-sufficient, and to provide labor for war industries. Guards clearly played an auxiliary role, but one that nonetheless could elicit criticism, such as for being too indulgent to prisoners at a time when Japanese children were being stunted from malnutrition.

When we think about masculinity during war, it is often in terms of the bravery of men under fire, or courage in attacking the enemy. But captivity, and the guarded masculinity that resulted from it, is also part of war, and for many soldiers it is the largest part of it. For the hundreds of thousands of prisoners and internees in the Pacific War, the defining experience of war was being prisoners of the Japanese. It should be no surprise that these bitter memories had lasting repercussions—not just in the war crimes trials, and in recasting the Geneva Conventions, but in how we recall and commemorate this history.

Emphasizing the savagery and barbarism of Japanese guards underscored the endurance and bravery of Allied POWs. It provided a way to restore the hierarchy of civilizations when Western empires were being overrun. Allied propagandists began to do this systematically in 1944, highlighting the trial and execution of captured bomber crews. They typically ignored altogether the much larger number of non-European prisoners— as many historians still do today. Instead, it was the emaciated American or British Commonwealth POW who became emblematic of the experience. Published photos of scantily clad and painfully thin prisoners shocked the public, and still retain this power.[11] But what impact did that have on the prisoners themselves?

During the war, correspondents portrayed the "forbearance of men in the face of atrocious mistreatment."[12] But this is not necessarily how others saw them at the time, or even how POWs saw themselves. As Christina Twomey has argued, tensions about masculinity could be seen in the self-doubt and shame through which former POWs recalled their experience.[13] Former POWs suffered physically and psychologically. Among British POWs, the most common condition was what is today known as post-traumatic stress disorder (PTSD) and hearing problems. A time-study of American POWs held by the Japanese found substantial health consequences. Although it is difficult to tell what was attributable to combat, to imprisonment, and to re-entry, one study found that "generalized anxiety disorder, alcoholism, and affective disorders" appeared with high frequency.[14] Another study of Pacific War veterans reported that "among the American POW survivors, almost ¾ suffered from PTSD, as compared to from ¼ to ⅓ of the combat veterans."[15] POWs could also experience sexual dysfunction, both as a direct result of their captivity—due to malnutrition—and from what one British doctor called "difficulties of readjustment."[16]

Reducing the complexity of the Pacific War captivity experience to a study of manly forbearance in the face of animalistic savagery therefore diminishes the suffering of POWs and internees. It was experienced as humiliating and traumatic for specific historical reasons, and exploring that history—however painful—is the only way we can learn from it.

It also bears lessons for later US wars in Asia, notably in Korea and Vietnam, where the plight of American POWs once again became emblematic of entire conflicts in which far larger numbers of non-Americans suffered and died. One of the most important lessons was how war crimes could result not from deliberate high-level decision making but from poor training, a lack of planning, and a callous disregard for anything but military priorities. This was the "lesson" of My Lai, where US troops had received little, if any, training in the laws of war. But it was a lesson that might have been learned decades earlier by examining the experience of the Pacific War.

The Pacific War did have an impact on the Geneva Conventions, but only in the wording of specific provisions, not in a more honest accounting of how military exigencies can actually determine the use and abuse of international law. It was therefore sadly ironic when, in 2002, as the United States launched a "global war on terror," and had to decide how it would treat its captives, then White House counsel Alberto Gonzales called some clauses of the Geneva Conventions "obsolete," and "quaint." The Bush administration concluded that al Qaeda and the Taliban were not entitled to its provisions.[17]

During the war in Iraq, another war launched with little advanced planning or consideration for POWs, American forces were once again stretched thin. What they did to captives at Abu Ghraib—who once again were deemed unworthy of the protections of the Geneva Conventions— seemed beyond comprehension, especially the way they were humiliated in ways meant to challenge their masculinity. But the military police who guarded them were poorly trained, underequipped, and outnumbered seventy-five to one.[18] Though Donald Rumsfeld eventually took responsibility, the only ones penalized were the eleven enlisted men and one officer tried.[19] Lawyers have argued that, according to the standards the United States applied at the Tokyo Tribunal, the Bush administration committed war crimes.

American courts ultimately rejected White House attempts to send alleged terrorists to indefinite detention without charge or due process of law. In 2006 the US Supreme Court cited Pacific War precedents, including the *Yamashita* case, to reject the contention that the Geneva Conventions did not apply to al Qaeda and the Taliban. A majority ruled in *Hamdan v. Rumsfeld* that any new tribunals must comply with the laws of war as encoded in the Geneva Conventions.[20] The justice who wrote the opinion, John Paul Stevens, himself served in the Pacific War with naval intelligence. Ironically, his main duty was decoding enemy communications to help find and sink Japanese ships.[21]

When the decision was handed down, and reporters asked the president if it meant he would have to close Guantanamo Bay, and stop subjecting people to indefinite detention, Bush insisted he would find a way to keep them locked up: "I'm not going to jeopardize the safety of the American people. People have got to understand that. I understand we're in a war on terror; that these people were picked up off of a battlefield; and I will protect the people."[22]

When he said this, Bush was standing next to the Japanese prime minister, Jun'ichirō Koizumi, who was at the White House on an official visit. During their press conference, the two men went on to marvel at how, some sixty years earlier, it was Japan and the United States at war, and "our respective fathers looked at each other with deep suspicion." Indeed, George H. W. Bush had narrowly escaped capture as a naval aviator. And Koizumi's own father had been expelled from politics during the American occupation.

The two men said nothing more about the prisoners in Guantanamo Bay. They instead talked about history. They insisted that they were deepening their alliance, including joint operations of US and Japanese military forces, because of their historic dedication to peace. For Bush, Japan was a model for what he was trying to achieve with two ongoing wars in the Middle East: "I firmly believe that the example that we show today will be repeated over the decades, particularly with newly-elected leaders in the Middle East. And the Prime Minister understands that. And I'm grateful for the contribution of the Japanese people to the cause of peace."[23]

"It's because we have learned the lessons of World War II," Koizumi explained. "It is because we've learned lessons from the past in our relations with the United States and determined to maintain friendly relations with the United States."

But what were these lessons? Koizumi annually visited the Yasukuni Shrine, enraging Chinese and Koreans for appearing to honor the memory of class-A war criminals. Bush, for his part, invited Japan's participation in America's military expeditions to Afghanistan and Iraq, which critics likened to an attempt to create a new empire. Presidents and prime ministers have come and gone, but Guantanamo Bay, and all it represents, remains open. Bush finally accepted that the Geneva Conventions applied to prisoners there, but ever since, government lawyers have found ways to argue that they are not actually entitled to its protections.

These are very nearly the opposite of the lessons learned by Ayusawa Iwao and other Japanese of his generation. Observing the sometimes unseemly negotiations that led to the 1949 Geneva Conventions, he realized that international law cannot in itself prevent war crimes, and that every war leads to new crimes. As for the Allied POWs of that era, few survive to tell their stories. But the stories themselves continue to be told and retold, both familiar and strange, and seemingly ever more remote.

At a time in which debates over torture and military tribunals have come to seem unending, we need to understand how and why they first began. The most important lesson of all may be that people who might otherwise seem worlds away from us, even people consigned to the remote past, can—indeed must—surprise and unsettle us, when we realize they are not actually so strange. Looking into the past, we find it looking back at us.

Notes

Archival Sources

Acknowledgments

Index

# Notes

## Introduction

1. Although I discuss female internees, here "Allied POWs" refers to male servicemen. Though not covered in this book, the major exception was the nurses stationed in the Philippines at the beginning of the war, members of the US Army Nurse Corps and the US Navy Nurse Corps who continued their work throughout the war.

2. Laura Hillenbrand, *Unbroken: A World War II Story of Survival, Resilience, and Redemption* (New York: Random House Trade Paperbacks, 2014); *The Bridge on the River Kwai,* directed by David Lean (London: Horizon Pictures GB Ltd., 1957); James Clavell, *King Rat* (Boston: Little, Brown, 1962).

3. John Grisham, *The Reckoning: A Novel* (New York, Doubleday, 2018).

4. J. G. Ballard, *Empire of the Sun* (New York: Simon and Schuster, 1984); *Empire of the Sun,* directed by Steven Spielberg (Burbank, CA: Warner Brothers, 1987).

5. See Bernice Archer, *The Internment of Western Civilians under the Japanese, 1941–1945: A Patchwork of Internment* (Hong Kong: Hong Kong University Press, 2008); Christina Twomey, *Australia's Forgotten Prisoners: Civilians Interned by the Japanese in World War Two* (Cambridge: Cambridge University Press, 2007); and A. Hamish Ion, "'Much Ado about Too Few': Aspects of the Treatment of Canadian and Commonwealth POWs and Civilian Internees in Metropolitan Japan 1941–1945," *Defence Studies* 6, no. 3 (2006): 292–317. Even those who see this as a problem themselves write national histories. See Karl Hack and Kevin Blackburn, eds., *Forgotten Captives in Japanese-Occupied Asia* (New York: Routledge, 2008), 4.

6. How large a proportion died from friendly fire is impossible to determine now with any precision, especially because estimates for the total number transported vary. According to the records of the Prisoner of War Information Agency, 14,790 men were shipped and 2,835–2,873 died. This includes the 1944 voyage of the *Ōryoku Maru,* which resulted in 308 deaths. Chaen Yoshio, ed., *Furyo Jōhōkyoku Furyo toriatsukai no kiroku: Tsuketari, Kaigun Heigakkō "Kokusaihō"* (Tokyo: Fuji Shuppan, 1992), 43–50. Michno calculates the number

of passages rather than the number of people transported, and some POWs made multiple voyages. He arrives at the figure of 126,064 passages to and from Guam, Singapore, Indonesia, and the Philippines, among other places. He estimates that 21,039 POWs died, 19,000 from friendly fire. Gregory F. Michno, *Death on the Hellships: Prisoners at Sea in the Pacific War* (Annapolis, MD: Naval Institute Press, 2001), viii–ix, 282–283, 317. Looking just at the Philippines, the American Defenders of Bataan and Corregidor Memorial Society, an organization of family members of former POWs, estimates that 3,600 American POWs lost their lives aboard hell ships and that some 700 others lost their lives soon after (http://www.dg-adbc.org/content/history).

7. After first describing the Japanese as following a strict code, Gavan Daws later asserts that "*Bushidō,* the way of the warrior, meant whatever officers wanted it to mean." Daws, *Prisoners of the Japanese: POWs of WWII in the Pacific* (New York: William Morrow, 1994), 83.

8. Oleg Benesch, *Inventing the Way of the Samurai* (Oxford: Oxford University Press, 2014), 208; John Dower, *War without Mercy: Nationalism, Internationalism, and Bushido in Modern Japan* (New York: Pantheon Books, 1986), 64–71.

9. As John Lynn put it, after observing the lack of military history in the most prominent academic journal and a preoccupation with "cutting edge" topics like race, class, and gender, "The fact is that they are out to get us, and military history has been compelled to receive the 'cutting edge' like a bayonet in the guts." Lynn, "The Embattled Future of Academic Military History," *Journal of Military History* 61, no. 4 (1997): 781.

10. Lynn, "The Embattled Future of Academic Military History," 783. But note that Lynn himself acknowledges that comparative masculinities is a useful way to analyze military history (784–787). In the years since, a number of military historians have taken up this challenge, even while military history itself remains "relatively marginalized within professional academic circles." For a survey, see Robert M. Citino, "Military Histories Old and New: A Reintroduction," *American Historical Review* 112, no. 4 (October 2007): 1070–1090.

11. Robert A. Nye, "Western Masculinities in War and Peace," *American Historical Review* 112, no. 2 (April 2007): 424.

12. Robin Gerster, "War by Photography: Shooting Japanese in Australia's Pacific War," *History of Photography* 40, no. 4 (2016): 445.

13. Gerster, "War by Photography," 442.

14. Dower, *War without Mercy,* 81–91; Gerstler, "War by Photography," 436.

15. Dower, *War without Mercy*, 78.

16. Dower, *War without Mercy*, 146.

17. Gerald Horne, *Race War! White Supremacy and the Japanese Attack on the British Empire* (New York: New York University Press, 2003), 46; Harumi Furuya, "Japan's Racial Identity in the Second World War: The Cultural Context of Japanese Treatment of POWs," in *Japanese Prisoners of War,* ed. Philip Towle, Margaret Kosuge, and Yoichi Kibata (London: Hambledon Press, 2000), 117–134.

18. Elizabeth Norman, *We Band of Angels: The Untold Story of American Nurses Trapped on Bataan* (New York: Simon and Schuster, 2000), 84.

19. The asterisk is in the original. Daws claims, by way of explanation, that "the great majority were released within months." Even if true—no more careful accounting is offered—their experience could be no less harrowing (*Prisoners of the Japanese,* 18, 22).

## 1. From Avatar of Modernization to Outlaw Nation

1. Sho Konishi, "The Emergence of an International Humanitarian Organization in Japan: The Tokugawa Origins of the Japanese Red Cross," *American Historical Review* 119, no. 4 (2014): 1129–1153. Olive Checkland, the rare scholar writing in English on the JRCS, never examined original Japanese-language archival documents, and her account mainly takes up its early successes—and late failures. Until recently, Japanese-language scholars (Inoue Tadao, Koike Masayuki, Masui Takashi, Yoshikawa Ryūko) were mostly concerned with the institutional history of the Japan Red Cross Society or its relationship with the ICRC. More recently, scholars such as Konishi Sho and Frank Käser have examined the documents and argued that the intellectual and humanitarian origins of the JRCS derive from a "preexisting humanitarian ethic" in the late Tokugawa period (Konishi, "The Emergence of an International Humanitarian Organization in Japan," 1134). This kind of scholarship is indebted to that of scholars such as David Howell and Karen Wigen. Greg DePies also takes up this kind of argument, pointing out that the JRCS was an exemplar of modern humanitarianism that sought to rescue ordinary people from disaster and to promote health and life.

2. Henri Dunant, *A Memory of Solferino* (Washington, DC: American National Red Cross, 1939, translation of *Souvenir de Solferino;* reprint, Geneva: International Committee of the Red Cross, 1939), https://www.icrc.org/en/doc/assets/files/publications/icrc-002-0361.pdf.

3. John F. Hutchinson, *Champions of Charity: War and the Rise of the Red Cross* (New York: Perseus, 1997), 25.

4. Hutchinson, *Champions of Charity*, 24–28.

5. Hutchinson, *Champions of Charity*, 31–37.

6. Hutchinson, *Champions of Charity*, 45.

7. D. Colin Jaundrill, *Samurai to Soldier: Remaking Military Service in Nineteenth-Century Japan* (Ithaca, NY: Cornell University Press, 2016), 5. During the Edo period (1603–1867) power was split between the shogunate in Tokyo and the provincial domains (the precursors of today's prefectures).

8. "Vienna International Exposition and Japonism," in *100 Years of Japanese Emigration to Brasil* (Tokyo: National Diet Library, n.d.), www.ndl.go.jp /exposition/e/s1/1873-2.html.

9. "Besuch bei der Gesellschaft vom Roten Kreuz, Geneva, July 1, 1873, Japanese Embassy," 493–497, and Aimé Humbert to the Comité international de secours aux militaires blessés, in *Bulletin International 5me Année,* no. 17 (October 1873): 11–16, as found in Kunitake Kume and Peter Panzer, *Die Iwakura-Mission: Das Logbuch des Kume Kunitake über den Besuch der japanischen Sondergesandtschaft in Deutschland, Österreich und der Schweiz im Jahre 1873* (Munich: Iudicum, 2002), 495–497.

10. Jaundrill, *Samurai to Soldier,* 147.

11. Konishi argues that this was the origin of the JCRC. Konishi, "The Emergence of an International Humanitarian Organization in Japan," 1142. On Japan's history with the Red Cross, also see Margaret Kosuge, "Religion, the Red Cross and the Japanese Treatment of POWs," in *Japanese Prisoners of War,* ed. Philip Towle, Margaret Kosuge, and Yoichi Kibata (London: Hambledon Press, 2000), 149–161.

12. Mizuno attributes this to "Meiji concerns over national security" as well as seeking primacy in the world. Eskildsen argues it is "mimetic imperialism." Norihiko Mizuno, "Early Meiji Policies towards the Ryukyus and the Tai-wanese Aboriginal Territories," *Modern Asian Studies* 43, no. 3 (May 2009): 685; Robert Eskildsen, "Of Civilization and Savages: The Mimetic Imperialism of Japan's 1874 Expedition to Taiwan," *American Historical Review* 107, no. 2 (April 2002): 388–418.

13. Barclay argues that "the process Ronald Niezen dubs 'indigenization' is a historical concomitant of competitive nation building in the age of high imperialism (1870s–1910s)." Idea discussed in Ronald Niezen, *The Origins of*

*Indigenism: Human Rights and the Politics of Identity* (Berkeley: University of California Press, 2003); Paul Barclay, *Outcasts of Empire: Japan's Rule on Taiwan's "Savage Border," 1874–1945* (Berkeley: University of California Press, 2018), 1–2.

14. Naoko Shimazu, "The Myth of the 'Patriotic Soldier': Japanese Attitudes towards Death in the Russo-Japanese War," *War & Society* 19, no. 2 (December 2013): 74.

15. Jaundrill, *Samurai to Soldier*, 148.

16. Konishi has argued that it emphasized "pioneering medical knowledge and the moral practice of medical healing for common people." Konishi, "The Emergence of an International Humanitarian Organization in Japan," 1150.

17. Konishi, "The Emergence of an International Humanitarian Organization in Japan," 1137–1142.

18. "Higashifushimi-no-miya Yoshiaki Hakuaisha sōchō shūnin shōdaku" [Prince Higashifumi Yoshiaki sends a letter of agreement to be president of the Hakuaisha], *Yomiuri Shimbun*, October 10, 1877, 2.

19. Frank Käser, "A Civilized Nation: Japan and the Red Cross 1877–1900," *European Review of History: Revue européenne d'histoire* 23, no. 1/2 (2016): 22.

20. Käser, "A Civilized Nation," 1–2, 16–32.

21. Käser, "A Civilized Nation," 22–23.

22. Konishi, "The Emergence of an International Humanitarian Organization in Japan," 1145; Käser, "A Civilized Nation," 21.

23. Käser, "A Civilized Nation," 25.

24. Edward Drea, "In the Army Barracks of Imperial Japan," *Armed Forces and Society* 15, no. 3 (April 1989): 329–348.

25. Drea, "In the Army Barracks of Imperial Japan," 330.

26. Sabine Frühstück, *Colonizing Sex: Sexology and Social Control in Modern Japan* (Berkeley: University of California Press, 2003), 28–32.

27. Theodore F. Cook, "Making 'Soldiers': The Imperial Army and the Japanese Man in Meiji Society and State," in *Gendering Modern Japanese History*, ed. Barbara Molony and Kathleen Uno (Cambridge, MA: Harvard University Asia Center, distributed by Harvard University Press, 2005), 269; Frühstück, *Colonizing Sex*, 28.

28. Obinata Sumio, "Teikoku guntai no kakuritsu to 'dansei'-sei no kōzō" [The establishment of the "Imperial Army" and the structure of "masculinity"], *Jendā Shigaku* 2 (2006): 21–23.

29. By the end the mid-1920s, attendance at the Staff College was a prerequisite for high status.

30. Jaundrill, *Samurai to Soldier*, 179.

31. Kawamata Seiichi, *The History of the Red Cross Society of Japan* (Tokyo: n.p., 1919), 112–119.

32. "War Items," *Japan Weekly Mail* (Yokohama), September 24, 1894, 361–362.

33. Yoichi Kibata, "Japanese Treatment of British Prisoners of War: The Historical Context," in Towle, Kosuge, and Kibata, *Japanese Prisoners of War*, 137.

34. The Japanese were acutely interested in following international law during the war. In a later examination, Professor Sakuyei Takahashi, who had served as legal officer to the commanding admiral aboard the *Matsushima*, wrote an account about Japan's law and consulted on a compilation of the official history of the war. In addition to Takahashi, Ariga, a professor at the military college, was attached to the troops on land. Sakuyei Takahashi, *Cases on International Law during the Chino-Japanese War* (Cambridge: Cambridge University Press, 1899), 117–118.

35. Kawamata, *The History of the Red Cross Society of Japan*, 114–125.

36. Rotem Kowner, "Imperial Japan and Its POWs: The Dilemma of Humaneness and National Identity," in *War and Militarism in Modern Japan: Issues of History and Identity*, ed. Guy Podoler (Folkestone: Global Oriental, 2009), 85; Takahashi, "Cases on International Law," 36–37.

37. Takahashi, "Cases on International Law," 35.

38. *New York Times*, December 17, 1894, 9.

39. As cited in Käser, "A Civilized Nation," 26.

40. Olive Checkland, *Humanitarianism and the Emperor's Japan, 1877–1977* (New York: St. Martin's Press, 1994), 9.

41. Julia Irwin, *Making the World Safe: The American Red Cross and a Nation's Humanitarian Awakening* (New York: Oxford University Press, 2013), 22.

42. "Convention (II) with Respect to the Laws and Customs of War on Land and Its Annex: Regulations concerning the Laws and Customs of War on Land. The Hague, 29 July 1899," International Committee of the Red Cross, https://ihl

-databases.icrc.org/ihl/INTRO/150?OpenDocument. The Conference of 1899 successfully adopted a Convention on Land Warfare, which was only slightly revised at the Second International Peace Conference in 1907. The Hague Conventions were rooted in the 1863 Lieber Code, which governed the conduct of Union troops.

43. Caroline Beth Reeves, "The Power of Mercy: The Chinese Red Cross Society, 1900–1937" (PhD diss., Harvard University, 1998). Europeans and Americans first organized an unofficial Red Cross mission in 1894. Five years later, the Chinese first made diplomatic moves to start a Red Cross organization, following the Japanese model (ibid., 55–77). The Qing government was split between internationalists (Japan as model where the formation of a national Red Cross Society was a diplomatic initiative) and isolationists (ibid., 84–91).

44. *New York Tribune,* December 29, 1902, 8N; *Chicago Daily Tribune,* December 15, 1901, 54.

45. Kibata, "Japanese Treatment of British Prisoners of War," 137–141.

46. "Furyo jōhōkyoku o setchi su," February 2, 1918, National Archives of Japan, 00963100, Japan Center for Asian Historical Records (hereafter cited as JACAR), reference code A01200935200.

47. Philip Towle, "Japanese Treatment of Prisoners in 1904–1905—Foreign Officers' Reports," *Military Affairs* 39, no. 3 (1975): 115–116.

48. Kowner, "Imperial Japan and Its POWs," 87; Towle, "Japanese Treatment of Prisoners in 1904–1905," 116; Masahiro Yamamoto, *Nanking: Anatomy of an Atrocity* (Westport, CT: Praeger, 2000), 30.

49. Caroline Moorehead, *Dunant's Dream: Switzerland and the History of the Red Cross* (New York: Harper Collins, 1998), 155.

50. Moorehead, *Dunant's Dream,* 154.

51. Yoshita Makita, "Professional Angels at War: The United States Army Nursing Service and Changing Ideals of Nursing at the Turn of the Twentieth Century," *Japanese Journal of American Studies,* no. 24 (2013): 79.

52. "Address of Thanks to the Mrs. Muggy's Party," Rikugun-shō Riku Mitsuru Shin dai nikki-41-2-12, JACAR reference code C03027616700.

53. "Red Cross in Japan: Miss Ethel McCaul's Book about Hospitals and Sanitary Arrangements," *New York Times,* March 18, 1905, 163.

54. Towle, "Japanese Treatment of Prisoners in 1904–1905," 116.

55. Reeves, "The Power of Mercy," 12.

56. Andrew Gordon, "The Crowd and Politics in Imperial Japan: Tokyo 1905–1918," *Past & Present* 121 (1988): 141.

57. Barclay, *Outcasts of Empire,* 4.

58. Leonard Humphreys, *The Way of the Heavenly Sword: The Japanese Army in the 1920's* (Stanford, CA: Stanford University Press, 1995), 12–15.

59. Obinata,"Teikoku guntai no kakuritsu," 24–26.

60. Sabine Frühstück, *Playing War: Children and the Paradoxes of Modern Militarism in Japan* (Oakland: University of California Press, 2017), 31.

61. Frühstück, *Playing War,* 32–35.

62. Edward Drea, *Japan's Imperial Army: Its Rise and Fall, 1853–1945* (Lawrence: University Press of Kansas, 2009), 119.

63. Drea, *Japan's Imperial Army,* 120.

64. Inoue Hikaru, Commander 19th Division, Rikugun-shō—riku mitsuru hisoka dai nikki, March 5, 1905, M39-1-10 (Holdings: National Institute for Defense Studies, Ministry of Defense), JACAR reference code C03020440100.

65. Oleg Benesch, *Inventing the Way of the Samurai: Nationalism, Internationalism, and Bushidō in Modern Japan* (Oxford: Oxford University Press, 2014), 105–106.

66. Benesch, *Inventing the Way of the Samurai,* 106–110.

67. The era is named after the Taishō emperor (1912–1926).

68. International Committee of the Red Cross, "The Archives of the International Prisoners of War Agency, 1914–1919," http://grandeguerre.icrc.org/Content/help/Introduction_en.pdf.

69. Moorehead, *Dunant's Dream,* 187–193.

70. Richard B. Speed, *Prisoners, Diplomats, and the Great War: A Study in the Diplomacy of Captivity* (Westport, CT: Greenwood Press, 1990), 37; Moorehead, *Dunant's Dream,* 184–186.

71. Moorehead, *Dunant's Dream,* 187–193.

72. Humphreys, *The Way of the Heavenly Sword,* 23.

73. Charles Burdick and Ursula Moessner, *The German Prisoners-of-War in Japan, 1914–1920* (Lanham, MD: University Press of America, 1984), 18.

74. Mahon Murphy, "Brücke, Beethoven, and Baumkuchen: German and Austro-Hungarian Prisoners of War and the Japanese Home Front," in *Other Fronts, Other Wars? First World War Studies on the Eve of the Centennial*, ed. Joachim Bürgschwentner, Gunda Barth-Scalmani, and Matthias Egger (Leiden: Brill, 2014), 129–130; Checkland, *Humanitarianism and the Emperor's Japan*, 72.

75. Burdick and Moessner, *The German Prisoners-of-War in Japan*, 9.

76. Burdick and Moessner, *The German Prisoners-of-War in Japan*, 8–11.

77. Baron Ishiguro to President ICRC, "First Page of a Letter from the Japanese Red Cross Announcing that ICRC Delegate Fritz Paravicini Is Authorized to Visit Prisoner of War Camps in Japan," August 11, 1918, https://www.icrc.org /eng/who-we-are/history/150-years/dam-files/1914-paravicini-33_277.pdf.

78. Burdick and Moessner, *The German Prisoners-of-War in Japan*, 8–10, 13–14, 71n32.

79. Burdick and Moessner, *The German Prisoners-of-War in Japan*, 61, 63.

80. Murphy, "Brücke, Beethoven, and Baumkuchen," 132.

81. Burdick and Moessner, *The German Prisoners-of-War in Japan*, 13.

82. Takahashi Terukazu, *Marugame Doitsuhei horyo shūyōjo monogatari* (Tokyo: Enishi Shōbo, 2014), 167–177; Burdick and Moessner, *The German Prisoners-of-War in Japan*, 25–61.

83. Burdick and Moessner, *The German Prisoners-of-War in Japan*, 8; Takahashi, *Marugame Doitsuhei horyo shūyōjo monogatari*, 9–20.

84. Takahashi, *Marugame Doitsuhei horyo shūyōjo monogatari*, 9–20.

85. It was the result of a merger of three other camps, among them Marugame.

86. Takahashi, *Marugame Doitsuhei horyo shūyōjo monogatari*, 203–211. See also "Ausstellung für Bildkunst und Handfertigkeit" [Exhibition of pictorial arts and handicrafts], Bando 1918, March 8, 1918, http://bando.dijtokyo.org/?page =object_detail.php&pn_id=237; *Die Baracke: Zeitung für das Kriegsgefangenenlager* [The barracks: Newspaper for POW camps], Bando Japan, no. 25, March 17, 1918; "Führer durch die Ausstellung für Bildkunst und Handfertigkeit Kriegsgefangenenlager," Bando 1918, March 8–18, 1918, in *Kokaido in Bando* [Guide for the exhibition of pictorial arts and handicrafts of POWs], http://bando.dijtokyo.org/?page=object_detail.php&p_id=277.

87. Murphy, "Brücke, Beethoven, and Baumkuchen," 136.

88. 100 yen = $1. Takahashi, *Marugame Doitsuhei horyo shūyōjo monogatari*, 213–220.

89. Murphy, "Brücke, Beethoven, and Baumkuchen," 145; Takahashi, *Marugame Doitsuhei horyo shūyōjo monogatari*.

90. The 2006 film *Baruto no gakuen* [Ode to joy] shows the relationships among the camp commander, local residents, and POWs.

91. Naraoka Sochi, *Hachigatsu no hōsei o kiita Nihonjin* (Tokyo: Chikura Shobō, 2013), 5–8, 107.

92. For more, see Naoko Shimazu, *Japan, Race, and Equality: The Racial Equality Proposal of 1919* (Abingdon, UK: Routledge, 1998).

93. Takahashi, *Marugame Doitsuhei horyo shūyōjo monogatari*, 213–220.

94. Takahashi, *Marugame Doitsuhei horyo shūyōjo monogatari*, 218.

95. Thomas Burkman, *Japan and the League of Nations: Empire and World Order, 1914–1938* (Honolulu: University of Hawai'i Press. 2008), xii.

96. Frederick Dickinson, "Toward a Global Perspective of the Great War: Japan and the Foundations of a Twentieth-Century World," *American Historical Review* 119, no. 4 (2014): 1162.

97. Kowner, "Imperial Japan and Its POWs," 100; Towle, "Japanese Treatment of Prisoners in 1904–1905," 2–3.

98. Obinata, "Teikoku guntai no kakuritsu to 'dansei'-sei no kōzō," 26–31.

99. Tachikawa Kyoichi and Shukuhisa Haruhiko, "Seifu oyobi gun to ICRC nado to no kankei," *NIDS Security Studies* 11, no. 2 (2009): 126–127.

100. Paul E. Dunscomb, *Japan's Siberian Intervention, 1918–1922: A Great Disobedience against the People* (Lanham, MD: Lexington Books, 2011), 56; Tatiana Linkhoeva, *Revolution Goes East: Imperial Japan and Soviet Communism* (Ithaca, NY: Cornell University Press, 2020), 39, 56–57.

101. N. Margaret Kosuge, "The 'Non-religious' Red Cross Emblem and Japan," *Revue Internationale de la Croix-Rouge* 85, no. 849 (2003): 84.

102. Tachikawa and Shukuhisa, "Seifu oyobi gun to ICRC nado to no kankei," 126–127.

103. Gordon, "The Crowd and Politics in Imperial Japan," 143, 147.

104. Sally Hastings, *Neighborhood and Nation in Tokyo, 1905–1937* (Pittsburgh: University of Pittsburgh Press, 1995), 39.

105. Hastings, *Neighborhood and Nation in Tokyo*, 39.

106. Humphreys, *The Way of the Heavenly Sword*, 50. If loyalty should be to one's class instead of to the emperor, then soldiers who served the emperor were unpopular.

107. Humphreys, *The Way of the Heavenly Sword*, 47.

108. Irwin, *Making the World Safe*, 149–150.

109. From 1919 until 1928, the two organizations contended for international recognition, and in 1928 they reached an agreement. Today the two, along with the national Red Cross/Red Crescent societies, make up the Red Cross movement. See Kimberly Lowe, "The League of Red Cross Societies and International Committee of the Red Cross: A Re-Evaluation of American Influence in Interwar Internationalism," in "Transnational Humanitarian Action: Atlantic and Global Voluntary Activities from Abolitionism to the NGOs, 1800–2000," special issue, *Moving the Social—Journal of Social History and the History of Social Movements/Mitteilungsblatt des Instituts für soziale Bewegungen* 57 (2017): 38.

110. Edward J. Drea, *In the Service of the Emperor: Essays on the Imperial Japanese Army* (Lincoln: University of Nebraska Press, 1998), 83.

111. Yamada Mami, "Oyama no iru fūkei Dainiji sekaitaisen-chū no Nipponhei sensō horyo shūyōjo no nichijō to 'otoko rashisa' no datsu kōchiku," *Ningen Bunka Sōsei Kagaku Sōron* 15 (March 31, 2013): 302.

112. Yamada, "Oyama no iru fūkei," 302.

113. Frühstück, *Playing War*, 52–55.

114. The concept of "hygienic modernity" is from Ruth Rogaski, *Hygienic Modernity: Meanings of Health and Disease in Treaty-Port China* (Berkeley: University of California Press, 2004). See Sheldon Garon, "Rethinking Modernization and Modernity in Japanese History: A Focus on State-Society Relations," *Journal of Asian Studies* 53, no. 2 (1994): 357.

115. Humphreys, *The Way of the Heavenly Sword*, 72.

116. Danny Orbach, *Curse on This Country: The Rebellious Army of Imperial Japan* (Ithaca, NY: Cornell University Press, 2017), 164.

117. Humphreys, *The Way of the Heavenly Sword*, 72.

118. Humphreys, *The Way of the Heavenly Sword*, 72–79, 90–99. The assignment of a lieutenant general of general staff background was a demotion. Commanding a division meant an officer was no longer on the inside track and even that he might soon be out of a job. Two thousand active-duty officers were assigned to secondary schools and colleges as military instructors.

119. Orbach, *Curse on This Country*, 165.

120. Humphreys, *The Way of the Heavenly Sword*, 122.

121. Benesch, *Inventing the Way of the Samurai*, 177.

122. As quoted in Dickinson, "Toward a Global Perspective of the Great War," 1181.

123. William Hitchcock, "Human Rights and the Laws of War: The Geneva Conventions of 1949," in *Human Rights Revolution: An International History*, ed. Akira Iriye et al. (Oxford: Oxford University Press, 2012), 93–112; "Convention Relative to the Treatment of Prisoners of War," Geneva, July 27, 1929, International Committee of the Red Cross, https://ihl-databases.icrc.org/ihl/INTRO/305.

124. Several International Conferences of the Red Cross (tenth in 1921, eleventh in 1923, and twelfth in 1925, all in Geneva) adopted resolutions inviting the ICRC to undertake action in this field.

125. "Draft International Convention on the Condition of Civilians of Enemy Nationality Who Are on Territory Belonging to or Occupied by a Belligerent, Tokyo, 1934," International Committee of the Red Cross, https://ihl-databases .icrc.org/ihl/INTRO/320?OpenDocument.

126. Orbach, *Curse on This Country*, 188.

127. The core membership of Araki Sadao's Kōdōha [Imperial Way faction] was men of the 1925, 37th class, of the Military Academy.

128. By 1928, factions in the Army were well developed as Ugaki continued to fight for modernization. Ultimately he lost this war, and Araki Sadao became Army Minister.

129. Drea, *Japan's Imperial Army*, 167.

130. Rustin Gates, "Meiji Diplomacy in the Early 1930s: Uchida Kōsai, Manchuria, and Post-withdrawal Foreign Policy," in *Tumultuous Decade: Empire, Society, and Diplomacy in 1930s Japan*, ed. Masato Kimura and Tosh Minohara (Toronto: University of Toronto Press, 2013), 189.

131. Drea, *Japan's Imperial Army*, 169.

132. Rana Mitter, *Forgotten Ally: China's World War II, 1937–1945* (Boston: Houghton Mifflin Harcourt, 2013), 35.

133. Drea, *Japan's Imperial Army*, 181.

134. Drea, *Japan's Imperial Army*, 173; Kowner, "Imperial Japan and Its POWs," 100.

135. Benesch, *Inventing the Way of the Samurai*, 177–178.

136. Benesch, *Inventing the Way of the Samurai,* 181.

137. Ben-Ami Shillony, *Revolt in Japan: Young Officers and the February 26, 1936 Incident* (Princeton, NJ: Princeton University Press, 1973).

138. Its instigators, Kita Ikki and Nishida Mitsugi, received death sentences. A purge of the military meant that many officers supporting the Imperial Way faction were moved to the reserves, empowering the Control faction. More obliquely, its result was to empower the military through the terror it caused.

139. Rustin Gates, "Solving the 'Manchurian Problem': Uchida Yasuya and Japanese Foreign Affairs before the Second World War," *Diplomacy and Statecraft* 23, no. 1 (2012): 32–43.

140. Stewart Brown, "Japan Stuns World, Withdraws from League," UPI, February 24, 1933.

141. Gates, "Meiji Diplomacy in the Early 1930s," 210.

142. Kimura and Minohara, *Tumultuous Decade,* xvii; Jessamyn R. Abel, "Cultural Internationalism and Japan's Wartime Empire: The Turns of the *Kokusai Bunka Shinkōkai,*" in Kimura and Minohara, *Tumultuous Decade,* 17–43.

143. Sven Saaler, *Pan-Asianism in Modern Japanese History: Colonialism, Regionalism and Borders* (London: Routledge, 2007), 11–12.

144. "The Japan Advertiser: XVth International Red Cross Conference Edition, Tokyo 1934," October 1934, Library of Congress.

145. Gaimu jikan Shigemitsu Rikugun jikan Kaigun jikan kaku tsū [Vice Minister Shigemitsu to Vice Minister of the Army and Vice Minister of the Navy], "Senchi guntai ni okeru shōsha oyobi byōsha no jōtai kaizen ni kansuru 1929 nen 7 gatsu 27 nichi no 'Junēvu jōyaku' oyobi 'furyo no taigū ni kansuru 1929 nen 7 gatsu 27 nichi no jōyaku' gohijungata sōsei ni kansuru ken" [Request to ratify the Geneva Convention for the Amelioration of the Condition of the Wounded and Sick in Armies in the Field of July 27, 1929 and the Geneva Convention relative to the treatment of prisoners of war of July 27, 1929], August 8, 1934, in *Bankoku sekijūji kaigi kankei ikken sekijūjijōyaku kaisei narabini furyo hōten hensan ni kansuru Junēvu kaigi* (1929), kankei/jōyaku hijun oyobi kanyū kanekei dai ni kan, bunkatsu 1 [Geneva Meeting on the Red Cross Treaty Revision and the Prisoner of War Code Compilation (1929)/Ratification and Accession to Treaty/Vol. 2/Part 1 of 5, exhibit 6], JACAR reference code B04122508300.

146. "Kaigun jikan hatsu gaimu jikan ate [Vice Minister of the Navy to Vice Minister of Foreign Affairs], "'Furyo no taigu ni kansuru 1929 nen 7 gatsu 27 nichi

no jōyaku' gohijungata seiso ni kansuru ken kaito" [Reply to the request to ratify the Geneva Convention Relative to the Treatment of Prisoners of War of July 27, 1927], Kanbō Kimitsu 1984 gō no 3 [Minister's Secretariat Secret Document No. 1984-3], November 15, 1934, in *Bankoku sekijūji kaigi kankei ikken sekijūjijōyaku kaisei narabini furyo hōten hensan ni kansuru Junēvu kaigi* (1929), kankei / jōyaku hijun oyobi kanyū kankei dai ni kan, bunkatsu 4 [Geneva Meeting on Red Cross Treaty Revision and Prisoner of War Code Compilation (1929) / Ratification and Accession to Treaty / Vol. 2 / Part 4 of 5], exhibit 338–339, JACAR reference code B04122508600.

147. Kaigun jikan hatsu gaimu jikan ate, "Furyo no taigu ni kansuru."

148. Rikugun jikan Hashimoto Toranosuke Gaimujikan Shigemitsu Aoi tono [Vice Minister of War Hashimoto Toranosuke to Vice Minister of Foreign Affairs Shigemitsu Aoi], "Senchi guntai ni okeru shōsha oyobi byōsha no jōtai kaizen ni kansuru 1929 nen 7 gatsu 27 nichi no 'Junēvu jōyaku' oyobi 'furyo no taigū ni kansuru 1929 nen 7 gatsu 27 nichi no jōyaku' gohijungata sōsei ni kansuru ken kaitō" [Reply to the request to ratify the Geneva Convention for the Amelioration of the Condition of the Wounded and Sick in Armies in the Field of July 27, 1929 and the Geneva Convention Relative to the Treatment of Prisoners of War of July 27, 1929], Rikumitsu dai 521 go [Army secret No. 521], September 6, 1934, in *Bankoku sekijūji kaigi kankei ikken sekijūjijōyaku kaisei narabini furyo hōten hensan ni kansuru Junēvu kaigi* (1929), kankei / jōyaku hijun oyobi kanyū kankei dai ni kan, bunkatsu 2 [Geneva Meeting on Red Cross Treaty Revision and Prisoner of War Code Compilation (1929) / Ratification and Accession to Treaty / Vol. 2 / Part 2 of 5], exhibit 127, JACAR reference code B04122508400.

149. Utsumi Aiko, *Nihongun no horyo seisaku* (Tokyo: Aoki Shoten, 2005), 130–132. The Soviet Union also did not ratify the 1929 Convention.

150. Nihon Sekijūjisha, *Daijugokai sekijūji kokusai kaigi shi* (Tokyo: Nihon Sekijūjisha, Shōwa 11 [1936]), 1–26, 96–103, 106, 161–164, 187–193, 238–257; Moorehead, *Dunant's Dream,* 292–294.

151. "Draft International Convention on the Condition of Civilians of Enemy Nationality"; Moorehead, *Dunant's Dream,* 294–295.

152. Minister of Foreign Affairs Hirota to Minister Counselor Hotta, Telegram, December 18, 1934, Dai 40 gō, in *Bankoku sekijūji kaigi kankei ikken / sekijūji jōyaku kaisei narabini furyo hōten hensan ni kansuru Junēvu kaigi* (1929) kankei / jōyaku hijun oyobi kanyū kanekei dai ni kan, bunkatsu 5, JACAR reference code B04122508700.

153. Vice Minister of the Navy to Vice Minister of Foreign Affairs, November 15, 1934, "Furyo no taigū ni kansuru 1929 nen 7 gatsu 27 nichi no jōyaku" gohijun-gata sōsei ni kansuru ken Kaitō, in *Bankoku sekijūji kaigi kankei ikken / sekijūji jōyaku kaisei narabini furyo hōten hensan ni kansuru juneevu kaigi* (1929) kankei / jōyaku hijun oyobi kanyū kanekei dai ni kan, bunkatsu 4 (1–2), JACAR reference code B04122508600; Utsumi, *Nihongun no horyo seisaku,* 130–131; Ulrich Straus, *The Anguish of Surrender: Japanese POWs of World War II* (Seattle: University of Washington Press, 2003), 21.

154. Bernard Kelly, *Military Internees, Prisoners of War, and the Irish State during the Second World War* (London: Palgrave Macmillan, 2015).

155. Boyd van Dijk, "'The Great Humanitarian': The Soviet Union, the International Committee of the Red Cross, and the Geneva Conventions of 1949," *Law and History Review* 37, no. 1 (2019): 214.

156. Sandra Wilson, *The Manchurian Crisis and Japanese Society, 1931–33* (New York: Routledge, 2002), 99.

157. Harukata Takenaka, *Failed Democratization in Prewar Japan: Breakdown of a Hybrid Regime* (Stanford, CA: Stanford University Press, 2014), 60–61.

158. Sheldon Garon, *The Molding of Japanese Minds: The State in Everyday Life* (Princeton, NJ: Princeton University Press), 141–142; Wilson, *The Manchurian Crisis,* 100.

159. Tsuchida Akio, "Declaring War as an Issue in Chinese Wartime Diplomacy," in *Negotiating China's Destiny in World War II,* ed. Hans van de Ven, Diana Lary, and Stephen MacKinnon (Stanford, CA: Stanford University Press, 2014), 126. According to Herbert Bix, the emperor supported the 1937 decision to neither apply nor act in accordance with the Geneva Conventions on Land Warfare. Herbert Bix, *Hirohito and the Making of Modern Japan* (New York: Harper-Collins, 2000), 359–360. By the end of the war there were fifty-six Chinese POWs, though of course many others had been kept captive (ibid., 360).

160. Mitter, *Forgotten Ally,* 67, 86. Beginning in 1940, Wang served as head of state for the Japanese puppet government in Chonqing.

161. Tsuchida, "Declaring War," 125–126.

162. Utsumi, *Nihongun no horyo seisaku* (Tokyo: Aoki Shoten, 2005), 126–128; JIMTE 1948, 1014–1015.

163. Huber to de Haller, August 8, 1942, International Committee for the Red Cross Archives, Geneva, G.8 / 76 II, delegation to Japan, September–December 1942, DSC03751.

164. André Durand, *From Sarajevo to Hiroshima: History of the International Committee of the Red Cross* (Geneva: Henry Dunant Institute, 1984), 377–383.

165. As quoted in Frank Dikötter, *Crime, Punishment and the Prison in Modern China* (New York: Columbia University Press, 2002), 347. See also Rana Mitter and Aaron William Moore, "China in WWII, 1937–1945: Experience, Memory, and Legacy," *Modern Asian Studies* 45, no. 2 (2011): 225–240; Matthew Johnson, "Propaganda and Sovereignty in Wartime China: Morale Operations and Psychological Warfare under OWI," *Modern Asian Studies* 45, no. 2 (2011): 317, 326.

166. Dikötter, *Crime, Punishment and the Prison in Modern China*, 346–347.

167. *Sources of Japanese Tradition*, ed. Wm. Theodore de Bary, Carol Gluck, and Arthur L. Tiedemann, 2nd ed., vol. 2 (New York: Columbia University Press, 2005), 968–969, 975.

168. Bary, Gluck, and Tiedemann, *Sources of Japanese Tradition*, 2:968–969, 975.

169. My discussion of bushidō is indebted to Benesch, *Inventing the Way of the Samurai*, 201.

170. Benesch, *Inventing the Way of the Samurai*, 207.

171. Benesch, *Inventing the Way of the Samurai*, 204–208.

172. John Dower, *War without Mercy* (New York: Pantheon Books, 1986), 64–71.

173. Benesch, *Inventing the Way of the Samurai*, 208.

174. Even more IJA men died due to the established policy that they were never supposed to surrender or be taken alive. Alvin D. Coox, *Nomonhan: Japan against Russia, 1939* (Stanford, CA: Stanford University Press, 1985), 1083.

175. Coox, *Nomonhan*, 929.

176. Coox, *Nomonhan*, 930–931.

177. Coox, *Nomonhan*, 951.

178. Coox, *Nomonhan*, 949.

179. Yamada, "Oyama no iru fūkei," 301.

180. Takenaka, *Failed Democratization in Prewar Japan*, 76.

181. Janis Mimura, *Planning for Empire: Reform Bureaucrats and the Japanese Wartime State* (Ithaca, NY: Cornell University Press, 2011), 7–8, 33–34.

## 2. Singapore

1. Paul Kratoska, *The Japanese Occupation of Malaya: A Social and Economic History* (Honolulu: University of Hawai'i Press, 1997), 21.

2. Kratoska, *The Japanese Occupation of Malaya*, 19. This is Kratoska's point, 19.

3. Kratoska, *The Japanese Occupation of Malaya*, 14. Eaton has argued that this group "supported the colonial system, not because they were overawed by white racial superiority, but because they accrued economic and social benefits from it." Clay Eaton, "Communal Welfare Associations and the Agricultural Settlements of Wartime Singapore," 45, http://www.tufs.ac.jp/ofias/caas/Clay %20EATON.pdf.

4. "Malaya Malady," 2 Loyals—Kingsley & Strange Collection, 1939–1945, Box 8, 1942–1945, Fulwood Barracks Archive (hereafter FB).

5. Kratoska, *The Japanese Occupation of Malaya*, 20.

6. On the expansion of the Japanese community in Malaya, see Yuen Choy Leng, "The Japanese Community in Malaya before the Pacific War: Its Genesis and Growth," *Journal of Southeast Asian Studies* 9, no. 2 (1978): 163–179. On intelligence, see Kratoska, *The Japanese Occupation of Malaya*, 28.

7. Kratoska, *The Japanese Occupation of Malaya*, 29–32. Kratoska: "the late 1930s."

8. Edward J. Drea, *Japan's Imperial Army: Its Rise and Fall, 1853–1945* (Lawrence: University Press of Kansas, 2009), 211.

9. Kratoska, *The Japanese Occupation of Malaya*, 36.

10. Kratoska, *The Japanese Occupation of Malaya*, 34.

11. "The Army That Was Betrayed," 2 Loyals—Kingsley & Strange Collection, 1939–1945, Box 8, FB.

12. "The Army That Was Betrayed."

13. Stanley Bryant-Smith, POWs, Accession Number 002613, National Archives of Singapore, 2.

14. Tomoyuki Yamashita, "Declaration of the Commander of the Nippon Army," *Shōnan Times*, February 20, 1942, 2, http://eresources.nlb.gov.sg/newspapers /Digitised/Article/syonantimes19420220-1.2.14.

15. "Tokyo Time All Over Malaya," *Syonan Shimbun*, March 3, 1942; "Malaya Officially Named Malai," *Syonan Shimbun*, December 10, 1942, 1.

16. "Lingua Franca of Malaya," *Syonan Shimbun*, February 28, 1942, 4.

17. Kratoska, *The Japanese Occupation of Malaya*, 57, 65.

18. Tomoyuki Yamashita, "Declaration of the Commander of the Nippon Army," 2.

19. Shingapōru Shiseikai, *Shōnan tokubetsushi shi* (Tokyo: Nihon Shingapōru Kyōkai, 1987), 20–21. This is a book written by former members of the municipal administration.

20. Shingapōru Shiseikai, *Shōnan tokubetsushi shi*, 20–21.

21. Hayashi Hirofumi, "The Battle of Singapore, the Massacre of Chinese, and Understanding of the Issue in Postwar Japan," *Asia-Pacific Journal* 7, iss. 28, no. 4 (2009): 6–7; Yōji Akashi, "Colonel Watanabe Wataru: The Architect of the Malayan Military Administration, December 1941–March 1943," in *New Perspectives on the Japanese Occupation in Malaya and Singapore, 1941–1945*, ed. Yōji Akashi and Mako Yoshimura (Singapore: NUS Press, 2008), 33–64.

22. Kratoska, *The Japanese Occupation of Malaya*, 95–99. Hayashi bases the 5,000 figure on Kawamura's diary. He notes that the larger figure is common in Singapore but that he has found no archival record supporting it. Hayashi, "The Battle of Singapore," 2.

23. Hayashi, "The Battle of Singapore," 6.

24. United Kingdom, Military jurisdiction, United Kingdom v. Takuma Nishimura et al., National Archives Kew, London, WO 00235 No. 01004, JAG No. 65189, http://www.legal-tools.org/doc/444a5a/pdf/; "Nishimura et al.—Schedule," May 20, 1947, https://www.legal-tools.org/en/doc/14a581/.

25. United Kingdom, Military jurisdiction, United Kingdom v. Takuma Nishimura et al.

26. "Trial against Nishimura Takuma et al.," Trial Report, Military Court for the Trial of War Criminals, http://www.legal-tools.org/doc/42a375/pdf/.

27. "Defendant Nishimura Takuma et al.," March 10, 1947, WO 235 / 1004, British National Archives, Kew, United Kingdom (hereafter BNA).

28. "Trial against Nishimura Takuma et al."

29. "Trial against Nishimura Takuma et al."

30. Felicia Yap, "Prisoners of War and Civilian Internees of the Japanese in British Asia: The Similarities and Contrasts of Experience," *Journal of Contemporary History* 47, no. 317 (2012): 318–319.

31. Lionel Wigmore, *The Japanese Thrust* (Canberra: Australian War Memorial, 1957), 519.

32. Utsumi Aiko, *Nihongun no horyo seisaku* (Tokyo: Aoki Shoten, 2005), 204–207.

33. C. Gorgé, February 6, 1943, 299E 2001 (D) 3 / 402, Swiss Federal Archives (SFA), Bern, Switzerland.

34. Sheila Bruhn-Allen, Accession Number 002740, interview by Zarina bte Yusof, Reel 2, 1–5, National Archives of Singapore.

35. R. P. W. Havers, *Reassessing the Japanese Prisoner of War Experience: The Changi POW Camp, Singapore, 1942–5* (London: RoutledgeCurzon, 2003), 32.

36. Van Waterford, *Prisoners of the Japanese in World War II: Statistical History, Personal Narratives, and Memorials concerning POWs in Camps and on Hellships, Civilian Internees, Asian Slave Laborers, and Others Captured in the Pacific Theater* (Jefferson, NC: McFarland, 1994), 266; Akashi and Yoshimura, *New Perspectives on the Japanese Occupation in Malaya and Singapore*, 186.

37. Captain Mohammed Ahmadi, "Liberated POW Interrogation Questionnaire," WO 344 / 36 / 1, BNA.

38. Mohan Singh, "Liberated POW Interrogation Questionnaire," WO 344 / 36 / 1, BNA.

39. Lieutenant Kenneth Addy, "Liberated POW Interrogation Questionnaire," WO 344 / 36 / 1, BNA.

40. Unlike other camps, the internee camp at Changi has been well documented. There are several reasons: there were many upper-class women who wanted to record the experience. They also made quilts. In Singapore and in the empire, historians have conducted many oral histories of these women, and it is an experience that even today is reported again and again in podcasts such as "Reply All."

41. R. L. G., "Deterior," *Changi Chimes,* March 22, 1942, no. 1, Changi Civilian Internment Camp Newspapers (RCMS 103 / 12 / 29), Cambridge Digital Archives, http://cudl.lib.cam.ac.uk/view/MS-RCMS-00103-00012-00029/428.

42. Havers, *Reassessing the Japanese Prisoner of War Experience,* 41.

43. James Clavell, *King Rat* (Boston: Little, Brown, 1962). Blackburn and Hack describe the situation in Changi as described by Clavell as a captive's dilemma: to cooperate or collaborate under uncertain moral conditions. Kevin Blackburn and Karl Hack, *Forgotten Captives in Japanese-Occupied Asia* (London: Routledge, 2011), 9.

44. John W. Dower, *War without Mercy: Race and Power in the Pacific War* (New York: Pantheon Books, 1986), 9, 41.

45. As quoted in Havers, *Reassessing the Japanese Prisoner of War Experience*, 26.

46. G. J. Douds, "The Men Who Never Were: Indian POWs in the Second World War," *South Asia: Journal of South Asian Studies* 27, no. 2 (2004): 184–185.

47. John Baptist Crasta and Richard Crasta, *Eaten by the Japanese: The Memoir of an Unknown Indian Prisoner of War* (Bangalore: Invisible Man, 1999), 21.

48. Matsuoka quoted in Jeremy A. Yellen, *The Greater East Asia Co-Prosperity Sphere: When Total Empire Met Total War* (Ithaca, NY: Cornell University Press, 2019), 4; Velauthar Ambiavagar, Communities of Singapore (pt. 2), Accession Number 000355, interview by Pitt Kuan Wah, Reel 7, 64, National Archives of Singapore.

49. "The Story of an Indian POW (Non-INA) Who Manned Guns for the Japanese," Report no. 16, File 379, pt. 3, INA Papers, Private Archives, National Archives of India (hereafter NAI).

50. "The Story of an Indian POW," Report no. 16, File 379, pt. 3.

51. "The Story of an Indian POW," Report no. 16, File 379, pt. 3.

52. One out of three subedar-majors, Falak Shar, volunteered. "The Story of an Indian POW," Report no. 16, File 379, pt. 3, 5.

53. Douds, "The Men Who Never Were," 199–200.

54. Wigmore, *The Japanese Thrust*, 513–514.

55. Wigmore, *The Japanese Thrust*, 524.

56. Douds, "The Men Who Never Were," 200.

57. No. 2 Interrogation Report, 13, August 30 1946, File 215, INA Papers, Private Archives, NAI.

58. Wild and Schweitzer, to ICRC, August 31, 1945, G8/76/xi, September to December 1945, International Committee of the Red Cross Archives (hereafter ICRC).

59. Shōnan Tokubetsushi Shi, *Shōnan tokubetsushi shi*, 22–24.

60. Wigmore, *The Japanese Thrust*, 520.

61. Wigmore, *The Japanese Thrust*, 522.

62. Wigmore, *The Japanese Thrust*, 515.

63. As quoted in Wigmore, *The Japanese Thrust*, 513.

64. For example, see Private Papers of A. V. Toze at the IWM, the Record of Alex R. C. Johnstone at the IWM, and the papers of Donald T. Giles at the Library of Congress.

65. Wigmore, *The Japanese Thrust,* 516.

66. Mary Dorothy Cornelius, *Changi* (Ilfracombe, UK: Arthur H. Stockwell, [1945?]), 71.

67. "Poster for Musical Show" by David Foster at Changi POW Camp, June 27, 1942, 2 Loyals, Kingsley & Strange Collection, 1939–1945, Box 8, FB.

68. Wigmore, *The Japanese Thrust,* 529.

69. Wigmore, *The Japanese Thrust,* 518; Clavell, *King Rat.*

70. "Liberated POW Interrogation Questionnaire," WO 344 / 36 / 1, BNA.

71. Capt. George Edward Guy Round, "The Road from Singapore," MSS 1370, Australian War Memorial (hereafter AWM).

72. As quoted in Havers, *Reassessing the Japanese Prisoner of War Experience,* 43.

73. Cornelius, *Changi,* 51, 58–59, 69.

74. "Tōjō rikugun daijin Zentsūji shidan shisatsu no sai dō shidanchō ni ataeraretaru kunjichū furyo ni kansuru jikō no bassui" [Excerpt from the part concerning the treatment of prisoners-of-war in War Ministry Tōjō 's instructions delivered to the commander of the Zentsuji Division on his visit of inspection], May 30, 1942, IMFTE Exhibit 1960, document 1547-A, https://www.legal-tools.org/doc/27ef18/pdf/.

75. Utsumi, *Nihongun no horyo seisaku,* 190–194.

76. In 1941, Tokyo agreed to follow the 1929 Geneva Conventions (which they had signed, not ratified) mutatis mutandis. Even so, earlier conventions, which they had ratified, prohibited forced labor. For more on the Geneva Conventions, see Chapter 6.

77. At these meetings, bureaucrats discussed a wide range of issues in detail. Minister Tōjō made the decisions and approved the regulations regarding treatment of POWs.

78. "Shinnin furyo shū yō shochō ni atau rikugun daijin kunji" [Instructions of War Minister Hideki Tōjō to the newly appointed commanders of the prisoner of war camps], June 25, 1942, Exhibit 1962, 1630-A, https://www.legal-tools.org/doc/eb36e4/pdf/.

79. For more on transportation on "hell ships," see Chapter 3. Note that captives became official POWs only upon arrival in POW camps.

80. "Summary of the Disposal of Prisoners of War," Doc 10591, Declassification Review Project 775011, Japanese Laws, Rules and Regulations to POWs, 37–62, SCAP Legal Section, Administrative Division, Miscellaneous Japanese File, 1942–1948, POW Camp Records, Records of Allied Operational and Occupation Headquarters, Record Group 331, US National Archives and Records Administration (hereafter NARA).

81. Statistics differ. According to Kinvig, it was 62,000 Allied POWs and 270,000 Asians. Clifford Kinvig, "Allied POWs and the Burma-Thailand Railway," in *Japanese Prisoners of War,* ed. Philip Towle, Margaret Kosuge, and Yoichi Kibata (London: Hambledon, 2000), 39–40.

82. "United States of America vs. Hiroshi Tamura," vol. 1 of 8 vols., exhibit 237, National Diet Library (NDL), Tokyo.

83. "Trial against Fukuei Shimpei Trial Reports," http://www.legal-tools.org/doc/bd5b8b/pdf/.

84. "Trial against Fukuei Shimpei Trial Reports."

85. "Liberated POW Interrogation Questionnaire," WO 344 / 36 / 1, BNA; Wigmore, *The Japanese Thrust,* 523.

86. Foreign Ministry official Dr. Kusama, POW Information Bureau official 1st Lt. Yotsumoto, and Prince Shimazu and Asst. Azumi of the Japan Red Cross helped at the port.

87. Paravicini to ICRC, August 30, 1942, G 8 / 76, Délégation au Japon, DSC03554-55-56, ICRC.

88. Wigmore, *The Japanese Thrust,* 515.

89. Havers, *Reassessing the Japanese Prisoner of War Experience,* 47.

90. Tachikawa Kyoichi, "Kyūgun ni okeru horyo no toritsukai: Taiheiyōsensō no jōkyō o chūshin ni," *Bōeikenkyūsho Kiyō* 10, no. 1 (2007): 108–109.

91. "Medical Appreciation concerning Aust. R.P.'s Now Concentration in Singapore," AWM 54, Control Symbol 555 / 2 / 2, Item Barcode 467227, AWM.

92. In April 1945 they were issued US Red Cross medicine. Prisoners were vaccinated for typhoid and dysentery. From Wild and Schweitzer (in Shonan), to ICRC in Japan, August 31, 1945, G8 / 76 / xi, September to December 1945, ICRC.

93. "Summary of the Disposal of Prisoners of War," Doc. 10591, Declassification Review Project 775011, Japanese Laws, Rules and Regulations to POWs, 37–62, SCAP Legal Section, Administrative Division, Miscellaneous Japanese File, 1942–1948, POW Camp Records, Records of Allied Operational and Occupation Headquarters, Record Group 331, NARA.

94. "Kōkyu jimukan kōkyu buin setsumei jikō," in *Furyo ni kansuru shorui tsuzuri* (September 1945), unpaginated, Bōeishō Bōei Kenkyūsho Senshi Kenkyū Sentā.

95. "Kōkyu jimukan kōkyu buin setsumei jikō."

96. "Kōkyu jimukan kōkyu buin setsumei jikō."

97. Drea, *Japan's Imperial Army*, 234.

98. Commission on Verification and Support for the Victims of Forced Mobilization under Japanese Colonialism in Korea, "unpublished report," vol. 2, 1st draft, Seoul, Korea, July 27, 20112011.

99. Wigmore, *The Japanese Thrust*, 524.

100. "The Story of an Indian POW," Report no. 16, File 379, pt. 8, 1–250, INA Papers, Private Archives, NAI.

101. Wigmore, *The Japanese Thrust*, 527–528.

102. "Official Statement of Interrogation," Doc. no. 25272-A, 2.05.116, 522, Dutch National Archives (DNA), The Hague, Netherlands.

103. As found in Havers, *Reassessing the Japanese Prisoner of War Experience*, 11.

104. "The Story of an Indian POW," Report no. 16 yes, File 379, pt. 8, 1–250.

105. Mehervan Singh, Communities of Singapore (pt. 2), Accession Number 000553, 67 reels, interview by Pitt Kuan Wah, 4, Oral History Centre, Singapore.

106. J. S. Singh, Joginder Japanese Occupation of Singapore, Accession Number 000365, 11 reels, 105, interview by Low Lay Leng, Oral History Centre, Singapore.

107. J. S. Singh interview, 6–10.

108. Velauthar Ambiavagar interview, 64.

109. Velauthar Ambiavagar interview, 64.

110. Douds, "The Men Who Never Were," 201.

111. *Greater East Asia Joint Declaration* (Osaka: Mainichi Shimbunsha, 1943). For more, see Yellen, *The Greater East Asia Co-Prosperity Sphere*.

112. *Greater East Asia Joint Declaration.*

113. No. 2 Interrogation Report 13, August 30, 1946, File 215, INA Papers, Private Archives, NAI.

114. No. 2 Interrogation Report 13, August 30, 1946.

115. When, in September 1943, Italian subs capitulated in Singapore harbor, the captives initially were treated in a superior manner but later were interned in Changi, where they received no special treatment. J. Oosterhuis, Diary, Collection 401, N. 313.1, NIOD (Instituut voor Oorlogs-, Holocaust- en Genocidestudies) (hereafter NIOD).

116. "Record of Number of Cases of Protests concerning POWs and the Steps Taken by the POW Information Bureau and the POW Administration Bureau," G8 / 76 xiii, April–June 1946, ICRC.

117. In 1945 it collapsed and petitions were no longer accepted. Tachikawa Kyoichi, "The Treatment of Prisoners of War by the Imperial Japanese Army and Navy Focusing on the Pacific War," *NIDS Security Reports,* no. 9 (2008): 57; Furyo Jōhōkyoku and Chaen Yoshi, eds., *Furyo toriatsukai no kiroku* (Tokyo: Fuji Shuppan, 1992), 45–46.

118. Wigmore, *The Japanese Thrust,* 528.

119. Wigmore, *The Japanese Thrust,* 528–531.

120. Official Netherlands and Netherlands Indies News Agency, "Untitled Report," September 13, 1945, 18 / A 1–11, 18 / 2, 846, Ministerie van Defensie, Nederlands Instituut voor Militaire Historie (NIMH).

121. Wild and Schweizer to ICRC, August 29, 1945, G8 / 76 / xi, September–December 1945, ICRC.

122. Wigmore, *The Japanese Thrust,* 532.

123. Tachikawa Kyoichi, "The Treatment of Prisoners of War," 67.

124. Wild and Schweizer to ICRC, August 30, 1945, G8 / 76 / xi, September–December 1945, ICRC.

125. Wild and Schweizer to ICRC, September 1, 1945, G8 / 76 / xi, September–December 1945, ICRC.

126. Wild and Schweizer to ICRC, August 31, 1945, G8 / 76 / xi, September–December 1945, ICRC.

127. Wild and Schweizer to ICRC, August 31, 1945.

128. "Records of the Office of the Provost Marshal General, Record Group 389, NARA.

129. "Changi PQ Camp, Singapore," Records of the Office of the Provost Marshal General, Record Group 389, NARA.

130. No. 2 Interrogation Report 13, August 30, 1946.

## 3. The Philippines

1. Ikehata Setsuo, "The Japanese Occupation Period in Philippine History," in *The Philippines under Japan: Occupation Policy and Reaction,* ed. Ikehata Setsuo and Ricardo Trota Jose (Honolulu: University of Hawai'i Press, 2009), 13.

2. Ikehata, "The Japanese Occupation Period in Philippine History," 5.

3. Lydia N. Yu-Jose, "World War II and the Japanese in the Prewar Philippines," *Journal of Southeast Asian Studies* 27, no. 1 (1996): 69–73.

4. Hayase Shinzo, "The Japanese Residents of 'Dabao-kuo,'" in Ikehata and Jose, *The Philippines under Japan,* 251–253.

5. Yu-Jose, "World War II and the Japanese in the Prewar Philippines," 71.

6. Hayase, "The Japanese Residents of 'Dabao-kuo,'" 253.

7. Yu-Jose, "World War II and the Japanese in the Prewar Philippines," 69. In 1927 there were 11,092 Japanese, in 1935 there were 21,468, and in 1941 there were 20,000 in Davao alone.

8. Yu-Jose, "World War II and the Japanese in the Prewar Philippines," 68–69; Ikehata, "The Japanese Occupation Period in Philippine History," 12; also see Ikehata Setsuo, "Mining Industry Development and Local Anti-Japanese Rule Resistance," in Ikehata and Jose, *The Philippines under Japan.*

9. Sven Matthiesen, *Japanese Pan-Asianism and the Philippines from the Late Nineteenth Century to the End of World War II: Going to the Philippines Is Like Coming Home?* (Leiden: Brill, 2015), 45–62. Japanese Pan-Asianists in particular argued that Nan'yō (the South Seas) was critical for solving problems, differing only in their logic.

10. Theorists had two different strategies: respecting the sovereignty of the Philippines and, as Togo Shigenori and the military argued, governing through Manuel L. Quezon. This idea was intended to end hostilities quickly, support the Quezon government, implement a military administration for a short time, and then turn the Philippines into a republic.

11. Yu-Jose, "World War II and the Japanese in the Prewar Philippines," 73–74.

12. Joyce Lebra, *Japanese-Trained Armies in Southeast Asia: Independence and Volunteer Forces in World War II* (New York: Columbia University Press, 1977), 6.

13. Kevin C. Murphy, "'Raw Individualists': American Soldiers on the Bataan Death March Reconsidered," *War & Society* 31, no. 1 (2012): 46.

14. Louis Morton, *The Fall of the Philippines* (Washington, DC: US Army, Center of Military History, 1953), 152–154, https://history.army.mil/books/70-7_06.htm.

15. Morton, *The Fall of the Philippines*, 155–158, quotation at 158.

16. Sayre to Hon. Charles A. Wolverton, *Congressional Record,* House of Representatives, January 26, 1948, 554, https://www.govinfo.gov/content/pkg/GPO-CRECB-1948-pt1/pdf/GPO-CRECB-1948-pt1-15.pdf.

17. Brian Masaru Hayashi, *Democratizing the Enemy* (Princeton, NJ: Princeton University Press, 2010), 81; Swiss Legation to the United States, "Reply by the United States to Japanese Allegations of Massacre of Japanese Residents of Mindanao, Philippines," December 29, 1942, *Foreign Relations of the United States* (hereafter cited as *FRUS,* with year and volume number), 1942, 1:855.

18. E. Carl Engelhart, "Trapped on Corregidor: An Autobiographical Story," unpublished manuscript, E. Carl Engelhart papers, 1950, Engelhart, E. Carl.1 box, US Army Heritage and Education Center, US Army War College (hereafter USAWC).

19. Engelhart, "Trapped on Corregidor," 19–20.

20. Kobayashi Shigeko, "Kaisen zengo ni okeru manira nihonjin gakkō ni miru kyōiku katsudō no henyō," *Nihon Kenkyū* no. 50 (2014): 250–251.

21. Hayase, "The Japanese Residents of 'Dabao-kuo,'" 274.

22. Swiss Legation to the United States, "Reply by the United States to Japanese Allegations of Massacre of Japanese Residents of Mindanao, Philippines," December 29, 1942; and Swiss Legation to the Department of State, January 27, 1942, *FRUS,* 1942, 1:855–856.

23. Morton, *The Fall of the Philippines,* 128.

24. Honma via Yuma Totani, *Justice in Asia and the Pacific Region, 1945–1952: Allied War Crimes Prosecutions* (New York: Cambridge University Press, 2015), 25.

25. Engelhart, "Trapped on Corregidor," 21–22.

26. Engelhart, "Trapped on Corregidor," 22.

27. Engelhart, "Trapped on Corregidor," 23.

28. Engelhart, "Trapped on Corregidor," 25.

29. Edward J. Drea, *Japan's Imperial Army: Its Rise and Fall, 1853–1945* (Lawrence: University Press of Kansas, 2009), 223.

30. Morton, *The Fall of the Philippines,* 236.

31. Kobayashi, "Kaisen zengo ni okeru manira nihonjin gakkō ni miru kyōiku katsudō no henyō," 248.

32. Kobayashi, "Kaisen zengo ni okeru manira nihonjin gakkō ni miru kyōiku katsudō no henyō," 251–252.

33. As quoted in Sven Matthiessen, *Japanese Pan-Asianism and the Philippines from the late 19th Century to the End of World War II: Going to the Philippines Is Like Coming Home?* (Leiden: Brill, 2016), 86.

34. Matthiessen, *Japanese Pan-Asianism and the Philippines,* 12.

35. Matthiessen, *Japanese Pan-Asianism and the Philippines,* 12.

36. Nakano Satoshi, "Appeasement and Coercion," in Ikehata and Jose, *The Philippines under Japan,* 23.

37. See the account by Benigno Aquino of Lt. Kimura in the Honma trial. Aquino stated that Kimura had said, "I saw he tried to deceive me and that he is a bad man. Therefore I ordered that the writ of execution be carried out." "Trial against Masaharu Honma," Public Trial, vol. 26, Doc. 296828, https://www .legal-tools.org/doc/c1f35b/pdf/; Totani, *Justice in Asia,* 29.

38. Totani, *Justice in Asia,* 29.

39. Li Yuk-Wai, "The Chinese Resistance Movement in the Philippines during the Japanese Occupation," *Journal of Southeast Asian Studies* 23, no. 2 (1992): 308–321.

40. Ikehata Setsuho, "Firipin ni okeru Nihon gunsei no ichikōsatsu—Rikarute shōgun no yakuwari o megutte," *Ajia kenkyū* 22, no. 2 (1975): 45–46.

41. Nakano, "Appeasement and Coercion," 27.

42. Nakano, "Appeasement and Coercion," 26–27.

43. Drea, *Japan's Imperial Army,* 223–224.

44. Paul P. Rogers and Arlene Hostetler Rogers, *The Good Years: MacArthur and Sutherland* (Westport, CT: Greenwood Press, 1990), 144.

45. Totani, *Justice in Asia,* 25.

46. Engelhart, "Trapped on Corregidor," 29.

47. Engelhart, "Trapped on Corregidor," 33.

48. Carol M. Petillo, "Douglas MacArthur and Manuel Quezon: A Note on an Imperial Bond," *Pacific Historical Review* 48, no. 1 (1979): 115. See also note 27 above.

49. As quoted in Rogers and Rogers, *The Good Years*, 218.

50. Walter R. Borneman, *MacArthur at War: World War II in the Pacific* (New York: Little, Brown, 2016), 132.

51. Rogers and Rogers, *The Good Years*, 215.

52. As quoted in Rogers and Rogers, *The Good Years*, 214.

53. Engelhart, "Trapped on Corregidor," 45.

54. Estimates vary widely, hovering around 75,000. Murphy, "'Raw Individualists,'" 42. A 1945 report by the provost Marshal found 65,000. This is a number that included US soldiers, sailors, and navy and marines, plus US civil servants and civilians, Filipino scouts, and members of the Philippine Commonwealth Army. The same report claimed that Japanese reports found 9,000 US servicemen and 30,000 Filipinos. Arthur Lerch, *American Prisoners of War in the Philippines,* November 15, 1945, Office of the Provost Marshal General Report, http://www.mansell.com/pow_resources/camplists/philippines/pows_in_pi -OPMG_report.html#Bataan. This document comes from the Roger Mansell collection, some of which is online and the remainder of which can be found at the Hoover Institution and Archives, Stanford University.

55. Totani, *Justice in Asia*, 26.

56. Office of the Provost Marshal General, "Report on American Prisoners of War Interned by the Japanese in the Philippines," November 19, 1945, http://www .mansell.com/pow_resources/camplists/philippines/pows_in_pi-OPMG_re port.html.

57. Jumpai Nobuo, "Weekly Report of Foreign Affairs" [Gaikō Jihō], May 15, 1942, WWII and POW treatment problems [Daitōa sensō to furyo toriatsukai mondai], Gaimushō Gaikō Shiryōkan (hereafter GGS).

58. Totani, *Justice in Asia*, 26.

59. Tachikawa Kyoichi, "Kyūgun ni okeru horyo no toriatsukai—Taiheiyōsensō no jōkyō o chūshin ni," *Bōeikenkyūsho Kiyō* 10, no. 1 (2007): 101–103.

60. As early as 1944, this was identified publicly as an outrageous act by the US, British, Canadian governments and in the British press.

61. Office of the Provost Marshal General, "Report on American Prisoners of War."

62. Dyess's original story first came to light in 1942 via a dispatch from a *New York Times* reporter, Byron Darnton. Dyess later told it to the *Chicago Tribune*. It was published as a book in 1944. See Lt. Col. Wm. E Dyess, *The Dyess Story* (New York: G. M. Putnam's Sons, 1944), 69–70, https://archive.org/details/in .ernet.dli.2015.59993/page/n5. As Murphy points out, its most profound impact may have come from an article in *Time* magazine that gave a precis of Dyess's experiences accompanied by commentary by elected officials, turning it into a "staple narrative." Murphy, "'Raw Individualists,'" 44.

63. Dyess, as quoted in "March of Death after Bataan Surrender," in *Daily Herald*, January 29, 1944, found in Bundesarchiv, E 2001 (D), 1968 / 74 BD:2, 1508–1509.

64. Office of the Provost Marshal General, "Report on American Prisoners of War."

65. As Kevin Murphy points out, the common narrative emphasizing US-Filipino solidarity derives in large part from its source base: POW narratives written years after the conflict. Murphy argues that there were a wide range of Filipino reactions: some were sympathetic, but others "exploited Americans in their time of weakness." Kevin Murphy, "'To Sympathize and Exploit': Filipinos, Americans, and the Bataan Death March," *Journal of American–East Asian Relations* 18, no. 3 / 4 (2011): 297, 307, 316.

66. Office of the Provost Marshal General, "Report on American Prisoners of War."

67. Office of the Provost Marshal General, "Report on American Prisoners of War."

68. Capt. Robert Edward Conn, "Perpetuation of Testimony of Robert Edward Conn, Jr.," http://mansell.com/pow_resources/camplists/fukuoka/fuk_01 _fukuoka/fukuoka_01/USAffA-C.htm#Conn.

69. Defense POW / MIA Accounting Agency, "Historical Report U.S. Casualties and Burials at Cabanatuan POW Camp #1," http://www.dpaa.mil/Portals/85 /Documents/Reports/U.S.Casualties_Burials_Cabanatuan_POWCamp1.pdf ?ver=2017-05-08-162357-013.

70. "Seishiki furyo shūyōsho" are those captured prior to the establishment of formal camps—for example, personnel captured at the time of, and after, the fall of Bataan. POW camps were not established prior to August 1942; therefore, those who died earlier were not reported to the ICRC during the war.

71. Morton, *The Fall of the Philippines*, 524.

72. "Review of the Staff Judge Advocate," United States of America vs. Yoshio Tsune-yoshi, March 24, 1949, http://www.mansell.com/pow_resources/camplists/philip pines/Cabanatuan/IMTFE_Case230_TSUNEYOSHI_Cabanatuan.pdf.

73. Gerald Linderman, *The World within War: America's Combat Experience in WWII* (New York: Free Press, 1997), 178–181.

74. Drea, *Japan's Imperial Army*, 224.

75. Office of the Provost Marshal General, "Report on American POWs Interned by the Japanese in the Philippines."

76. Hull, Memorandum, Record Group 153, SCAP Legal Section, Declassification Review Project NND 735027, War Crimes Branch, Entry 132, Box 6, 184, US National Archives and Records Administration, College Park, MD (hereafter NARA).

77. For another two days, US-Filipino forces remained on Mindanao. Brig. Gen. William F. Sharp—Sixty-First, Eighty-First, and 101st Divisions—surrendered on May 8. Filipinos evaded capture, and the Americans were imprisoned at Del Monte or Malabalay.

78. Hull, Memorandum.

79. Engelhart, "Trapped on Corregidor," 57.

80. Engelhart, "Trapped on Corregidor," 58.

81. Engelhart, "Trapped on Corregidor," 57–61.

82. Engelhart, "Trapped on Corregidor," 66–70.

83. Author interview with Leland Chandler, Albuquerque, NM, 2018.

84. Engelhart, "Trapped on Corregidor," 73.

85. Engelhart, "Trapped on Corregidor," 72. This may reflect his postwar knowledge.

86. Totani, *Justice in Asia*, 27.

87. Conn, "Perpetuation of Testimony."

88. "Defense POW/MIA Accounting Agency, "Historical Report U.S. Casualties." Senior officers were moved to Tarlac, the rest to Cabanatuan or work details. Camp O'Donnell was called "Camp O'Death." The 1,547 Americans who died at Camp O'Donnell remained in the camp cemetery until Allied forces regained control of Luzon, when they were disinterred.

89. Totani, *Justice in Asia*, 28.

90. "Memorandum by the Ambassador in Japan (Grew)," February 4, 1938, *FRUS, 1931–1941*, vol. 1, Document 418, https://history.state.gov/historicaldocuments/frus1931-41v01/d418.

91. The Third Secretary of Embassy in China (Allison) to the Secretary of State, February 2, 1938, *FRUS,* 1938, vol. 4, Document 321, https://history.state.gov /historicaldocuments/frus1938v04/d321.

92. The Consul General at Shanghai (Gauss) to the Secretary of State, January 18, 1940, *FRUS,* 1940, vol. 4, Document 313, https://history.state.gov/historical documents/frus1940v04/d313.

93. Engelhart, "Trapped on Corregidor," 72.

94. Engelhart, "Trapped on Corregidor," 71–72.

95. Engelhart, "Trapped on Corregidor," 71–74.

96. Engelhart, "Trapped on Corregidor," 72.

97. Engelhart, "Trapped on Corregidor," 72.

98. William J. Fossey to Paul Geissler, "Crimes and Atrocities Committed by Japanese on American Prisoners of War," September 25, 1946, http://mansell .com/pow_resources/camplists/fukuoka/fuk_01_fukuoka/fukuoka_01/USA ffD-H.htm#Fossey.

99. Conn, "Perpetuation of Testimony of Robert Edward Conn." According to Conn, men had been executed for leaving the camp to obtain food and for trading for food. However, the six who were executed were not the men who had been trading.

100. Fossey to Geissler, "Crimes and Atrocities Committed by Japanese on American Prisoners of War."

101. Cabanatuan remained open until the Japanese defeat in the Philippines, closing on January 30, 1945.

102. "Summary of the Disposal of Prisoners of War," Doc. 10591, Declassification Review Project 775011, Japanese Laws, Rules and Regulations to POWs, 37–62, SCAP Legal Section, Administrative Division, Miscellaneous Japanese File 1942–1948, POW Camp Records, Records of Allied Operational and Occupation Headquarters, Record Group 331, NARA.

103. POW Information Office, December 1955, The Record of POW Treatment [Furyo toriatsukai no kiroku], 12, Bōeichō Bōeikenkyūsho.

104. Robert W. Phillips, interview by Elaine Blatt et al., Herndon, Virginia, April 13, 2007, Oral history at Rutgers University, New Brunswick, NJ, https://oralhistory .rutgers.edu/images/PDFs/phillips_robert.pdf.

105. POW Information Office, "The Record of POW Treatment."

106. POW Information Office, "POW: Hell Ship Nagato Maru," chap. 13, http://www
.k4ext.com/military/chap13.asp.

107. Russell Brines, ed., *Santo Tomas Internment Camp Gazette,* Internews, May 5,
1942, Library of Congress.

108. Paravicini, "Telegram," November 15, 1943, G.8 / 76 / v, November 1943 to January 1944, g8 / pa, ICRC.

109. Totani, *Justice in Asia,* 31.

110. "Telegram," January 10, 1944, G.8 / 76 / v, November 1943 to January 1944,
g8 / pa, ICRC.

111. Yu-Jose, "World War II and the Japanese in the Prewar Philippines," 79.

112. Hayase, "The Japanese Residents of 'Dabao-Kuo," 256–259.

113. Hayase, "The Japanese Residents of 'Dabao-Kuo," 262–267. Of 5,027 conscripted from Davao, only 374 survived the war.

114. Ricardo T. Jose, "The Association for Service to the New Philippines (KALIBAPI)
during the Japanese Occupation: Attempting to Transplant a Japanese Wartime
Concept to the Philippines," *Journal of Sophia Asian Studies* 19 (2001): 153–154.

115. Jose, "The Association for Service," 156–160. It was also required to work to
establish the "bagong Pilipinas" (new Philippines) as a unit of the Greater East
Asia Co-Prosperity Sphere. It is hard to know membership numbers, but in
1943 they claimed to have 23,000 to 25,000 members.

116. Jose, "The Association for Service," 169–170; Matthiessen, *Japanese Pan-
Asianism and the Philippines,* 150–154.

117. Jose, "The Association of Service," 174–175.

118. Ken'ichi Goto, *Tensions of Empire: Japan and Southeast Asia in the Colonial
and Postcolonial World* (Athens: Ohio University Press, 2003), 66.

119. Goto, *Tensions of Empire,* 66–67.

120. Ikehata, "The Japanese Occupation Period in Philippine History," 6.

121. Nakano, "Appeasement and Coercion," 43.

122. Nakano, "Appeasement and Coercion," 23.

123. Leocadio de Asis, *From Bataan to Tokyo: Diary of a Filipino Student in Wartime Japan, 1943-1944* (Lawrence: University of Kansas Center for East Asian
Studies, 1979), 55.

124. Totani, *Justice in Asia*, 31–32.

125. Totani, *Justice in Asia*, 32.

126. Lebra, *Japanese-Trained Armies*, 141.

127. Lebra, *Japanese-Trained Armies*, 141.

128. Ricardo Jose, "Food Production and Food Distribution Programmes in the Philippines during Japanese Occupation," in *Food Supplies and the Japanese Occupation in South-East Asia*, ed. Paul H. Kratoska (London: Macmillan, 1998), 67–72.

129. Hayase, "Japanese Residents of 'Dabao-Kuo,'" 277.

130. After the war, residents knew them and named them in war crimes. Hayase, "Japanese Residents of 'Dabao-Kuo,'" 277.

131. Department Telegram, May 15, 1945, A.I. No. 11488 / No. 1789, NND 765006, 711.6–814.2, Records of Foreign Service Posts of the Department of State, Record Group 84, NARA.

132. From Secretary of State, to Bern, May 12, 1945, "Telegram," SCAP Legal Section, War Crimes Branch, Declassification Review Project NND 735027, Records of the Office of the Judge Advocate General (Army), Record Group 153, NARA.

133. According to Japan, the number of Allied citizens in the Philippines at the beginning of 1944 was 11,200 POWs and 11,740 others. N.A., beginning of 1944, Honpō oyobi Daitōa ken'nai ni okeru tekikokujin sū [The number of people from the Allies in Greater East Asian region], Diplomatic Archives [Daitōa-sensō kankei ichi-ken 11], 23, GGS.

134. Gladwin A. Lee, "Did Sigint Seal the Fates of 19,000 POWs?," *Cryptologia* 30, no. 3 (2006): 202–203.

135. So were the British. See "Telegram 646, Bombing of Hospital Ships," WO 208 / 1506, Governor (Sir S. Thomas) to Secretary of State for the Colonies, BNA.

136. Gregory Michno, *Death on the Hellships: Prisoners at Sea in the Pacific War* (Annapolis, MD: Naval Institute Press, 2016), 179–182, 315.

137. Michno, *Death on the Hellships*, 188–190.

138. Eleanor D. Gauker and Christopher G. Blood, "Friendly Fire Incidents during World War II Naval Operations," *Naval War College Review* 48, no. 1 (1995): 115–122.

139. It is difficult to tell which US submarine sunk which ship—Japanese and American sources disagree, and it was often a melee.

140. Yamashita testified that "guerrilla actions increased more and more, and it became so that they interfered with military operations at quite a few places." Totani, *Justice in Asia,* 32.

141. "Report of Interview with Lt. Col. Karl H. Houghton, MC," ASN 20411, interview by Lt. Larson on March 6, 1946.

142. Dwight E. Gard, "Notebook," and Col. John R. Vance, marginalia and explanatory notes, Dwight E. Gard papers, 1941–1945, USAWC.

143. "Report of Interview with Lt. Col. Karl H. Houghton," March 6, 1946, http:// mansell.com/pow_resources/camplists/fukuoka/fuk_01_fukuoka/fukuoka_01 /USAffD-H.htm#Houghton.

144. Dwight E. Gard, "Notebook," USAWC.

145. Lee A. Gladwin, "American POWs on Japanese Ships Take a Voyage into Hell," *Prologue* 35, no. 4 (2003): unpaginated, https://www.archives.gov/publications /prologue/2003/winter/hell-ships-1.html.

146. Engelhart, "Trapped on Corregidor," 208.

147. Dwight E. Gard Papers, notebook.

148. Fossey to Geissler, "Crimes and Atrocities Committed by Japanese on American Prisoners of War."

149. Gladwin, "American POWs on Japanese Ships Take a Voyage into Hell."

150. Engelhart, "Trapped on Corregidor," 214.

151. Engelhart, "Trapped on Corregidor," 223–224.

152. "Report of Interview with Lt. Col. Karl H. Houghton," March 6, 1946.

153. Scholars disagree about exact figures, and archival records kept by the Japanese are incomplete. Because the ships carrying POWs were unmarked, it is especially difficult for scholars to agree on numbers. Sources include Komamiya Shinshichirō, *Senji yusō sendanshi* (Tokyo: Shuppan Kyōdōsha, 1987), but he does not list which ships carried POWs. Other sources that can be used to reconstruct the numbers include ICRC lists, reports of air crews, escaped prisoners, captured documents, and Japanese POWs. During the war, intelligence units used intercepted and decrypted materials, as well as decoded radio broadcasts. The US National Archives has information for only five ships, perhaps because the cards they had of POWs who died were on those ships: the

*Shinyo, Arisan, Ōryoku, Enoura,* and *Brazil.* Gladwin, "American POWs on Japanese Ships Take a Voyage into Hell."

154. How large a proportion died from friendly fire is impossible to determine with any precision, especially because estimates for the total number transported vary. According to the records of the Prisoner of War Information Agency, 14,790 men were shipped, and of those, 2,835 to 2,873 died. This includes the 1944 voyage of the *Ōryoku Maru,* which resulted in 308 deaths. Chaen Yoshio, ed., *Furyo Jōhōkyoku Furyo toriatsukai no kiroku: Tsuketari, Kaigun Heigakkō "kokusaihō"* (Tokyo: Fuji Shuppan, 1992), 43–50. Michno calculates the number of passages rather than the number of people transported, and some POWs made multiple voyages. He arrives at the figure of 126,064 passages to and from Guam, Singapore, Indonesia, and the Philippines, among other places. He estimates that 21,039 POWs died, 19,000 from friendly fire. Leaving them out of the total figure for POWs who died at Japanese hands would make the mortality rate comparable to that of Allied POWs in German custody. Michno, *Death on the Hellships,* 282–283, 317. Looking just at the Philippines, the American Defenders of Bataan and Corregidor Memorial Society, an organization of family members of former POWs, estimates that 3,600 American POWs lost their lives aboard hell ships and some 700 others lost their lives soon after. http://www.dg-adbc.org/content /history.

155. Hayashi Hiroshi, "Nihongun no meirei denpō ni miru Manira-sen, Kantō Gakuin Daigaku keizaigakubu sōgō gakujutsu ronsō," *Shizen Ningen Shakai* 48 (2010): 83.

156. Hayashi, "Nihongun no meirei denpō ni miru Manira-sen," 83.

157. Hayashi, "Nihongun no meirei denpō ni miru Manira-sen," 76.

158. Hayashi, "Nihongun no meirei denpō ni miru Manira-sen," 77.

159. Dodis, E 1004.1 1 / 456 Federal Council, Département politique, Proposition du 27 avril 1945, "Entraves à l'activité de la légation de Suisse au Japon: Traitement des Suisses établis au Japon et dans les territoires occupés par ce pays; Atteinte à la personne, à la liberté et à la propriété des Suisses aux Philippines," http:// dodis.ch/48037.

160. Ikehata, "The Japanese Occupation Period in Philippine History," 9.

161. As quoted in Hayashi, "Nihongun no meirei denpō ni miru Manira-sen," 87.

162. Hayashi, "Nihongun no meirei denpō ni miru Manira-sen," 92.

163. Ikehata, "The Japanese Occupation Period in Philippine History," 1–18.

164. Ikehata, "The Japanese Occupation Period in Philippine History," 1.

165. Ikehata, "The Japanese Occupation Period in Philippine History," 1–18.

## 4. A War of Words

1. Hull to American Legation, December 18, 1941, SCAP Legal Section, War Crimes Branch, Declassification Review Project NND 735027, Records of the Office of the Judge Advocate General (Army), Record Group 153, US National Archives and Records Administration (hereafter NARA).

2. Civilians were also included. See Hull to Department of State, "Establishment of Prisoner of War Services," January 13, 1942, US Legation, Bern, American Interest Section, Supplemental General Records, 1942–1945, Foreign Service Posts of the Department of State, Switzerland, Record Group 84, NARA; and Secretary of State to Huddle, January 13, 1942, *Foreign Relations of the United States,* 1942 (hereafter cited as *FRUS,* with year and volume number) (Washington, DC: Government Printing Office, 1960), 1:793–794.

3. In his excellent 1987 account of the State Department's Special Section for internee exchanges, P. Scott Corbett showed how some of these connections worked. P. Scott Corbett, *Quiet Passages: The Exchange of Civilians between the United States and Japan during the Second World War* (Kent, OH: Kent State University Press, 1987), 42. At the beginning of the war, the Special Section had planned for several internee exchanges of officials and non-officials. The first had returned some 268 State Department employees. Though thousands were repatriated in the first two exchanges, there were only two of them, far fewer than anyone had expected. Corbett, *Quiet Passages,* 96, 114–116.

4. Huddle to Secretary of State, February 4, 1942, *FRUS,* 1942, 1:796. The term was widely used in both the United States and Japan, and is usually translated as "with the necessary changes," and in Japanese as "junyō."

5. Utsumi Aiko, *Nihongun no horyo seisaku* (Tokyo: Aoki Shoten, 2005), 176–179; Secretary of State to Harrison, Washington, December 17, 1942, *FRUS,* 1942, 1:839.

6. Max Huber to President Comité Central Croix rouge japonaise, December 27, 1941, G.8 / Par Correspondance diverse, International Committee of the Red Cross Archives (hereafter ICRC); Ōkawa Shirō, *Ōbeijin horyo to Sekijūji katsudō: Parabichīni Hakushi no fukken* (Tokyo: Ronsōsha, 2006).

7. Quoted in Utsumi Aiko, "The Japanese Army and Its Prisoners, Relevant Documents and Bureaucratic Institutions," Australia-Japan Research Project, Australian War Memorial, http://ajrp.awm.gov.au.

8. Margaret Kosuge, "Religion, the Red Cross, and Japanese Treatment of POWs," in *Japanese Prisoners of War,* ed. Philip Towle and Yoichi Kibata (London: Hambledon, 2000), 159.

9. "Affidavit of Odashima, Tadashi," January 30, 1948, SCAP Legal Section, Administrative Division, Miscellaneous Japanese File, 1942–1948, POW Camp Records, SCAP Legal Section, Records of Allied Operational and Occupation Headquarters, Record Group 331, NARA.

10. Brian Masaru Hayashi, *Democratizing the Enemy: The Japanese-American Internment* (Princeton, NJ: Princeton University Press, 2010), 81.

11. Secretary of State to Huddle, January 20, 1942, *FRUS,* 1942, 1:794; Corbett, *Quiet Passages,* 48–49.

12. Huddle to Secretary of State, February 19, 1942, *FRUS,* 1942, 1:846–847.

13. Huddle to Secretary of State, February 19, 1942.

14. Harrison to the Secretary of State, Telegraph No. 733, February 24, 1942, *FRUS,* 1942, 1:799.

15. Karl Hack and Kevin Blackburn, eds., *Forgotten Captives in Japanese-Occupied Asia* (Abingdon, UK: Routledge, 2008), 13; Felicia Yap, "Prisoners of War and Civilian Internees of the Japanese in British Asia: The Similarities and Contrasts of Experience," *Journal of Contemporary History* 47, no. 2 (2012): 322–323.

16. Joseph C. Green to Edward MacDougall, February 25, 1942, Special War Problems Division Subject Files, 1939–1955, POW Americans in Japan to Miyoshi, Department of State Central Files, Record Group 59, NARA.

17. John DeWitt, *Final Report: Japanese Evacuation from the West Coast, 1942* (Washington, DC: U.S. Government Printing Office, 1943), 33.

18. Greg Robinson, *By Order of the President: FDR and the Internment of Japanese Americans* (Cambridge, MA: Harvard University Press, 2001), 108.

19. Corbett, *Quiet Passages,* 55.

20. Hayashi, *Democratizing the Enemy,* 81.

21. Robinson, *By Order of the President,* 7, 116–117, 120–123.

22. Corbett, *Quiet Passages,* 54.

23. Huddle to Secretary of State, February 24, 1942, SCAP Legal Section, Declassification Review Project NND 735027, War Crimes Branch, Records of the Office of the Judge Advocate General (Army), Record Group 153, NARA.

24. D. C. Brody to J. P. M. Bland, September 22, 1942 [Office of Censorship, USA], Special War Problems Division Subject Files, 1939–1955, POW Americans in Japan to Miyoshi, Department of State Central Files, Record Group 59, NARA.

25. Michael Sherry, *The Rise of American Airpower: The Creation of Armageddon* (New Haven, CT: Yale University Press, 1987), 123–125.

26. Embajada de Espana (España), "Protection of Civil Belligerent Internees," May 9, 1942, Special War Problems Division Subject Files, 1939–1955, POW Americans in Japan to Miyoshi, Department of State Central Files, Record Group 59, NARA.

27. "Copy of Cable Received July 8, 1942," NLT Intercross Washington, Special War Problems Division Subject Files, 1939–1955, POW Americans in Japan to Miyoshi, Department of State Central Files, Record Group 59, NARA.

28. Tom Francis to Friends, April 15, 1943 [Extract, Office of Censorship, USA], Special War Problems Division Subject Files, 1939–1955, POW Americans in Japan to Miyoshi, Department of State Central Files, Record Group 59, NARA.

29. "Summary of Number of American Civilians Held by Japan, as of May 23, 1944," Special War Problems Division Subject Files, 1939–1955, POW Americans in Japan to Miyoshi, Department of State Central Files, Record Group 59, NARA.

30. "Memorandum of Conversation," September 12, 1942, Special War Problems Division Subject Files, 1939–1955, POW Americans in Japan to Miyoshi, Department of State Central Files, Record Group 59, NARA.

31. Paravicini to ICRC, May 15, 1942, G 8 / 76 I, Délégation au Japon, Janvier–aôut 1942, ICRC.

32. Hull to Bern, August 27, 1942; US Legation, Bern, American Interest Section, Supplemental General Records, 1942–1945, Foreign Service Posts of the Department of State, Switzerland, Record Group 84, NARA.

33. Hull to American Legation, August 12, 1942, SCAP Legal Section, War Crimes Branch, Declassification Review Project NND 735027, Records of the Office of the Judge Advocate General (Army), Record Group 153, NARA.

34. Ulrich Straus, *The Anguish of Surrender: Japanese POW's in World War II* (Seattle: University of Washington Press, 2003), 134–141.

35. "Kūshū-ji no teki kōkūki tōjō-in ni kansuru ken," issued on July 28, 1942, Furyo ni kansuru sho hōki ruishū, December 1946, Japan Center for Asian Historical Records (JACAR), exhibit 1981–1982, reference code C13070714700, https://www

.jacar.archives.go.jp/aj/meta/image_C13070714700?IS_KIND=summary_normal&IS
_STYLE=default&IS_TAG_S1=iFi&IS_KEY_S1=F2013071117181973242&.

36. Harrison to Secretary of State, August 8, 1942, SCAP Legal Section, War
    Crimes Branch, Declassification Review Project NND 735027, Records of the
    Office of the Judge Advocate General (Army), Record Group 153, NARA.

37. Harrison to Secretary of State, September 9, 1942, SCAP Legal Section, War
    Crimes Branch, Declassification Review Project NND 735027, Records of the
    Office of the Judge Advocate General (Army), Record Group 153, NARA.

38. Corbett, *Quiet Passages,* 32.

39. Harrison to Secretary of State, September 26, 1942, *FRUS,* 1942, 1:822–823.

40. Tachikawa Kyoichi and Shuku Haruhiko, "Seifu oyobi Gun to ICRC nado tō
    tono kankei: Nisshin sensō kara Taiheiyō sensō made," *Bōei Kenkyūjo Kiyō* 11,
    no. 2 (January 2009): 127, 147.

41. Its employees as well as others so testified. For example, see the testimony of
    one employee, Captain Saito Yoichi: Interrogation of Captain Saitō Yoshichi,
    September 23, 1947, in *Kokusai kensatsu-kyoku (IPS) jinmon chōsho,* ed. Awaya
    Kentarō and Yoshida Yutaka, vol. 49 (Tokyo: Nihon Tosho Sentā, 1993), 221.

42. Utsumi, *Nihongun no horyo seisaku,* 183–185.

43. Tachikawa Kyoichi, "The Treatment of Prisoners of War by the Imperial Japa-
    nese Army and Navy focusing on the Pacific War," *NIDS Security Reports* no. 9
    (2008): 75–76; Harumi Furuya, "Dai niji sekai taisenki ni okeru Nihonjin no
    jinshu identity" [The racial identity of the Japanese people during the period of
    the World War II], in *Sensō no kioku to horyo mondai* [The memory of war and
    the POW issues], ed. Yoichi Kibata, Margaret Kosuge, and Philip Towle (Tokyo:
    Daigaku Shuppankai, 2003), 166.

44. "Interrogation of Odashima, Tadashima," October 18, 1948, SCAP Legal
    Section, Administrative Division, Miscellaneous Japanese File, 1942–1948,
    POW Camp Records, Records of Allied Operational and Occupation Head-
    quarters, Record Group 331, NARA.

45. The Japanese cited this factor in answering American charges. "Treatment
    Given American Citizens in Japan," May 11, 1944, No. J-96, Ex. 119.01, SCAP
    Legal Section, War Crimes Branch, Declassification Review Project NND
    735027, Records of the Office of the Judge Advocate General (Army), Record
    Group 153, NARA. See also Ichimata Masao, "Senpan saiban kenkyū yōron (2):
    Taiheiyō sensō teisen shori kansuru kokusaihō sōsatsu," *Kōkusaihō gaikō
    zasshi* 66, no. 2 (1967); Adachi Sumio, *Unprepared Regrettable Events: A Brief*

*History of Japanese Practices on Treatment of Allied War Victims during the Second World War* (Yokosuka: National Defense Academy, 1982).

46. Tachikawa and Shuku, "Seifu oyobi Gun to ICRC nado tō tono kankei," 127–128.

47. War Department, "Lists of Japanese Officers Connected with the Japanese Prisoner of War Camps," September 10, 1945, SCAP Legal Section, War Crimes Branch, Declassification Review Project NND 735027, Records of the Office of the Judge Advocate General (Army), Record Group 153, NARA.

48. Park Byeong Suk, interview with the author, August 1, 2011; Lee Hak Rae, interview with the author, December 16, 2011.

49. The Commission on Verification and Support for the Victims of Forced Mobilization under Japanese Colonialism in Korea, unpublished report, vol. 2, 1st draft, Seoul, Korea, July 27, 2011, 15.

50. "Interrogation of Odashima, Tadashima," October 18, 1948.

51. Paravicini to ICRC, August 30, 1942, G 8/76, Délégation au Japon, ICRC.

52. "Conseil Fédéral Procès-verbal de la séance du 27 avril 1945," in *Documents Diplomatiques Suisses,* vol. 15 (Bern: Benteli, 1992), 1086–1089.

53. "Renforcement de la Délégation au Japon," April 14, 1942, J G.8/Par, Correspondance diverse, ICRC.

54. J. Duchosal, Transcription of Phone Call from Edouard de Haller, April 21, 1942, G-8/76 I, Délégation au Japon, Janvier–août 1942, ICRC.

55. Paravicini to ICRC, August 30, 1942.

56. Squire to Tait, November 13, 1942, US Legation, Bern, American Interest Section, Supplemental General Records, 1942–1945, Foreign Service Posts of the Department of State, Switzerland, Record Group 84, NARA.

57. "Memorandum," March 29, 1943, US Legation, Bern, American Interest Section, Supplemental General Records, 1942–1945, Foreign Service Posts of the Department of State, Switzerland, Record Group 84, NARA.

58. "Note pour les délégués du Comité international de la Croix-rouge," October 20, 1942, DT/AMG G.6/PP. G.4, Swiss Federal Archives (hereafter SFA).

59. *La Sentinelle,* June 7, 1944, Extrait de la Séance du Conseil National, SFA.

60. Jean-Claude Favez, *The Red Cross and the Holocaust* (Cambridge: Cambridge University Press, 1999), 14–15.

61. "Note pour les délégués."

62. Max Huber to Monsieur le Conseiller fédéral, May 9, 1942, G.6 / PP / S, SFA.

63. Favez, *Red Cross and the Holocaust,* 46–52.

64. Tachikawa and Shuku, "Seifu oyobi Gun to ICRC nado tō tono kankei," 126.

65. "Interrogation of Odashima, Tadashi," October 18, 1948.

66. "Téléphone de M. Edouard de Haller le mardi 21 avril 1942 à 18h30," April 21, 1942, G-8 / 76 I, Délégation au Japon, Janvier–août 1942, ICRC.

67. De Saussure to ICRC, February 6, 1942, G-8 / 76 I, Délégation au Japon, Janvier–août 1942, CICR; Gorgé to Politque Intérêts, June 22, 1945, D.C.56A B.24.20, Karuizawa 760 XI, SFA.

68. Conseil fédéral, "Procès-verbal de la séance du 27 avril 1945," in *Documents Diplomatiques Suisses,* vol. 15 (Bern: Benteli, 1992), 1087.

69. Gorgé to Département politique, February 6, 1943, in *Documents Diplomatiques Suisses,* vol. 15, 991–993.

70. Conseil fédéral, "Procès-verbal de la séance du 27 avril 1945," 1087–1088.

71. Gorgé to Politique Intérêts, June 27, 1945, D.C.56A B.24.20, SFA.

72. Paravicini to ICRC, May 15, 1942, G 8 / 76 I, Délégation au Japon, Janvier–août 1942, ICRC.

73. Daha seyo, 'Shinchū no 'beikoku': Bei furyo ni 'okawaisōni' towa nanigoto zo," *Asahi Shimbun,* December 5, 1942, radio script available at http://binder.gozaru .jp/radio/19421204-akiyama.htm.

74. Hull to American Legation, October 23, 1942, SCAP Legal Section, War Crimes Branch, Declassification Review Project NND 735027, Records of the Office of the Judge Advocate General (Army), Record Group 153, NARA.

75. Hull to American Legation, December 12, 1942, SCAP Legal Section, War Crimes Branch, Declassification Review Project NND 735027, Records of the Office of the Judge Advocate General (Army), Record Group 153, NARA; Hull to Harrison, December 17, 1942, *FRUS,* 1942, 1:839.

76. Harrison to Secretary of State, February 23, 1943, SCAP Legal Section, War Crimes Branch, Declassification Review Project NND 735027, Records of the Office of the Judge Advocate General (Army), Record Group 153, NARA.

77. Hull to American Legation, April 5, 1943, SCAP Legal Section, War Crimes Branch, Declassification Review Project NND 735027, Records of the Office of the Judge Advocate General (Army), Record Group 153, NARA.

78. Sherry, *The Rise of American Airpower,* 109.

79. For example, Grew to Bern, March 19, 1945, SCAP Legal Section, War Crimes Branch, Declassification Review Project NND 735027, Records of the Office of the Judge Advocate General (Army), Record Group 153, NARA.

80. Gorgé to Berne, March 14, 1944, E 2001 (D), 1968 / 74 BD:1, B.24.USA. (13)6 J / R0, SFA.

81. Corbett, *Quiet Passages,* 119, 133.

82. Sherry, *The Rise of American Airpower,* 169–170.

83. Corbett, *Quiet Passages,* 119, 132–134.

84. R. M., "Memorandum," dated December 5, 1944 [incorrect], SCAP Legal Section, War Crimes Branch, Declassification Review Project NND 735027, Records of the Office of the Judge Advocate General (Army), Record Group 153, NARA.

85. "Interrogation of Odashima, Tadashima," October 18, 1948.

86. Untitled document [interrogation of Hoda Haruo], April 9, 1948, SCAP Legal Section, Administrative Division, Miscellaneous Japanese File, 1942–1948, POW Camp Records, Records of Allied Operational and Occupation Head-quarters, Record Group 331, NARA.

87. André Durand, *From Sarajevo to Hiroshima: History of the International Committee of the Red Cross* (Geneva: Henry Dunant Institute, 1984), 534.

88. Relevant examples include issues of the POWIB's monthly journal from 1942 and memoranda from Tamura Hiroshi, head of the POWIB. Utsumi Aiko and Nagai Hitoshi, eds., *Tokyo Saiban shiryō: Furyo jōhōkyoku kankei bunsho* (Tokyo: Gendai Shiryō Shuppan, 1999); and Chaen Yoshio, ed., *Furyo Jōhō-kyoku Furyo toriatsukai no kiroku: Tsuketari, Kaigun Heigakkō "kokusaihō"* (Tokyo: Fuji Shuppan, 1992).

89. Gorgé to de Haller, February 28, 1944, Bern, E2001-02 1000-110 BD-9, SFA; de Saussure to Tokio, February 17, 1944, Gbr.(15)6.A.1.-J / Ha, SFA; Durand, *From Sarajevo to Hiroshima,* 529.

90. Gorgé to de Haller, Politique Intérêts, February 28, 1944, Bern, E2001-02 1000-110 BD-9, SFA.

91. Gorgé to Politique Intérêts, June 21 and June 22, 1945, D.C.56A B.24.20, SFA.

92. Gorgé to Politique Intérêts, June 21 and June 22, 1945.

93. "Traitement des prisonniers de guerre au Japon," March 2, 1944, E 2001 (D), 1968 / 74 BD:1, B.52.49.2, SFA.

94. Eden speech to the House of Commons, January 28, 1944, Parliamentary Debates, Commons, 5th ser., vol. 396 (1944), cols. 1029–1033.

95. Bertram D. Hulen, "Hull Demands Japan Halt Abuse of U.S. Prisoners," *New York Times,* February 12, 1944, 1.

96. Transcript of Glen speech before the House of Commons, January 28, 1944, E 2001 (D), 1968 / 74 BD:1, B.52.49.2, Bundesarchiv, p. 1585. Also see Dyess, as quoted in "March of Death after Bataan Surrender," *Daily Herald,* January 29, 1944, found in Bundesarchiv, E 2001 (D), 1968 / 74 BD:2, 1508–1509.

97. John H. Crider, "Ruin Japan! Is Cry," *New York Times,* January 29, 1944, 1; Roger Dingman, *Ghost of War: The Sinking of the Awa Maru and Japanese-American Relations, 1945–1955* (Annapolis, MD: Naval Institute Press, 1997), 22–23.

98. "Primitive Japan," *Washington Post,* February 2, 1944, 8.

99. Gregson to Dublin, January 30, 1944, DFA / 4 / 241 / 402, Irish National Archives, Dublin.

100. Secretary of State to Harrison, January 27, 1944, *FRUS,* 1944, 5:921–932; Japanese Foreign Office to the Swiss Legation, April 28, 1944, *FRUS,* 1944, 5:942–965; Dingman, *Ghost of War,* 22–23.

101. Memo to Files, AI Note No. 8429, to D.P.I., May 10, 1944, American Legation, Bern American Interests Section, Foreign Service Posts of the Department of State, US Embassies, Legations, Consulates General, Consulates, and Missions, Record Group 84, NARA.

102. Hull to Bern, March 24, 1944, SCAP Legal Section, War Crimes Branch, Declassification Review Project NND 735027, Records of the Office of the Judge Advocate General (Army), Record Group 153, NARA.

103. "International Military Tribunal for the Far East the United States of America et al. vs. Araki Sadao et. al.," Def. Doc. #2173 (revised), August 29, 1947, SCAP Legal Section, Administrative Division, Miscellaneous Japanese File, 1942–1948, POW Camp Records, Records of Allied Operational and Occupation Headquarters, Record Group 331, NARA.

104. "Excerpt from International Military Tribunal for the Far East Transcript, 27,866–27,876, Cross-Examination of Odashima Tadashi," SCAP Legal Section, Administrative Division, Miscellaneous Japanese File, 1942–1948, POW Camp

Records, Records of Allied Operational and Occupation Headquarters, Record Group 331, NARA.

105. Chunghee Sarah Soh, *The Comfort Women: Sexual Violence and Postcolonial Memory in Korea and Japan* (Chicago: University of Chicago Press, 2008), 20–22.

106. Pierre-Yves Donzé, Claude Hauser, Pascal Lottaz, and Andy Maître, eds., *Journal d'un témoin: Camille Gorgé, diplomate suisse dans le Japon en guerre (1940–1945)* (Geneva: Documents Diplomatiques Suisses (Dodis), 2018), 65–67, https://www.dodis.ch/res/doc/QdD-Bd10.PDF.

107. Donzé et al., *Journal d'un témoin,* 65–67.

108. Donzé et al., *Journal d'un témoin,* 65–67.

109. Nagai, "Tamura Hiroshi chūjō 'kenkyūbibōroku' ni kansuru oboegaki," in Utsumi Aiko and Nagai Hitoshi, eds., *Tokyo Saiban shiryō: Furyo jōhōkyoku kankei bunsho* (Tokyo: Gendai Shiryō Shuppan, 1999), 46–49.

110. Nagai, "Tamura Hiroshi chūjō 'kenkyūbibōroku' ni kansuru oboegaki," 46–49.

111. Nagai, "Tamura Hiroshi chūjō 'kenkyūbibōroku' ni kansuru oboegaki," 46–49, 58–62.

112. Utsumi, "The Japanese Army and Its Prisoners."

113. Dingman, *Ghost of War,* 23–29, 34–36.

114. Harrison to the Secretary of State, July 8, 1944, *FRUS,* 1944, 5:989–990.

115. "Japan's Proposal for Reciprocal Visits to Internee Camps," *Department of State Bulletin* 12, no. 191 (1945): 61.

116. Huddle to the Secretary of State, December 18, 1944, *FRUS,* 1944, 5:1012–1013.

117. Secretary of State to Harrison, March 16, 1945, *FRUS,* 1945, 6:328–329.

118. Bruce Makins to the Acting Secretary of State, February 28, 1945, *FRUS,* 1945, 6:322–323.

119. Dingman, *Ghost of War,* 100–106.

120. "Conseil Fédéral Procès-verbal de la séance du 27 avril 1945," 1086–1089.

121. Swiss citizens had died at Japanese hands earlier in the war. For example, in 1943 the Japanese Navy had executed the Red Cross delegate Karl Matthias Vischer and his wife in Borneo. See Margaret Kosuge, "The 'Non-religious' Red Cross Emblem and Japan," *International Review of the Red Cross* 85, no. 849 (2003): 91.

122. The Acting Secretary of State (Grew) to the Secretary of War (Stimson), June 18, 1945, *FRUS,* 1945, 6:345.

123. Gorgé to Politique Intérêts, July 6, 1945, D.C.56A B.24.20, SFA.

124. This was Gorgé's estimate. The Minister in Switzerland (Harrison) to the Secretary of State, September 29, 1945, *FRUS,* 1945, 6:405–406, doc. 274.

125. Germany offers a useful comparison. While Germany's treatment of Soviet prisoners is notorious, and it also forced French and Eastern European POWs to work in harsh conditions, Hitler was persuaded not to repudiate the Geneva Conventions outright. When it came to British and American POWs, Berlin was strict in its adherence, with few exceptions, for fear that violations would bring reciprocal (mis)treatment of German POWs. Vasilis Voukoutiotis, *Prisoners of War and the German High Command: The British and American Experience* (New York: Palgrave Macmillan, 2003), 10, 192.

## 5. Korea

1. "Check List for Col. Schwartz," April 9, 1946, Record Group 331, Box 920, US National Archives and Records Administration, College Park, Maryland (hereafter NARA), on Mansell.com.

2. "Riku-a-Mitsu-ju no. 1910," Secret Telegram 2-28, From Chief of Staff, Korean Army, to Vice Minister of War, March 1, 1942 [received March 4 1942], in *The Tokyo War Crimes Trial, Proceedings of the Tribunal,* 22 vols. ed. R. John Pritchard and Sonia Magbanua Zaide (New York: Garland, 1981–1987), 6:14512–14513; Utsumi Aiko, *Furyo toriatsukai ni kansuru shogaikoku kara no kōgishū* (Tokyo: Fuji Shuppan, 1989), 14–15.

3. "Report regarding Plans for the Internment of POWs in Korea, from Commander in Chief of the Korean Army, Seishiro Itagaki to Minister of War, Hideki Tōjō," March 23, 1942, [*International Military Tribunal for the Far East,* 14514–14516]; "A-Mitsu [Asia Secret] No. 1910, Part II," received Army Secretariat April 23, 1942, in Pritchard and Zaide, *The Tokyo War Crimes Trial,* 6:14, 517.

4. "Report regarding Plans for the Internment of POWs in Korea"; "A-Mitsu [Asia Secret] No. 1910, Part II."

5. A selection of these photos can be found at the Imperial War Museum (hereafter IWM), London. See also Fran de Groen and Helen Masterman-Smith, "2002 History Conference—Remembering 1942, Prisoners on Parade: Japan Party 'B,'" Australian War Memorial (hereafter AWM), https://www.awm .gov.au/visit/events/conference/remembering-1942/japan-party-b.

6. Utsumi Aiko, *Kimu wa naze abakareta no ka: Chōsenjin BC-kyū senpan no kiseki* (Tokyo: Asahi Shimbun Shuppan, 2008), 67–78, esp. 74.

7. "The Commission on Verification and Support for the Victims of Forced Mobilization under Japanese Colonialism in Korea," unpublished report, 2011; Cho Gun, "Ilje kangjŏm malgi chosŏnchudunilbon'gunŭi chosŏnin p'orokamsiwŏn tongwŏn'gwa yŏnhapkun p'orosuyongso unyŏnng," *Han'gukkŭnhyŏndaesahakhoe* 67 (Winter 2013).

8. "Camp Division, Jinsen, Corée," Archives du Service des Camps, Rapports originaux CICR, International Committee of the Red Cross Archives (hereafter ICRC), vols. 783–786, 790–799, 807–811, Dépouillements des camps par matières, Japon (Corée, Taiwan), ICRC.

9. Chief of Staff of the Korean Army Ihara Junjirō to Vice-Army Minister Kimura Heitarō, August 13, 1942 [received by Army Secretariat August 19], "Reactions among the General Public Following Internment of British Prisoners of War"; Pritchard and Zaide, *The Tokyo War Crimes Trial,* 6:14521–14524; de Groen and Masterman-Smith, "2002 History Conference"; de Groen, citing David Bergamini, *Japan's Imperial Conspiracy* (London: Heinmann, 1971), 964–965, also notes this material but draws a different conclusion.

10. Chief of Staff of the Korean Army Ihara Junjirō to Vice-Army Minister Kimura Heitarō, August 13, 1942 [received by Army Secretariat August 19], "Reactions among the General Public following Internment of British Prisoners of War."

11. Guy Round, "The Road from Singapore," unpublished manuscript, 1943–1947, MS 1370, 191, AWM; Herbert Stanley Geldard, "Diary / Notebook," 1942, PR 91 / 194, AWM.

12. De Groen and Masterman-Smith, "2002 History Conference."

13. Korea initially had two POW camps, the main camp at Keijō and the No. 1 branch camp at Jinsen. A third camp, the No. 1 dispatched camp, was later opened at Kōnan (Hŭngnam), in the heavily industrialized north. There were also a number of internee camps, which held missionaries and other civilians.

14. "Instructions Given by Col. Y. Noguchi, Superintendent of the Chōsen War Prisoners' Camp," September 1942, Chōsen POW Camp, IWM.

15. To Elrington, Col. Noguchi "seemed to be a mild middle-aged man and anxious for a quiet life." Alan Vernon Toze, "Diary," Doc. 1133, IWM (hereafter Toze, "Diary").

16. Camp principal Keijō-Chōsen, "Dépouillements des camps par matières: Japon, Coree, Formose," Archives du Service des Camps, Rapports originaux CICR, vols. 783–786, 790–799, 807–811, Tel. 207 du 27.12.42 G 8 / Pa G 17 / Ja., ICRC.

17. "Prisoners in Far East: Camp Conditions," *Advocate* (Burnie, Tasmania), June 24, 1943, 2.

18. Dick Swarbrick, "Dick Swarbrick's War," Second Battalion, Loyal Regiment, http://www.far-eastern-heroes.org.uk/Richard_Swarbricks_War/html/jinsen _camp_-_korea.htm.

19. Archives du Service des Camps, Rapports originaux CICR, vols. 790–799, 807–811, CICR SC 023, Folder RV 23, 1, RR (CICR) 783–795, Rapports: Pestalozzi-Angst-Paravicini, 790 Japon-Manchukuo, novembre 1943–fev.– mars.–av. 1944, ICRC.

20. Guy Round describes such an unsuccessful attempt in 1944 by Sgt. Griffiths and Private Broughton. Round, "The Road from Singapore," 347.

21. Sgt. S. Strange and A. V. Toze, "In Defense of Singapore: Scenes and Personal Images before and after the Fall of Singapore: A Series of Drawings with Brief Notes," plate XVII, Fulwood barracks (hereafter FB).

22. Guy Round, "I Was a Prisoner in Korea," *Western Mail* (Perth, WA), August 17, 1950, 3.

23. Harry Kingsley, "Prisoner of War Drawings at Keijō P.O.W. Camp, Korea: 1942 to 1945," 67038, IWM.

24. Dick Swarbrick, "Dick Swarbrick's War," https://www.far-eastern-heroes.org .uk/Richard_Swarbricks_War/; Gerald Rosenberg, September 22, 1943, MSS 1737, AWM.

25. Prisoners of War Camp, Chōsen, Visited by M. Pestalozzi, November 15, 1943, ICRC.

26. Toze, "Diary," November 23, 1943, Docs. 1133, 57, IWM.

27. Toze, "Diary," June 27, 1943, Docs. 1133, 39, IWM.

28. Alex Johnstone, "Diary," November 7, 1942, PRO 1044, AWM.

29. Alex Johnstone, "Diary," November 12, 1942, PRO 1044, AWM.

30. Dépouillements des camps par matières: Japon, Corée, Formose, Archives du Service des Camps, Rapports originaux CICR, vols. 783–786 790–799, 807–811, Tel. 207 du 27.12.42 G 8 / Pa G 17 / Ja., 429–437, ICRC.

31. "Camp Division Jinsen," Archives du Service des Camps, Rapports originaux CICR, vols. 783–786, 790–799, 807–811, Dépouillements des camps par matières: Japon (Corée, Taiwan), ICRC.

32. Utsumi Aiko, *Nihongun no horyo seisaku* (Tokyo: Aoki Shoten, 2005), 219.

33. In November 1944, another shipment arrived from Rashin via Vladivostok, containing 1,670 wrapped packages, meaning four boxes each. Utsumi, *Nihongun no horyo seisaku*, 219–220.

34. Dépouillements des camps par matières: Japon, Corée, Formose, Archives du Service des Camps, Rapports originaux CICR, February 15, 1945, vols. 783–786 790–799, 807–811, Tel. 1645 du 15.2.45 G 17 / 76 ExO G 8 / Pa, Fev 45, Rap 1179, ICRC.

35. *The Daily News* (Perth, WA, 1882–1950), December 7, 1943; Utsumi, *Nihongun no horyo seisaku*, 212–221.

36. "Camp PG Chōsen," Detached Camp No. 1, Dépouillements des camps par matières: Japon, Corée, Formose, Archives du Service des Camps, Rapports originaux CICR, vols. 783–786 790–799, 807–811, Tel. 1645 du 15.2.45 G 17 / 76 ExO G 8 / Pa Fev 45, Rap 1179, ICRC.

37. Utsumi, *Nihongun no horyo seisaku*, 212–221.

38. Swarbrick, "Dick Swarbrick's War."

39. Swarbrick, "Dick Swarbrick's War."

40. Archives du Service des Camps, Rapports originaux CICR, vols. 783–786, 790–799, 807–811, Dépouillements des camps par matières: Japon (Corée, Taiwan), ICRC.

41. Archives du Service des Camps, Rapports originaux CICR, vols. 783–786, 790–799, 807–811, Dépouillements des camps par matières: Japon (Corée, Taiwan), ICRC; see especially February 15, 1945.

42. Camp de Zinsen (Jinsen), (Camp division de Keijō), Archives du Service des Camps, Rapports originaux CICR, vols. 783–786, 790–799, 807–811, Dépouillements des camps par matières. Japon (Corée, Taiwan), ICRC.

43. Utsumi, *Nihongun no horyo seisaku*, 214.

44. "Camp PG Chōsen." Others worked as miners or stevedores. For commissioned officers, work would be voluntary and unpaid. Utsumi, *Nihongun no horyo seisaku*, 214.

45. "Camp PG Chōsen."

46. Toze, "Diary," Doc. 1133, IWM.

47. ICRC inspector Angst was sick the day of the scheduled inspection, and the Japanese "inspected" it in his absence.

48. *United States of America vs. Yuzuru Noguchi,* Review of the Staff Judge Advocate, September 13, 1945, as found at Forschungs- und Dokumentationszen trum für Kriegsverbrecherprozesse, 7, http://www.uni-marburg.de/icwc.

49. Lionel John Apps and Leonard George Mills, "Affidavit," Military Agency Records, The War Department and the Army Records, Records of the Adjutant General's Office, 1917–, Record Group 407, NARA.

50. Alex Johnstone, private record, November 4, 1942, PRO 1044, AWM, p. 82, and November 6, 1942, PRO 1044, AWM.

51. Toze, "Diary," Doc. 1133, IWM.

52. Gerald Rosenberg, MSS 1737, AWM, unpaginated.

53. Swarbrick, "Dick Swarbrick's War."

54. "Hygiene in Jinsen Camp, Korea," Archives du Service des Camps, Rapports originaux CICR, vols. 783–786, 790–799, 807–811, Corée, Japon (Corée, Taiwan), ICRC.

55. Richard Biggs, "Affidavit," Military Agency Records, The War Department and the Army Records, Records of the Adjutant General's Office, 1917–, Record Group 407, NARA.

56. Leonard George Mills, "Affidavit," Military Agency Records, The War Department and the Army Records, Records of the Adjutant General's Office, 1917–, Record Group 407, NARA.

57. Toze, "Diary," IWM 1133, IWM, 86.

58. Round, "The Road from Singapore," 201.

59. *United States of America vs. Yuzuru Noguchi,* 31.

60. *United States of America vs. Yuzuru Noguchi,* 50.

61. *United States of America vs. Yuzuru Noguchi.*

62. On September 12, 1945, Recovery Team 70 visited the prison and found twelve prisoners. "Report of Recovery Team 70," Military Agency Records, The War Department and the Army Records, Records of the Adjutant General's Office, 1917–, Record Group 407, NARA.

63. *United States of America vs. Yuzuru Noguchi,* 58.

64. *United States of America vs. Yuzuru Noguchi,* 34.

65. Round, "The Road from Singapore," 347.

66. Round, "The Road from Singapore," 344.

67. "Check List for Col. Schwartz."

68. "Check List for Col. Schwartz."

69. "Check List for Col. Schwartz."

70. Shreve transcribed his diary as evidence for the War Crimes Tribunal in 1948. For the War Crimes Office, Judge Advocate General's Department, Department of the Army, United States of America, "Perpetuation of Testimony of Arthur L. Shreve, Lt Colonel, 011176, Taken at: Baltimore, Maryland, Dated: 16 January 1948, In the Presence of: Jack S. Kelly, Special Agent, 109th CIC Det, Second Army," http://www.mansell.com/pow_resources/camplists/fukuoka /fuk_01_fukuoka/fukuoka_01/Shreve.html.

71. "Check List for Col. Schwartz."

72. "Defense Motion for Disapproval of Findings and Modification of Sentence as to Yasutoshi Mizuguchi," March 25, 1948, 18, Records of Allied Operational and Occupation Headquarters, WWII, Record Group 331, NARA.

73. Gerald Rosenberg, August 9, MSS 1737, AWM.

74. Gerald Rosenberg, August 12, MSS 1737, AWM.

75. Gavan Daws, *Prisoners of the Japanese: POWs of WWII in the Pacific* (New York: Harper, 1994), 324-325.

76. See also In Sŭnggab for this sentiment: "Our plan was to persuade POWs to be on our side. Korean guards and POWs numbered 90,000 and Japanese soldiers were only 20,000." In Sŭnggab, "Waenomdŭl sone chungnŭni nararŭl wihae ssautaga chukketta," in *Nambang kihaeng: Kangje tongwŏn kunsok sugijip,* ed. Yi Seil et. al (Seoul: Ilche Kangjŏmha Kangje Tongwŏn P'ihae Chinsang Kyumyŏng Wiwŏnhoe, 2008), 230-231.

77. This document is frequently used to argue that the Japanese had such a policy. See Daws, *Prisoners of the Japanese,* 324-325, and translation and explanatory text on Mansell website: "Taiwan furyo shūyōjo honbu nisshi" [Journal of the Taiwan POW Camp HQ in Taihoku], August 1, 1944, Doc. 2701, Exhibit "O" [The order to murder all the POWs], Record Group 24, Box 2015, US Naval Academy, http://www.mansell.com/pow_resources/Formosa/taiwandocs.html and http://www.mansell.com/pow_resources/Formosa/doc2701-trans.html. The document was introduced into the prosecution of Araki Sadao, Dohihara Kenji, Hashimoto Kingoro, Hata Shunroku, Hiranuma Kiichiro, Hirota Koki, Hoshino Naoki, Itagaki Seishiro, Kaya Okinori, Kido Koichi, Kimura Heitarō, Koiso

Kuniaki, Matsui Iwane, Matsuoka Yosuke, Minami Jiro, and Muto Akira by American prosecutor Col. Gilbert Woolworth on January 9, 1947: https://www .legal-tools.org/doc/6bba81/pdf/; UNWCC10.csv:3205 (IMTFE Transcript pages 14684–14848, 14724–14727).

78. "Taiwan furyo shūyōjo honbu nisshi."

79. Utsumi claims that this Taiwan POW camp document was based on a central order, dated September 11, 1944, from the Vice Minister of the War Ministry (Utsumi, *Nihongun no horyo seisaku,* 318–320). In the *International Military Tribunal for the Far East (IMTFE)*, the document was cited as "written evidence of an order from higher authority to kill POWs" (*IMTFE,* 49644). But the document Utsumi cites is actually quite vague and does not provide the basis for an order directing a specific massacre. Moreover, Utsumi herself says that central order could be from 1945 (Utsumi, *Nihongun no horyo seisaku,* 318). Even in the Tokyo tribunal, the prosecutor dates the Taiwan document as August 1944, meaning it could not have been based on a central order that only came later (https://www.legal-tools.org/doc/6bba81/pdf/, 14725). Also, this document states that it reports to the "Army Commander." But from September 1944, the Taiwan Army changed its name to "Tenth Area Army," a designation that lasted until the end of the war. If this Taiwan POW camp document was issued in 1945, it should have been reported to "Area Army Commander" not "Army Commander," providing further evidence that it actually dated to August 1944, preceding the central order. Page numbers refer to *IMTFE,* Judgment of November 12, 1948, in Pritchard and Zaide, *The Tokyo War Crimes Trial,* vol. 22. At the trial, additional evidence included Soldiers' diaries (*IMTFE,* 49644) and Shibayama order (*IMTFE,* 49645).

80. Likely Odashima Tadashi. " Documents Demonstrating Orders for Those Who Abused POWs to Flee," undated, SCAP Legal Section, Administrative Division, Miscellaneous Japanese File, 1942–1948, POW Camp Records, Records of Allied Operational and Occupation Headquarters, Record Group 331, NARA.

81. Neil Boister and Robert Cryer, eds., *Documents on the Tokyo International Military Tribunal: Charter, Indictment and Judgments* (Oxford: Oxford University Press, 2008), 550. The Sandakan march happened in the wake of this order.

82. Boister and Cryer, *Documents on the Tokyo International Military Tribunal,* 550.

83. During the war crimes trials, the Australian prosecutor argued that this was high-level policy. The Japanese government and Japanese Army admitted that there had been abusive treatment of POWs. Despite a prosecutorial focus (or obsession) with prosecuting the Japanese government and its leadership for the abuse of Allied POWs, the verdict was that the Japanese government tacitly

allowed abusive treatment of POWs. Only the Ministry of War and some of its leadership were convicted of Allied POW abuse. Utsumi Aiko, *Tokyo saiban to horyo mondai* (Osaka: Osaka University of Economics and Law [Osaka keizai hōka daigaku], Asia Pacific Center, 2013–2014), 27, 30.

84. Odajima Tadashi, "Circumstances Leading to the Draft of Riku-A-Mitsu no. 2257," SCAP Legal Section, Administrative Division, Miscellaneous Japanese File, 1942–1948, POW Camp Records, Records of Allied Operational and Occupation Headquarters, Record Group 331, NARA.

85. Chief, POW Camps, to Chief of Staff, Formosa Army, August 20, 1945, Doc. No. 2697, SCAP Legal Section, Administrative Division, Miscellaneous Japanese File, 1942–1948, POW Camp Records, Records of Allied Operational and Occupation Headquarters, Record Group 331, NARA.

86. Chief, POW Control Division, to Seoul POW Commander, August 22, 1945, SCAP Legal Section, Administrative Division, Miscellaneous Japanese File, 1942–1948, POW Camp Records, Records of Allied Operational and Occupation Headquarters, Record Group 331, NARA.

87. "Documents concerning Cessation of Hostilities," 2 Loyals, Kingsley & Strange Collection, 1939–1945, Box 8, FB.

88. The statistics on fatalities are problematic—records are incomplete, and prisoners were transported throughout the war. Toru Fukubayashi, "POW Camps in Japan Proper," http://www.powresearch.jp/en/archive/camplist/index.html.

89. *Chuhan Migunsa: HUSAFIK* (Seoul: Tolbegae, 1988), 32.

## 6. Captivity on the Home Front

1. "Checklist," March 29, 1946, US National Archives and Records Administration, College Park, Maryland (hereafter NARA), http://mansell.com/pow-index.html. Goodpasture's account was a source for the July 31 Gibbs Report, "Prisoner of War Camps in Japan and Japanese Controlled Areas as Taken from Reports of Interned American Prisoners Liaison and Research Branch American Prisoner of War Information Bureau," Record Group 389, Records of the Office of the Provost Marshal Records, NARA. It is critical to note that Goodpasture's account was given to an attorney to be used as prosecutorial evidence. For more on how to consider these kinds of documents, see Sandra Wilson, Robert Cribb, Beatrice Trefalt, and Dean Aszkielowicz, *Japanese War Criminals: The Politics of Justice after the Second World War* (New York: Columbia University Press, 2017).

2. In the last twenty-five years, Kyushu has been the center of redress movements as Allied, Chinese, and Korean forced laborers have sought compensation for which progressive Japanese citizens have also fought. As Yukiko Koga has recently written, "traumatic casualties of the colonial past are 'inherited' and 'redeemed' in the present." Yukiko Koga, *Inheritance of Loss: China, Japan, and the Political Economy of Redemption after Empire* (Chicago: University of Chicago Press, 2016). William Underwood, "Names, Bones and Unpaid Wages (1): Reparations for Korean Forced Labor in Japan" (pt. 1 of 2), *Asia-Pacific Journal Japan Focus* 4, no. 9 (2006), https://apjjf.org/-William-Underwood/2219 /article.html; Fujita Yukihisa, "Aso Mining's Indelible Past: Prime Minister Aso Should Seek Reconciliation with Former POWs," *Asia-Pacific Journal Japan Focus* 7, no. 16 (2009), https://apjjf.org/-Fujita-Yukihisa/3127/article.html; Underwood, "Mitsubishi, Historical Revisionism and Japanese Corporate Resistance to Chinese Forced Labor Redress," *Asia-Pacific Journal Japan Focus* 4, no. 2 (2006), https://apjjf.org/-William-Underwood/1823/article.html.

3. J. Oosterhuis, "Diary," November 23, 1944, Collectie 401, Dagboeken Neder-lands—Indie N. 313.1, *Nederlands instituut voor oorlogsdocumentatie,* Amsterdam. Oosterhuis wrote in his diary—written on Japanese-style paper and complete with cigarette and food wrappers—that he was held captive at Fukuoka 1, but evidence indicates that at this point he may have been held in a different camp in Fukuoka. The original is kept at the Museon in The Hague.

4. Maj. Gen. Archer Lerch, in Utsumi Aiko and Nagai Hitoshi, *Tōkyō Saiban shiryō: Furyo Jōhōkyoku kankei bunshō* (Tokyo: Gendai Shiryō Shuppan, 1999), 22 [324].

5. Shunsuke Tsurumi, *An Intellectual History of Wartime Japan, 1931–1945* (London: KPI, 1986), 56.

6. Yoshiko Miyake, "Doubling Expectations: Motherhood and Women's Factory Work under State Management in Japan in the 1930s and 1940s," in *Recreating Japanese Women, 1600–1945,* ed. Gail Lee Bernstein (Berkeley: University of California Press, 1991), 288.

7. The Imperial Japanese Navy ran its own camps, most infamously Ōfuna in Kanagawa, which held POWs before they were transferred to the Army. The naval camps were established to gather intelligence.

8. Utsumi Aiko, *Nihongun no horyo seisaku* (Tokyo: Aoki Shoten, 2005), 190–194, 255–257, 327–334.

9. In 1943–1944, dispatch camps were set up to address a lack of manpower.

10. "Application for Permission to Employ Dispatched Prisoners of War," Declassification Review Project 775011, Japanese Laws, Rules and Regulations to POWs, 37–62, SCAP Legal Section, Administrative Division, Miscellaneous Japanese File, 1942–1948, POW Camp Records, Records of Allied Operational and Occupation Headquarters, Record Group 331, NARA.

11. "Interrogation of Tadashi Odashima," October 18, 1948, Declassification Review Project 775011, Japanese Laws, Rules and Regulations to POWs, 37–62, SCAP Legal Section, POW Camp Records, Box 1324, Records of Allied Operational and Occupation Headquarters, Record Group 331, NARA.

12. Established as Kumamoto Branch Camp of Yawata Temporal POW Camp at Aza-Saburōtsuka, Kengun-chō, Kumamoto City, Kumamoto Prefecture, on November 26, 1942.

13. Utsumi, *Nihongun no horyo seisaku*, 182–183.

14. Robert Metcalf, "In the Matter of War Crimes Committed by Japanese Nationals and in the Matter of Ill-Treatment of Prisoners of War at Kumamoto Prisoner of War Camp," from the Center for Research on Allied POWs under the Japanese: http://mansell.com/pow-index.html.

15. Arthur Edward Chalkey, "Perpetuation of Testimony," JAG War Crimes Case File, Records of the Office of the Judge Advocate General (Army), Record Group 153, NARA.

16. Metcalf, "In the Matter of War Crimes Committed by Japanese Nationals."

17. Although the ICRC was supposed to visit all Japanese POW camps, they visited only a small number. ICRC representatives never visited Fukuoka 1, although they visited the camps in the Fukuoka region three times in 1942–1945. War Office, "Report," May 5, 1944, FO 916/1095/1944, British National Archives.

18. E. Vesey, Affidavit, "In the Matter of War Crimes Committed by Japanese Nationals and in the Treatment of Prisoners of War at No. 1. Subcamp, Prisoner of War Camp, Fukuoka, Island of Kyūshū, Japan," from the Center for Research on Allied POWs under the Japanese, http://mansell.com/pow-index.html.

19. Vesey, Affidavit. In Japanese, Wakamoto tablets, which are still used.

20. Col. William D. North, "Perpetuation of Testimony of William D. North, Colonel, 017345," June 28, 1946, taken by Jacques M. P. Wilson, http://www.mansell.com/pow_resources/camplists/fukuoka/fuk_01_fukuoka/fukuoka_01/USAffJ-P.htm#North.

21. North, "Perpetuation of Testimony of William D. North."

22. Frederick Chilton, "In the Matter of Japanese War Crimes and in the Matter of the Ill-Treatment of Prisoners of War at Fukuoka Camp," May 23, 1946, JAG War Crimes Case File, Records of the Office of the Judge Advocate General (Army), Record Group 153, NARA.

23. US policy was outlined in "The War Department Policy with Respect to Labor of Prisoners of War," published January 10, 1943. Arnold Krammer, *Nazi Prisoners of War in America* (Briarcliff Manor, NY: Stein and Day, 1979), 81.

24. Among other jobs, German POWs in the United States picked cotton and worked in foundries and mines. Krammer, *Nazi Prisoners of War in America,* 88–94. In Kyushu, POWs manufactured landing wheels (Report no. XVII). "USSBS Report no. 15, the Japanese Aircraft Industry, Aircraft Division," May 1947, from "Japan Air Raids," https://www.scribd.com/doc/70239551/USSBS-Report-15-The-Japanese-Aircraft-Industry.

25. Lt. Col. M.D.S. Saunders, "Preliminary Report on P.O.W. Camps in Which Certain Allied Personnel Have Spent 3½ Yrs Captivity," September 8, 1945, from the Center for Research on Allied POWs under the Japanese, http://mansell.com/pow_resources/camplists/fukuoka/fuk_01_fukuoka/fukuoka_01/Saunders_report_1945-09-08.pdf.

26. Lt. Col. Martin Dustan Sedgwick Saunders, "Perpetuation of Testimony," JAG War Crimes Case File, Records of the Office of the Judge Advocate General (Army), Record Group 153, NARA.

27. Saunders, "Preliminary Report on P.O.W. Camps."

28. Saunders, "Preliminary Report on P.O.W. Camps."

29. Galixtro Garcia, "Perpetuation of Testimony," JAG War Crimes Case Files, Records of the Office of the Judge Advocate General (Army), Record Group 153, NARA.

30. Lt. Col. Martin Dunstan Sedgwick Saunders, "In the Matter of Japanese War Crimes and the Matter of Japanese War Crimes and the Matter of No. 1 Sub Camp Fukuoka Area," http://mansell.com/pow_resources/camplists/fukuoka/fuk_01_fukuoka/fukuoka_01/Page03.htm#Saunders.

31. Saunders, "Preliminary Report on P.O.W. Camps."

32. Utsumi, *Nihongun no horyo seisaku,* 296–297.

33. Utsumi, *Nihongun no horyo seisaku,* 295. Prisoner of War Punishment Provisions (*Furyo shobatsu kitei*), originally enacted in 1905, updated the regulations

from the Russo-Japanese War and sought to ensure the control of what was now massive numbers of POWs laboring.

34. "Affidavit of Odashima Tadashi," January 30, 1948, WOT Doc. no. 11104, SCAP Legal Section, Administrative Division, Miscellaneous Japanese File, 1942–1948, POW Camp Records, Records of Allied Operational and Occupation Headquarters, Record Group 331, NARA.

35. Utsumi, *Nihongun no horyo seisaku*, 296–297.

36. George Dowling, "Perpetuation of Testimony," JAG War Crimes Case File, Records of the Office of the Judge Advocate General (Army), Record Group 153, NARA. Dowling alleged that Bucktooth was "cross-eyed and always had a silly grin on his face and was always finding fault with us prisoners. My cap wasn't on just to suit him so he beat me over the head with his gun until the blood ran down my face. Then he smashed me in the face with his fist which knocked me out."

37. Tachikawa Kyoichi, "The Treatment of Prisoners of War by the Imperial Japanese Army and Navy Focusing on the Pacific War," *NIDS Security Reports*, no. 9 (2008): 77–78, http://www.nids.mod.go.jp/english/publication/kiyo/pdf/2008/bulletin_e2008_5.pdf.

38. Tachikawa, "The Treatment of Prisoners of War," 77–78.

39. Utsumi, *Nihongun no horyo seisaku*, 295–300. Koreans tell a different story: see Sarah Kovner, "Allied POWs in Korea: Life and Death during the Pacific War," in *The Dismantling of Japan's Empire in East Asia: Deimperialization, Postwar Legitimation, and Imperial Afterlife*, ed. Barak Kushner and Sherzod Muminov (New York: Routledge, 2017), 107–124.

40. Gerry Nolthenius, *Home by Christmas: Memoirs 1940-1948* (1998), as cited on http://mansell.com/pow_resources/camplists/fukuoka/fuk_01_fukuoka/fukuoka_01/Page09.htm.

41. The ratio of guards to prisoners was highest in 1942 and 1944. In 1942, each guard was responsible for 60 POWs; in 1943, 25; in 1944, 47; and in 1945, 23. Tachikawa, "The Treatment of Prisoners of War."

42. There is little contemporary evidence of such disobedience among Russians. See Chapter 1 for this history.

43. Doc. no. 1567A, "Extract from the Imperial Diet Proceedings of February 17th, 1943, concerning the Draft of Invasion of a Part of Military Service Law and These Other Matters," from the Dutch National Archives (DNA): *International Military Tribunal of the Far East: Papers from the International Prosecution*

*Section, Netherlands Division, and Judge BVA Röling,* https://www.archieven.nl
/nl/zoeken?mivast=0&mizig=210&miadt=298&micode=402_ENG&milang
=nl&mizk_alle=war%20crimes%20tribunal&miview=inv2.

44. Ultimately, 2,711 POWs were dealt with in military courts, 150 white POWs
were executed, and 64 were found guilty of escape attempts. Utsumi, *Nihongun
no horyo seisaku,* 295–300.

45. Utsumi, *Nihongun no horyo seisaku,* 194–198.

46. "Telegram," from Bern to DC, November 4, 1942, Project Number NND
765006, 921–922, Records of Foreign Service Posts of the Department of State,
Record Group 84, NARA.

47. "Interrogation of Odashima Tadashi," January 30, 1948, WOT Doc. no. 11104,
SCAP Legal Section, Administrative Division, Miscellaneous Japanese File,
1942–1948, POW Camp Records, Records of Allied Operational and Occupation Headquarters, Record Group 331, NARA.

48. Utsumi, *Nihongun no horyo seisaku,* 195–196.

49. Utsumi, *Nihongun no horyo seisaku,* chap. 4; McIntosh, Affidavits and Testi-
mony, JAG War Crimes Case File, Records of the Office of the Judge Advocate
General (Army), Record Group 153, NARA; "List of Personnel Punished for
Committing Personal Punishments," and "Investigation Chart concerning
Personal Punishments," SCAP Legal Section, Administrative Division, POW
Camp Records, Record Group 331, NARA.

50. Accounts disagree on when the move happened, probably because the official
move happened earlier than the POWs actually moved. For example, according
to the POW Research Network, the camp moved in September 1943. According
to POWs such as Lt. Col. Martin Saunders, the move occurred in November:
http://www.powresearch.jp/en/archive/camplist/index.html#fukuoka; Saunders,
"Perpetuation of Testimony."

51. Saunders, "Preliminary Report on P.O.W. Camps."

52. Judge Advocate Report Cont'd 2, Masato Hada Trial Records—JAG War
Crimes Case File, Records of the Office of the Judge Advocate General (Army),
Record Group 153, NARA, from the Center for Research on Allied POWs under
the Japanese: http://mansell.com/pow-index.html.

53. Felicia Yap, "Prisoners of War and Civilian Internees of the Japanese in British
Asia: The Similarities and Contrasts of Experience," *Journal of Contemporary
History* 47, no. 2 (2012): 317–346; "Affidavit," JAG War Crimes Case File, Records
of the Office of the Judge Advocate General (Army), Record Group 153, NARA.

54. Kostecki, "Affadavit," JAG War Crimes Case File, Records of the Office of the Judge Advocate General (Army), Record Group 153, NARA; Saunders, "Perpetuation of Testimony."

55. Tachikawa Kyoichi, "Kyūgun ni okeru horyo no toriatsukai: Taiheiyō sensō no jōkyō o chūshin ni," *Bōeikenkyūsho kiyō* 10, no. 1 (2007): 118.

56. Oosterhuis, "Diary," November 23, 1944, 192–197.

57. Telegram from Mouravieff to Geneva, July 25, 1944, G876 / vii, June–September 1944, ICRC.

58. Telegram from Mouravieff to Geneva, July 25, 1944.

59. "Report on Visit to Sub-camp no. 11 of Fukuoka War Prisoners Camp, July 27th, 1944," DNA.

60. "Report on Visit to Sub-camp no. 11."

61. Oosterhuis, "Diary," December 20, 1944, 198–204.

62. Oosterhuis, "Diary," December 20, 1944, 198–204.

63. Oosterhuis, "Diary," December 20, 1944, 198–204.

64. Oosterhuis, "Diary," January 1, 1945, 204–205.

65. Oosterhuis,"Diary," January 2, 1945, 205–206.

66. Oosterhuis, "Diary," December 20, 1944, 198–204.

67. Oosterhuis, "Diary," January 2, 1945, 205–206.

68. Oosterhuis, "Diary," September 4, 1945, 206–208.

69. As of August 15, 1945, Fukuoka 1 held 381 captives, both POWs and civilians (the civilians were mostly American contractors from Wake): 140 British, 153 Americans, 58 Dutch, 28 Australians, 1 Norwegian, and 1 Canadian. List of Hukuoka Camp Strength as of August 15, 1945, SCAP Legal Section, Administrative Division, Miscellaneous Japanese File, Records of Allied Operational and Occupation Headquarters, Record Group 331, NARA.

70. "Saunders Affidavit," Record Group 153, Entry 143, Box 1035, NARA.

71. E. Carl Engelhart, unpublished manuscript, 242, E. Carl Engelhart Papers, 1950, US Army War College, Carlisle, Pennsylvania (USAWC).

72. Engelhart, unpublished manuscript, 245.

73. Engelhart, unpublished manuscript, 242–243.

74. William J. Fossey to Paul Geissler, "Crimes and Atrocities Committed by Japanese on American Prisoners of War" (notarized), September 25, 1946, http://mansell.com/pow_resources/camplists/fukuoka/fuk_01_fukuoka /fukuoka_01/USAffD-H.htm#Fossey.

75. Robert McIntosh, "Perpetuation of the Testimony of James Robert McIntosh, in the Matter of the Atrocities Committed by the Japanese to Allied Interned POWs," JAG War Crimes Case File, Records of the Office of the Judge Advocate General (Army), Record Group 153, NARA.

76. Engelhart, unpublished manuscript, 245.

77. Gerry Noltenius, "Home by Christmas: Memoirs 1942–1945," http://mansell .com/pow_resources/camplists/fukuoka/fuk_01_fukuoka/fukuoka_01/Page07 .htm.

78. McIntosh, "Perpetuation of the Testimony of James Robert McIntosh."

79. McIntosh, "Perpetuation of the Testimony of James Robert McIntosh."

80. Henry Forsberg, "Perpetuation of Testimony," JAG War Crimes Case File, Records of the Office of the Judge Advocate General (Army), Record Group 153, NARA.

81. Forsberg, "Perpetuation of Testimony."

82. North, "Perpetuation of Testimony of William D. North"

83. North, "Perpetuation of Testimony of William D. North."

84. Fossey to Geissler, "Crimes and Atrocities Committed by Japanese on American Prisoners of War."

85. Fossey to Geissler, "Crimes and Atrocities Committed by Japanese on American Prisoners of War."

86. Kenneth Wheeler, "Affidavit of Kenneth R. Wheeler, Lieut," November 26, 1945, http://mansell.com/pow_resources/camplists/fukuoka/fuk_01_fukuoka /fukuoka_01/USAffR-W.htm#Wheeler.

87. "Clemency Report," US Embassy, Japan, Japanese War Crimes Cases: Sanematsu Yuzuru to Saito Kyosuke, Records of Foreign Service Posts of the Department of State, Switzerland, Record Group 84, NARA.

88. "Canadian Government Wishes to Be Informed re Parole or Clemency of This Offender, Parole Documents," n.d., US Embassy, Japan, Japanese War Crimes Cases: Sanematsu Yuzuru to Saito Kyosuke, Records of Foreign Service Posts of the Department of State, Switzerland, Record Group 84, NARA.

89. "Current Intelligence Study Number 19," OSS, R&A Branch, May 18, 1945, https://www.cia.gov/library/readingroom/docs/DOC_0000709790.pdf.

90. "Affidavit of Odashima Tadashi."

91. Tachikawa, "Kyūgun ni okeru horyo no toriatsukai," 117–118.

92. Kumano Iso, *Kyūshū Daigaku seitai kaibō jiken: 70-Nen-me no shinjitsu* (Tokyo: Iwanami Shoten, 2015), 6–7, 18–20.

93. Kumano, *Kyūshū Daigaku seitai kaibou jiken,* 6–7, 18–20; Tōno Toshio, *Omei: "Kyūdai seitai kaibō jiken" no shinsō* (Tokyo: Bungei Shunshū, 1979), 27–42.

94. Kumano, *Kyūshū Daigaku seitai kaibou jiken,* 18–30; Tōno, *Omei,* 42–45.

95. Kumano, *Kyūshū Daigaku seitai kaibou jiken,* 24–47.

96. Kamisaka Fuyuko, *"Seitai kaibō" jjiken: B 29 hikō-shi, igaku jikken no shinsō* (Tokyo: PHP Kenkyūjo, 2005), 100.

97. Tachikawa, "Kyūgun ni okeru horyo no toriatsukai," 117–119; Hata Ikuhiko, Sase Masamori, and Tsuneishi Keiichi, *Sekai sensō hanzai jiten* (Tokyo: Bungei Shunjū, 2002), 196–197; Kamisaka Fuyuko, *Sabakareta sensō hanzai: Sugamo Purizun 13-gō teppi* (Tokyo: PHP Kenkyujo, 2004), 228–232, 238–239.

98. Tachikawa, "Kyūgun ni okeru horyo no toriatsukai," 119; Kosuge Nobuko and Nagai Hitoshi, *B-C-kyū sensō hanzai saiban* (Tokyo: Nihon Tosho Sentā, 1996), 61, 126–127; Kobayashi Hirotada, *"Tōbō"—Aburayama jiken' senpan kokuhaku-roku* (Tokyo: Mainichi Shinbunsha, 2006), 100–105.

99. Tachikawa, "Kyūgun ni okeru horyo no toriatsukai," 119; Kobayashi, *"Tōbō,"* 140, 107, 125–130; Kosuge and Nagai, *B-C-kyū sensō hanzai saiban,* 131–134.

100. Furyo Johokyoku, "Personnel of Detainees in POW Camps," in Strahler, letter to ICRC, October 11, 1945, G8 / 76 / xi, September–December 1945, ICRC.

101. Burton C. Ellis, "Affidavit," December 5, 1946, before Arthur Fry, http://man sell.com/pow_resources/camplists/fukuoka/fuk_01_fukuoka/fukuoka_01/USA ffD-H.htm#Ellis.

102. Edwin B. Moss, "Perpetuation of Testimony," August 20, 1946, http://www .mansell.com/pow_resources/camplists/fukuoka/fuk_01_fukuoka/fukuoka_01 /USAffJ-P.htm#North.

103. Tachikawa, "The Treatment of Prisoners of War," 59.

104. Approved and sanctioned by Tamura and Lt. Gen. Shibayama, Vice Minister of War. The next draft was submitted to the Secretariat, then issued in the name

of the Vice Minister of War. RM 2257, June 17, 1945, addressed to army commanders in Japan, Manchuria, and Korea. Odajima Tadashi, undated, "Circumstances Leading to Draft of Riku-a-mitsu no. 2257 and POW Management Bureau of War Ministry Questionnaire on Abuses," SCAP Legal Section, Administrative Division, Miscellaneous Japanese File, 1942–1948, POW Camp Records, Records of Allied Operational and Occupation Headquarters, Record Group 331, NARA.

105. Toward the beginning of March 1945, Lt. Gen. Tamura ordered the drafting of a memorandum that specified how POWs should be treated after Allied landings in Japan and Manchuria, if air raids became more intense. This document was written with reference to Mitsu 1633, which specified that all means should be taken to prevent the enemy from getting POWs. Thus they should be transferred, as long as labor was not affected. If enemy attacks arose, POWs should be liberated and "positively no atrocity such as killing and injuring shall be committed."

106. Mitsu 1633, Odajima Tadashi, June 17, 1945, "Memorandum on Japanese Policy toward POWs as War Situation Intensifies," Army policy—Riku-A-Mitsu 2257, SCAP Legal Section, Administrative Division, Miscellaneous Japanese File, 1942–1948, POW Camp Records, Records of Allied Operational and Occupation Headquarters, Record Group 331, NARA.

107. For example, 900 were moved on May 15, 1945; 465 were moved on March 30, 1945; and 455 and 600 were moved on June 4, 1945. In the Tokyo-Yokohama area, perhaps 3,000 to 4,000 POWs were moved to avoid bombing.

108. John W. Dower, *Embracing Defeat: Japan in the Wake of WWII* (New York: W. W. Norton/New Press, 1999), 92.

## 7. Endings and Beginnings

1. Speech by Emperor Hirohito accepting the Potsdam Declaration, radio broadcast, August 14, 1945, transmitted by Dōmei and recorded by the Federal Communications Commission, https://www.mtholyoke.edu/acad/intrel/hirohito.htm.

2. Mark Selden, "A Forgotten Holocaust: US Bombing Strategy, the Destruction of Japanese Cities and the American Way of War from World War II to Iraq," *Asia-Pacific Journal* 5, no. 5 (2007): 13; John Dower, *Embracing Defeat: Japan in the Wake of World War II* (New York: W. W. Norton/New Press, 1999), 45–47. On air raids, see the encyclopedic website run by Cary Karacas, David Fedman, Eri Tsuji, and Bret Fisk, http://www.japanairraids.org.

3. In Korea, on August 14, newspapers printed handbills and the radio announced that a great declaration was coming on August 15 at noon. Excerpt from the *Korean Times* (undated), found in "Documents concerning Cessation of Hostilities," 2 Loyals, Kingsley & Strange Collection, 1939–1945, Box 8, Fulwood Barracks.

4. Dower, *Embracing Defeat,* 48–53.

5. Stephen Connor, "Side-Stepping Geneva: Japanese Troops under British Control, 1945–7," *Journal of Contemporary History* 45, no. 2 (2010): 389–405. Connor argues that the idea came from Japanese diplomats in Europe reported to Tokyo on Germans and Surrendered Enemy Personnel.

6. Connor, "Side-Stepping Geneva," 398.

7. Connor, "Side-Stepping Geneva," 401–402.

8. Lori Watt, "The 'Disposition of Japanese Civilians': American Wartime Planning for the Colonial Japanese," *Diplomatic History* 41, no. 2 (2017): 392–414; thirty-five-page draft convention on the repatriation of nonmilitary personnel, July 30, 1946, ICRC Documentation to 17th International Red Cross Conference, Records of the Office of the Provost Marshal General, Record Group 389, US National Archives and Records Administration, College Park, Maryland (hereafter NARA).

9. "Relief of Prisoners of War and Internees," in *Reports of General MacArthur: MacArthur in Japan: The Occupation, Military Phase,* prepared by his General Staff, 1966, facsimile reprint (Washington DC: 1994). https://history.army.mil/books/wwii/MacArthur%20Reports/MacArthur%20V1%20Sup/ch4.htm.

10. Commander in Chief, US Pacific Fleet (CINPAC) to Chief of Naval Operations, "CINPAC Report of Surrender and Occupation of Japan, February 11, 1946," 134, https://apps.dtic.mil/dtic/tr/fulltext/u2/a438971.pdf.

11. United States Armed Forces in Korea (USAFIK), "History of the United States Armed Forces in Korea," compiled under the supervision of Harold Larsen [*sic*], chief historian, Tokyo and Seoul, 1947, 1948, manuscript in the Office of the Chief of Military History, Washington, DC, 7–8/301–302, n15, https://history.army.mil/books/wwii/MacArthur%20Reports/MacArthur%20V1%20Sup/ch4.htm.

12. Operation "Blacklist," https://apps.dtic.mil/dtic/tr/fulltext/u2/a438112.pdf.

13. "Memorandum," F. Sinclair to F. Shedden, August 27, 1945, "Appendix A: Recovery of Australian Prisoners of War Held by Japan," A816, 54/301/294, National Archives of Australia (NAA).

14. CINPAC to Chief of Naval Operations, "CINPAC Report of Surrender and Occupation of Japan," 2.

15. CINPAC to Chief of Naval Operations, "CINPAC Report of Surrender and Occupation of Japan," 10.

16. CINPAC to Chief of Naval Operations, "CINPAC Report of Surrender and Occupation of Japan," 19.

17. CINPAC to Chief of Naval Operations, "CINPAC Report of Surrender and Occupation of Japan," 19.

18. CINPAC to Chief of Naval Operations, "CINPAC Report of Surrender and Occupation of Japan," 21.

19. By March 1945, the Allies, including the British and the Americans, were aware of this and protested to the Japanese government. The British believed it was a "set purpose" that caused the Japanese to locate camps near docks, warehouses, war factories, railway marshalling yards, and other military objectives on the Thai-Burma Railway. March 14, 1945, British Legation to Foreign Interests Division, US Legation, Bern, American Interest Section, Supplemental General Records, 1942–1945, Foreign Service Posts of the Department of State, Switzerland, Record Group 84, NARA.

20. The Navy supported these plans and agreed to support them with permanently stationed surface vessels on the flight routes.

21. CINPAC to Chief of Naval Operations, "CINPAC Report of Surrender and Occupation of Japan," 26–27.

22. Bilfinger to ICRC, January 20, 1947, G8 / 76 xiv, July–September 1946, ICRC.

23. Marcel Junod, "The Hiroshima Disaster, a Doctor's Account," International Committee of the Red Cross, September 12, 2005, https://www.icrc.org/eng/resources/documents/misc/hiroshima-junod-120905.htm.

24. Bilfinger to Junod, September 2, 1945, G8 / 76 / x, June–August 1945, ICRC.

25. Bilfinger to Junod, August 31, 1945, G8 / 76 / x, June–August 1945, ICRC.

26. Bilfinger to Junod, August 28, 1945, G8 / 76 / x, June–August 1945, ICRC.

27. Bilfinger to Junod, June 12, 1945, G8 / 76 / x, June–August 1945, ICRC.

28. Bilfinger to Junod, August 28, 1945, G8 / 76 / x, June–August 1945, ICRC.

29. Bilfinger to Junod, June 12, 1945, G8 / 76 / x, June–August 1945, ICRC.

30. To Chief Delegate, August 28, 1945, Geneva G8 / 76 / x, June–August 1945, ICRC.

31. Bilfinger to Junod, n.d., G8 / 76 / x, June–August 1945, ICRC.

32. The Swiss made early observations of just how much Japan had changed. They tried to help the Americans with what they knew, and complained at how little the Americans used them. Bilfinger to Junod, September 6, 1945, G8 / 76 / x, June–August 1945, ICRC.

33. Bilfinger to Junod, September 6, 1945, G8 / 76 / x, June–August 1945, ICRC.

34. Bilfinger to Junod, September 12, 1945, G8 / 76 / x, June–August 1945, ICRC.

35. Christopher Bayly and Tim Harper, *Forgotten Wars: Freedom and Revolution in Southeast Asia* (Cambridge, MA: Belknap Press of Harvard University Press, 2007), 3.

36. Bilfinger to Junod, September 12, 1945, G8 / 76 / x, June–August 1945, ICRC.

37. When Bilfinger arrived at headquarters at the New Osaka Hotel, he found that the last of the Osaka sector camps were just in the process of completing evacuation. Bilfinger to Junod, September 12, 1945, G8 / 76 / x, June–August 1945, ICRC.

38. The plan was for US Army Forces in the Pacific (AFPAC) to operate and train liaison, recovery, and final processing teams; the Recovered Personnel Detachment organized the teams.

39. A joint Army-Navy conference East Honshu, West Honshu, North Honshu, Hokkaido. Southern Honshu, Shikoku, and Kyushu would come later.

40. CINPAC to Chief of Naval Operations, "CINPAC Report of Surrender and Occupation of Japan," 21.

41. James F. McGlincy, "Visitors View Tokyo's Ruins: Blasted City's People Appear Still to Be Suffering from Shock," *Los Angeles Times,* August 31, 1945, 2.

42. *Reports of General MacArthur, MacArthur in Japan: The Occupation, Military Phase,* prepared by the General Staff (Washington, DC: U.S. Government Printing Office, 1966), https://history.army.mil/books/wwii/MacArthur%20 Reports/MacArthur%20V1%20Sup/ch4_notes.htm#e40.

43. *Reports of General MacArthur, MacArthur in Japan.*

44. *Reports of General MacArthur, MacArthur in Japan.*

45. *Reports of General MacArthur, MacArthur in Japan,* 113. Daily radio reports were sent to the Commander-in-Chief United States Army Forces in the

Pacific, Tokyo, Commander-in-Chief Army Forces Manila, and the Attorney General in Washington, DC. Relatives in the United States and other UN countries found out within a few days. The challenge for Recovery Teams was identifying UN POWs eligible for evacuation and recovery. According to guidelines, a UN POW was a "person who was an Allied soldier or accompanying person," except for China, a serviceman of a Japan-occupied country serving a UN country (Dutch, Vietnamese), a member of an armed force of a country occupied by Japan who had been serving the UN country, or a member of the merchant marine. This was not the same set of people considered POWs by the Geneva Conventions or by Japan.

46. *Reports of General MacArthur: MacArthur in Japan.*

47. War Department data were obtained by supplemental processing teams aboard the hospital ships, *Reports of General MacArthur: MacArthur in Japan.*

48. Alfred A. Weinstein, MD, *Barbed-Wire Surgeon* (1948; repr., Atlanta: Deeds, 2014), 340.

49. Weinstein, *Barbed-Wire Surgeon*, 340–341.

50. CINPAC to Chief of Naval Operations, "CINPAC Report of Surrender and Occupation of Japan," 51–52.

51. CINPAC to Chief of Naval Operations, "CINPAC Report of Surrender and Occupation of Japan," 50.

52. PFC J. W. Gianes, "Log of Recovery Team no. 9," September 12–November 5, 1945, Declassified NND 883078 Philippine Archives Collection, Records of the Adjutant General's Office, Individual Rosters, Japanese POW Information, 85–108, Military Agency Records, the War Department and the Army Records, Records of the Adjutant General's Office, 1917–, Record Group 407, NARA.

53. Gianes, "Log of Recovery Team no. 9."

54. Gianes, "Log of Recovery Team no. 9."

55. "List of Fukuoka POW Camp Strength as of August 14, 1945," August 14, 1945, SCAP Legal Section, Records of Allied Operational and Occupation Headquarters, Record Group 331, NARA.

56. Gianes, "Log of Recovery Team no. 9."

57. The recovery team next checked lists of ashes against Japanese "list of the dead." They failed to find those of nine flyers, but eventually found the remains of forty-eight British and Dutch soldiers in a temple.

58. CINPAC to Chief of Naval Operations, "CINPAC Report of Surrender and Occupation of Japan," 115.

59. CINPAC to Chief of Naval Operations, "CINPAC Report of Surrender and Occupation of Japan," n3.

60. HQ Eighth US Army, Office of the Surgeon, Medical Report on the Occupation of Japan for September 1945, Annex 4.

61. According to "Blacklist," there were 36,000 Allied POWs in around 140 camps. The numbers were generally correct in the end.

62. (1) Rad 060535 / z, CinC BPF to CinC Hong Kong, 7 Sep 55; (2) Rad 081117 / z, CinC BritPacFlt to COMGEN AFWESPAC, 9 Sep 45; (3) Rad 060533 / z, SHA No. 404 to GHQ Manila, 9 Sep 45; (4) Rad 140211 / z, VABPF to COM 3rd FLT, 15 Sep 45. In G-3 GHQ Adm 383.

63. "1648 Allied Recovered Prisoners of War evacuated by air to Okinawa 7 Sep 45 signed Eichelberger" (Rad 71531, Eighth A ADV to Navy Okinawa, 9 Sep 45. In G-3 GHQ Adm 383.6).

64. CINPAC to Chief of Naval Operations, "CINPAC Report of Surrender and Occupation of Japan."

65. Col. Wibb E. Cooper, "Medical Report," Folder: Jinsen, Korea, Records of the Office of the Provost Marshal General, Record Group 389, NARA.

66. A. V. Toze, "Private Papers of A. V. Toze," August 18, 1945, typescript, IWM.

67. Guy Round, "The Road to Singapore," unpublished manuscript, 367, AWM.

68. United States Armed Forces in Korea (USAFIK), *Chuhan Migunsa: HUSAFIK* (Seoul: Tolbegae, 1988), 4, courtesy of Lori Watt.

69. USAFIK, *Chuhan Migunsa,* 51–52.

70. USAFIK, *Chuhan Migunsa,* 50–53, 51.

71. USAFIK, *Chuhan Migunsa,* 40.

72. Extract from Reports of Recovered Personnel Teams, Keijō POW Camp 1, Record Group 389, Entry 460A, Box 2134, Records of the Office of the Provost Marshal General, American POW Information Bureau Records Branch, General Subject File, 1942–46, Camps: Korea to Netherlands East Indies NARA.

73. USAFIK, *Chuhan Migunsa,* 13.

74. USAFIK, *Chuhan Migunsa,* 13.

75. CINPAC to Chief of Naval Operations, "CINPAC Report of Surrender and Occupation of Japan," 112; USAFIK, "History of the United States Armed Forces in Korea."

76. ["Our Own Correspondent"], "Americans In Korea," *Times* (London), September 10, 1945, 4.

77. "Total Military POWs Recovered in Korea," Record Group 389, Entry 460A, Box 2134, Records of the Office of the Provost Marshal General, American POW Information Bureau Records Branch, General Subject File, 1942–1946, Camps: Korea to Netherlands East Indies, NARA.

78. James O'Connor, "U.S. Troops Land in Korea," *The Argus* (Melbourne, Australia), September 10, 1945, 16.

79. USAFIK, *Chuhan Migunsa*, 7.

80. "Held by Japan," *The West Australian* (Perth), June 28, 1947, 5.

81. USAFIK, "History of the United States Armed Forces in Korea," n29.

82. USAFIK, "History of the United States Armed Forces in Korea," 2, 52.

83. CINPAC to Chief of Naval Operations, "CINPAC Report of Surrender and Occupation of Japan," 114 for Korea; USAFIK, "History of the United States Armed Forces in Korea," 2.

84. CINPAC to Chief of Naval Operations, "CINPAC Report of Surrender and Occupation of Japan," 126.

85. Rana Mitter, *Forgotten Ally: China's World War II, 1937–1945* (Boston: Houghton Mifflin Harcourt, 2013), 363.

86. CINPAC to Chief of Naval Operations, "CINPAC Report of Surrender and Occupation of Japan," 120–123.

87. Chaen Yoshio, ed., *Furyo jōhōkyoku Furyo toriatsukai no kiroku: Tsuketari, Kaigun Heigakkō "Kokusaihō"* (Tokyo: Fuji Shuppan, 1992). CINPAC made radically different estimates (CINPAC to Chief of Naval Operations, "CINPAC Report of Surrender and Occupation of Japan," 120–123, 126).

88. CINPAC to Chief of Naval Operations, "CINPAC Report of Surrender and Occupation of Japan," 124.

89. CINPAC to Chief of Naval Operations, "CINPAC Report of Surrender and Occupation of Japan," 126–132.

90. Included Java and Sumatra and Vietnam south of 16th parallel.

91. Connor, "Side-Stepping Geneva," 390–393.

92. Connor, "Side-Stepping Geneva," 391.

93. William J. Rust, "Operation Iceberg: Transitioning into CIA; The Strategic Services Unit in Indonesia," *Studies in Intelligence* 60, no. 1 (2016): 5.

94. Rust, "Operation Iceberg," 1–22.

95. R. P. W. Havers, *Reassessing the Japanese Prisoner of War Experience: The Changi POW Camp, Singapore, 1942–5* (London: RoutledgeCurzon, 2003), 165.

96. Suzanne Hall, "Politics of Prisoner of War Recovery: SOE and the Burma-Thailand Railway during WWII," *Intelligence and National Security* 17, no. 2 (2002): 69. The Thai Resistance movement was led by Field Marshal Phibun Songkram. During the war Songkram had been in contact with both the British Special Operations Executive and the Office of Strategic Services and assisted them. By August 1945, some 90,000 guerrillas helped facilitate the POW recovery program with their knowledge of terrain and language. Hall, "Politics of Prisoner of War Recovery," 68.

97. Hall, "Politics of Prisoner of War Recovery," 51–80. Hall is laudatory about the SOE.

98. Some captives lacked information, and for others escape was arduous.

99. Hall, "Politics of Prisoner of War Recovery," 70–72.

100. Hall, "Politics of Prisoner of War Recovery," 10, n134, 72.

101. "Singapore Is British Again!," *Straits Times*, September 7, 1945, Cambridge Digital Archive from Changi and Sime Road Civilian Internment Camps, RCMS 103 / 12 / 15 / 4 / 5, http://cudl.lib.cam.ac.uk/view/MS-RCMS-00103-00012 -00015/1795.

102. Bayly and Harper, *Forgotten Wars*, 52–53.

103. "Japanese in Malaysia Surrender at Singapore," *Straits Times*, September 13, 1945, http://eresources.nlb.gov.sg/newspapers/Digitised/Article/straitstimes 19450913-1.2.2.

104. Bayly and Harper, *Forgotten Wars*, 53.

105. "Japanese in Malaysia Surrender at Singapore."

106. Bryce Abraham, "Bringing Them All Back Home," Australian War Memorial, SVSS paper, 2015, 14–15.

107. Abraham, "Bringing Them All Back Home," 14–15.

108. Rust, "Operation Iceberg," 6.

109. "Medical Appreciation concerning Aust R.P.'s Now Concentrating in Singapore," Reports from Singapore by Lt. Col. G. Gibson and Lt. Col. Glyn White, "Article on Return of Ex Prisoners of War," 1945 AWM 54 555 / 2 / 2 DPI, AWM.

110. Nederlands Instituut voor Militaire Historie, Ministerie van Defensie, "Pamflet getitled Allied Prisoners / Geallieerde gevangen," Official Netherlands and Netherlands Indies Press Agency, untitled press report, September 13, 1945, 846, 18 / A / 1-11, 18 / 2.

111. "Medical Appreciation concerning Aust R.P.'s Now Concentrating in Singapore."

112. "Medical Appreciation concerning Aust R.P.'s Now Concentrating in Singapore"; "Article on Return of Ex Prisoners of War."

113. "Medical Appreciation concerning Aust R.P.'s Now Concentrating in Singapore."

114. "Medical Appreciation concerning Aust R.P.'s Now Concentrating in Singapore."

115. Bayly and Harper, *Forgotten Wars*, 6, 111, 123.

116. Connor, "Side-Stepping Geneva," 399.

117. Connor, "Side-Stepping Geneva," 403.

118. Bayly and Harper, *Forgotten Wars*, 271.

119. Rust, "Operation Iceberg," 1–22.

120. "Pamflet getitled Allied Prisoners / Geallieerde gevangen," August 28, 1945, 846, folder 18 / 1, Nederlands Instituut voor Militaire Historie, Ministerie van Defensie, the Hague, Netherlands.

121. "The Imperial Japanese Army Proclamation to the Allied Prisoners of War and Civilian Internees in Java, 6 September 2605 [1945]," Overzichtkaart van krijgsgevangenkampen in Japan z.d., 8 / 59, Commander in Chief of the Imperial Army in Java, Nederlands Instituut voor Militaire Historie, Ministerie van Defensie, the Hague, Netherlands.

122. "Overzichtkaart van krijgsgevangenkampen in Japan z.d., 8 / 59 "Proclamation to All Prisoners of War and Internees on Java," September 6, 2605 [1945], 8 / 59, Nederlands Instituut voor Militaire Historie, Ministerie van Defensie, the Hague, Netherlands.

123. Bayly and Harper, *Forgotten Wars,* 167.

124. Bayly and Harper, *Forgotten Wars,* 168–170; Rust, "Operation Iceberg," 7.

125. Rust, "Operation Iceberg," 6.

126. In Sŭnggab, "Waenomdŭl sone chungnŭni nararŭl wihae ssautaga chukketta," in *Nambang kihaeng: Kangje tongwŏn kunsok sugijip,* ed. Yi Seil et. al (Seoul: Ilche Kangjŏmha Kangje Tongwŏn P'ihae Chinsang Kyumyŏng Wiwŏnhoe, 2008).

127. Opgetsled statements by the Netherlands Indies Red Cross Society of Allied Prisoner of War and Internees in Far East, May 1945, 023 / 6, Nederlands Instituut voor Militarie Historie, Ministerie van Defensie, The Hague, Netherlands.

128. Connor, "Side-Stepping Geneva," 400.

129. Rust, "Operation Iceberg," 16.

130. Connor, "Side-Stepping Geneva," 400.

131. Bayly and Harper, *Forgotten Wars,* 168–170.

132. Nationaal Archief, "RAPWI, Recovery of Allied Prisoners of War and Internees," http://www.en.afscheidvanindie.nl/archieven-onderwerpen-rapwi.aspx. On January 26, 1946, RAPWI disbanded and Dutch relief Allied Military Administration-Civil Affairs Branch (AMACAB) filled in.

133. Rust, "Operation Iceberg," 14.

134. Bayly and Harper, *Forgotten Wars,* 61.

135. Connor, "Side-Stepping Geneva," 395.

136. Bayley and Harper, *Forgotten Wars,* 240.

## 8. Undue Process

1. Commander in Chief, US Pacific Fleet and Pacific Ocean Areas (CINPAC), to Chief of Naval Operations, "CINPAC Report of Surrender and Occupation of Japan," February 11, 1946, 51, http://www.mansell.com/Resources/special_files /FOLD3/CINCPAC%20Report%20of%20Surrender%20and%20Occupation%20 of%20Japan%201946-02-11.pdf.

2. Leland Chamberlain, interview with author, May 3, 2018, Albuquerque, New Mexico.

3. "Affidavit of Odashima, Tadashi," January 30, 1948, WOT Doc. no. 11104, SCAP Legal Section, Administrative Division, Miscellaneous Japanese File, 1942–1948,

POW Camp Records, Records of Allied Operational and Occupation Headquarters, Record Group 331, US National Archives and Records Administration, College Park, Maryland (hereafter NARA). The War Ministry sent a
telegram directing the destruction of confidential documents. It was left up to
specific command, and the POWIB chief decided personally what to burn. The
International Military Tribunal for the Far East, "Burning of Documents
June 2, 1947," http://imtfe.law.virginia.edu/collections/tavenner/5/1/burning
-documents-june-2-1947.

4. Sandra Wilson, Robert Cribb, Beatrice Trefalt, and Dean Aszkielowicz, *Japanese War Criminals: The Politics of Justice after the Second World War* (New
York: Columbia University Press, 2017), 53.

5. Riku-mitsu 5931, in *Furyo ni kansuru shorui tsuzuri* (September 1945), unpaginated, Bōeishō Bōei Kenkyūsho Senshi Kenkyū Sentā.

6. Riku-mitsu 5931.

7. Nagai Hitoshi, "Tamura Hiroshi chūjō 'Kenkyū bibōroku' ni kansuru oboegaki,"
in *Tōkyō Saiban shiryō: Furyo Jōhōkyoku kankei bunsho,* ed. Utsumi Aiko and
Nagai Hitoshi (Tokyo: Gendai Shiryō Shuppan, 1999), 50.

8. Chaen Yoshio, ed., *Furyo Jōhōkyoku, Furyo toriatsukai no kiroku: Tsuketari,
Kaigun Heigakkō "Kokusaihō"* (Tokyo: Fuji Shuppan, 1992), 196; Hara Takeshi
and Yasuoka Akio, eds., *Nihon Riku-Kaigun jiten* (Tokyo: Shin Jinbutsu
Ōraisha, 1997), 171.

9. On May 14, 1946, they were shipped to Japan.

10. Trial record, Yokohama no. T187, June 26, 1946, Legal Section, Administrative
Division, Records of Allied Operational and Occupation Headquarters, Record
Group 331, NARA. The first commander in Fukuoka, Col. Sugasawa Iju, was
tried at Yokohama, held responsible for those he commanded, and hanged.

11. Wilson et al., *Japanese War Criminals,* 74; Franziska Seraphim, "Carceral Geo-
graphies of Japan's Vanishing Empire: War Criminals' Prisons in Asia," in
*The Dismantling of Japan's Empire in East Asia: Deimperialization, Postwar
Legitimation and Imperial Afterlife,* ed. Barak Kushner and Sherzod Muminov
(London: Routledge, 2017), 134.

12. Margherita Straehler, "War Criminals," February 8, 1946, CR 240–241, CR
240–242, D AO Japon 1-047, War Criminals in Japan, 9/14/1945–5/11/1946,
International Committee of the Red Cross Archives (hereafter ICRC).

13. Chaen, *Furyo Jōhō-kyoku.*

14. "Office Memo," December 1945, G8/76/xi, September–December 1945, ICRC.

15. Affidavits could be of varying quality, dependent as they were on the questions being asked, the circumstances in which they were asked, and the goals of both the interviewer and the interviewee.

16. "Seek POW Testimony on Jap War Crimes," *Newsday,* August 15, 1946, 10.

17. Wilson et al., *Japanese War Criminals,* 53.

18. "Additional Arrests Ordered," December 10, 1945, CR 240–241, CR 240–242, D AO Japon 1-047, War Criminals in Japan, 9/14/1945–5/11/1946, ICRC.

19. Wilson et al., *Japanese War Criminals,* 63.

20. John R. Pritchard, "The Gift of Clemency Following British War Crimes Trials in the Far East, 1946–1948," *Criminal Law Forum* 7, no. 1 (1996): 15, 20.

21. The IMTEE laid out three kinds of offenses: crimes against peace, war crimes, and crimes against humanity. Scholars and citizens argue over whether these trials were "victor's justice." On the international military tribunal in Tokyo that tried the twenty-eight men accused of planning and executing the war (Class A), see Yuma Totani, *The Tokyo War Crimes Trial: The Pursuit of Justice in the Wake of World War II* (Cambridge, MA: Harvard University Press, 2008). On the trials that judged conventional war crimes (Class B) and crimes against humanity (Class C), see Barak Kushner, "Pawns of Empire: Postwar Taiwan, Japan and the Dilemma of War Crimes," *Japan Studies* 30, no. 1 (2010): 111–113; Barak Kushner, *Men to Devils, Devils to Men: Japanese War Crimes and Chinese Justice* (Cambridge, MA: Harvard University Press, 2015); Sandra Wilson, "Koreans in the Trials of Japanese War Crimes Suspects," in *Debating Collaboration and Complicity in War Crimes Trials in Asia, 1945–1956,* ed. Kirsten von Lingen (New York: Springer Berlin Heidelberg, 2017), 19–40; and Wilson et al., *Japanese War Criminals.* Von Lingen and Cribb point out that it is all in how you measure: the trials may have been a bargain compared to the International Criminal Tribunals for the former Yugoslavia and Rwanda, and the International Criminal Court. See Kerstin von Lingen and Robert Cribb, "Justice in the Time of Turmoil: War Crimes Trials in Asia in the Context of Decolonization and Cold War," in *War Crimes Trials in the Wake of Decolonization and Cold War in Asia, 1945–1956: Justice in Time of Turmoil,* ed. Kerstin von Lingen (Cham, Switzerland: Palgrave Macmillan, 2016), 21.

22. The Australians ran 310 trials, beginning November 20, 1945, and ending April 9, 1951. David Sissons, "Sources on Australian Investigations into Japanese War Crimes in the Pacific," *Journal of the Australian War Memorial,* no. 30 (1997), https://www.awm.gov.au/articles/journal/j30/sissons.

23. Estimates in Wilson et al. derive from a 1973 estimate by *Hōmu daijin kanbō shihō hōsei chōsabu* together with archival estimates. See Wilson et al., *Japanese War Criminals*, 78–79. Kushner discusses the politics of the 1973 book in *Men to Devils, Devils to Men*, 231–232.

24. Office of the Resident Commissioner of the Philippines to the United States, "Report on the Destruction of Manila and Japanese Atrocities, February 1945" (Washington DC, 1945); Wolfgang Form, "Colonization and Postcolonial Justice: US and Philippine War Crime Trials in Manila after the Second World War," in von Lingen, *War Crimes Trials in the Wake of Decolonization*, 143–166.

25. Form, "Colonization and Postcolonial Justice," 145.

26. Form, "Colonization and Postcolonial Justice," 145.

27. Wilson et al., *Japanese War Criminals*, 116; Form, "Colonization and Postcolonial Justice," 149.

28. Allan A. Ryan, *Yamashita's Ghost: War Crimes, MacArthur's Justice, and Command Accountability* (Lawrence: University Press of Kansas, 2012), 134.

29. Ryan, *Yamashita's Ghost*, 183–188, 223–224.

30. Ryan, *Yamashita's Ghost*, 184–188.

31. Ryan, *Yamashita's Ghost*, 61–65, quotation at 65.

32. Yuma Totani, *Justice in Asia and the Asia Pacific Region, 1945–1952: Allied War Crimes Prosecutions* (New York: Cambridge University Press, 2015), 33.

33. Ironically, the United States failed to use it for itself, where it would have likely justified the conviction of generals in Vietnam and Abu Ghraib. Yet it has been added to the Geneva Conventions and used by international tribunals for the former Yugoslavia and adopted by the International Criminal Court. Ryan, *Yamashita's Ghost*, preface.

34. Ryan, *Yamashita's Ghost*, 310–311. This means "a personal dereliction of duty."

35. As quoted in Ryan, *Yamashita's Ghost*, 29.

36. Form, "Colonization and Postcolonial Justice," 165–166.

37. Form, "Colonization and Postcolonial Justice," 152.

38. Form, "Colonization and Postcolonial Justice," 153.

39. Form, "Colonization and Postcolonial Justice," 153–157.

40. Trefalt and Form differ slightly on these statistics. Beatrice Trefalt, "Hostages to International Relations? The Repatriation of Japanese War Criminals from the Philippines," *Japanese Studies* 31, no. 2 (2011): 193; Form, "Colonization and Postcolonial Justice," 162.

41. They ended in 1948. Pritchard, "The Gift of Clemency," 15.

42. "Prison and Camp Cases," *Singapore War Crimes Trials,* https://www.singa porewarcrimestrials.com/case-summaries#prison-and-camp-cases.

43. United Kingdom, Military jurisdiction, United Kingdom v. Shimpei Fukuei, Reference the proceedings of the trial by military court, National Archives, Kew, London, WO 00235 No. 00825, JAG No. 65012, http://www.legal-tools.org /doc/1aef12/; [Trial against Fukuei Shimpei] Trial Reports, February 2, 1946, Singapore, UNWCC10.csv:147, United Nations War Crimes Commission (UNWCC), http://www.legal-tools.org/doc/bd5b8b/; Synopsis of Case No. 235 / 825; From the Trials of Japanese War Crimes in Singapore, U.C. Berkeley War Crimes Studies Center, http://www.legal-tools.org/doc/3c81c9/.

44. Film of this exists; see "Execution of Japanese General by Firing Squad at Changi and Lady Mountbatten Visits Hospitals in Surabaya (27 / 4 / 1946)," in *Colonial Film: Moving Images of the British Empire,* film courtesy of the Imperial War Museum, http://www.colonialfilm.org.uk/node/6290.

45. Graham Bettany, Keith Bettany, and Ruth Flaherty, "Des' Sketch Book Confiscated by Major General Saito," at *The Changi POW Artwork of Des Bettany,* https://changipowart.com/archives/1097.

46. United States, *Chuhan Migunsa: HUSAFIK* (Seoul: Tolbegae, 1988), 53–54.

47. This was not unusual. According to Wilson et al., *Japanese War Criminals,* around half of the trials dealt with more than one defendant. See Sarah Kovner, "Allied POWs in Korea: Life and Death during the Pacific War," in Kushner and Muminov, *The Dismantling of Japan's Empire in East Asia,* 118.

48. United States of America vs. Yuzuru Noguchi, 62, https://www.legal-tools.org /doc/ebfe21/pdf/. Rules governing trials differed: some used only documents, some used witnesses brought from abroad, some included local men and women. Original Japanese-language documents, many of which had been destroyed, were rarely used. It was common for Japanese defendants to not testify or to only give unsworn testimony, so they could not be cross-examined. And all Japanese-language material had to be translated. Though defense lawyers pointed out procedural shortcomings, such as hearsay testimony and affidavits, these arguments were often ignored. Wilson et al., *Japanese War Criminals,* 81–82.

49. "Defense Motion for Disapproval of Findings and Modification of Sentences as to Yuzuru Noguchi, Kajuro Okazaki and Goro Uchida," October 7, 1948, 16, Records of Allied Operational and Occupation Headquarters, WWII, Record Group 331, NARA.

50. "Defense Motion for Disapproval of Findings," 4; See also "Rule 153, Command Responsibility for Failure to Prevent, Repress or Report War Crimes," Customary IHL, https://www.icrc.org/customary-ihl/eng/docs/v1_cha_chapter43 _rule153.

51. "Military Commission," Orders No. 303, October 2, 1948, Series: US versus Japanese War Criminals Case Files, 1945–1949, Records of Allied Operational and Occupation Headquarters, Record Group 331, NARA.

52. "Clemency Report," US Embassy, Japan, Japanese War Crimes Cases: Sanematsu Yuzuru to Saito Kyosuke, Records of Foreign Service Posts of the Department of State, Switzerland, Record Group 84, NARA.

53. "Clemency Report."

54. "Canadian Government Wishes to Be Informed re Parole or Clemency of This Offender, Parole Documents," n.d., US Embassy, Japan, Japanese War Crimes Cases: Sanematsu Yuzuru to Saito Kyosuke, Records of Foreign Service Posts of the Department of State, Switzerland, Record Group 84, NARA.

55. "Clemency Report."

56. "Clemency Report."

57. Lt. Col. Martin Dustan Sedgwick Saunders, "Perpetuation of Testimony," Entry 143, Box 1035, Record Group 153, NARA.

58. Hada Masato, "Case Synopses from Judge Advocate's Reviews: Yokohama Class B and C War Crimes Trials," *U.C. Berkeley War Crimes Studies Center: World War II Pacific Theater,* https://www.ocf.berkeley.edu/~changmin/Japan /Yokohama/Reviews/PT-yokohama-index.htm.

59. "Katsura Trial Record," Case Files, War Crimes Branch, 1944–1949, Records of the Office of the Judge Advocate General (Army), Record Group 153, NARA.

60. United States of America vs. Hiroshi Tamura, vol. 1 of 8 vols., National Diet Library (NDL), https://dl.ndl.go.jp/info:ndljp/pid/9884763.

61. Andrew G. Russell to Mr. Roy Morgan, undated, as found in *Kokusai kensatsu-kyoku (IPS) jinmon chōsho,* ed. Awaya Kentarō and Yoshida Yutaka, 52 vols. (Tokyo: Nihon tosho sentā, 1993), 49:124.

62. "List of Personnel Punished for Committing Personal Punishments," and "Investigation Chart concerning Personal Punishments," Doc. 2662, pt. 17, Supplement No.1, Legal Section, Administrative Division, Records of Allied Operational and Occupation Headquarters, Record Group 331, NARA.

63. United States of America vs. Hiroshi Tamura, vol. 3, NDL, https://dl.ndl.go.jp /info:ndljp/pid/9884765.

64. Chief of POW Control Department, War Ministry, to General Chief of Staff, "I" Group, Commander of the Southern Field–Railway Corps, Chief of Thai POW camp, Chief of Malay POW Camp, Communication from Chief of POW Control Department re Matters for Investigation of POW Treatment on Thai-Burmese Railway Construction, January 7, 1945, Exhibit 236, 795; United States of America vs. Hiroshi Tamura, vol. 5, NDL, https://dl.ndl.go.jp/info:ndljp /pid/9884420.

65. Chief, Prisoner of War Controls Division, War Ministry, to Commander, Korean Prisoner of War and Internment Camps, Seoul, Korea, August 22, 1945, SCAP Legal Section, Administrative Division, Miscellaneous Japanese File, 1942–1948, POW Camp Records, Records of Allied Operational and Occupation Headquarters, RG 331, NARA.

66. Barak Kushner, review of Totani, *Justice in Asia and the Pacific Region, 1945–1952, H-Net Reviews in the Humanities and Social Sciences,* January 2016, https:// www.h-net.org/reviews/showrev.php?id=44358; Tachikawa Kyoichi, "The Treatment of Prisoners of War by the Imperial Japanese Army and Navy Focusing on the Pacific War," *NIDS Security Reports* 9 (2008): 77, http://www.nids.mod .go.jp/english/publication/kiyo/pdf/2008/bulletin_e2008_5.pdf.

67. Tachikawa, "The Treatment of Prisoners of War," 75–76; Harumi Furuya, "Dai niji sekai taisenki ni okeru Nihonjin no jinshu identity" [The racial identity of the Japanese people during the period of the World War II], in *Senso no kioku to horyo mondai* [The memory of war and the POW issues], ed. Yoichi Kibata, Margaret Kosuge, and Philip Towle (Tokyo: Daigaku Shuppankai, 2003), 166.

68. Its employees as well as others so testified. For example, see the testimony of one employee, Capt. Saito Yoichi: Interrogation of Captain Saitō Yoshichi, September 23, 1947, as found in Awaya and Yoshida, *Kokusai kensatsu-kyoku (IPS) jinmon chōsho,* 49:221.

69. Adjutant notification to the chief of POWIB.

70. United States of America vs. Hiroshi Tamura, vol. 2, 182, NDL, https://dl.ndl.go .jp/info:ndljp/pid/9884764.

71. United States of America vs. Hiroshi Tamura, vol. 2, 182, NDL.

72. See note 68.

73. Hiroshi Tamura to Prosecutor Col. G. S. Woolworth, "Copy of Petition," September 15, 1947, as found in Awaya and Yoshida, *Kokusai kensatsu-kyoku (IPS) jinmon chōsho,* 49:129.

74. Tamura recommended witnesses of his own: Col. Odashima Tadashi, Col. Yamasaki Shigeru, Lt. Col. Yamanouchi Haru, Lt. Col. Hoda Haruji, Maj. Takata Masaru, Maj. Tokoi Takaji, and Lt. Yotsumoto Masanori. Hiroshi Tamura to Prosecutor Col. G. S. Woolworth, "Copy of Petition," September 15, 1947, as found in Awaya and Yoshida, *Kokusai kensatsu-kyoku (IPS) jinmon chōsho,* 49:129.

75. Tōjō also addressed how important it was for Japanese workers to instruct the POWs effectively.

76. Odajima Tadashi, "Circumstances Leading to Draft of Riku-a-mitsu no. 2257," n.d., SCAP Legal Section, Administrative Division, Miscellaneous Japanese File, 1942–1948, POW Camp Records, Records of Allied Operational and Occupation Headquarters, Record Group 331, NARA.

77. Tachikawa, "The Treatment of Prisoners of War," 77.

78. For example, the atrocities on the Thai-Burma Railway, the Bataan Death March, Sandakan, and the September 1944 decapitation of airmen in Aitape, April 1945.

79. United States of America vs. Hiroshi Tamura, vol. 1, NDL, https://dl.ndl.go.jp/info:ndljp/pid/9884763.

80. Totani, *Justice in Asia and the Asia Pacific Region,* 75.

81. Totani, *Justice in Asia and the Asia Pacific Region,* 76.

82. Wilson et al., *Japanese War Criminals,* 117, 120–124, 237.

83. Charged with War Crimes, Toyoda was eventually acquitted.

84. Wilson et al., *Japanese War Criminals,* 119.

85. Kushner, *Men to Devils, Devils to Men,* 9.

86. Sherzod Muminov, "Prejudice, Punishment, and Propaganda, Post-Imperial Japan and the Soviet Versions of History and Justice in East Asia, 1945–1956," in Kushner and Muminov, *The Dismantling of Japan's Empire in East Asia,* 155. See also Valentyna Polunina, "From Tokyo to Khabarovsk: Soviet War Crimes

Trials in Asia as Cold War Battlefields," in von Lingen, *War Crimes Trials in the Wake of Decolonization,* 239–241.

87. Wilson et al., *Japanese War Criminals,* 119. In 1949, NOPAR (National Offenders' Prevention and Rehabilitation Commission) was established as part of the Japanese attorney general's office (it handled only Japan, not Okinawa).

88. Wilson et al., *Japanese War Criminals,* 106–111.

89. Utsumi Aiko, "Changing Japanese Views of the Allied Occupation of Japan and the War Crimes Trials," *Journal of the Australian War Memorial* no. 30 (1997), https://www.awm.gov.au/articles/journal/j30/utsumi.

90. Sandra Wilson, "The Shifting Politics of Guilt: The Campaign for the Release of Japanese War Criminals," in Kushner and Muminov, *The Dismantling of Japan's Empire in East Asia,* 88.

91. Utsumi, "Changing Japanese Views of the Allied Occupation."

92. Wilson, "The Shifting Politics of Guilt," 102.

93. Trefalt argues that this was based on political discussions that centered on reparations. Trefalt, "Hostages to International Relations?," 191–209.

94. "Undated Parole Documents," US Embassy, Japan, Japanese War Crimes Cases: Sanematsu Yuzuru to Saito Kyosuke, Records of Foreign Service Posts of the Department of State, Switzerland, Record Group 84, NARA.

95. "Undated Parole Documents."

96. Note Verbale, Ministry of Foreign Affairs to US Embassy, Japan Bei 2271, November 22, 1955, US Embassy, Japan, Japanese War Crimes Cases: Sanematsu Yuzuru to Saito Kyosuke, Records of Foreign Service Posts of the Department of State, Switzerland, Record Group 84, NARA.

97. Note Verbale, Ministry of Foreign Affairs to US Embassy, Japan Bei 2271, November 22, 1955.

98. Seraphim, "Carceral Geographies of Japan's Vanishing Empire," 126.

99. "Kōkyu jimukan kōkyu buin setsumei jikō," in *Furyo ni kansuru shorui tsuzuri,* unpaginated (September 1945), Bōeishō Bōei Kenkyūsho Senshi Kenkyū Sentā.

100. "Kōkyu jimukan kōkyu buin setsumei jikō."

101. "Kōkyu jimukan kōkyu buin setsumei jikō."

## 9. Prisoners of History

1. Iwao Frederick Aysuawa to Mrs. Margaret L. Thomas, May 6, 1949, Ms. Coll. 969, Box 7, Haverford College Libraries.

2. Other observers included the Dominican Republic, Poland, San Marino, and Yugoslavia. Federal Political Department, *Final Record of the Diplomatic Conference of Geneva of 1949,* vol. 1 (Berne: Federal Political Department, n.d.), 71, http://www.loc.gov/rr/frd/Military_Law/pdf/Dipl-Conf-1949-Final_Vol-1.pdf. The United States banned Germany—see Geoffrey Best, *War and Law since 1945* (Oxford: Clarendon Press, 1994), 95.

3. See, for example, Sandra Wilson, "Koreans in the Trials of Japanese War Crimes Suspects," in *Debating Collaboration and Complicity in War Crimes Trials in Asia, 1945–1956,* ed. Kirsten von Lingen (New York: Springer Berlin Heidelberg, 2017), 19–40; and Sarah Kovner, "War of Words: Allied Captivity and Swiss Neutrality in the Pacific," *Diplomatic History* 41, no. 14 (2017): 719–746.

4. Joyce A. C. Gutteridge, "The Geneva Conventions of 1949," *British Yearbook of International Law* 26 (1949): 294.

5. For example, Sir Robert Craigie, British ambassador to Japan in 1937–1944, was in 1945 chair of the War Crimes Commission.

6. Best, *War and Law since 1945,* 143.

7. See, for example, David P. Forsythe, *The Humanitarians: The International Committee of the Red Cross* (Cambridge: Cambridge University Press, 2005). Also see Jean-Claude Favez, *The Red Cross and the Holocaust,* trans. and ed. John Fletcher and Beryl Fletcher (Cambridge: Cambridge University Press, 1999); and Caroline Moorehead, *Dunant's Dream: War, Switzerland, and the History of the Red Cross* (New York: Caroll and Graf, 1999). On the ICRC in Japan during the war, see, for example, Keiko Tamura's case study, "Being an Enemy Alien in Kobe: Civilian Experiences of War and the Work of the International Committee of the Red Cross and the Swiss Government in Japan," *History Australia* 10, no. 2 (2013): 35–55; Tachikawa Kyoichi and Shukuhisa Haruhiko, "Seifu oyobi gun to ICRC nado to no kankei: Nisshin sensō kara taiheiyō sensō made," *Bōei Kenkyūjo Kiyojo* 11, no. 2 (2009): 105–150; and Sho Konishi, "The Emergence of an International Humanitarian Organization in Japan: The Tokugawa Origins of the Japanese Red Cross," *American Historical Review* 119, no. 4 (2014): 1129–1153.

8. For two important exceptions, see Best, *War and Law since 1945;* and William Hitchcock, "Human Rights and the Laws of War: The 1949 Geneva Conventions,"

in *The Human Rights Revolution: An International History,* vol. 3., ed. Iriye Akira, Petra Goedde, and William Hitchcock (Oxford: Oxford University Press, 2012), 93–112. See also Paul de la Pradelle, *La Conférence Diplomatique et les Nouvelles Conventions de Genève du 12 août, 1949* (Paris: Éditions internationales, 1951).

9. Sherzod Muminov, "Eleven Winters of Discontent: The Siberian Internment and the Making of the New Japan, 1945–1956" (PhD diss., Corpus Christi College, 2015), 186; Sandra Wilson, Robert Cribb, Beatrice Trefalt, and Dean Aszkielowicz, *Japanese War Criminals: The Politics of Justice after the Second World War* (New York: Columbia University Press, 2017), 238. From 550,000 to 600,000 men were initially captured and gradually repatriated. See Muminov, "Eleven Winters of Discontent," 116; and Andrew Barshay, *The Gods Left First: The Captivity and Repatriation of Japanese POWs in Northeast Asia, 1945–56* (Berkeley: University of California Press, 2013), appendix.

10. Jean S. Pictet, "The New Geneva Conventions for the Protection of War Victims," *American Journal of International Law* 45, no. 3 (1951): 464.

11. Kovner, "War of Words," 725–743.

12. Best, *War and Law since 1945,* 81.

13. International Committee of the Red Cross, "Preliminary Documents Submitted [to the] Commission of Government Experts for the Study of Conventions for the Protection of War Victims, Geneva, April 14 to 26, 1947" (Geneva: International Committee of the Red Cross, 1947), 1.

14. Diplomatic Conference for the Establishment of International Conventions for the Protection of Victims of War, Jean S. Pictet, ed., *Geneva Conventions of 12 August 1949. Commentary, Published under the General Editorship of Jean S. Pictet, Director for General Affairs of the International Committee of the Red Cross,* 4 vols. (Geneva: ICRC, 1949), 1:105, Translated from the original French.

15. The Swiss Federal Council, trustee of the Geneva Conventions, convened the conference in Geneva, headquarters of the ICRC. For more on the tensions between the ICRC and Switzerland, see Kovner, "War of Words."

16. International Committee of the Red Cross, "Preliminary Documents," 2.

17. Pictet, "The New Geneva Conventions for the Protection of War Victims," 466; Best, *War and Law since 1945,* 92.

18. International Committee of the Red Cross, "Preliminary Documents," 4.

19. Pictet, "The New Geneva Conventions for the Protection of War Victims," 467.

20. "Draft International Convention on the Condition and Protection of Civilians of Enemy Nationality Who Are on Territory Belonging to or Occupied by a Belligerent. Tokyo, 1934," https://www.icrc.org/ihl/INTRO/320?Open Document.

21. See, for example, Raymond Palmer, "Felix Kersten and Count Bernadotte: A Question of Rescue," *Journal of Contemporary History* 29, no. 1 (1994): 39–51.

22. Best, *War and Law since 1945,* 82–83.

23. US recommendations originated in the interdepartmental POW committee, which included State, Army, Navy, Air Force, Justice, Treasury, the Post Office, and the American Red Cross. R. W. Dillon, "Development of Law Relative to Treatment of Prisoners of War," Administrative Division; Mail and Records Branch, Geneva Convention 1946–1949, Records of the Office of the Provost Marshal General, 1941–, Record Group 389 (Provost Marshal General), US National Archives and Records Administration, College Park, Maryland (hereafter NARA).

24. Diplomatic Conference for the Establishment of International Conventions for the Protection of War Victims, at Geneva, *Seventeenth International Red Cross Conference at Geneva, Switzerland, April 21–August 12, 1949: Report of the United States Commission,* compiled by William H. McCahon, Division of Protective Services, State, Delegation from the United States, October 3, 1949; Secretary of State to Basil O'Connor, General Records of the Department of State, Record Group 59 (Office of the Legal Advisor), NARA.

25. Best, *War and Law since 1945,* 89–90.

26. As cited in Best, *War and Law since 1945,* 81. See also Vernon E. Davis, *The Long Road Home: U.S. Prisoner of War Policy and Planning in Southeast Asia* (Washington, DC: Historical Office, Secretary of Defense, 2000), 4–5.

27. Best, *War and Law since 1945,* 85.

28. Best, *War and Law since 1945,* 84–86.

29. Federal Political Department, *Final Record of the Diplomatic Conference of Geneva of 1949,* vol. 2A (Berne: Federal Political Department, n.d.), 274.

30. Federal Political Department, *Final Record of the Diplomatic Conference of Geneva of 1949,* vol. 2A, 274; vol. 2B, 13.

31. For more on the French in Indochina, see Beatrice Trefalt, "Japanese War Criminals in Indochina and the French Pursuit of Justice: Local and International Constraints," *Journal of Contemporary History* 49, no. 4 (2014): 727–742.

See also Kiyoko Kurusu Nitz, "Japanese Military Policy towards French Indochina during the Second World War: The Road to the 'Meigo Sakusen' (9 March 1945)," *Journal of Southeast Asian Studies* 14, no. 2 (1983): 328–353.

32. Trefalt, "Japanese War Criminals in Indochina," 727–729.

33. Best, *War and Law since 1945*, 88.

34. Frank T. Cleverley to B. de Rouge, October 6, 1948 ICRC, CRI 2 / II et 25 / III.

35. "Opinions of the Ministry of Foreign Affairs on the Red Cross Conventions Revised or Drafted by the Conference of Governmental Experts for the Study of Convention for the Protection of War Victims, Held in Geneva, April 16–26, 1947," ICRC, CRI 2 / II et 25 / III.

36. "Opinions of the Ministry of Foreign Affairs."

37. William H. McCahon, "Report of the United States Delegation," October 1949, Office of the Legal Adviser; Records Relating to the Red Cross and Geneva Conventions, 1941–1967, General Records of the Department of State, Record Group 59, NARA.

38. McCahon, "Report of the United States Delegation."

39. Saito So'ichi to the Chairman of the ICRC, April 9, 1949, G.3 / 78, ICRC.

40. Best, *War and Law since 1945*, 100–102.

41. US Committee on Foreign Relations, *Geneva Conventions for the Protection of War Victims* (Washington, DC: US Government Printing Office, June 27, 1955), 4.

42. This issue was emphasized in US Committee on Foreign Relations, *Geneva Conventions for the Protection of War Victims.*

43. Pictet, *Geneva Conventions of 12 August 1949*, 3:196–197.

44. Arnold Krammer, *Nazi Prisoners of War in America* (New York: Stein and Day, 1979), 84, 110–111.

45. Mr. Moll (Venezuela) considered that the New Zealand amendment—which said POWs should not be subject to "unhealthy or dangerous labour" but could be exposed to the "normal risks of civilian employment"—satisfactory, but regarded "normal risks of civilian employment" as too vague. If the New Zealand amendment were adopted, it should at all events be supplemented by a clause regarding climatic conditions, as proposed in the Canadian amendment. Federal Political Department, *Final Record,* 2B:274–275.

46. US Committee on Foreign Relations, *Geneva Conventions for the Protection of War Victims*, 4.

47. He accordingly proposed that the words "without witnesses" in the first paragraph should be omitted. Federal Political Department, *Final Record*, 2A:303.

48. Wing Commander Davis (Australia), in Federal Political Department, *Final Record*, 2A:264.

49. M. Straehler to Madam Morier, December 15, 1945 G 8 / 76, ICRC.

50. Federal Political Department, *Final Record*, 2B:513.

51. Anthony Eden, British Secretary of State for Foreign Affairs, January 28, *Parliamentary Debates*, House of Commons, 5th Ser., vol. 396, cols. 1029–1033, 1029.

52. Yuma Totani, *Justice in Asia and the Pacific Region, 1945–1952: Allied War Crimes Prosecutions* (New York: Cambridge University Press, 2015), 21–23.

53. Joyce A. C. Gutteridge (United Kingdom), in Federal Political Department, *Final Record*, 2B:515.

54. *Geneva Convention Relative to the Treatment of Prisoners of War, August 12, 1949*, chap. 2, art. 26.

55. They did not achieve as much as they wished, but successfully provided minimum protection for those not actively involved in hostilities. Pictet, *Geneva Conventions of 12 August 1949*, 1:469.

56. US Committee on Foreign Relations, *Geneva Conventions for the Protection of War Victims*.

57. McCahon, "Report of the United States Delegation."

58. Pictet, *Geneva Conventions of 12 August 1949*, 1:16.

59. Pictet, *Geneva Conventions of 12 August 1949*, 1:18.

60. Barshay, *The Gods Left First*, 35–37, 48.

61. Straehler to Geneva, September 9, 1946, "Communication by Japanese in Soviet Controlled Territories," 8 / 76, ICRC.

62. Acheson to Acting Political Adviser, December 23, 1949, Office of the Legal Adviser, Records Relating to the Red Cross and Geneva Conventions, 1941–1967, General Records of the Department of State, Record Group 59, NARA.

63. "MacArthur's Request for Neutral Assistance in Repatriation of Japanese from the USSR," Office of the Legal Adviser, Records Relating to the Red Cross and Geneva Conventions, 1941–1967, General Records of the Department of State, Record Group 59, NARA.

64. Muminov, "Eleven Winters of Discontent," 12.

65. Muminov, "Eleven Winters of Discontent," 165–166.

66. Aysuawa to Mrs. Thomas. April 30, 1949, Ms. Coll. 969, Box 7, Haverford College Libraries.

67. Aysuawa to Mrs. Thomas. April 30, 1949.


## Conclusion

1. Park Byeong Suk, interview with author, August 1, 2011, Seoul.

2. In July 1945 the Americans let 2 million go, but another 1.5 million were sent to France and the United Kingdom to labor there. In 1948 the last German POW in French hands was returned; in 1956 the last German POW in Soviet hands was returned. Giles MacDonogh, *After the Reich: The Brutal History of the Allied Occupation* (New York: Basic Books, 2009), 394–399.

3. James Weingartner, "War against Subhumans: Comparisons between the German War against the Soviet Union and the American War against Japan, 1941–1945," *The Historian* 58, no. 3 (1996): 565.

4. Kowner's analysis is particularly insightful. See Rotem Kowner, "Imperial Japan and Its POWs: The Dilemma of Humaneness and National Identity," in *War and Militarism in Modern Japan: Issues of History and Identity,* ed. Guy Podoler (Folkestone, UK: Global Oriental, 2009), 88–89.

5. Kowner, "Imperial Japan and Its POWs," 88–89.

6. From Chief of Malay POW camp, to Chief of POW Control Dept., "The Presentation of Matters Investigated regarding the Treatment of POWs Engaged in the Construction of the Thai-Burmese Railway" (Ma-fu-fu no.238), "Chief of Malay Reply to Exhibit 236," February 7, 1945, "United States of America vs. Hiroshi Tamura," Exhibit 237, WOT. Doc. 11152-B, vol. 5, NDL. This document is part of an explicit cover-up. In interviews, this was a point that former POWs (or their children) stressed consistently. When Korean guard Lee Hank Rae arrived at Hintok (Hintoku) in Thailand, he found the camp unfinished. There were shortages of food or medicine. According to Korean Guard Park Byeong Suk, Korean guards were treated the same as

POWs. There was little rest, the climate was bad, and there were many tropical diseases. Specifically, he remembered that the food was so poor that he "went to bathroom once a week." Ogawa Matsuhiro, the son of a Japanese sailor, stressed that conditions on the hell ships were as bad for Japanese sailors as for American POWs. Ogawa Matsuhiro, interview with author, May 3, 2018, Albuquerque, NM; Lee Hang Rae, interview with author, December 6, 2011, Tokyo; Park Byeong Suk, interview with author, August 1, 2011, Seoul.

7. George Edward Guy Round, "The Road from Singapore," unpublished manuscript, 255–256, MSS1370, AWM.

8. "Searchu," *Nor Iron Bars,* 1943, 2 Loyals, Kingsley & Strange Collection, 1939–1945, Box 8, Fulwood Barracks Archive (hereafter FB).

9. Racist slurs also included anti-German and anti-Italian comments. "Things I Wouldn't Like to Be," *Nor Iron Bars,* July 1943, 2 Loyals, Kingsley & Strange Collection, 1939–1945, Box 8, FB. The magazine also featured a "Korean Fauna" section that featured animalistic representations of both captives and guards.

10. "Things I Wouldn't Like to Be."

11. Christina Twomey, "Emaciation or Emasculation: Photographic Images, White Masculinity and Captivity by the Japanese in World War Two," *Journal of Men's Studies* 15, no. 3 (2008): 304–305.

12. Robin Gerster, "War by Photography: Shooting Japanese in Australia's Pacific War," *History of Photography* 40, no. 4 (2016): 446.

13. Twomey, "Emaciation or Emasculation," 307.

14. John C. Kluznik, MD, et al., "Forty-Year Follow-Up of United States Prisoners of War," *American Journal of Psychiatry* 143, no. 11 (1986): 1445.

15. Patricia B. Sutker, PhD, Albert N. Allain Jr., MS, and Daniel K. Winstead, MD, "Psychopathology and Psychiatric Diagnoses of World War II Pacific Theater Prisoner of War Survivors and Combat Veterans," *American Journal of Psychiatry* 150, no. 2 (1993): 240–245.

16. S. Leonard Simpson, "Impotence," *British Medical Journal* 1, no. 4655 (1950): 693.

17. In 1984 the United States ratified the 1984 United Nations Convention against Torture. Alberto Gonzales, "Memorandum for the President," January 25, 2002, https://nsarchive2.gwu.edu//NSAEBB/NSAEBB127/02.01.25.pdf.

18. In *Hamdan v. Rumsfeld* (548 U.S. 557, 2006, https://www.supremecourt.gov /opinions/05pdf/05-184.pdf), a slim majority in the US Supreme Court held

that then-operating US military commissions complied neither with the Uniform Code of Military Justice nor with the International Laws of War. The majority reasoned that Common Article 3 of the Geneva Conventions, which applies to noninternational armed conflicts, should be interpreted broadly, therefore, rendering its protections applicable to the petitioner (Salim Ahmed Hamdan, a detainee in the US military facility in Guantanamo Bay). However, subsequent case law has failed to establish consistent criteria for identifying the presence or absence of "armed hostilities" in the fluid context of military efforts to suppress terrorism and repressive forms of religious extremism. This has resulted in continued confusion and arguable inconsistencies in the grounds on which individual detainees are held. Harvard Law School Program on International Law and Armed Conflict (HLS PILAC), "Section 7—International Law and the End of the United States' War on Terror," https://pilac.law.harvard .edu/indefinite-war-legal-briefing//section-7-international-law-and-the-end-of -the-united-states-war-on-terror.

19. Gonzales, "Memorandum for the President"; *Third Geneva Convention Relative to the Treatment of Prisoners of War, Geneva, 12 August 1949,* Focus on Part I, "General Provisions," Article 17, http://www.icrc.org/ihl.nsf/7c4d08d9b287a421 41256739003e63bb/6fef854a3517b75ac125641e004a9e68; *UN Convention against Torture and Other Cruel, Inhuman or Degrading Treatment or Punishment,* December 10, 1984, https://treaties.un.org/doc/Treaties/1987/06/19870626%2002 -38%20AM/Ch_IV_9p.pdf; "Leadership Failure: Firsthand Accounts of Torture of Iraqi Detainees by the U.S. Army's 82nd Airborne Division," *Human Rights Watch* 17, no. 3 (September 2005), http://hrw.org/reports/2005/us0905/.

20. *Hamdan v. Rumsfeld.*

21. Erin Miller, "John Paul Stevens and the U.S. Navy at War," *SCOTUSblog,* April 22, 2010, https://www.scotusblog.com/2010/04/john-paul-stevens-and -the-u-s-navy-at-war/.

22. "President Bush and Japanese Prime Minister Koizumi Participate in a Joint Press Availability," June 29, 2006, https://georgewbush-whitehouse.archives .gov/news/releases/2006/06/print/20060629-3.html.

23. "President Bush and Japanese Prime Minister Koizumi Participate in a Joint Press Availability."

# Archival Sources

**Australia**

Australian War Memorial (AWM)
National Archives of Australia (NAA)

**India**

National Archives of India (NAI)

**Ireland**

Irish National Archives

**Japan**

Bōeichō Bōeikenkyūsho Senshi Kenkyū Sentā (National Institute for Defense Studies
[NIDS] Center for Military History)
Ministry of Foreign Affairs Diplomatic Archives
National Diet Library (NDL)

**Netherlands**

Dutch National Archives (DNA)
Nederlands Instituut voor Militarie Historie (NIMH)
NIOD (Instituut voor Oorlogs-, Holocaust- en Genocidestudies)

**Republic of Korea**

The Commission on Verification and Support for the Victims of Forced Mobilization
under Japanese Colonialism in Korea

**Switzerland**

International Committee of the Red Cross Archives (ICRC)
Swiss Federal Archives (SFA)

**United Kingdom**

British National Archives (BNA)

Fulwood Barracks (FB)
Imperial War Museum (IWM)

## United States

Haverford College Archives
Library of Congress (LOC)
US Army War College, Carlisle, PA (USAWC)
US National Archives and Records Administration (NARA)
US Naval Academy (USNA)

## Interviews by Author

Henry Chamberlain, May 3, 2016, Albuquerque, NM
Kang (son of Kang Taehyo), July 29, 2011, Seoul
Lee Hang Rae, December 16, 2011, Tokyo
Leland Chandler, May 3, 2016, Albuquerque, NM
Ogawa Matsuhiro, May 3, 2016, Albuquerque, NM
Park Byeong Suk, August 1, 2011, Seoul

# Acknowledgments

One hot summer in Geneva at the International Committee of the Red Cross Archives, I sought in vain to find out what Swiss men thought about the brothels and streetwalkers that became ubiquitous in occupied Japan, the subject of my first book. I was planning to follow up with a history of efforts to combat the international sex trade. Instead, I discovered Red Cross delegates' reports about POW camps. Shortly thereafter, I found myself in Sydney, where a newscaster reported on a review of the latest book on POWs, another reminder of how frequently the subject figured in popular fiction and films. Older relatives and friends often asked me about it when the topic of World War II came up. I was struck by how, on the other hand, I had never heard it mentioned in a graduate history class, or an academic conference. Soon thereafter, I jettisoned the year I had spent researching the history of "white slavery" and decided to write a book on Allied POWs. I quickly realized how little I knew.

Realizing how little I knew was not an unfamiliar experience. As a professor at the University of Florida, I was kindly reminded by colleagues that the world was bigger than Japan. That experience was invaluable to me, as were my writing partners, Michelle Campos and Jessica Harland-Jacobs. Senior colleagues, including Luise White and Ida Altman, helped me survive the tenure process. Helen Lee provided me not only with companionship and tea, but also with invaluable introductions in Seoul. After I moved to Columbia, the Saltzman Institute of War and Peace Studies offered me a welcome home and more reminders of how the world is even bigger than history. Bob Jervis and Dick Betts have always made time for me and answered my questions, simple though they may be. Ingrid Gerstman and Alba Tavaras make everything seem easy.

Writing a multinational and multiarchival book cannot be accomplished without librarians and archivists, and I was lucky to have met some who were incredibly helpful. I especially thank Jane Davies at the Lancashire Infantry Museum, Jeroen Kemperman at NIOD, Fabrizio Bensi and Daniel Palmieri at the ICRC Archives, Cho Gun at the Commission on Verification and Support for the Victims of Forced Mobilization under Japanese Colonialism in Korea, and Tonai Yuzuru at the Slavic-Eurasian Research Center Library, Hokkaido University. I also want to thank the veterans and their children who spoke with me, including Park Byeong Suk, Mr. Kang, and Lee Hank Rae, as well as Mindy Kotler, Leland Chandler, Ogawa Matsuhiro, and Henry Chamberlain.

Patient audiences at the University of Basel, Cambridge University, the University of Chicago, Columbia University, the European University Institute, Fudan University, Leiden University, the University of Manchester, the Naval War College, Stanford University, the University of Sydney, and Yale University, among other places, listened to my talks and provided useful feedback. Students in my War and Captivity seminar allowed me to work out my ideas and, in some cases, shared their own remarkable wartime experiences. Many historians helped shape parts of the manuscript, invited me to present chapters, and provided introductions. I especially thank Asano Toyomi, Matt Augustine, Eveline Buchheim, Robert Cribb, Tadashi Ishikawa, Yukiko Koga, Barak Kushner, Matthieu Leimgruber, Aaron William Moore, Dirk Moses, Sherzod Muminov, Christina Twomey, and Sandra Wilson. With little notice, Lori Watt, Richard Betts, and Robert Jervis read all the draft chapters and workshopped them with me. Two anonymous readers improved the manuscript tremendously.

I received generous funding from Columbia University, the University of Florida, and Yale International Security Studies. At Harvard University Press, Joyce Seltzer took a chance on me, while Kathleen McDermott shepherded the manuscript through the publication process. Special thanks go to my indefatigable production editor, John Donohue. Though all mistakes are my own, my research assistants, among them Brit Felsen-Parsons, Kirara Nakamura, Ariella Napoli, Yosuke Nasu, Natan Rabinowitz, Namiko Sawaki, and Rohan Shah, prevented me from making many others.

Most importantly, I thank my family. Long ago my parents, Chris and Tony, set a high standard, encouraging me to use the NYU research library for my high school papers. My sister Anna, ever the optimist in a dismal science, dispensed pep talks and quantitative advice. Above all, this book could not have been written without Matt, who is everything I am not, and more besides. It is dedicated to Lily, who is the best.

# Index

*Note:* page numbers in *italics* refer to maps, figures, and tables.

Japanese support for Philippine independence, 68, 69; as justification for Japanese
imperialism, 34

Paravicini, Fritz: assistant to, 106; death of, 112;
difficulty of seeing POWs, 108; and distribution of relief packets, 59, 106; emphasis on
positive aspects of POW treatment, 109;
experience in Japan, 97; on fragmented
Japanese bureaucracy in charge of POWs,
106; on ICRC neutrality, 109; on obstacles to
ICRC work in Japan, 108; poor health of, 108;
as Red Cross representative, 6, 25, 97–98; on
treatment of POWs in Japan, 102

Park Byeong Suk, 7, 209

Patriotic Labor Corps, 138

Patriotic National labor Cooperation Ordinance, 138

Peace Preservation Law, 47

Pearl Harbor attack: and Japan as seemingly
distant threat, 1; oil embargo as provocation
for, 41–42; vulnerability of Singapore following, 45

Philippines: broad support for United States in,
88; defense preparations, 68; and Greater
East Asian Conference (1943), 63–64; history
of colonial rule, 67; important natural resources in, 69; Japanese-language newspapers in, 87; and Pan-Asianism, lack of
interest in, 73; special relationship with
United States, 67; strategic importance to
United States, 68; traditional Japanese
support for US rule in, 68–69; US bases in,
68; US plan for defense of, 69–70, 72; war
deaths in, 182

Philippines, civilians interned by Japan in,
86–87; camps for, 86; limited interest of
Japanese in, 87; living conditions for, 86;
number and nationalities of, 86

Philippines, Japanese civilians in, 68; control
of, by occupation government, 87; support
for Japanese invasion and occupation, 69, 72,
73, 87, 90

Philippines, Japanese civilians interned by
United States, 67, 70–71; attacks on, 70;
confiscation of property from, 71; forced
work by, 70; as one cause of Japanese abuse
of POWs, 79–80

Philippines, Japanese-held POWs in: better
treatment of, after turn to use of POWs for
labor, 85; disease as greatest threat to, 84;
executions of, 93; Japanese failure to plan for,
67, 73, 76, 79, 81, 95; Japanese refusal to allow
neutral inspections of, 99; as largest number
of US servicemen held by Japanese, 67; living
conditions of, 77–78; names of, as not reported
to ICRC, 79; number of, 76; requirement to
salute guards, 83, 84; transport to forced labor
camps, 85–86; treatment compared to Filipinos,
95. See also Freeing of POWs, in Philippines;
Transport of POWs to work sites, from
Philippines

Philippines, Japanese-held POWs, abuses of:
executions of offenders, 84; and high number
of deaths, 67; Honma's knowledge of, 82; and
humiliation of Americans as goal, 80, 98–99;
IJA experience in China and, 81–82; Japanese
classification as prisoners without POW
status, 79; and Japanese ignorance of Geneva
Conventions, 83; Japanese resentment of US
internment and, 79–80; lack of Japanese
planning and, 67, 79, 81; POWs' inability to
understand guards and, 83, 84; punishment
of Filipinos supporting United States, 80;
reasons for, 78–85; reductions over time in, 85;
toll taken on Japanese forces by US defense
and, 80. See also Bataan Death March

Philippines, Japanese invasion of, 72–74;
bombing of docks and ships, 72; destruction
of US fighter planes, 71; Filipinos' lack of
support for, 73–74; initial bombing, 71; lack
of planning for POWs, 67, 73, 76, 79, 81, 95,
118; losses in fight for Bataan Peninsula,
74–75; occupation of Manila, 73; preparations
for, 69; priorities in, 73; and SS *Corregidor*,
sinking of, 71; troop landings, 72; US air
power and, 70; US doubts about potential
for, 70; US withdrawal to Bataan Peninsula,
72. See also Corregidor (Philippines)

Philippines, Japanese occupation of: Allied
bombing after August 1944, 91; atrocities
committed in, 182; and Chinese, targeting of,
74; crumbling Japanese defense perimeter
and, 90; and establishment of independent
Republic of Philippines, 89–90; establishment

with change of camp staff, 151; CINPAC summary of, 177; and colonial view of Asians, 143; complex factors affecting, 5–6; denial of POW protections to some prisoners, 79, 105; as detrimental to overall war strategy, 209; different cultural expectations and, 101; difficulty of coordinating in widespread empire, 105; and disruption of military structure, 214; food shortages and, 105; general Japanese deprivation as explanation for, 135, 138, 154, 156, 211; vs. German treatment of Russian POWs, 210; humane, Japanese interest in appearance of, 119; ICRC positive spin on, 109, 118; improvement of, with impending Allied victory, 131; as inadvertent consequence of policy, 8; vs. Japanese treatment of their own soldiers, 4, 211; Japanese view of POWs as cowards and, 1–2, 40, 41, 142, 194; and Japanese vs. Western norms, 137; Japan's concern about Western perception of, 4; and lawless warfare against China, impact of, 5; limited government awareness of, 106, 115; limited impact on Japanese memory of war, 2; as major issue beginning in 1944, 101; medical experimentation on, 137, 154; military control over, 103; as more complex than popular account, 7; neutral observers' difficulty in evaluating, 108; outsized impact on Allied memory of war, 2; poor Japanese decision making on, 117–118; poor planning of expansion and, 3, 5, 42, 54, 105, 118, 209; popular account of, 1–2; power politics in military and, 145; POW executions, vs. Allied war crimes, 2–3; as product of leaders' inattention rather than malice, 3, 190, 191, 201, 209; and public outrage in Allied nations, 113–115; racial component in mental anguish, 212–213; range of perspectives needed to understand, 6–7; and refusal to supply list of POWs, 108; vs. suffering of Japanese civilians, 177; and toughening of War Prisoners Punishment Act of 1905, 144; treatment of Chinese, as deliberately harsh, 4, 210; and US airmen, debate on status of, 144–145; US internment of Japanese and, 2, 100, 112; US sinking of *Awa Maru* and, 117; variations with time

and place, 208, 210, 211. *See also* Geneva Conventions on POWs, Japan and; Korean POW camps; Philippines, Japanese-held POWs, abuses of; POW policy of Japan; POWs from Singapore

Treatment of Japanese POWs, Japanese views on: bitterness and, 156; internal debate on, 4, 98; postwar characterization as cultural misunderstanding, 194; public's resentment of good treatment, 109–110, 131, 154, 210

Treatment of Japanese POWs, US views on: downplaying of abuses to avoid reprisals, 101; and hope to shame Japanese into better treatment, 114–115; and restoring primacy of Western civilization, 214–215; as strategy to justify bombing Japanese cities, 13, 111, 118, 214–215

Treaty of Versailles (1919), Japanese disappointment with, 27

Tsuneyoshi Yoshio, 77, 79, 178, *179*

Uemura Mikio, 56, 98, 179
*Unbroken* (Hillenbrand), 1, 2
Unit cohesion, and survival of POWs, 134
Universal Declaration of Human Rights, 195
US Army in the Far East (USAFE): and defense of Philippines, 68; MacArthur as commander of, 69
Ushihara Tatsumi, 130, 180, 185–186
US relations with Japan, war criminals as issue in, 193, 194
US soldiers: belief in Japanese surrender offers as traps, 8, 39–40; desecration of Japanese dead, 40

Vienna Exhibition of 1874, Japanese pavilion in, 16
Vietnam War, and war crimes lessons of Pacific War, 215–216

Wainwright, Jonathan, 72, 75, 76, 80, 84, 182
War, development of international law on, 15
War crimes: clemency policy of United States and United Kingdom, 192–193; commission by both sides in Pacific War, 197; early release of those convicted of, 193–194, 208–209; international law as insufficient protection